SEEKING SECURITY AND DEVELOPMENT

SEEKING SECURITY AND DEVELOPMENT

The Impact of Military Spending and Arms Transfers

edited by

Norman A. Graham

LYNNE
RIENNER
PUBLISHERS

BOULDER
LONDON

Table 7.3 is reprinted with permission from Samuel P. S. Ho,
Economic Development in Taiwan, 1860–1970, Yale
University Press, 1978.

Published in the United States of America in 1994 by
Lynne Rienner Publishers, Inc.
1800 30th Street, Boulder, Colorado 80301

and in the United Kingdom by
Lynne Rienner Publishers, Inc.
3 Henrietta Street, Covent Garden, London WC2E 8LU

Library of Congress Cataloging-in-Publication Data
Seeking security and development : the impact of military spending and
    arms transfers / edited by Norman A. Graham.
        p.   cm.
    Includes bibliographical references and index.
    ISBN 1-55587-416-9 (alk. paper)
    1. National security—Developing countries.   2. Developing
countries—Defenses—Economic aspects.   3. Arms transfers—
Developing countries.   4. Developing countries—Economic policy.
I. Graham, Norman A.
UA10.5.S428   1994
355'.033'001724—dc20   93-41148
                                                                    CIP

British Cataloguing in Publication Data
A Cataloguing in Publication record for this book
is available from the British Library.

Printed and bound in the United States of America

        The paper used in this publication meets the requirements
 ∞   of the American National Standard for Permanence of
        Paper for Printed Library Materials Z39.48-1984.

❖ Contents ❖

❖ Preface ❖

This volume presents the results of a series of workshops sponsored by the Midwest Consortium for International Security Studies (MCISS) under a grant from the MacArthur Foundation and by the Center for the Advanced Study of International Development (CASID), the Center for European and Russian Studies (CERS), and James Madison College, all at Michigan State University. MCISS was established to develop a closer network of scholarship and academic exchange on arms control and security issues among several midwestern universities, including Michigan State, Indiana University, Northwestern University, Ohio State University, Purdue University, the University of Chicago, the University of Illinois, the University of Iowa, the University of Kansas, the University of Michigan, the University of Minnesota, the University of Notre Dame, the University of Wisconsin, and several others that vary from year to year. MCISS is administered by the Midwest Center of the American Academy of Arts and Sciences in Chicago and is funded by modest yearly allocations from the member universities and by external grants, principally from the MacArthur Foundation.

As editor of this volume and convenor of the workshops that led to it, I would like to acknowledge the crucial role played by MCISS and its capable executive secretary, Marian Rice. I would also like to acknowledge the financial support provided for these workshops by the MacArthur Foundation and the helpful guidance of its project officer, Kimberly Stanton. Responsibility for the contents of the volume, however, belongs to the editor and the individual chapter authors, not MCISS, the American Academy of Arts and Sciences, or the MacArthur Foundation.

Credit must be given to Nicole Ball, who visited the campus of Michigan State University shortly after the publication of her important book, *Security and Economy in the Third World*. In her short time as a guest of CASID and James

Madison College, she succeeded in galvanizing emerging interest among several contributors to this volume in the complex interrelationships involved in simultaneously "seeking security and development."

I would also like to express gratitude to the editorial staff of Lynne Rienner Publishers. The meticulous copyediting provided by Cheryl Carnahan and the general support and guidance offered by Lynne Rienner and Michelle Welsh are examples of professionalism well beyond that which I have previously experienced in work with a range of academic and commercial publishers. Finally, I would like to acknowledge the thoughtful, substantive comments made by the anonymous external reviewer(s) selected by Lynne Rienner.

Norman A. Graham

❖ ONE ❖

Introduction

Norman A. Graham

The economic performance of many developing countries has seemed to decline significantly in recent years in the face of international debt crises, recession, and resource scarcity. At the same time, military expenditures in much of the developing world have continued to grow, with no sign of a slump in sight. Indeed, despite the easing of security concerns among the major world powers as a result of relaxed East-West tensions, arms imports by developing countries continue at a rapid pace, and the burden of military expenditures on the economies of many countries appears substantial and seems to be growing.

Given these apparent trends, what are the causal links, if any, between military expenditures and economic development? Do military expenditures retard economic growth and development; do they contribute to or enhance the development process; or are they irrelevant, at least in any systematic and predictable way? How effective are military and military-dominated regimes in promoting economic development? What is the impact of military expenditures and arms acquisitions on security and conflict patterns in the Third World? The scholarly literature to date (lacking in longitudinal, multidisciplinary, and international-team research designs) has contributed little clarity to these crucial questions. Our principal aim in this volume is to address them systematically through a series of comparative, longitudinal, and interregional studies.

Previous Research[1]

The impact of military spending on economic performance has received much attention in recent years. Research on nations with "advanced" economies has tended to show that the military burden has an overall negative effect on public and private investment, reduces private consumption, and causes inflation and

1

a variety of other problems (Degrasse, 1983; Melman, 1978; 1985; see also Szymanski, 1973a).

Indeed, Seymour Melman, who for the past three decades has written on the negative effects of military spending, has argued that:

> The permanent war economy, far from solving problems of capital and labor surplus in the American economy, as suggested by the conventional wisdom . . . performs as a prime generator of uninvestable capital, unemployable labor, and industrial inefficiency. . . . The permanent war economy . . . [is] a prime cause of the inflation of the 1970s, a development that is inexplicable to those trained in contemporary economics that classifies military outlays as just another species of government spending. (1985, 21)

However, social scientists generally believe military spending has at least two possible positive effects on advanced-economy nations: the creation of domestic demand and the possibility for technological "spin-offs." Much skepticism exists, however, about these apparently positive effects, because defense firms have often had considerable difficulty in developing technologies with direct application to the production of consumer goods.

Military spending in the advanced economies has a number of effects that are tied directly to industrial inefficiency, including corrosion of the capital stock, increased national debt, and increased capital flight. It is important to note, however, that many aspects of these arguments pertain to nations that manufacture weapons systems as opposed to those that purchase them in completed form. It may be that those who purchase weapons avoid such problems at the cost of severe balance of payments problems. What, then, is the true cost of a new weapons system to the nation that develops it?

When we consider the poorer nations of the world, a number of new arguments arise concerning the impact of military spending. These are connected, generally speaking, to several variants of development theory.

First, a demand-creation argument was developed by Marxists as an explanation for military spending in the advanced economies, that is, as an effort by advanced-economy nations to avoid the underconsumption crisis. In transferring this model to the Third World, it is argued that aggregate demand in poorer nations may be inadequate to attain the highest levels of potential aggregate supply. Thus, military demand may lead to increased use of labor or of capital, reducing the overall resource cost. Military demand for particular products may also induce the development of extra domestic supply and thus create subsequent backward linkages.

Turning to the political and coercive sphere, Saadet Deger and Ron Smith suggest that a strong military enables the state to exercise an expanded coercive capacity, which in turn

> may enable the state to increase the rate of exploitation of available resources. Surplus labor may be mobilized, raw material production developed in the face of opposition, agrarian surplus allocated to industry, consumption restricted,

industrial disputes suppressed, and the rate of work increased. (Deger and Smith, 1983, 338)

Without an organized military force, the state might not have the same capacity to mobilize or exploit these potential resources. The critique of this view is extensive and tends to focus on the repression involved and on the validity of the supposed efficiency of coercive mobilization (see, for example, Ball, 1988, chapter 8).

Also, consistent with this argument, the military may be instrumental in the extension of the market by breaking down traditional patterns of political and social organization. This hypothesis is frequently described as the "military as modernizing institution" hypothesis. The military, it is argued, is in some cases the only modern institution in the peripheral economy (see the discussion of the South Korean case in Graham, 1991 and Ball, 1988, chapter 9).

To the contrary, research on the role of the military in development frequently shows that the amount of expertise and technical ability inside the military is highly variable by nation and is not necessarily greater than the amount found in civilian bureaucracies or academic institutions. Where military regimes exist, civilian structures are often required to perform technical, welfare, and representation functions that the military is either unable or unwilling to perform. Even when the military has skills, these skills are not always transferable to what is required for rule. Development research has generally traced the failures of the military back to its corporate interests. These bureaucratic requirements and needs are displayed in the way in which the military acquired power, both as a bargainer and as an administrator (Ball, 1983a; 1983b).

The military may serve as the conduit through which new technology is introduced into the society and as the means by which the infrastructure of the economy is developed. Opponents contend, however, that military investment in technology is frequently restricted to highly capital-intensive venues, which have minimal chance for civilian-sector spin-off. Further, military facilities and infrastructure are often located in the hinterlands of the nation where there is little prospect for use by the civilian population (see Louscher and Salomone, 1987a).

The military may provide technical training and may socialize the peasantry into accepting the norms of industrial discipline. It is widely argued that the military is an efficient school for teaching basic skills and discipline and for inculcating the habit of obeying orders (Benoit, 1973; 1978a; Pye, 1962). Some argue, however, that such training may also develop the necessary skills for violent protest and revolution (Wolpin, 1986). Military expenditures may be necessary to guarantee the general societal conditions that are essential for production and to prevent disintegrative conflicts, but the military's ability to modernize a nation appears highly variable.

Finally, the military may provide security from threats by regional neighbors that could discourage confidence in production and accumulation. This argument is certainly relevant in the case of Taiwan and the Republic of Korea. Additionally, the military is often the poorer nation's major link with major powers, and it may be instrumental in orchestrating the transfer of technology and the provision of aid, both civilian and military.

It has been argued, however, that the military often develops overly strong ties with the major powers—ties that may operate against the popular forces within the peripheral society (Baran and Sweezy, 1966). Dependent elites have historically sided with the interests of the United States or the USSR and sometimes perhaps against the interests and needs of their own citizens. Examples that are frequently mentioned in this context include post-1964 Brazil, Honduras, the Philippines, and the Republic of Korea.

Unfortunately, there is little consensus among the scholars engaged in systematic empirical research. The initial empirically based analyses of the impact of military spending on economic growth and development in the Third World generally focused on or flowed from the "Benoit hypothesis." Emile Benoit cautiously contended that a positive correlation found between military spending and economic growth was caused by demand creation, increases in human capital and physical capital, the mobilization of resources, and the inculcation of modern norms and values. In his words:

> The military establishment, which in the developed countries often appears as rather archaic and tradition-bound, can in the LDC (less-developed country) context have quite a different significance, being an important force for modernization. If it is to be at all effective, it has to be largely utilitarian and efficiency-oriented in its approach. It also inculcates in those it trains a great many modern attitudes and aptitudes (e.g., using and conserving machinery, following and transmitting precise instructions, living "by the clock," earning, spending and saving money, understanding and working with bureaucracy). Even more fundamental is its revolutionary effect in destroying unquestioned acceptance of local custom and tradition, in substituting a national for a local, ethnic, tribal, or caste consciousness, in promoting a common language, and introducing a host of modern ideas and interests. (1973, 88)

Benoit calculated the simple correlation between military spending and economic growth during the period 1950–1965 for a sample of forty-four less-developed nations (Benoit, 1973; see also Benoit, 1978a). He argued that although the connection between military spending and growth was complex and multifaceted, there were clear benefits to military institutions and military spending. This study set the stage for a number of succeeding empirical analyses because of the counterintuitive nature of Benoit's conclusions and the primarily economic framework of his work (see, for example, the work of Ball, 1983a; 1988; Deger, 1986a; Lim, 1983; Looney, 1986; Weede, 1986; and Wolpin, 1986).

These later studies frequently yielded results that conflicted with Benoit's findings. David Lim's (1983) replication, using data from the period 1965–1973, with an expanded sample and differing measures, found an overall negative relationship between military spending and growth. Similarly, Riccardo Faini, Patricia Annez, and Lance Taylor (1984) found that military spending had an overall negative effect on economic growth in a sixty-nine–nation panel study. These authors found no evidence for beneficial military spending effects through short-term lagged human capital, demand creation, or capital utilization. In fact, the studies provided evidence of negative effects of military spending within most regional subsamples. In the Asian sample (which did not include Taiwan), there were very weak effects.

A series of studies by Saadet Deger has yielded mixed results (Deger and Smith, 1983; see also Deger, 1986a and b; Deger and Sen, 1983). Deger found that military spending has a positive direct effect and a negative indirect effect on economic growth; military spending itself was determined to be endogenous, with levels influenced by oil, war, and economic size. Deger argued that we must look at the simultaneous effect of military spending on different areas of the economy—something previous researchers had often failed to do. Deger's research was rather narrowly focused on a limited number of variables, some of which seemed to suffer from measurement problems.

B. Biswas and R. Ram (1986) found very weak effects of military spending in their research. Estimating the defense spending–growth relationship for a number of country samples over two time periods (1960–1970 and 1970–1977), they found a relationship that varied from slightly negative to significantly positive. They concluded that "military expenditures neither help nor hurt economic growth" (1986, 370).

Wayne Joerding's (1986) time series study also arrived at a "no effect" conclusion. Joerding employed a Granger causality framework in his examination of fifty-seven poorer nations during the period 1962–1977. In spite of the technical innovations he introduced, Joerding failed to examine many possible effects of military spending, in particular balance-of-payments issues, domestic consumption, and capital formation. He also failed to include some explanatory variables of interest to noneconomists in the model's specification. Joerding's major conclusion was that military spending is strongly influenced by, but has no effect on, growth.

In a more recent cross-sectional study, Robert Looney (1989a) found significant differences between civilian and military regimes in the "styles" of economic management. He concluded that military regimes tend to create an environment in which military expenditures have a positive overall impact on economic growth. Civilian regimes, which have less control over "rent-seeking" groups, do not appear to be able to generate a similar impact.

Studies of single nations have also had conflicting results. Stephanie Neuman (1978), for example, concluded that military spending in Iran had a beneficial impact; Dan Smith and Ron Smith's results (1979) provided a direct criticism of this conclusion. Peter Terhal (1981) arrived at a negative assessment of the impact of military spending in India. James Lebovic and Ashtaq Ishaq (1987) concluded that military spending suppressed economic growth in the Middle East (their cases and time period were selected in an effort to examine a cluster of cases that had very high levels of military expenditures).

The lack of consensus among researchers on the effects of military expenditures on economic development is rooted in a number of factors, all of which have clear implications for further research on this topic. First, as John Hartman (1989) has argued, analysts have commonly utilized less than perfect measures for key variables and concepts. Poor operationalization of variables relating to human capital and economic growth and development in particular is likely to be responsible for erroneous or misleading findings. Economists have often been ineffective in measuring political variables—when they seek to measure them or analyze them at all—and political scientists, sociologists, and military and strategic analysts have often used overly simplistic measures of economic variables relating to concepts they do not thoroughly understand. Most analysts express some dissatisfaction with gross national product (GNP) per capita as a key measure, but few try to include rigorous measures of distribution in their analyses. Miles Wolpin (1986), for example, notes that measures of the "physical quality of life" differ from GNP per capita but speculates only briefly as to why this is the case.

Similarly, measures of military spending are problematic. Some agreement exists among U.S. Arms Control and Disarmament Agency (ACDA), World Bank, United Nations (UN), Stockholm International Peace Research Institute (SIPRI), International Institute for Strategic Studies (IISS), and World Military and Social Expenditures (WMSE) data, but there are also significant differences in the range of coverage. More comprehensive data bases that carefully combine these sources to construct large-scale longitudinal series are clearly needed.

Second, and relatedly, cross-sectional research designs analyzing large numbers of disparate countries in a limited time frame and countries often selected more on the basis of data availability than with a theoretical structure or policy evaluation design in mind are clearly unsatisfactory. Time series analysis is underused despite its obvious advantages, and the use of time series of cross-sections of nations or even a truly comparative research design involving several time series analyses of different countries selected on the basis of theory or carefully framed hypotheses is almost totally absent in this area.

Third, the interpretation of results in the typical cross-sectional research effort tends to suffer from the lack of field research input or, in many cases, even from the analysts' lack of significant knowledge about most of the countries in question. Area study expertise or field research experience in developing countries is rarely evident in the analysts who have dominated this area of inquiry to date.

Finally, the lack of consensus also reflects the considerable variability in the conditions and the political and economic processes in Third World countries (see Ball, 1988, for illustrations of the importance these differences can have). Clear insight as to the differences and specific structures involved must be brought into future research design processes. Countries must be chosen carefully to reflect these differences, and systematic analysis should proceed on a country-by-country basis. The specific channels by which military spending has an impact on development in key countries must be known before a detailed behavioral model (whether econometric or otherwise) can be specified and estimated. The absence of this crucial step goes far to explain the inconclusive and unsatisfactory results of previous research.

This effort must also include, however, sensitivity to and exploration of differences in the way elements of the international system and external security situations impinge upon Third World states. To what extent do variations in external and internal threat perceptions affect military expenditures and their impact on the domestic economy? How have the arms transfer policies of major suppliers affected national military expenditures? What are the patterns of arms transfers and indigenous arms production in Third World countries, and how do they relate to patterns of conflict? What are the determinants of each of these patterns, and how do they relate to the expenditure/development relationships?

There are no easy solutions to these problems and constraints. The workshops that formed the basis for this volume struggled with them continually. It is hoped that some initial steps have been made and that subsequent work both by the members of the working group and by others with whom we have been engaged or have sought to address in this effort will bear more fruit.

Key Questions

The workshops and literature review raised the following key questions for research:

1. What are the general determinants of military expenditures in developing countries?
2. What is the impact of differences in the security environment and perceived threats; the budgetary allocation and decisionmaking process; the role of military assistance and arms suppliers; financial and economic constraints; military versus civilian regimes; domestic defense industry development?
3. What is the impact of military expenditures on economic growth; public consumption, savings, and investments; nonmilitary govenment expenditures and programs; employment; technological transfers and productivity; balance of payments, foreign exchange, and external debt; income distribution and welfare?
4. How do these relationships and impacts vary according to regime type, access to natural resources, and industrial development?
5. What are the implications of trends in conventional arms production and transfers for arms control and security in the Third World and beyond?
6. What are the patterns of arms transfers and indigenous arms production in Third World countries, and how do they relate to patterns of conflict?

7. What are the determinants of each of these patterns, and how do they relate to the expenditure and development relationships in the previous questions?

Workshop Membership and Schedule

The workshops that led to the conceptualization and research reported in this volume were sponsored by the Midwest Consortium for International Security (MCISS) under a grant from the MacArthur Foundation, and the Center for the Advanced Study of International Development (CASID) and the Center for European and Russian Studies (CERS), both at Michigan State University. The workshops began in winter 1991 and included the following participants:

Itty Abraham, University of Illinois (political science)
Mohammed Ayoob, Michigan State University (James Madison College, political science)
Michael Barnett, University of Wisconsin (political science)
Tom W. Carroll, Michigan State University (Center for the Advanced Study of International Development)
Marcus Cheatham, Michigan State University (political science)
Greg Cline, Michigan State University (political science)
Chris Crantz, Wayne State University (Center for Peace and Conflict Studies)
Donald K. Crone, Scripps College (political science)
Ahmed El-Kholei, University of Illinois (urban planning)
Patrice Franko-Jones, Colby College (economics)
Deborah Gerner, University of Kansas (political science)
Norman A. Graham, Michigan State University (James Madison College, political science)
Amit Gupta, University of Illinois (political science)
Kwabena Gyimah-Brempong, Wright State University (economics)
John Hartman, SUNY-Buffalo (sociology)
Subbiah Kannappan, Michigan State University (economics)
V. N. Krishnan, Bowling Green State University (political science)
Robert Leh, Illinois Wesleyan University (political science)
Peter Lewis, Michigan State University (James Madison College, political science)
David J. Louscher, University of Akron (political science)
John Nutter, Michigan State University (James Madison College, political science)
Warren Phillips, University of Maryland (political science)
Linda Racioppi, Michigan State University (James Madison College, political science)

Patrick M. Regan, University of Michigan (political science)
Marian Rice, Midwest Consortium for International Security Studies
Michael Rubner, Michigan State University (James Madison College, political science)
Lewis W. Snider, Claremont Graduate School (political science)
Andrew Wallace, University of Chicago (political science)
Jonas Zoninsein, Michigan State University (James Madison College, economics)

Overview

In this volume we begin to address the questions and limitations discussed earlier in this chapter with Mohammed Ayoob's continuation of his substantial work on security in the Third World. Ayoob sharpens the concept of security, warning against undue broadening of its meaning, and describes the security problematic of the Third World as a "multilayered cake." The layers include the multiple balances of the present international system, the regional dimension, and the important internal dimension of security. This formulation allows him to stress the relevance of the processes of state formation and legitimation and to criticize the previous research and commentary that have suggested that the problematic is simply, or even largely, a guns-for-butter tradeoff.

John Nutter continues the exploration of the international environment for military spending and security policy by developing a general concept of threat. He then focuses on the subcomponent of military threat and suggests relevant propositions and empirical measures. Nutter examines numerous issues relevant to the systematic measurement of threat and the prospects for incorporating such measures into future quantitative studies. Although the search for these measures and for appropriate statistical tools for incorporating them effectively into studies of military spending and economic development may still require substantial attention, Nutter clearly helps to move us in that direction. This is particularly important given Ayoob's arguments on the importance and complexity of the role of conceptions of threat and security and the notable lack of careful attention to the measurement of threat and threat perception in previous quantitative studies.

Part II opens with an overview by David Louscher and James Sperling that discusses past and prospective patterns of arms and related technology transfers. Based on substantial and long-term data base development and trend analysis efforts, the authors describe these patterns in terms of change in the structure of power in the international system, noting four distinct phases: U.S. Hegemony (1947–1962), Bloc Competition (1962–1974), Bloc Competition Modified (1975–1985), and Bloc Erosion–Incongruent Multipolarity (1986 to present). They present substantial data on major suppliers and recipients, depicting change in the international arms transfer system largely in tandem with these four phases. Accordingly, in their view the arms transfer system has progressed from a phase of U.S. dominance, relying largely on grants of equipment and support, to one characterized by U.S.-USSR competition through the mid-1970s. This was followed by a phase of "industrial supplier competition" leading to the present phase of "diffuse economic competition."

Warren Phillips and Linda Racioppi focus more specifically on trends and prospects in Soviet-Russian arms transfers in the context of broader relations with the Third World. Of great interest here is an effort to examine the extent to which patterns and determinants evident (although still the subject of considerable scholarly debate) during the Soviet period remain relevant today and for the future. While tracing the historical patterns and regional distribution of arms, the authors stress the rising importance (after the Khrushchev years) of efforts to promote relations that are of "mutual economic benefit." They note that as the Soviet economy weakened generally, the importance of arms production and sales grew substantially. The authors stress the continuing importance of this sector in describing the dilemmas faced as the post–Cold War government attempts to restructure the domestic economy and to consider defense-industrial conversion in a demanding foreign economic environment.

Amit Gupta offers a careful discussion and explanation of the arms procurement policy and patterns of a major Third World recipient and producer, India. Systematically considering a broad range of internal and external factors, Gupta stresses the importance of India's relationship with the former Soviet Union for its outright arms purchases and substantial licensed production arrangements. This relationship was crucial, particularly through much of the 1970s, in part because of the constraints on the availability of hard currency for purchases from Western suppliers. Gupta concludes with an assessment of the prospects both for the Indian-Soviet/Russian defense equipment relationship and for the independent efforts of India to arm itself in the context of worsening economic conditions.

Part II closes with a longitudinal analysis of military spending in Taiwan. John Hartman and Wey Hsiao attempt to escape from some of the limitations of previous research and to examine systematically the impact of both internal and external influences. They model the expansion of military spending in Taiwan from 1953 to 1988, finding that it was related less to perceptions of external threat than to the general level of economic activity in the country, particularly given Taiwan's security relationship with the United States The evolution of the defense industry is traced, as are the variation in alliance patterns and the external threat environment.

In Part III we turn to the impact of military spending and military regimes on development. Jonas Zoninsein explores the relationship among military spending, investment funds, and economic growth. He makes special reference to the demands and opportunities of the post–Cold War international environment, but he also draws upon his previous work on the Latin American world model. Zoninsein assesses the "opportunity cost" of military expenditures and addresses the obstacles to demilitarization, which—along with Ayoob, Phillips and Racioppi, Gupta, and others—he finds are substantial and are often not related to elites' real concern about development and investment.

Lewis Snider then examines the relationship between military spending and the ability of developing countries to meet economic stabilization and adjustment targets. Snider follows up on Ayoob's arguments on the multifaceted nature of Third World security choices and gives careful consideration to the impact of relative levels of security concerns. In effect, he provides a systematic approach to addressing the question of how we can know if a government is spending more than it "should" on its military establishment. Snider stresses the need to examine the impact of the political dimension (political weakness, distributive politics, and similar concerns) and the security dimension (domestic and external), as well as the economic or structural dimension.

In the next two chapters the impact of military regimes on development in a comparative context is examined. Donald Crone compares Thailand and Indonesia in an examination of "patrimonialism versus the market." Stressing the need for a comparative case method to examine the idiosyncratic and subtle effects of the military, he focuses on the degree of military predominance within the ruling regime and the resulting conception of development. Military predominance shapes other aspects of society and leads to a patrimonial "security coalition," but when the regime is broadened to include significant civilian elements, a "growth coalition" may emerge.

Norman Graham and Peter Lewis compare Brazil, Nigeria, Pakistan, and the Republic of Korea in a longitudinal effort to examine the impact of internal and external factors. The authors provide a broad comparison of the economic performance of four military regimes from the mid-1960s through the 1980s, finding that strong security challenges prompted a more statist and authoritarian direction in development strategy. But the difference in economic performance resulted from an array of other factors, most notably progress in state-building and variation in security concerns and in the global context within which each state could operate, including access to foreign assistance.

Marcus Cheatham concludes Part III with a study of the impact of war and military spending on food security in Africa, exploring the development of what he terms *military famine* in the context of internal and external security factors. Cheatham explicitly adopts Ayoob's multilayered cake conception of security as a framework for understanding the durability of military famine in Africa. Here, he describes and models the ways in which militarization can undermine political security when "food security" deteriorates to the point that insurgents can claim greater legitimacy.

In a brief conclusion, I attempt to draw together recurring themes and lessons from this comparative and interdisciplinary enquiry. An effort is also made to sketch the key questions that remain unanswered or only partially answered as a guide and a call for future research.

Note

1.   The author acknowledges the important contribution of John Hartman to an earlier version of this section during the course of the preparation for the workshops.

❖ PART I ❖

Concepts and Trends

❖ TWO ❖

Security in the Third World:
Searching for the Core Variable

Mohammed Ayoob

Before we start searching for the variable that lies at the core of Third World security, we should be clear as to what we mean by the term *security* itself. I adopt here what can be characterized as an essentially state-centric concept of security that emphasizes the primarily political content of the term. I adopt this definition on the basis of an argument I have made elsewhere, which concluded:

> It is preferable to define security in relation to vulnerabilities that threaten to, or have the potential to, bring down or significantly weaken state structures, both territorial and institutional, and regimes which preside over these structures and profess to represent them internationally.... This is a definition which assumes the basic primacy of political variables in determining the degree of security states and regimes enjoy. Different types of vulnerability, including those of the economic and ecological varieties, become integral components of this definition of security only if and when they become acute enough to take on overtly political dimensions and threaten state boundaries, state institutions or regime survival. In other words, debt burdens, or even famines, do not become part of the security calculus for the purpose of this definition unless they threaten to have political outcomes that affect the survivability of states, in either the territorial or institutional sense or both, or of governing elites within those states. (Ayoob, 1991a, 259)

This argument is based on the conviction that an undue broadening of the concept of security makes the concept so elastic that it loses all analytical utility. It is based further on the assumption that other words can be used for economic and ecological phenomena that are increasingly discussed under the umbrella term *security*; for example, we could use terms such as economic deprivation and environmental degradation to describe what are now discussed as problems of economic and environmental security.[1] Such usage would allow for a clear, political definition of security with the understanding that economic, ecological, and other phenomena could become essential parts of the security calculus if and when they are eventually seen to directly threaten state institutions or boundaries or the survivability of regimes.

It has also become fashionable to equate security with other values many analysts consider intrinsically more important than, and morally superior to, the political-military phenomena and objectives traditionally encompassed by the concept of security. For example, Ken Booth has argued that security should be equated with "emancipation." According to Booth, "Emancipation is the freeing of people (as individuals and groups) from the physical and human constraints which stop them carrying out what they would freely choose to do. . . . Security and emancipation are two sides of the same coin. Emancipation, not power or order, produces true security. Emancipation, theoretically, is security" (Booth, 1991, 319).

The problem with such semantic jugglery is that by a sleight of hand it totally obfuscates the meanings of the concepts of both security and emancipation. Booth's definition refuses to acknowledge that a society or a group can be emancipated without being secure; the reverse is also true. Moreover, specifically in the case of the Third World, such semantic acrobatics tend to impose a model of contemporary Western polities—of national states that have largely solved their legitimacy problem and possess representative and responsive governments that preside over socially mobile populations within societies that are usually affluent and free from want—that are far removed from Third World realities. It may, therefore, be possible to equate emancipation with security in Western Europe (although even that is debatable), but it would be extremely far-fetched and, indeed, intellectually disingenuous to do the same in the case of the Third World, where basic problems of state legitimacy, political order, and capital accumulation are not only far from being solved but may even be becoming more acute. In the context of the Third World, where the legitimacy of states and regimes is constantly challenged, and where demands for economic redistribution and political participation perennially outrun state capacities and create major overloads on political systems, an explicitly political definition of security provides a highly valuable analytical tool that should not be sacrificed at the altar of utopian thinking, even if it is termed utopian realism (Booth, 1991, 317).

The Security Problematic of the Third World

Workings of the International System

Used in the explicitly political and state-centric sense I have outlined here, the security problematic of the Third World is like a multilayered cake. The topmost, and, therefore, the most easily visible, layer is provided by the workings of the international system—until recently the bipolar system that exacerbated conflict in the Third World for a variety of reasons, including the relative unimportance of the Third World to the global balance of power. Among other things, this led to the prevalence of proxy wars in the Third World so that the superpowers could probe the adversary's political will and military reach, as well as test new weapons systems in a wide variety of locales ranging from the paddy fields of Vietnam to the mountain passes of Afghanistan.In other words, the workings of the post–World War II international system and the global balance of power permitted—indeed, encouraged—conflict in the Third World at the same time violent interstate conflict was ruled out in the core strategic and economic areas, namely the industrial heartland comprising Europe, North America, and Japan./ The linkage of the security of industrial states with systemic security in the thermonuclear age made it imperative that as the "amity lines" (Wight, 1977, 125) were preserved in Europe, the great game of international politics should continue to be played out in the Third World in order to protect the superpowers' spheres of influence, to reinforce their standing as great global powers, and to constantly explore whether any changes in the global balance of power were imminent.

Some of these systemic inputs into Third World security began to change in the late 1980s as the Cold War wound down and the global political balance shifted radically in favor of one pole of power—the United States. The Soviet retrenchment in the Third World (especially its decision to withdraw from Afghanistan) provided the first firm indication that the global balance of power was undergoing radical transformation. The changes in Eastern Europe in 1989 and 1990 confirmed that this trend was irreversible. The disintegration of the Soviet Union in 1991 made it unmistakably clear that the bipolar balance of power that was the hallmark of the post–World War II global political landscape had been irrevocably transformed.

What has come to be called the post–Cold War system is based upon a three-dimensional global balance of power whose three dimensions are often out of sync with each other. A continuation of strategic bipolarity is based upon Washington's and Moscow's nuclear—including second-strike—capabilities, which still give them the capacity to inflict unacceptable damage on each other's territorial and demographic domains in case of a direct military confrontation. One could argue that strategic bipolarity has been much diluted by the disintegration of the Soviet Union and its replacement with a loose commonwealth of independent states. However, Russia's insistence that it remain the only successor state to the Soviet Union and that it maintain control of much, if not all, of the erstwhile superpower's nuclear arsenal and delivery capabilities indicates that strategic bipolarity still exists and that the Mutual Assured Destruction (MAD) doctrine is likely to be reasserted as a central theme of global politics when Russia organizes its economic and political systems—possibly by the end of the 1990s.

The decline and final demise of the Soviet Union have had much more dramatic effects on the political balance than on the strategic balance and have also had more immediate consequences for the Third World. Moscow's decision under Mikhail Gorbachev first to reduce its political and military commitments outside the borders of the former Soviet Union and then to remove itself from the superpower competition in both Europe and the Third World has led to the emergence of a politically unipolar world with the United States as the lone political superpower relishing its "unipolar moment" (Krauthammer, 1991).

In the political realm, "being a superpower involves more than owning nuclear weapons: it requires a state of mind that has the will to project power" (*The Economist*, March 9, 1991). As the 1990–1991 Gulf War demonstrated beyond doubt, the United States has indeed emerged, even if temporarily, as the only political superpower if we base this status upon considerations of global interests, global military reach, and the political will to protect and enhance global interests with the exercise of the available military reach. Major questions have been raised about Washington's ability to replictate its actions in the Gulf in future situations. Much of this skepticism is related to U.S. domestic political constraints, declining economic capacity, and reduced leverage with Japan and Germany—which might be insufficient for the United States to persuade those two countries to underwrite much of the financial costs of a future venture as they did during the Gulf War. However, despite these qualifications, the U.S. position as the lone political superpower is established until a future crisis demonstrates U.S. inability to repeat its military and political success in the Gulf.

The third dimension of the current global balance—the economic one—is characterized by multipolarity or, more precisely, tripolarity, with its three poles being the United States, the European Community, and Japan. It is interesting to note that although with the demise of the Soviet Union the United States has emerged for the moment as the undoubted dominant political power, it has lost (by a process of gradual erosion) the predominant position it had occupied in the international economy for a quarter of a century after the end of World War II. At its apex the international economic hierarchy now consists of three near-equals, with Japan potentially the weakest pole of economic power given its paucity of indigenous resources, its smaller market, and its smaller pool of manpower.

The recent Gulf Crisis and the war that followed demonstrated that economic multipolarity was used in the service of political unipolarity (with Japan contributing $13 billion and Germany $9 billion to the U.S.-led war effort) and that strategic bipolarity had for the moment become almost irrelevant to the major security issues in the Third World. Whether the United States will ever again be able to use the economic muscle of Japan and Europe to serve its own geopolitical purposes is, however, a moot question. The Iraqi occupation of Kuwait had placed the huge oil wealth of both countries under the control of a maverick Arab ruler. If this act had gone unchallenged, Saddam Hussein would also have been in a position to dictate Saudi oil pricing and production policy given Riyadh's military vulnerability vis-à-vis Iraq. Because of Japan's and Europe's much higher dependence on oil imports from the Gulf and the Middle

East, this scenario appeared even more alarming to them than it did to the United States. This European and Japanese apprehension explains at least in part the huge Japanese and German financial commitment to the allied war effort, as well as the British and French decision to actively take part in the military campaign against Iraq.

At another level, the struggle over Kuwait can be viewed as one of an aspiring regional hegemon (Iraq) whose regional aspirations ran counter to those of the global political hegemon (the United States). Moreover, in the Iraq-Kuwait crisis the United States found the opportunity to demonstrate its global political hegemony not only to the Third World and the former Soviet Union but, more important, to its political allies that were also its economic competitors. This was essential to emphasize to Europe and Japan that U.S. political will and military power were vital for the protection of the industrialized world's economic and strategic interests from threats by Third World predators such as Iraq and that, therefore, Japan and Europe should bear this in mind when competing economically with the United States.

This does not mean that the pattern of U.S. military involvement in the Iraq-Kuwait crisis will be repeated in every instance in which an aspiring regional Third World hegemon decides to translate its preeminence into predominance by the use of force or the threat of the use of force. The strategic and economic importance of the region to the United States and Washington's perception of the exercise of such hegemony as benign or malign to U.S. interests will determine U.S. reaction. For example, if India decides to annex the Himalayan kingdom of Bhutan, which is plagued by internal turmoil, it is doubtful that the United States would launch Operation Himalayan Blunder to reinstate the king of Bhutan on his throne in Thimpu. Moreover, given the faltering performance of the U.S. economy in recent years, much would also depend upon Europe's and Japan's ability and will to bear the financial burden of future U.S.-led military ventures.

The unique combination of circumstances that made the successful projection of U.S. power possible in the 1990–1991 Gulf Crisis is unlikely to be repeated in routine fashion in other Third World crises and crisis-areas. In fact, arguments are now being made that a reversal of roles might occur between the United States and its major allies, Germany and Japan. This feeling is related to the fact that "relative to its allies, the United States is confronted with a diminished capacity to generate and deploy economic resources in pursuit of foreign policy objectives. . . . Today, Germany and Japan have the economic capacity to constrain U.S. policy should they so choose. . . . U.S. influence [today] is largely dependent on allied toleration of U.S. aims" (Borrus et al., 1992, 197–198). Great-power influence on, and involvement in, regional problems and conflicts in the Third World is, henceforth, more likely to be subjected to a variety of complex pulls and pressures emanating from within the group of major powers than was the case either during the Cold War or during the fleeting moment of U.S. unipolarity.

The Regional Dimension of Third World Security

I now discuss the intermediate layer of the security cake, the regional dimension of Third World security. One can argue that the end of the Cold War should have freed the regional power balances from the oppressive domination of the global balance and allowed the inherent power of preeminent regional states to reassert itself by reducing the capacity of the regional challengers to "borrow" power from one or the other superpower. Such a conclusion, however, must be heavily qualified by considerations of U.S. and other major powers' responses to assertions of regional hegemony. In some cases the United States and the other major powers may be relatively indifferent to such hegemonic aspirations (South Asia), in other instances positively opposed (the Gulf), and in some cases supportive to different degrees (Israel). However, the translation of these regional hegemonic aspirations into concrete realities will depend greatly on the internal capabilities—political and economic, in addition to military—of the regionally preeminent powers (Ayoob, 1991b). Regional colossi with feet of clay do not make successful hegemons.

We should also be aware that many interstate security issues (in other words, actual or potential regional conflicts) are embedded in the domestic political structures and processes of the regional states. Examples of such interconnectedness, in which domestic causes and considerations have led to interstate conflict, are the India-Pakistan war over Bangladesh in 1971 and the Iraq-Iran War of 1980–1988. The former resulted primarily from political breakdown within Pakistan (Sisson and Rose, 1990), and the latter was intimately connected both to the 1979 Iranian Revolution and to the crisis of political legitimacy faced by the Baathist regime in Iraq following the revolution in Iran (Chubin and Tripp, 1988).

All of this does not imply that no autonomous interstate factors lead to regional conflicts. Many Third World conflicts result from dissonance between the views of competing states regarding their own and their rivals' legitimate roles and positions within regional balances of power. This applies both to the India-Pakistan rivalry in South Asia and to the Iran-Iraq rivalry in the Gulf. Such a lack of perceptual congruence among regional rivals is often buttressed by the heritage of colonial rule, which includes unresolved territorial issues (for example, Kashmir, Palestine, the Western Sahara), contested boundaries (for example, Iran-Iraq, China-India), and divided populations (for example, Kurds, Somalis). Artificially drawn and arbitrarily imposed colonial boundaries provide much of the raw material for interstate conflict in the Third World.

The diffusion of nuclear technology and the resulting prospects for nuclear proliferation have further contributed to the climate of conflict in various regions of the Third World. Possession of nuclear-weapons capability is seen by threshold nuclear powers as an avenue to enhance their status both regionally and globally, especially in light of the Chinese experience since 1964. However, nuclear proliferation also threatens to escalate qualitatively the level of violence and the magnitude of destruction in future Third World conflicts. Such potential for escalation is particular cause for concern, because some nuclear-capable Third World states have intense adversarial relationships with other similarly capable states. The India-Pakistan relationship is the classic case that proves this point (Chellaney, 1991).

These relatively autonomous dynamics of interstate conflict should not, however, blind us to the interconnection between issues of regional and domestic security, because the latter often generate the causes that lead to regional conflict by spilling over state boundaries, including moving refugees from one country to another (for example, from Afghanistan to Pakistan), or by forcing regimes that are acutely insecure internally to try to legitimize their repressive behavior by portraying their principal source of insecurity as emanating from external sources (for example, Iraq following the Iranian Revolution). Furthermore, artificially drawn boundaries usually provide sympathetic constituencies for one state's dissidents in one or more neighboring countries, thereby transforming intrastate conflicts into interstate ones.

The Internal Dimension of Security

The interconnection between interstate and intrastate sources of conflict and insecurity leads us to the last, and most important, layer of the Third World security cake. This layer consists of the internal dimension of security, which in the case of the Third World is often derived from the stage of state-making in which Third World states find themselves and is, therefore, related to the lack of unconditional legitimacy of Third World states and regimes.[2] This is a major distinguishing characteristic of the early stage of state-making that is adequately documented by the European experience (Tilly, 1975).

State-making in the Third World, as the earlier European experience demonstrates, can be defined primarily in terms of what has been termed "the primitive accumulation of centralized state power" (Cohen, Brown, and Organiski, 1981, 902)—the expansion and consolidation of centralized control over demographic and territorial space, which is often contested either by elements within postcolonial societies that refuse to accept the legitimacy of the postcolonial state or by neighboring states that are engaged in their own state-making enterprise, which involves similar expansion of control and brings them into conflict with their neighbors. As with the states of early modern Europe, Third World states are not nation-states and are, therefore, engaged in nation-building as well as state-making. The dichotomy between nation-states and state-nations, as propagated by some analysts of the Third World (Rejai and Enloe, 1969), is a false one, because the European states—with the exception of the Balkans (which explains many of the problems in the Balkans today)—had the same experience of states preceding nations that Third World states are undergoing today. Even latecomers such as Germany and Italy were welded into *national states* by the policies of "blood and iron" pursued by Prussia and Savoy before the German and Italian *nation-states* came into existence.[3] This sequence was succinctly summarized by Massimo d'Azeglio, who is reported to have remarked at the first meeting of the Italian parliament, "We have made Italy, now we have to make Italians" (*The Economist*, December 22, 1990).

In Europe, with the exception of the Balkans, this process was largely conducted sequentially (although with a significant degree of overlap in many cases) and over a period of centuries. It still entailed much violence and trauma for the societies undergoing it. The major difference between Europe and the Third World involves the amount of time available to complete the process of building national states. States of Western and Northern Europe took several centuries for the successful completion of the state-making enterprise; Third World states, however, are expected to duplicate and complete the same process within an artificial time frame imposed by their own people and donor nations of ridiculously short duration, encompassing a few decades at the most.

A further important difference, and a corollary of the first, is the attempt in the Third World, unlike in Europe, simultaneously to undertake all of the phases of nation-state–building—standardization, penetration, participation, and distribution (Rokkan, 1975). The last two of these phases involve mass mobilization and populist politics whose demands often run counter to the major requirement of state-making—the imposition of order and central control. The problem for the Third World has been compounded by the already mentioned colonial legacy of artificial boundaries and the multiethnic composition of Third World societies. As a result, most of the violence in the Third World today is of an intrastate rather than an interstate character and is intimately related to the accumulation of centralized power by the state and the resistance to this process by important segments of Third World societies (Ayoob, 1992).

This conclusion is borne out by the data published in the 1991 SIPRI Yearbook. According to this highly respected source, in 1990 there were thirty-one major armed conflicts around the globe (almost all of them in the Third World), of which only one was interstate in nature—that between India and Pakistan on the cease-fire line in Kashmir. SIPRI defines a major armed conflict "as prolonged combat between the military forces of two or more governments or of one government and at least one organized armed group, involving the use of weapons and incurring battle-related deaths of at least 1,000 persons." This criterion of battle-related deaths is, however, applied from "the beginning of the conflict between the current fighting parties" (Lindgren et al., 1991, 345). Such a criterion has led to two anomalies in the 1990 data, one of which involves the inclusion of the India-Pakistan conflict over Kashmir as the only major interstate conflict, although in 1990 battle-related deaths between these two countries were minimal. On the other hand, it has led to the exclusion of the Iraqi invasion of Kuwait, because battle-related deaths between August and December 1990 were below one thousand. Only in 1991 did battle-related deaths escalate into the thousands or even the hundreds of thousands following the decision by the U.S.-led alliance to launch a massive air and land invasion of Iraq and Iraqi-occupied Kuwait.

SIPRI further subdivides intrastate conflicts into those for the control of the government (where the legitimacy of regimes is challenged) and state-formation conflicts (where the legitimacy of existing states is challenged). In 1990 intrastate conflicts were divided almost equally between these two categories (Lindgren et al., 1991, 346–348). We should note that in many cases it is extremely difficult to distinguish between the two categories of intrastate conflicts, because they often overlap with one another and sometimes move from one category to another depending primarily upon how states and regimes decide to respond to the initial challenges.

State-Making and Security Expenditure

The central importance of the internal dimension of security, which is inextricably linked to the state-making process in the Third World, is also demonstrated by the data presented by Nicole Ball in her wide-ranging study of the relationship between security expenditure and development in the Third World (Ball, 1988). Ball makes three interrelated arguments: (1) that many Third World states spend substantial proportions of their relatively meager resources on the security sector; (2) that although expenditure on costly weapon systems and military technologies forms a part of security expenditure, it is not the major part in the overwhelming majority of Third World states, and the major part of this expenditure is on operating costs; and (3) that such security expenditure is frequently undertaken at the expense of the developmental objectives of Third World states, and that such resources would be better utilized for developmental purposes.

Her first assertion is in one sense noncontroversial, because in the late twentieth century security is not attained cheaply. In another sense it is open to criticism on the grounds that states in different regions of the Third World spend different proportions of their gross national products (GNP) or gross domestic products (GDP) on security. Most sub-Saharan African countries, for example, spend a fraction of what several countries in the Middle East and South Asia spend on defense and security. Even within South Asia, defense expenditure in 1990 varied, according to official figures, between a high of 7.2 percent of GDP for Pakistan and a low of 1.5 percent of GDP for Bangladesh, with India occupying the middle ground at 3.2 percent of GDP (Cheung and Friedland, 1991, 52–53).

However, Ball's point about security expenditure going beyond mere defense expenditure is well taken, because the former includes expenditure on paramilitary forces, which is not included in defense budgets. These paramilitary forces—such as the Border Security Force and the Central Reserve Police Force in India or the praetorian guards in countries such as Syria and Iraq—play extremely important roles in the sphere of internal security and regime maintenance in the Third World. It is instructive to note that the strength of the paramilitary forces in India has almost doubled between 1970 and 1990, whereas the strength of the regular military has stayed constant (Thomas, 1991).

Ball's second point about Third World states spending "a very high proportion of their security budgets on operating costs, particularly salaries and emoluments for the troops" (Ball, 1988, 393) merits further discussion. Ball examined the evolution of operating costs as a percentage of total security expenditure of twenty selected Third World countries for the years 1951–1979 and found that in all cases except one (Iran under the shah), operating costs clearly dominated in the mix of security expenditures for these countries (1988, 396–402). She therefore concluded that although "in the public mind, security expenditure in the Third World is firmly linked with the arms trade . . . for most of the Third World, the arms trade and security expenditure are not synonymous: Operating costs, particularly personnel-related outlays, form a large and permanent portion of most developing countries' security budgets" (Ball, 1988, 107, 111). This, Ball suggests, is connected to the fact that "the internal security role of the armed forces is considerable throughout the Third World and, in many cases, is their primary function" (Ball, 1988, 393).

Although Ball's sample omits such oil-rich and population-poor countries as Saudi Arabia and Kuwait, in which capital costs—including expenditure on defense infrastructure and weapons procurement—would be appreciably higher than reflected in her data, her basic point regarding high operating costs and their relationship with internal regime and state security is valid for most of the Third World countries. This reflects not merely the relatively low level of technology and the high level of manpower required by Third World states for the maintenance of internal control but also the stage they are at in terms of their state-making enterprise.

As the European experience has demonstrated, taxation (extracting resources under the protection of coercive state agencies), policing (maintaining domestic order where it has already been imposed), and warfare (extending and consolidating a particular political order by the use of force against potential as well as dissident subjects and fending off rival claimants to the same territorial and demographic space) together characterize the bulk of the activities undertaken by early state-makers. These are all labor-intensive activities that engage relatively large numbers of persons in the security arena, thereby raising the ratio of operating (including personnel) costs relative to the total expenditure on security. Security-sector costs in the Third World are understandably linked to the performance of these essential functions in the current early stage of state-making.

In this context, Ball's third assertion regarding the relationship between security expenditure and development makes sense, although her conclusion that if such expenditure were diverted to developmental purposes it could produce better returns is rather misplaced. Despite the declaratory commitment of Third World state elites to the goal of development (defined as economic growth plus some degree of distributive justice), most of them feel this is an instrumental value that helps them achieve their primary objectives of political legitimacy and state and regime security. Therefore, Ball's conclusion that "available evidence does suggest that expenditure in the security sector is more likely to hinder than to promote economic growth and development in the Third World" (Ball, 1988, 388), although possibly valid, misses the essential motivation behind such expenditure. This motivation has to do primarily with the "primitive central state power accumulation" mentioned previously and secondarily with meeting threats from the regional environment. As a result, development, measured as a serious objective in its own right and not merely on the basis of Third World leaders' rhetoric, places a poor third in the policy priorities of most Third World elites and is rarely considered a goal that deserves to be fulfilled autonomously of internal and external security considerations.[4]

Furthermore, given the fragility of many Third World polities, it is no wonder that "one negative effect of security expenditure," as Ball terms it, has been "the strengthening of the armed forces at the expense of civilian groups within society" (Ball, 1988, 390). Once again, this is almost inevitable, given the stage of state-making at which most Third World states currently find themselves. No other institution is more important than the military (which in this case includes paramilitary forces as well) where the interface between issues of state-making and those of internal and external security is concerned. As the early modern European experience has demonstrated, the role of the coercive apparatuses of state, which means primarily of military and paramilitary institutions, in the early phase of state-making is considerable (Finer, 1975).

In the case of most Third World states, the problem has been compounded by the existence and combination of two further factors. The first is the weakness of civil society and other political institutions, which precludes the emergence of strong checks on the natural proclivity of the security apparatuses to usurp as much of the state's power and resources as possible. Second, the encapsulation of the various phases of state-building and nation-building into one all-encompassing phase, and the drastic curtailment of the time available to Third World states to complete these twin processes of state-making and nation-building, enhance the political importance of the coercive functions of the state and, therefore, of the agencies that perform such functions. Even in the one country in which a democratic political system has operated more successfully than possibly anywhere else in the Third World—India—the important and increasingly dominant role of the security apparatus is clearly visible in states such as Punjab and Kashmir, in which the Indian state faces major overt challenges in the state-building and nation-building arenas. Therefore, it should come as no surprise that the security sector hogs a large share of the state's disposable resources without regard for the impact this may have on the process of economic development in most Third World states.

It is interesting to note in this context that little difference seems to exist between the overtly military-dominated polities in the Third World and those under civilian control in the allocation of scarce resources to the security sector. This is demonstrated by Ball's data, which include several states under civilian rule within the category of the heaviest spenders on security (Ball, 1988, 387,

Fig. 10-1). It is also corroborated by a study of defense spending by the member-states of the Association of Southeast Asian Nations (ASEAN), which, despite several caveats and qualifications, concluded that "the countries [in ASEAN] in which the military has the largest political role (Thailand and Indonesia) are the ones in which defence spending has grown more slowly than the ASEAN average" (Denoon, 1987, 49). State-making and the violence that accompanies it obviously cut across the distinction between military-dominated and civilian-ruled polities in the Third World.

Conclusion

The SIPRI data, as well as those provided by Nicole Ball, support the conclusion that state-making and the violence it entails dominate the political, and certainly the security, landscape in the Third World. With the end of the Cold War and the demise of the Soviet Union, the internal dimension of security will likely take on even greater salience as the overlay of Cold War rivalries is removed from Third World conflicts. Although in some cases this may make Third World conflicts more amenable to solution (at least temporarily), in most cases the removal of Cold War constraints—on superpower rivalry as well as on exacerbated conflict in the Third World—will likely lead to their intensification in the short term or, at the least, to a much clearer assertion of the intrinsic reasons propelling such conflicts.

In any case, although global rivalries, and the recent changes introduced into those rivalries as a result of the collapse of the Soviet Union, did (and do) provide important inputs into the total security picture in the Third World, they do not form the core of the Third World's security problematic and do not determine its basic character. This core is provided by the internal dimension of security. Internal threats to the security of states and regimes in the Third World are, in turn, determined by the state-making enterprise in which almost all Third World countries are engaged. The nature of these threats is particularly influenced by state-building strategies adopted by Third World state elites—strategies that range from primarily coercive to primarily persuasive in character. However, given the nature of the state-making enterprise, even in those cases (such as India) in which state-building strategies have traditionally fallen near the persuasive end of the persuasive-coercive continuum, they inevitably include a considerable amount of coercion (Ayoob, 1991c). This preoccupation with state-making on the part of Third World state elites, and the reaction to state-building strategies by various segments of the Third World's populations, dictate, and will continue to dictate in the foreseeable future, much of these countries' political and security agendas. This is the main reason that any paradigm that attempts to explain Third World security issues without making state-making its central concern will have only a limited degree of explanatory power.

I need to reiterate that the internal security dimension of Third World states, as reflected most dramatically in instances of attempted secession, should be analyzed not in isolation but in conjunction with the reality of regional power balances and the workings of the global balance of power. ¡This is essential because these last two variables provide major external inputs into the process of state-making in the Third World, which is supported by the fact that attempts at secession come closer to being successful when they garner effective support from important external sources—either regional powers or major global powers. This is the reason Donald Horowitz concluded that "secession lies squarely at the juncture of internal and international politics." At the same time, Horowitz made it clear that "whether and when a secessionist movement will emerge is determined mainly by domestic politics, by the relations of groups and regions within the state. Whether a secessionist movement will achieve its aims, however, is determined largely by international politics, by the balance of interests and forces that extend beyond the state" (Horowitz, 1985, 230). Origins of most forms of conflict in the Third World, especially of secession, therefore usually lie in the domain of domestic rather than international politics, although their success or failure is often determined by the interplay of external and domestic forces.

Unfortunately, as a result of a misconstruction of priorities, in much of the international relations literature concerned with Third World security, the regional and global dimensions of security often receive analytical primacy over issues of state-making and internal security. This usually tends to distort our perceptions of the Third World security problematic. The prevailing tendency to emphasize external at the expense of internal factors in discussions of Third World security results from two factors. First, the Western intellectual bias reflected in the literature on the subject defines security almost exclusively in external terms (and, therefore, sees it as a function of threat or lack of threat from outside state boundaries). Second, most analysts are fascinated with the impact of great-power rivalry (in other words, global systemic factors) on the security of Third World states.

This analytical tendency needs to be corrected if we are to fully comprehend the security predicament facing Third World states at this historical juncture when, as stated earlier, the principal preoccupation of Third World state elites is with the consolidation and legitimation of state power and authority, which are constantly under challenge from powerful segments of their populations. This preoccupation forms the core of the state-making process. Therefore, analyzing the security of Third World states without giving adequate—which in this case means primary—attention to this factor is like ena
prince of Denmark.

Notes

I would like to thank my colleague Michael Schechter for h
earlier draft of this chapter.

1. For a cogent case made by a scholar who is sympath

agenda against linking environmental concerns with national security, see Daniel Deudney (1990).

2. I have explained elsewhere that the "late development of modern state structures has meant that they still lack legitimacy . . . in large parts of the Third World. Defined, as they have been, primarily by boundaries drawn by the colonial powers for the sake of administrative convenience or in some form of trade-off with colonial competitors, these structures have not yet developed the capacity to ensure the habitual identification of their populations with their respective states and the regimes that preside over the post-colonial structures within colonially-dictated boundaries" (Ayoob, 1983–1984, 45). For an insightful analysis of the colonial inheritance and its impact on Third World "stateness," see Joel Migdal (1988).

3. A clear distinction should be made between national states, which are "relatively centralized, differentiated, and autonomous organizations successfully claiming priority in the use of force within large, contiguous, and clearly bounded territories" (Tilly, 1990, 43), and nation-states, which are states "whose people share a strong linguistic, religious, and symbolic identity" (Tilly, 1990, 3).

4. For an interesting discussion of the relationship between economic development and national security in the Third World that reaches similar conclusions, see Ethan B. Kapstein (1988).

❖ THREE ❖

Unpacking Threat: A Conceptual and Formal Analysis

John Jacob Nutter

"Threat" seems such a self-evident concept that it is often discussed as though we all know what it means and thus does not merit the same careful consideration as, say, distinguishing tactical from strategic missiles or removing autocorrelation. Although threat has received much attention in the Realist literature (which generally focuses on military threat), even there a lack of precision has created numerous disputes arising from conceptual ambiguity. This is an important lacuna, because threat is generally the reason given (and accepted) for the creation of national armed forces. Because this process generally has two results—the stimulation of counterthreat (one's own military buildup) and the diversion of often critical economic, social, and intellectual resources—any clarity we can bring to the concept of threat is a tangible social benefit.[1]

In this chapter I do two things. First, I develop a general concept of threat, working from an Eastonian understanding of politics, as elaborated by Richard Mansbach and John Vasquez (1981) in their "issues-based paradigm." Second, I examine one component of threat—external military threat—focusing on the nexus of threat, counterthreat, capability, and hostility. I formally develop a set of propositions and suggest empirical measures.

Three observations should be made at this time. First, my work here is conceptual in nature and thus does not address specific issues such as the threat resulting from changing warhead accuracy, ten-thousand-foot runways, and the like. Second, I focus on military threat, because even given an Eastonian approach, this chapter is part of a project that focuses on Third World security and arms spending. Because military threat should be a primary determinant of arms spending, it remains the most important concept to clarify. Third, my focus here is on external threat. This last point requires some explication.

Internal threats are not irrelevant to any state and are often paramount to Third World states (Ayoob, 1991a; Chapter 2 in this book). However, I do not address them here for two reasons. First, the internal dimension of security is dealt with elsewhere in this volume (Chapter 2; see also Nutter, 1992). Second, and more important, this volume focuses on the "guns-butter" tradeoff in the Third World. The most expensive military items are generally high-tech hardware (especially the paraphernalia that create a disproportionate share of external debt), which is most appropriate for two purposes: countering external threats and providing status. Internal security is generally the province of labor-intensive military forces (that is, infantry, paramilitary units, death squads) and therefore is a less important consideration in decisions to acquire expensive military technologies. Therefore, I focus here on external military threat.

Threats and Values

Mansbach and Vasquez (1981) have explicated a new paradigm for international politics by returning to the question What is politics? and employing Easton's answer that the domain of politics is the authoritative allocation of valued things. This diverges substantially from the classic Realist definition of politics as the "struggle for power" (for example, Morgenthau, 1973, 27, 5–8). The effect of this different starting point is profound:

> The Eastonian definition moves the analysis of global politics away from conceptions of power and security and toward the assumption that demands for value satisfaction through global decision making must be at the heart of any theory . . . [and reorients us] toward more basic questions of how dissatisfaction is generated. (Mansbach and Vasquez, 1981, 29)

For a Realist, power is the raison d'être of the state, and conflict is the result of power grabs or disagreements over power. Conversely, in an issue-based framework, threats are perceived over many different spheres of value. Power is one of these but not the only one: Other values—such as status, prosperity, peace, and justice—have intrinsic worth and are contended for. Further, this approach also guides us toward some useful solutions of conceptual and theoretical problems that are generally avoided in the literature, such as a general definition of threat.

The Pursuit of Values

An' it's one, two, three,
what're we fightin' for?
—*Country Joe McDonald*

"Values are the desired events, objects, and conditions for which people strive" (Gurr, 1970, 25). Thus, any state's policies can be analyzed as (1) the processes by which it selects and rank orders values to pursue, and (2) the means it uses to attain those values. When Third World States choose Tomcats over John Deeres, they are revealing something about their hierarchy of values.

What kinds of values do states pursue? Here we may benefit from the efforts of previous scholars, whose compilations of national values are presented in Table 3.1.

Although these authors have not always used identical labels, classification of values from their texts is straightforward. These values may not represent every object a nation might pursue, but they are a good starting point for sorting out the tangled skein of international relations research. Two of these values, physical security and autonomy, have been the focus of Realism and most international relations research,[2] although even here the concept has been highly elastic.

The Elements of Threat

In a values-based context, threat has three components: the likelihood of value deprivation, the salience of the value at stake, and the proportion of the value at stake.[3] The product of these elements defines threat. In formal terms:

$$(1) \quad \text{Threat} = \begin{array}{c} \text{probability} \\ \text{of value} \\ \text{deprivation} \end{array} \times \begin{array}{c} \text{value} \\ \text{salience} \end{array} \times \begin{array}{c} \text{value} \\ \text{proportion} \\ \text{at stake} \end{array}$$

I now briefly examine these.

Within a values context, threat is the likelihood that one will be deprived of some valued thing. Threat by its very nature refers to some future act. It should be considered a probability, because if an actor will attempt to deprive one of a

Table 3.1   Primary National Values

Value	Mansbach	Wilkenfeld	Spanier	Holsti
Wealth	X	X	X	X
Security	X	X	X	X
Autonomy	X	X	X	X
Peace	X	X		
Order	X			
Status	X	X	X	X
Justice	X	X		
Unity		X	X	X
Ideology		X	X	X

Sources: Mansbach and Vasquez, 1981, 58; Wilkenfeld et al., 1980, 52; Spanier, 1987, 87–97; Holsti, 1972, 130–153. See also Lasswell and Kaplan, 1950, 55–56; Gurr, 1970, 24–26; and Cobb and Elder, 1972, 40. Categories coded by author.

value, then the attempt may succeed or fail. However, until the attempt is either successful or unsuccessful, one cannot know whether one will be deprived. Thus, like Schrödinger's cat, the object is neither alive nor dead but is merely a probability.[4]

Salience of a value is simply the importance an actor attaches to it (Mansbach and Vasquez, 1981, 102). One perceives less threat over minor values and is less compelled to respond to such threats, whereas potential deprivation of a high-salience value elicits substantially different responses.

Within this context, the perception of threat can change over even a short time, because of either an increase or decrease in value saliency or the creation of new values. Moreover, action over the same persisting value can vary, because the saliency of that value changes over time. These changes are often produced when new opportunities are created by the capacity of humans to transform previously valueless objects into objects with value (Mansbach and Vasquez, 1981, 88). For example, although the Middle East was somewhat important to Europe as a navigation short cut, the region attained a much higher saliency because of the need for oil created by the internal combustion engine.

Values can also decline in saliency,[5] often due to the same human progress. The utility of an object can decrease if some better or cheaper means of value satisfaction becomes available. For example, British presence in the Falkland Islands allowed them to use the islands as a coaling station for the steam-driven Royal Navy of the nineteenth and early twentieth centuries. With the advent of newer technologies, such as oil and nuclear power, as well as the decline of the British Empire, the strategic value of the Falklands has declined proportionately.

Another consideration is the ability of a deprived actor to create, demand, or seize greater value satisfaction, which is usually conceived of as the actor's capability. If an actor perceives that nothing can be gained by overt conflict behavior because one is too weak to demand a new disposition of value, then the actor is unlikely to contest the issue until more favorable circumstances arise. Conversely, when changes in opportunity occur—for example, when the "haves" weaken or the "have nots" grow stronger—then the appetite for the value deprived is whetted (see Mansbach and Vasquez, 1981, 91). Conflict arising because of changing opportunities is a basic premise of much disparate research, including that of Ashley (1980), Gilpin (1981), Allan (1983), Maoz (1982), Organski and Kugler (1980), Blainey (1973), and Kennedy (1987). The important relationship of this point to military spending is that acquisition of military capability creates changes in opportunity. Therefore, the expansion of one country's military threatens other nations' valued things.

Finally, an important element of threat is the scarcity of the value at risk. A 1 percent loss of market share in auto exports is important but not critical, whereas a 10 percent decline could be disastrous. Similarly, the deployment of fifty MX missiles with CEP under 100 meters would constitute some threat yet alone would not present a credible first-strike capability. However, deployment of several hundred such missiles could be perceived as depriving Russia of virtually all of its land-based nuclear capability, thus posing a substantially greater threat.

In summary, threat as the likelihood of deprivation of value is a useful concept in all political contexts. It includes the probability of deprivation, the salience of the value at stake, and the proportion of the value at stake. Because military threat is the threat most logically connected to military spending and arms acquisition, I discuss it next.

Refining Military Threat

Threat as an Issue

Military threat occupies the central thrust of explanation in international relations theory. Realism—the nearest thing to an international relations paradigm—emphasizes the primacy of power, and military force is the wellspring of power, not because power is viewed as a way to attain peace but because it is the vital instrument in maximizing state survival and autonomy (Spykman, 1942, 7; Morgenthau, 1973; Bull, 1977, 107).

Within an issues framework, the military capability of an opposing actor may be interpreted as the potential to threaten the deprivation of many values. A militarily superior nation might defeat another, inflicting death and destruction and thereby compromising the primary value of physical security. Credible threats to physical security in turn imply potential deprivation of other values: Autonomy can be constrained, to the point of permanent occupation or the imposition of a political-economic structure; economic values can be extracted; loss of status is automatic. Because so many values are safeguarded by security, decisionmakers are highly responsive to external military threats.

Threat as Opportunity

Before going further, I should observe that not everyone treats threat as an issue. Threat is often viewed as a measure of opportunity or a situational variable rather than as an issue of contention per se between actors. Maoz, for example, describes the relationship between the initiation of serious international disputes and increases in threat as part of a model of "self-generated opportunities" (1982, 94–95).

It is precisely because the establishment of threat through the creation of capability is self-generated (for example, nations build armies and navies) that we treat it as an issue in and of itself. Nations resent the existence of other nations' military capability because such capability inherently conveys an opportunity for one actor to deprive another of some desired value. Such opportunity is not, however, an act of God. We do not find T-72 Main Battle Tanks as we would find gold nuggets. Actors must take specific, directed action to produce such tanks and, therefore, to produce threat.[6]

Threat: Intention, Capability, and Time

Threat can be analyzed in terms of four basic propositions. First, immediate threat is the product of an adversary's capability and intentions. Second, decisionmakers prefer a situation in which an opponent has no capability to threaten over one in which an opponent has the capability but not the intention (that is, they prefer weakness to friendship). Therefore, threat assessment focuses on the capability of the antagonist. Third, the relationship between military capability and military threat is relative. We cannot determine the degree of threat by looking at the capability of only one actor. Only in comparison does capability meaningfully translate as threat.[7] Fourth, time is an important element of threat. Decisionmakers not only act on immediate threat but also move to anticipate and head off potential threats in the environment.

A Formal Definition of Military Threat

The core concept of threat is usefully formalized in J. David Singer's widely cited definition (1958; see also Kissinger, 1977, 347):

(2)   THREAT = CAPABILITY × INTENTION

This formulation is purposely constructed so that if either capability or intention is zero, no threat exists.

For our purposes, the important feature of this construct is that capability and intention are substitutable for each other. In other words, any given level of threat can be conveyed from two possible combinations of capability and intention. A (hypothetical) threat level of 2 can be produced by a capability level of 2 and an intention level of 1 or by a capability level of 1 and an intention level of 2. Therefore, when an actor wishes to convey a threat to another, it may do so by increasing either its capability or its intention (or some combination thereof).

Threat Means Capability

However, the two components—capability and threat—are not perfectly interchangeable, at least from the perspective of the threatened. Without capability, no threat is possible; without intention, threat is possible, even though the belligerent makes no (current) effort to use its capability to threaten.

Therefore, capability can be regarded differently from intention in making threat assessments. In particular, because it creates the possibility, capability is inherently threatening. There are three arguments for this interpretation.

First, hostility is irrelevant if one cannot act on it. Benin, for example, fancies itself the "graveyard of capitalism," but its six-thousand-man army makes its intentions an incredible threat.

Second, intentions can change rapidly. Although this is less likely to occur between close allies, we often find rapid changes of affect and foreign policy orientation; examples include Ethiopia and Somalia switching alignment in 1977, China breaking with the USSR in 1963, and Egypt evicting the Soviets in 1972 (see Center for Defense Information, 1980). In general, decisionmakers are averse to relying on another actor's goodwill.

Third, the creation or enhancement of military force is often viewed as de facto evidence of hostile intent. Howard observes, "It was not so much the German Naval program itself that gave rise to so much alarm in Britain. It was the intention that lay behind it" (Howard, 1984, 18).

In an international state of nature, how else can we view the development of military capability? In practice, therefore, Singer's threat equation is often treated as

(3)   THREAT = CAPABILITY

In the following sections, I formally develop a basic theory of threat, including the relationship among capability, threat, counterthreat, and interstate hostility. This last element is vital, because hostility reflects the immediacy of the need to arm oneself even at the expense of other important values.

Capability Is Relative

Military capability must be assessed as a relative concept. We cannot accurately appreciate the degree of threat represented by such capability without considering the context, which involves comparing capability against the capabilities of opponents (Morgenthau, 1973, 154–56; Herz, 1976, 157–158; Choucri and North, 1975, 22; Gilpin, 1981, 187; Ferris, 1973; Bremer, 1977, 44–50). One hundred M-1 tanks is a minuscule number against the Warsaw Pact but is mighty against Yemen. Unlike nuclear weapons, conventional capability can largely "cancel out"; in other words, to get at your cities and valued things, I must go through your armed forces. If your forces can stop me—that is, if your defensive capability can destroy my offensive capability—I am no threat. The absolute size of my forces reveals nothing unless we know the size of yours, and, therefore, capability must be assessed as relative capability.

Threat Stimulates Counterthreat

Capability stimulates counterthreat (and, therefore, arms acquisition) in three ways. First, the difference, or gap, between two actors represents an imbalance of bargaining power, from which one actor might deprive the other of some value. Second, large differences in capability are likely to deter expressions of intense, overt hostility, or counterthreat. Third, if the gap between the two is changing, greater counterthreat is a likely result (under certain conditions). The first two propositions are static, asserting that behavior is predicated on threats from here and now. The last is dynamic, proposing that nations also act on what might be.

Capability Gaps Create Fear and Counterthreat

An important reason for hostility and the exchange of threat between nations is the disparity in capability between them. If one actor has more capability than the other, the more capable is commonly assumed to have a greater chance of success in disputes over the disposition of value (Allan, 1983, Chapter 5; Blainey, 1973; Nixon, 1981, Chapter 7; Kissinger, 1977, Chapter 14). To avoid making repetitive concessions (which might encourage the aggressor to threaten other, perhaps more salient, values), the weaker actor is likely to compensate for a lack of capability by increasing the level of intention in the threat equation, "as if to replace with expressed resolve what it lacks in firepower" (Ashley, 1980, 35). In other words, to redress perceived weakness, the nation compensates with "open, often conflictful assertions of strength and resolve" (Ashley, 1980, 188; see also Gilpin, 1981, Chapter 2; Choucri and North, 1975, Chapters 6, 7, 11, 15; Rummel, 1979b, 247; Morgenthau, 1973, 65; Ferris, 1973, Chapter 1).

According to this proposition, we should expect, ceteris paribus, to see a certain level of expressed hostility associated with a certain level of disparity. In other words, the greater the capability gap between two nations (ingo and jingo, or i and j), the greater the hostility of the weaker toward the stronger, or formally:

(4)   Capability gap_{ij} = Capability_i − Capability_j

(5) $\text{Hostility}_{i \rightarrow j}$ = $b_1 \times \text{Capgap}_{ij}$

Preponderance Creates Deterrence

It is apparent, however, that the relationship expressed in Equation 5 does not hold for all values of capability difference. Hostility does *not* increase indefinitely as the capability gap becomes overwhelming. Instead, we hypothesize and empirically observe a distinct decline in hostility at high levels of disparity as the stronger nation attains "preponderance" (an overpowering capability advantage (see Ferris, 1973, 116; Weede, 1976; Garnham, 1976a, 1976b; Singer, Bremer, and Stuckey, 1979).

In general, the weaker nation stops trying to compensate—that is, becomes deterred—when it becomes clear that no amount of hostility can credibly balance the threat equation. This happens because one can only express hostility to a given intensity before having to back up words with force or back down. In a situation of gross capability disadvantage, one does not want to force the issue.

Neither would one want to verbally retreat, because the accompanying loss of credibility might only reinforce the perception of weakness, thereby compounding the problem (see Payne, 1981, Chapter 3; Morgenthau, 1973, Chapter 6; Jervis, 1976, 46–47; White, 1970, 206–215).

Therefore, we should expect a nonlinear relationship[8] to exist between capability gap and hostility. When a disparity in capability exists between two actors, the weaker will express hostility toward the stronger in proportion to the size of the disparity. When the disparity reaches preponderance, however, the weaker nation will sharply reduce the amount of capability gap hostility it expresses.

Precisely when a capability gap becomes a deterrent is a matter of some dispute. Erich Weede (1976) uses a 10:1 ratio as "overwhelming preponderance," whereas Wayne Ferris (1973) employs a 2:1 ratio. The standard military rule of thumb is that an attacker requires at least a 3:1 advantage to assure success and preferably a 6:1 advantage or greater (Dunnigan, 1982, 420; Dupuy, 1979, 11–12); below this level, presumably one ought to be deterred.

There is probably no precise, general (noncontingent) deterrent ratio. Instead of deterrence occurring at a specific level, it more likely takes place over a range of values, mediated by the grievance that ignited the dispute. In other words, what deters hostility for a small dispute might not do so if the issue is critical. Therefore, because there is no a priori reason to select a particular ratio at which deterrence occurs, that value ought to be determined empirically.

It is also theoretically unclear whether this reduction in hostility is a real reduction, a leveling out, or simply a decrease in the marginal hostility rate. This is an important question, because the functional form of the relationship differs depending on which relationship is "true."

If nations express less hostility once the preponderance range is reached, then we would expect the data to fit a parabolic function and be modeled as a quadratic equation, as in Figure 3.1. The mathematical expression of this function is:

(6) $\text{Hostility}_{i—>j} = a_0 + (a_1 \times \text{Capgap}_{ij}) + (a_2 \times \text{Capgap}_{ij}^2)$

where Capgap_{ij} is the capability gap, or disparity, between nations i and j, and where $a_1 > 0$, $a_2 < 0$. Naturally, the sign of a_2 is an empirical matter, but theoretically it should be negative in order to produce the hypothesized direction of the parabola.

If there is a leveling off or change in the marginal increase of hostility related to increasing capability—that is, hostility continues to increase but much more slowly—then we would expect the data to approximate a logarithmic function as depicted in Figure 3.1. This is best fitted as a logarithmic function as in Equation 7:

(7) $\text{Hostility}_{i—>j} = a_0 + (a_1 \times \text{Log}(\text{Capgap}_{ij}))$

Figure 3.1 Relationship Between Capability Gap and Hostility

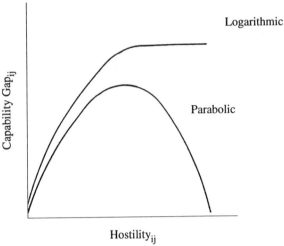

The precise form of the function is, of course, a matter for empirical determination.

Dynamic Capability Creates Potential Threat

When the gap in capability between two actors changes, a number of responses are possible for the lagging actor. One possibility is to increase its own production of capability—that is, to engage in an arms race.[9] This is an academically popular proposition, although the evidence for the existence of arms races is mixed. This relationship seems, at least, the most logical explanation for arms spending by any nation.

Another possible reaction, which has received less attention than arms races, is to increase one's own expression of hostility toward the faster-growing nation. The purpose of such an increase in hostility is to maintain an existing level of counterthreat despite declining relative capability or, again, to compensate for failing military power with increased evidence of will or credibility (that is, intention) (Ashley, 1980, 35, 188). In this section, I focus on the problem of changing capabilities over time and on the hostility stimulated by such potential threat.

One of the most important developments in international relations research in the past two decades has been the maturation of a large and diverse body of literature theoretically and empirically linking growth (especially differential capability growth) with international conflict and war. "The growth of the power of Athens," wrote Thucydides, "and the alarm which this inspired in Lacedaemon, made war inevitable" (1951, 15). Twenty-four hundred years later, another historian, Michael Howard, would observe, "It was the general perception of the growth of German power . . . and the fear that a German hegemony on the Continent would be a first step to a challenge to her own hegemony on the oceans, that led Britain to involve herself in the continental conflict on the side of France and Russia" (1984, 19). The link between rapidly changing power and internation tension typified in Thucydides and Howard pervades both our historiography (see Kennedy, 1987; Gilpin, 1981; Brodie, 1973: Chapter 8; Blainey, 1973; Morgenthau, 1973, 209) and our quantitative models of international politics (Choucri and North, 1975; Ashley, 1980; Organski and Kugler, 1980; Rummel, 1979b; Ferris, 1973; Maoz, 1982, 152; Wallace, 1979, 1982; Smith, 1980).[10]

Military capability is inherently dynamic. Nations constantly build, scrap, upgrade, buy, sell, and deploy capability. People are enlisted and discharged, training is updated, hardware is developed, and so on. Nations may fall behind, catch up, pass, or nearly overtake others and then fall off (see Kissinger, 1977, Chapter 14; McNeil, 1982; Holmes, 1988).

In 1984, seventeen nations spent more than 10 percent of their gross national products (GNP) on military expenditures (six exceeded 20 percent), and only three of these were at war. Moreover, clearly these expenditures were not generally used for personnel (see United States Arms Control and Disarmament Agency, 1986, 5). About 6 percent of gross world product is contributed for the creation and maintenance of military capability. Aside from simple spending measures, the military technology contest continues at a sprint. The list of technological marvels is impressive: the F-117 stealth fighter, "smart" bombs, binary chemical weapons, fuel air explosives, Patriot missiles, and so on (see Bellamy, 1987).

If everyone spent the same amount on or developed capability proportionally, we would need only to consider static relationships. However, capability grows differentially across nations, both quantitatively and qualitatively, because nations produce hardware and enlist manpower at different rates. Some produce highly advanced weaponry (for example, the M1 tank, the M-16 assault rifle), whereas others emphasize cheaper but more plentiful alternatives (for example, the T-62 tank, the AK-47 assault rifle). Furthermore, nations change in their ability to produce military capability. Some simply grow faster than others industrially and are, therefore, able to win the war of production lines. Others gain increased capability because of economic developments, such as changes in commodity prices (like oil), and are able to buy more capability. The end result of these processes is that everyone's force capability is constantly changing, and the way armed forces would interact in trial of arms becomes increasingly less predictable as time passes.

This ebb and flow of capability is a constant source of threat, as decisionmakers attempt to head off anticipated threats. In addition to containing current threats, represented by the current ratio of capabilities (as in Equation 4), governments also act on the basis of what might become a threat: "Political leaders hanker to be known as 'statesmen', which requires that they be 'far-sighted'. To be far-sighted is by definition to see threats well ahead of the time they develop into immediate perils" (Brodie, 1973, 350). As capability changes over time, things that are less known or predictable are perceived as more threatening, especially given the prevalence of worst-case analysis (see also Gilpin, 1981, 13, Chapter 2; Choucri and North, 1975, Chapters 6, 7; Maoz, 1982, 152; Ferris, 1973, 28; Brodie, 1973, Chapter 8).

In particular, when a nation increases its capabilities relative to another nation, the very act of growth is often interpreted as a prerequisite for challenging the status quo.

> Both domestic and international developments undermine the stability of the status quo . . . the most destabilizing factor is the tendency in an international system for the powers of the member states to change at different rates because of political, economic, and technological developments. In time, the differential growth in power of the various states in the system causes a fundamental redistribution of power in the system. (Gilpin, 1981, 13)

Changing capabilities are important not only because of the physical threat they contain but also because of the message they convey. Therefore, the creation of capability is often interpreted by itself as a threat. But what does it threaten?

Geoffrey Blainey (1973, Chapter 8) argues that the distribution of values (the status quo) in the international system is based on a commonly accepted "balance of power" empirically determined in the "last war." Such values include physical security, territory, autonomy and sovereignty, economic benefits and security, and structural values (control or influence over the "rules" of the international system, such as liberalism or mercantilism). When the balance of power changes, previously superior nations can find formerly settled values once again in dispute: "As its relative power increases, a rising state attempts to change the rules governing the international system, the division of spheres of influence, and most important of all, the distribution of territory" (Gilpin, 1981, 187). Heretofore weaker nations are apt to dredge up old disputes (for example, the Sudetenland or Shatt al-Arab) or create new ones (for example, the production of fissile material) to attain values consistent with their new position. In either the pull-ahead or the catch-up situation, then, we may expect an increase in internation hostility (see Organski and Kugler, 1980; Choucri and North, 1975, Chapter 1; Ashley, 1980, Chapters 2, 4; Howard, 1984, 7–22; Gilpin, 1981, Chapters 2, 3, 5; Rummel, 1979b, 266–268, 283; Ferris, 1973, 28–29; Vasquez, 1984, 13; Brown, 1987, 105).

Conceptualizing Potential Threat

Most research in this area has focused on the study of change over time, generally measured as the increase of one actor's capability relative to another's over some period of time (for example, Ferris, 1973, 52; Ashley, 1980, Chapter 8). The general form of the dynamic variable has been:

(8) $$\frac{Capgap_t - Capgap_{t-k}}{Capgap_t}$$

where Capgap is the difference in capability between two actors at some given time, t, and k is the time over which change occurs (Ferris calculates change over a five-year period, whereas Ashley uses yearly change).

An often overlooked problem with this formulation is that the time element is purely arbitrary. Why should change be looked at over one year rather than five years, or vice versa? This is an important question, because an underlying assumption of all of the theories in this area is that the more rapid the change (gaining or losing ground), the greater the hostility generated (Brown, 1987, 105; Choucri and North, 1975, Chapter 15; Ferris, 1973, 28; Organski and Kugler, 1980, 56). When the time element is short, the threat seems even greater.

A more important theoretical reason for exploring the time element is that potential threat is an innately temporal concept. We do not assess threat simply by the difference in growth rates of different actors. A 10 percent difference in growth rate is crucial if the actors are 1 percent apart and negligible if the gap is 1,000 percent. Therefore, potential threat must be assessed as the difference in growth rates and how far apart the actors are: A measure of potential threat must take both considerations into account simultaneously.[11]

Capability Vectors: Time as Threat

How can we combine disparity and growth? One way to think about dynamic capability relationships is to conceive of the two arsenals as vectors, each with a given level and rate of change. A monadic (single-nation) capability vector

Figure 3.2 Capability Growth over Time for One Actor

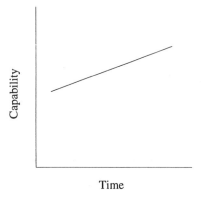

Time

incorporates both a level and a rate of change (see Figure 3.2). This might be represented by a difference equation:

(9) $Cap_t = Cap_{t-1} + (a_1 \times Cap_{t-1})$

where Cap_t and Cap_{t-1} represent military capability levels and the coefficient a_1 is the change in level per time increment. We can represent a dyadic capability relationship with two vectors on the same axes, as in Figure 3.3. The monadic

Figure 3.3a Closing Gap

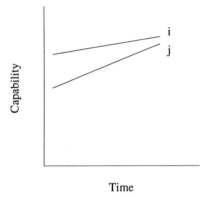

Figure 3.3b Opening Gap

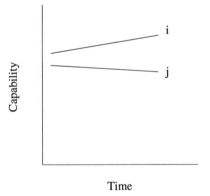

Equation 9 is easily extended to the dyadic case as a pair of simultaneous equations, depicted in Figure 3.3 (monadic means applying to one nation at a time, whereas dyadic means the equations apply to a pair of nations simultaneously):

(10i) $Cap_{i,t} = Cap_{i,t-1} + (a_i \times Cap_{i,t-1})$
(10j) $Cap_{j,t} = Cap_{j,t-1} + (a_j \times Cap_{j,t-1})$

where $Cap_{i,t}$ and $Cap_{j,t}$ are the capabilities of two nations i and j and a given time, t, and the coefficients a_i and a_j are the respective rates of change in capability per unit of time.

There are four possible situations for such a dyadic relationship:

1. $Cap_i > Cap_j$, $a_i > a_j$
2. $Cap_i < Cap_j$, $a_i < a_j$
3. $Cap_i < Cap_j$, $a_i > a_j$
3. $Cap_i > Cap_j$, $a_i < a_j$

In situation 1, the capability of ingo is greater than that of jingo, and ingo is growing faster (because $a_i > a_j$). From this we conclude that the capability gap between ingo and jingo is increasing (as depicted in Figure 3.3b). Situation 2 is similar to 1 but with the positions of ingo and jingo reversed. In 3 the weaker nation, ingo, is growing faster than jingo and is therefore closing the gap between them (as in Figure 3.3a). Again, 4 is analogous to 3, with roles reversed. We can see, then, that the four situations actually reduce to two: The gap is either being closed or opened.[12] These equations convey several bits of information: (1) the disparity between the nations, (2) whether the disparity is opening or closing, and (3) how rapidly this is occurring.

All of this information is contained in the concept Time to Parity, which is the amount of time until parity exists between two actors, given observed rates of change. For any pair of nations, we can find the time to parity by rewriting Equations 10i and 10j with time as a variable (t):

(11i) $Cap_i = Cap_i + (b_i \times t)$
(11j) $Cap_j = Cap_j + (b_j \times t)$

where Cap_i and Cap_j are still levels of capability, t is a number of time increments, and b_i and b_j are the amounts of capability added to current capability every time increment (not the growth *rate*). We can find time to parity by solving for t where Cap_i equals Cap_j, which is simply a way of asking, What is the value of time (t) when capabilities are equal, given current rates of change? If $Cap_i = Cap_j$, then:

(12) $Cap_i + (b_i \times t) = Cap_j + (b_j \times t)$

We can rewrite this as:

(13) $(b_i \times t) - (b_j \times T) = Cap_j - Cap_i$

Gathering terms yields:

(14) $t(b_i - b_j) = Cap_j - Cap_i$

which is equivalent to:

(15) $T = \dfrac{Cap_j - Cap_i}{b_i - b_j}$

In words, the number of time periods until equality equals the difference in capabilities divided by the difference in change to capabilities per time period, or t is equal to the number of times the difference in growth goes into the gap.

This equation results in positive numbers if the weaker side is gaining (and the gap is, therefore, narrowing) and in negative numbers if the gap is widening. For example, if the value of t for a given nation is –6, parity is projected to have occurred, given current levels and rates of change, six time periods in the past. Conversely, if the value of t is 6, we estimate that parity will occur six periods in the future.

We can determine this by referring to the four possible situations following Equations 10i and 10j. Suppose nation jingo has the greater capability, but nation ingo is growing faster (that is, $Cap_j > Cap_i$ and $b_i > b_j$). The sign of the numerator would be positive, and the sign of the denominator would also be positive, resulting in a positive number (indicating intersection of capabilities in the future). The other situations work out analogously.

In summary, counterthreat is created not only by current threat but also by potential threat, which is represented by the time to parity. The operational variable time to parity (TTP) is created similarly to Equation 15:

(16) $TTP = \dfrac{Cap_{it} - Cap_{jt}}{Capgro_i - Capgro_j}$

where Cap_{it} is the capability of nation i at time t and $Capgro_i$ is the rate of growth of nation i's capability, calculated as a three-year moving average (see Nutter, 1991, Chapter 7), and the values for nation j are created identically.

Measuring Threat

Power is generally asserted to be the essence of politics, yet it is a source of controversy. For the economist, money is an easily measurable stock; for the political scientist, power is not. There is even disagreement over how measurable power is. Some researchers assume that decisionmakers accurately perceive balances and imbalances of power (Ferris, 1973; Bueno de Mesquita, 1981). Others argue that one of the primary causes of war is the fact that decisionmakers often miscalculate power (Blainey, 1973). To effectively utilize the refinements to the concept of threat presented earlier, we must also make an effort to refine our measurement.

Threat is not the same as power. To simplify, I focus on threat as defined previously: the impending or potential deprivation of some desired value. The means by which threat is created is military capability, defined as that value that has the capacity to destroy value. Any military capability, because it contains the potential to destroy another actor's valued things, is potentially threatening, and therefore I focus here on measuring capability.[13]

There are several commonly employed measures of capability, including gross national product (see Organski and Kugler, 1980), military expenditures, and composite indices agglomerating various economic, demographic, and military variables (see Singer, Bremer, and Stuckey, 1979; Maoz, 1982; Rummel, 1979b; Wilkenfeld et al., 1980; for intriguing nonacademic efforts, see Dunnigan and Bay, 1985; Cline, 1980). I focus on two measures: military expenditures and the GLOBUS Military Capability Index. The former was selected as the most common measure, whereas the latter is an excellent example of bringing together concept and measurement (for a thorough discussion of many measures, see Nutter, 1991, Chapter 7).

Military Expenditures

The most common measure of capability is military expenditures (for example, Allan, 1983; Wallace, 1982; Ashley, 1980; Choucri and North, 1975; Newcombe and Klaassen, 1977; and numerous other sources). However, as a measure military expenditures have several drawbacks, including severe data problems (they are generally estimates, frequently of dubious reliability and comparability [see U.S. ACDA, 1984, 107–108]); they generally reflect more about the costs of military production than about output (Cusack, 1990, 156–157); and they are far more volatile than the underlying capability they approximate (for a thorough discussion, see Nutter, 1991, Chapter 7).

The GLOBUS Military Capability Index

The most direct measure of military capability is the conventional military capability index created by Thomas Cusack as part of the GLOBUS project (see Cusack, 1981, 1990). This index is a composite score based on the quantity of a nation's military manpower and actual military hardware. The latter element, military capital, was measured as the number of main battle tanks, major surface combat ships, and combat (nonstrategic) aircraft possessed by a nation (as defined in *The Military Balance* [see International Institute for Strategic Studies,

1963 through 1980]). The four elements (manpower, tanks, ships, and aircraft) were combined using principal components into a single-factor score of military capability (this was then rescaled so that the lowest possible score is zero [0.0]) (see Cusack, 1990, 157–163).

Cusack's index has several advantages. First, it is a direct measure of that which we seek, military capability. Second, it is available from 1962 through 1980 in machine-readable form, and its constituent elements are available to the present. Although it has limitations—for example, no qualitative differences are accounted for—it still represents a tremendous advance in the quantitative study of international politics. To provide the reader with a benchmark, in Table 3.2 I present the values of this variable for 1980.

The development and selection of a measure for capability are not the final steps in the process of assessing threat. Although nations may create and stockpile military capability, the mere existence of such capability is not automatically threatening. Brazil, for example, will not perceive the same degree of threat from the Chinese People's Liberation Army that Vietnam will perceive. In general terms, in a particular circumstance total capability and disposable capability are distinctly different.

Table 3.2   Conventional Military Capability, 1980

Soviet Union	552.7
China	357.8
United States	309.9
India	67.7
France	59.8
West Germany	58.0
Turkey	55.4
Italy	45.6
United Kingdom	41.7
Japan	41.6
Poland	40.8
Pakistan	34.2
Egypt	33.8
Czechoslovakia	28.7
Iran	28.4
Brazil	28.3
East Germany	22.5
Argentina	17.8
Indonesia	12.0
Canada	10.7
South Africa	8.6
Mexico	7.5
Venezuela	6.5
Saudi Arabia	6.4
Nigeria	4.8

Source: Adapted from Cusack, 1990, 160–162.

Threat, Capability, and Opportunity

Unless an actor can physically apply armed force to an opponent, threats are hollow and will be perceived as such. One central requisite for capability to be threatening is that the threatening nation must be able to physically apply its capability to the prospective prey—that is, "project" its force.[14]

Force Interface and the Projection of Threat

The possibility of military engagement is a necessary condition for the perception of military threat (and the concomitant stimulation of hostility) (see Blainey, 1973, 117; Zinnes, 1980, 349; Richardson, 1960, x, xiii; Spykman, 1942, 448; Garnham, 1976a; Weede, 1976). I have labeled this condition a "force interface." If a force interface cannot be established, then military threat is discounted. For example, Mexico will perceive no threat from Pakistan, because neither can directly attack the other nor send force to areas of mutual interest. This is an example of a symmetrical (negative) force interface.

A force interface can also be asymmetrical. Nation B (Britain) might be able to deliver armed force upon Nation A (Argentina), but Argentina might not be able to reciprocate, because only Britain has adequate transport capability. Such a situation is common when one actor is a major power and the other is not. In such cases, the major power can engage the smaller nation by using naval or air power or by sea or air transport of ground forces. Smaller nations typically have no such long-range capability. Examples of conflicts involving asymmetrical force interfaces include the Falklands-Malvinas conflict, the Vietnam War, Afghanistan and the USSR, and Nicaragua and the United States in the 1980s.

The force interface concept is similar, but not identical, to Kenneth Boulding's Loss-of-Strength gradient (LOS) (1962, 230). Boulding argues that the extension of power beyond one's borders is largely a function of distance (see also Spykman, 1942, 448; Baugh, 1984, 5–10). Bruce Bueno de Mesquita uses this idea, formulating LOS as a nonlinear drop-off in military capability as a function of distance: The larger the military capability is to begin with, the smaller the power loss over a given distance. In *The War Trap*, he discounts military power for distance and transportation capability by using the logarithm of the travel time from one combatant to the other (Bueno de Mesquita, 1981, 40–44).

There is another, simpler, yet perhaps more realistic approach to this problem. Albert Wohlstetter has persuasively argued that military power does *not* decline as a linear function of distance: "The lift capacity of the major powers massively exceeds that for short distance lift inside the theatre" (1968, 242–244). Moreover:

> Adding several thousand miles to the distance at which remote wars are fought increases the total cost of the fighting by only a very tiny percentage. It appears, for example, that if the support of the US forces in Korea had been 2000 miles

> further away, it would have meant adding less than three-tenths of a percent to the total annual cost of the war. (Wohlstetter, 1968, 245)

In other words, once the people and the equipment are physically in the ships, there is little difference, in terms of actual loss of capability, between moving them 100 miles and 6,000 miles. In particular, by far the most efficient means of delivering armed forces is by using large ships. Table 3.3 shows the costs, in terms of fuel consumption, of sending 1 ton of men and materiel a distance of 100 kilometers.

Although the data in Table 3.3 are only a rough guide, they are sufficient to make clear why Wohlstetter argued that distance is not especially relevant to the application of power (at least for some nations). Capability does not decline continuously (linearly or logarithmically) over distance, because it is frequently harder to move and supply armed forces within a theater of war than it is to get them there. Instead, Wohlstetter implies that the decline of capability occurs primarily as a "step-function," or a discrete variable. Either a nation can project power over a long distance (essentially, overseas) or it cannot. Most important, either it has ships or it does not. If it does not, then distance is irrelevant, because any actor can transport only a small amount of force any distance by air. If it does so, then distance is also irrelevant, because any loss of capability involved in travel will result from enemy action (attrition) rather than being a function of distance per se. The difference between LOS and force interface is that force interface represents the decline in capability as an either-or, rather than a continuous, variable.

Operationalizing Force Interface

A force interface can be established in a number of ways. The most obvious of these occurs when two nations are geographically contiguous. This concept has been explored empirically as contiguity and opportunity. Both David Garnham (1976a) and Erich Weede (1976) "control" for geographic contiguity by including only contiguous dyads in their samples (see also Zinnes, 1980, 349; Richardson, 1960, x, xiii; McGowan and Shapiro, 1973, 163–164). However, this requirement severely restricts the sample of dyads and also excludes most

Table 3.3   Relative Transport Efficiency

Vehicle	Load (in tons)	Distance (in kilometers)	Average Fuel Consumption (in gallons)
Ship	1	100	0.44
Train	1	100	0.85
Truck	1	100	13.50
Plane	1	100	26–65

Source: Calculated by the author from Dunnigan, 1982, 311, Chapters 23, 26, 27.

major-power conflicts, which generally occur in third areas (Siverson and Sullivan, 1983).

A second way force interface can be established occurs when one of the nations is an overseas power. Overseas powers have several advantages that enable them to project military power to noncontiguous areas and thus to project more power (and inherently, threat) than less powerful countries. First, major powers generally have substantial naval capability. The United States, Great Britain, France, and Russia all have global ("blue water") navies. Naval power alone provides the ability to apply destructive force, but equally important, it is also generally accompanied by a large military transport and amphibious capability. Thus, an actor cannot only destroy using naval power but can also occupy territory by moving an army to the scene.

Only four nations are true overseas powers: the United States, Russia, Great Britain, and France. This classification is made on the basis of size, quality, and seagoing capability of naval forces. Although the People's Republic of China (PRC) may have more ships (335) than Great Britain (99) (as of 1985 [Dunnigan and Bay, 1985]), the British ships are oceangoing vessels (about 3,600 tons average displacement), whereas the Chinese navy is a coastal defense force (about 810 tons average). James Dunnigan and Austin Bay (1985) have reached the same conclusion; they code only four nations (the United States, the former USSR, Britain, and France) as having "strategic, global oriented navies." Michael Kidron and Dan Smith (1983, Map 12) similarly code the major powers, with the category being "navies with global reach."[15]

Overseas powers also tend to maintain a widespread military presence through a network of foreign bases (see SIPRI, 1972, Chapter 7; Kidron and Smith, 1983, Map 17), sometimes of a voluntary nature and sometimes through outright occupation. This is another way of reaching noncontiguous nations. The establishment of bases and staging areas may occur before or after hostilities begin, as the result of the overseas power simply overrunning any countries that happen to be in the way. During the Cold War, the ability of the USSR to threaten West Germany depended on the occupation of East Germany. A case during war was the German attack on Poland as a means of establishing a staging area for Barbarossa, the German invasion of the USSR in 1941. I generally ignore occupation here, because the set of occupying nations is identical to the set of overseas powers, and such an additional consideration would therefore be redundant.

In summary, a force interface is a necessary condition for an actor to perceive threat from another's military capability. Such an interface only exists if one or both of the nations is an overseas power or both nations are physically contiguous. Military threat only exists between actors if one or both of these conditions pertains.[16]

Operationally, force interface can be coded as a dichotomous variable, as 1 (one) if a force interface exists—that is, if the above conditions apply—and as 0 (zero) if the conditions do not apply. This dummy variable then serves as an interaction term with the variables Capgap and time to parity.

Gauging Threat: A Summary

The preceding refinements to threat measurement can be implemented as follows. First, each nation must have its capability measured using Cusack's Military Capability Index. Then, the effect of military capability gaps on military spending would be taken into account, along with consideration of the deterrent effects of very large capability gaps. Moreover, the creation of potential threat would be estimated employing the concept of time to parity. The estimates of both immediate and potential threat would be mediated by force interface, which represents the inability of nations to deploy their military over distances.

Conclusion

I have presented here a set of refinements in the effort to make theoretical constructs, formal concepts, and operational measures more consonant. The process of doing so can only help to clarify our thinking about the idea of threat and, more important, may help in sorting through competing theories to discern how the world works. This theoretical endeavor has not taken place detached from the arduous empirical world, because these concepts have already been implemented in empirical research (Nutter, 1991, Chapters 11, 13; Nutter, 1992). Although even more remains to be accomplished (for example, incorporating internal threat), it is hoped that my work here provides a small step toward understanding our common heritage and our prospect.

Notes

This research was supported in part by the Gordon Scott Fulcher Chair for Decisionmaking in International Affairs at Northwestern University, held at the time by Harold Guetzkow. I am grateful for that support. I also thank Phil Schrodt for helpful discussions in the early part of this work.

    1. As important, the measurement of threat is a possible cause of war. Rational actors, at least, would not start wars without the ability to attain their objectives (see Bueno de Mesquita, 1981; Payne, 1981); therefore, the ability to accurately gauge threat seems crucial.

    2. Of course, these are also the foundation for Ayoob's (1991a) arguments.

    3. I should note that value salience and value proportion are related but not identical. Salience is simply the importance of a value and is probably related to the amount of a value one possesses or has threatened. When Japanese auto imports occupied 1 percent of the U.S. market, the issue was less salient, because the threat to the values of employment or prosperity was small. As the Japanese market share increased, the threat became more salient, because a larger share of these values was jeopardized. However, even though some values increase in salience as they become more scarce, they still may not jump ahead of other (previously more preferred) values.

    4. Although, unlike Schrödinger's cat, we might enjoy values we currently possess. What we do not know is whether we will continue to enjoy them.

    5. Actually, a nonissue is simply an issue with zero saliency.

6. The subject here is threatening capability, not threat perception. The latter can occur without any action on the part of any actor.

7. This point applies mainly to conventional military capability. A discussion of threat from nuclear weapons can be found in Nutter, 1991, Chapter 8.

8. This relationship might also be discontinuous, but that is left for another time.

9. Also, an arms race does not necessarily imply changing capability balances. For example, if two "racers" were producing arms at proportional rates, the level of arms might increase but the disparity remain constant (that is, the production functions are parallel). This is known as a "stable" arms race.

10. The arms race literature (Wallace and Smith) is cited not because all arms races involve changing capability gaps but because these particular works are about unstable arms races, which are germane.

11. An even more sophisticated approach would also take differential mobilization capabilities into account. That complication is left for another time, however.

12. There is one other possibility: that the respective arsenals are growing exactly proportionately, in which case the time to parity is undefined (the result of division by 0 [see Equation 15]).

13. See the argument related to Equation 3.

14. There are other considerations, including geography, doctrine, the so-called "intangibles," the constraint of other commitments, and similar factors (see Nutter, 1991, Chapter 7).

15. This list is also consistent with the major powers as defined by many scholars, including Levy (1983, 47), and Maoz (1982, 54). The only discrepancies between these lists and the overseas powers are China, for reasons explained in the text, and the former West Germany, which was constitutionally forbidden from projecting force.

16. Another way to look at this is that the Loss-of-Strength gradient is 100 percent at the first wide body of water. In the future a war may be fought at long distance by two opposing air forces (perhaps an upscaled version of the recent Iranian–Saudi Arabian air engagements), but, Douhet to the contrary, to date only a few such (minor) clashes have been fought. Also, such considerations would greatly complicate research, for relatively little return.

❖ PART II ❖

Arms Transfers and Military Spending

❖ FOUR ❖

Arms Transfers and the Structure of International Power

David J. Louscher & James Sperling

The future patterns of arms and technology transfers to the Third World will reflect not only the changing structure of power in the post-Yalta international system but also the economic security requirements of European and North American states. Likewise, the past patterns of these transfers to the Third World reflected the multiple structures of power that emerged during different periods of the competition between the United States and the Soviet Union (Louscher, 1987). The most striking change that has taken place in the post-Yalta security system is the renewed emphasis on the economic requirements of security—requirements that are linked to the maintenance of domestic political tranquility and the continued functioning of parliamentary democracies in the West and the survival of democracy in the East.

Arms sales are increasingly viewed as an important source of economic security and domestic tranquility (Hammond et al., 1983). They have been viewed as fulfilling multiple and essential functions in advanced capitalist states: contributing to full employment, serving as an instrument of domestic and foreign political influence, supporting industrial policies by providing a legitimate venue for the financial support of high-technology industries, and sustaining national autonomy by supporting an indigenous arms industry. Yet changes that took place in the 1980s have wrought changes in the international arms transfer system as well: Established suppliers are under considerable financial strains and face emerging threats to their industrial bases, not only from traditional competitors but also from suppliers that were formerly recipients.

The international arms transfer system has been transformed into a buyer's market: The large number of potential suppliers in the 1980s has supplanted the arms monopoly of the 1950s and the narrow oligopoly of the 1960s and 1970s. Today, recipients are no longer satisfied with obsolescent, surplus, or nonstate-of-the-art equipment (Laurance, 1992). Moreover, since about 1980, a shift has occurred in the acquisition strategy of Third World nations: Military technology is in greater demand than military hardware among the major buyers (Louscher, 1987). Whereas the Europeans have largely adapted to the new international arms transfer system and treat arms sales and the transfer of military technology more like a trade issue than like an issue complicated by strategic or moral considerations, the United States has only recently begun to recognize that the contemporary international arms market is driven increasingly by the logic of domestic political economy rather than by considerations of power and diplomacy. In the recent past, compared with the other major arms suppliers, the United States has treated the transfer of arms and arms technology more as a political than a mercantile issue—a position that placed at risk not only the continued viability of U.S. arms manufacturers but also the influence and leverage arms sales still provided to U.S. diplomacy.

The Structure of International Power and the Arms Transfer System: Overview

The connection between the structure of international power and the evolution of the arms transfer system is critical to understanding not only the contemporary international arms transfer system but the preceding postwar arms transfer systems as well. Understanding the interconnection between the successive international systems and arms transfer systems and assessing the contemporary arms transfer system require a systematic treatment of the evolution of the international system since 1945.

The structure of the postwar international systems may be defined by the distribution of resources (economic, military, and political), the diplomatic agenda of the dominant power(s) (issue areas, actors), and the patterns of alignment (formal alliances, tacit or explicit informal alignments). By focusing on these variables, we can identify four discrete international systems: U.S. hegemony (1947–1962), bloc competition (1963–1974), muted bloc competition (1975–1985), and bloc erosion and economic multipolarity (1986 to present) (Louscher, 1990).

The period 1947–1962 was characterized by U.S. dominance of tangible resources: The United States controlled over 50 percent of the world's gold reserves, produced 45 percent of the world's gross national product (GNP), enjoyed energy self-sufficiency, possessed the most technologically advanced industrial base in the world, and had an effective nuclear monopoly until the mid-1950s. U.S. policy was directed toward the containment of Soviet power and the spread of communism outside the Soviet sphere of influence agreed to at Yalta. It was supported by the largesse of the U.S. economy and was implemented with a series of defensive alliances surrounding the Sino-Soviet perimeter (the North Atlantic Treaty Organization [NATO], the Central Treaty Organization [CENTO], the Southeast Asia Treaty Organization [SEATO], and bilateral alliances with Japan, Korea, and Taiwan).

By 1962 U.S. hegemony was replaced with intense competition between the Soviet and U.S. military-economic blocs. U.S. economic dominance, a key characteristic of the earlier international system, diminished with the emergence of economic equality between North America and Europe and military-strategic parity between the United States and the former Soviet Union. The emergence of Europe as an economic power reflected the success of the European Recovery Program, the economic stability lent to the international system by the Bretton Woods monetary and associated trade arrangements, and the phenomenal success of the European Economic Community in fostering growth among the nations of Western Europe.

Although the U.S. monopoly in nuclear weapons was broken as early as 1949, and the former Soviet Union did not pose a credible nuclear threat to the continental United States until 1957 with the successful launching of Sputnik, U.S. dominance in the area of nuclear weapons was not significantly eroded until the early 1960s when military-strategic parity emerged between the two super-powers. This period also ushered in the decolonialization of the Third World and the transformation of a contest for allies in resource-rich areas of the world into an intense ideological competition in the Third World between liberal democracy and communism, which intensified an already deadly competition between the Soviet Union and the United States. The delicate balance of power between the East and West at this time generally defined international politics in terms of being in an alliance with or against one of the superpowers and led to the political and military stabilization of the two European alliances, NATO and the Warsaw Pact. The tight bipolarity between 1962 and 1973 yielded to a system of muted competition between the two blocs after the 1973 oil crisis, which persisted until the ascendancy of Soviet President Mikhail Gorbachev in 1985.

In 1973, the international system underwent an upheaval that radically changed the distribution of resources within that system. The largely bipolar distribution of power gave way to a more complex international system in which the sinews of power were either economic or military in nature. The three poles of economic power—North America, Europe, and Japan—entered into an open competition restrained only by economic self-interest and a (tattered) security consensus; and the three poles of military power—the United States, the former Soviet Union, and China—witnessed the slow dissolution of the Richard Nixon–Henry Kissinger détente, which was eventually replaced by the bellicose rhetoric of the first Reagan administration. The complexity of the international structure of power, the absence of a clear hierarchy, and the divergence of interests between allies (particularly between Americans and their continental European allies) produced an international politics that strained the preexisting fabric of interstate relations. These structural developments were magnified by (1) questioning on both sides of the iron curtain of the value of the existing military alliances; (2) the recognition that ideological conformity was irrelevant to the challenges facing the European states; (3) the manifest enfeeblement of the former Soviet Union, reflecting over 65 years of economic mismanagement; and (4) the growing U.S. realization that its political commitments outstripped its economic capacity.

This stage in the evolution of the international system foreshadowed the contemporary international system: The locus of competition shifted decidedly away from the United States and the former Soviet Union. Power was now located in commerce rather than in the barrel of a gun. This shift has worked to the advantage of the West vis-à-vis its former adversaries in the East; it has had the paradoxical effect of giving way to an intensely competitive multipolar system in which interstate relations are conducted in the idiom of monetary and commercial competition. These four discrete international systems, and the changes in the structure and sources of power supporting them, have shaped the contours and sustained four postwar international arms transfer systems.

An international arms transfer system may be defined by six key elements: the global market shares held by suppliers, the motives driving suppliers, the motives driving recipients, the modes of arms and technology transfers, the recipient's capacity and commitment to acquire arms and technology, and the level of technology transfer. Changes in these variables, set in motion by changes in the larger structure of power in the international system, produced four international arms transfer systems: the U.S.-dominant grant system (1950s to mid-1960s), the U.S.-USSR competition system (mid-1960s to mid-1970s), the industrial supplier competition system (mid-1970s to 1989), and the contemporary diffuse economic competition system (post-1989). These four systems are rooted in and parallel the four systems of international power identified earlier (see Figure 4.1).

Figure 4.1   Systemic Conceptual Overview

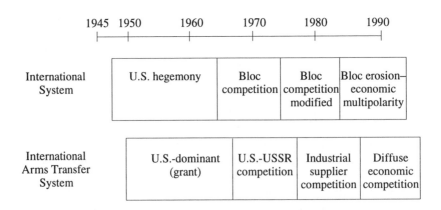

During the period of U.S. hegemony, the United States was the dominant purveyor of arms to its European and Asian allies. The former Soviet Union was a minor player in the arms trade during this period and did not begin the armament of its European allies and China until the late 1950s. Outside of the Soviet sphere of influence, the United States was the only major worldwide supplier of arms. Except to its NATO allies, the United States only offered surplus equipment; arms transfers were largely restricted to those countries perceived to be under threat from the expansion of Soviet power; and arms were provided primarily on a grant basis. Arms transfers were first and foremost a political instrument in the larger struggle with the Soviet Union and only served an incidental economic purpose.

The consolidation of the Soviet sphere of influence, cojoined by the rapid decolonialization of the French and British empires in the late 1950s and early 1960s, introduced an arms transfer system that reflected the sharpened political and ideological competition between the United States and the former Soviet Union. Arms sales and transfers became an important idiom in which the diplomacy of both superpowers was conducted, and that idiom was most clearly and effectively employed in the emerging Third World, the focal point of the Soviet-U.S. competition. The Soviet Union, unable to compete with the United States economically, could compete in the supply of weapons—instruments of statecraft and symbols of sovereignty highly valued by the newly independent Third World states. This competition was particularly sharp in the Middle East. In fact, the Soviet-U.S. competition to win friends and sustain allies exerted an astounding influence upon the pattern of U.S. arms sales to that region. The emerging Russian requirement for hard currency makes U.S.-Russian competition in the region no less intense. Although both superpowers supplied weapons to their clients on a concessionary basis, the Americans were able to offset the cost in part by changing the existing arms transfer relationship with the Europeans: The U.S. began to insist upon arms purchases by Europe and phased out the preexisting grant program.

This change in U.S. policy also had the effect of creating alternative sources of arms supply: The phasing out of grants to Europe gave the British and the French budgetary and balance-of-payments incentives to create an export-oriented arms industry. Moreover, economic recovery in Europe provided a sufficiently broad and technologically advanced basis for an indigenous arms industry capable of competing with the United States; the Americans fostered this development with licensing agreements that enabled the Europeans to produce state-of-the-art equipment (Louscher, 1987).

As the ideological ardor of the 1960s dissipated and was replaced with the rhetoric of détente, the competition between the United States and the Soviet Union became muted, and the international arms transfer system underwent yet another change: From the mid-1970s to the mid-1980s, competition in the arms bazaar occurred between industrial suppliers, without regard to ideological or alliance relationships. The arms transfer system was becoming transformed into a commodity market much like any other, without the political or moral opprobrium applied to such sales during the height of the Cold War.

Yet the U.S. government risked transforming the United States into a "reluctant supplier" (Hammond et al., 1983)—out of step with the exigencies of the evolving international system. The decision criteria for supplying or selling arms were determined increasingly by domestic political considerations rather than by either the geostrategic or the strictly mercantile benefits of supplying (or the costs of not supplying) arms to many areas of the world, particularly to the littoral states of the Gulf.

The market opportunities created by the U.S. failure to supply arms were exploited by the Europeans, even though the former Soviet Union receded as a U.S. competitor in the supply of arms outside the Middle East during this period. Nonetheless, all suppliers now faced budgetary constraints that made it more difficult for recipient countries to gain preferential financing of their purchases, which led to a small revolution in recipient nations' expectations. In the mid-1970s, recipients increasingly demanded licensing and offset agreements, a demand that reflected the desire to reduce the overall cost of arms procurement, to relieve budgetary pressures, and to enhance the productive capabilities of the national economy (Louscher and Salomone, 1987b). The demand for licensing agreements and technological assistance was matched by an additional demand for state-of-the-art equipment. Supplier acquiescence to these demands had the perverse effect of not only abetting the recipient strategy of import-substitution for national consumption but also of encouraging a strategy of export competition in an arms market already suffering from surplus capacity (McLaurin, 1989). The collapse of the postwar system in Europe established at Yalta, combined with the trend toward the proliferation of arms suppliers—not only in the industrial West but also in the nations of the Third World—established the basic structure of the emerging international arms transfer system of the 1990s.

The industrial nations no longer exercise a stranglehold on the production and export of arms. Europe and North America now compete with the newly industrialized Third World nations and emerging regional powers (Ross, 1989). The market competition in the contemporary is increasingly diffuse. Unlike the preceding international arms transfer systems, the current major suppliers cannot exercise their market power to serve discrete political ends. Today, nearly all arms suppliers are driven by economic considerations, which range from the desire to sustain an indigenous arms industry to the funding of industry research and development to the protection of employment in critical sectors of either the economy or the electoral map.

These economic pressures are especially acute in the heretofore major suppliers of arms to the world market: Italy, France, the United Kingdom, Russia, and the United States. Only the United States remains driven primarily by political considerations—considerations that work to the advantage of the other major suppliers in the Middle East, the major market for arms sales that can afford to make substantial purchases of state-of-the-art equipment. But even the United States is increasingly under pressure, for economic reasons, to sell in the Middle East (Bajusz and Louscher, 1988). Outside of this region, future arms sales will be severely circumscribed and will be dependent upon advantageous financial arrangements and attractive offsets. Moreover, the traditional suppliers of the industrial West will compete with newly industrialized nations in the supply of the most basic and middle-level defense equipment to nations that lack an indigenous arms industry. This trend will only intensify as import-substitution strategies are supplemented with export-oriented strategies to ensure the viability of indigenous arms industries (Klare, 1993).

These new producers will remain dependent upon the traditional suppliers of arms for advanced subsystems, components, and exotic materials. This dependence will not give the United States appreciable political leverage, however, because the major suppliers of these technologies—France, the United Kingdom, Italy, Japan, and Germany—provide readily alternative suppliers unencumbered by the U.S. moral or political agenda. The alternative arms suppliers should, therefore, enjoy considerable autonomy in the production and export of arms in the 1990s: Those producers with sufficient foreign exchange should have relatively free access to whatever state-of-the-art technologies are required for their arms industry.

The logic of this development leads to yet another incentive for a free market in such technologies: As more arms producers enter the global market, the traditional suppliers will be forced to exploit aggressively their comparative advantage, state-of-the-art technologies. Moreover, competition for market share and the absence of sufficient domestic demand should become even more intense as surplus capacity in the arms sector of the global economy grows—a development that could even lead to the new suppliers acting as subcontractors or vendors for the traditional suppliers of basic and middle-level defense equipment.

The locus of arms sales competition in the 1990s and beyond will be the Middle East; the oil-rich nations of the Gulf are the only countries that have the perceived need and income to afford large-scale purchases of state-of-the-art equipment. The limited market opportunities even these nations offer suggest that there will be a large-scale rationalization of the arms sector by the traditional suppliers. Such rationalization will either be taken on a national basis—defense firms will either be allowed to fail or be forced into shotgun marriages to create more competitive arms manufacturers—or it will duplicate the pattern of production found in every other sector of manufacturing—the extensive globalization of production and control. This development, along with the entry of nontraditional suppliers and of the market forces supporting their role into the international arms transfer system, casts doubt on any unilateral or multilateral effort to control either the proliferation of advanced equipment or the diffusion of technology to the pariah nations of the international community.

The International Arms Transfer Systems: Elements of Change

How did the elements of the international arms transfer system change and evolve during the postwar period? What are the implications of the patterns of change for the contemporary arms transfer system? What are the policy implications for the United States? These questions frame the remaining sections of this chapter.

Alignment Patterns: A Determinant of Market Share

States were generally aligned with either the Soviet Union or the United States for most of the period between 1947 and 1989. These patterns of alignment, in turn, provide very good indicators of the arms transfer patterns of these two nations. The United States and the Soviet Union, both anxious to protect their client states or alliance partners, were willing to sell or finance the sale of arms to bolster their defensive capability. Neither superpower used arms sales as a mechanism for "poaching" its opposite's client states; arms transfers were viewed as a reward to the virtuous or as a reinforcement of an unguarded frontier of the Cold War. As alignments changed over the course of the Cold War period, major shifts occurred in the structure of arms transfers: As the Soviet Union lost influence in Egypt, Ethiopia, Somalia, and China, the arms sales of U.S. manufacturers filled the void. Likewise, as the United States lost influence in Cuba, Nicaragua, Vietnam, and Iran, arms sales from the Soviet Union displaced those of the United States. The European suppliers and the suppliers from the newly industrializing Third World nations were not as constrained by patterns of alignment between the two superpowers, regardless of the intensity of their tie to or dependence upon either a U.S. or a Soviet security guarantee.

Clearly, however, the U.S. share of the global arms market (excluding domestic sales) remained stagnant in absolute terms and declined precipitously in relative terms. The United States sold $10.372 billion worth of arms during the period 1968–1972 on an annual basis; during the period 1983–1987, it sold $12.545 billion annually. The U.S. share of the global arms market (excluding domestic sales) fell from 51.84 percent (1968–1972) to 23.14 percent (1983–1987). The Soviet Union sold $5.26 billion worth of arms on an annual basis during the period 1968–1972; during the period 1983–1987, it sold $21.973 billion annually. The Soviet market share rose from 26.29 percent (1968–1972) to 40.54 percent (1983–1987). Nonetheless, the combined market share of the two superpowers fell from 78 percent in the period 1968–1972 to 63.68 percent in the period 1983–1987 (see Table 4.1 and Figure 4.2).

The drop in the Soviet and U.S. share was captured primarily by the increased sales of seven major supplier nations with exports over $1 billion per annum. These nations increased their exports from $3.347 billion on an annual basis during the period 1968–1972 to $13.097 billion annually during the period

Table 4.1 Share of Market by Type of Supplier (five-year average)[a]

Type of Supplier	1968–1972	%	1973–1977	%	1978–1982	%	1983–1987	%
Soviet Union	5,260	26.29	10,715	34.38	22,917	43.82	21,973	40.54
United States	10,372	51.84	11,389	36.54	10,622	20.31	12,545	23.14
Other major suppliers	3,472	16.72	6,579	21.10	12,732	24.34	13,097	24.16
Significant suppliers	947	4.73	2,025	6.50	5,292	10.00	5,946	10.97
Minimal suppliers	667	0.33	3,535	1.13	7,219	1.38	627	1.15
Insignificant suppliers	16	0.08	106	0.34	761	0.15	21	0.04
Totals	20,734		34,349		59,543		54,209	

Source: U.S. ACDA; calculations by David J. Louscher and Michael D. Salomone.
Note: a. In millions of dollars (1989, constant).

Figure 4.2 Share of Market by Type of Supplier (five-year average, percentage)

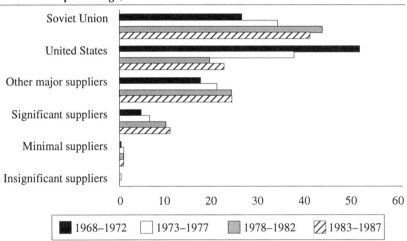

Source: U.S. ACDA; calculations by David J. Louscher, Michael D. Salomone, and James Sperling.

1983–1987, a 291 percent increase. These states' share of the global arms market grew from 16.72 percent (1968–1972) to 24.16 percent (1983–1987).

The twenty-five states comprising the significant suppliers also ate into the Soviet-U.S. share. These states increased their exports from $947 million on an annual basis over the period 1968–1972 to $5.946 billion annually over the period 1983–1987, a 527 percent increase. These states' share of the global arms market grew from 4.73 percent (1968–1972) to 10.97 percent (1983–1987) (see Table 4.1, and for a more detailed breakdown, Table 4.2). As the former Soviet Union comes to grip with its economic diffi-culties, and as the United States continues to reduce its own military establishment, it is likely, given the internal dynamics of the other suppliers, that the Russian-U.S. share of the international arms market will remain stagnant at best.

Table 4.2   Ranking of Arms Exporters, 1968–1987 (five-year average, millions of U.S.$, 1989)

Country	1968–1972	1973–1977	1978–1982	1983–1987
Soviet Union	5,260	10,715	22,917	21,973
United States	10,372	11,389	10,622	12,545
Other Major Suppliers				
France	889	1,913	4,030	4,541
West Germany	513	942	1,748	1,865
United Kingdom	660	1,359	2,708	1,737
China	707	348	625	1,500
Poland	101	565	1,150	1,280
Czechoslovakia	338	891	1,139	1,231
Italy	139	561	1,332	943
Significant Suppliers				
Bulgaria	3	35	210	553
Spain	30	94	230	485
Israel	17	121	362	450
Brazil	0	51	327	435
Yugoslavia	14	197	454	430
North Korea	1	43	510	390
East Germany	23	104	184	375
Romania	15	72	412	365
Switzerland	41	319	711	308
Belgium	58	210	213	272
South Korea	2	45	471	258
Hungary	10	109	130	251
Japan	26	46	171	212
Sweden	69	112	209	198
Austria	8	65	22	196
Canada	548	225	223	186
Finland	0	0	31	160
Pakistan	3	4	32	151
Portugal	6	34	60	139
Netherlands	73	139	267	132
Minimal Suppliers				
Egypt	2	20	98	92
Turkey	6	10	16	84
Libya	2	9	127	64
Chile	0	0	0	62
Australia	19	99	55	62
Argentina	5	7	8	52
Greece	0	2	33	41
South Africa	2	45	31	35
Singapore	6	15	27	23
Cuba	0	63	8	23
India	10	26	33	20
Saudi Arabia	3	10	183	20
Norway	11	46	69	19
Syria	0	1	33	14
Philippines	0	0	0	12

(continues)

Table 4.2 (continued)

Country	1968–1972	1973–1977	1978–1982	1983–1987
Insignificant Suppliers				
Vietnam	5	1	4	5
Denmark	4	18	15	5
Jordan	0	17	3	3
United Arab Emirates	0	4	0	3
Iran	2	61	7	1
Iraq	1	0	6	1
Nigeria	0	1	0	1
Oman	0	0	0	1
Sudan	0	0	1	1
Indonesia	0	0	3	0
Ireland	0	0	3	0
Malaysia	0	0	11	0
Morocco	0	4	1	0
New Zealand	0	0	1	0
Peru	0	0	15	0
Thailand	0	0	1	0
Yemen (Sanaa)	0	0	5	0
Algeria	2	0	0	0
Kuwait	2	0	0	0
Total Annual Average	20,008	31,167	52,297	54,205

Source: U.S. ACDA; calculations by David J. Louscher and Michael D. Salomone.

Supplier Motives

Arms suppliers may be driven by three types of motives, singly or in unison, for transferring military hardware and technologies: the promotion of foreign policy objectives, the promotion and protection of domestic economic objectives, and the promotion and protection of domestic defense industrial base objectives (Hammond, et al., 1983). During the first two decades of the Cold War, the arms sales policy of both the United States and the former Soviet Union were driven by their respective foreign policy strategies. The United States armed its allies and clients either to stop the direct expansion of the Soviet Union or its proxies in Europe and Northeast Asia or to combat wars of national liberation in Latin America or Southeast Asia. The Soviet Union armed its client states in Europe and Asia to support the people's democracies, which did not have the support of the people and were not democracies. The entrance of new suppliers in the 1970s, particularly the ostensible political and economic allies of the two superpowers, altered the logic of the international arms transfer system: Now only the two superpowers exported weapons for political purposes; the other nations exported arms in the service of mammon or in the pursuit of a national industrial or employment policy. By the early 1980s, the former Soviet Union also was forced to forgo an arms export policy driven solely by politics, which left the United States as the only arms supplier driven primarily by political considerations.

The logic of economics began to dominate the international arms transfer system, because of the entry of new suppliers into the market that lacked an indigenous market to produce at cost-effective levels. Although "cost-effective" varies from state to state and reflects a political as well as an economic calculus, the Europeans recognized that their national requirements were too small for efficient or sustainable production and to justify the lavish research and development budgets necessary to produce state-of-the-art weapons. Thus, European arms exports serve four economic objectives: to subsidize defense industries to maintain indigenous weapons development capabilities, to generate economies of scale or at least raise production to minimal sustaining rates, to offset trade deficits, and to achieve employment security in the defense sectors of the European economies. These motivations are unlikely to change in the foreseeable future, and it seems more likely that the pressures to continue exporting arms will intensify as the European economies struggle with the twin economic problems of slow growth and high levels of unemployment.

The logic of U.S. sales has been and has remained unremittingly political: As Figure 4.3 suggests, the initial burst of U.S. arms sales between 1950 and 1965 was to U.S. North Atlantic Treaty Organization (NATO) allies; in the next decade, the majority of U.S. arms went to the Republic of South Vietnam; after the Yom Kippur War, arms were directed to Israel (and Egypt after the Camp David Accords); and in the 1980s, U.S. attention was redirected to the rearmament of the NATO allies. These nations have accounted for 58 percent of total U.S. arms sales since 1950.

Recipient Motives

The motives for recipients are more protean and ambiguous. In the 1950s, recipients were driven to procure arms not only to meet the immediate and tangible need for possessing the instruments of internal and external security; they also viewed arms as a tangible measure of alliance commitment to the supplier. As the need for alliance reassurance declined by the late 1960s, the recipient states sought to reduce their sole-supplier relationships, particularly with the United States and the former Soviet Union. These states began to seek a security of supply by diversifying arms suppliers in the early 1970s. This decision by recipients reflected a number of calculations and opportunities: (1) The increased cost of weapons systems encouraged these nations to seek alternative suppliers with a lower cost; (2) the tendency of traditional suppliers to attach political conditions to the transfer of arms was viewed as an unnecessary cost; (3) recipient nations were able to lower the potential of a disrupted arms supply by increasing the number of suppliers; (4) suppliers, to enhance their market position in the transfer of technology, encouraged recipients to embark upon a policy of self-reliance; (5) recipient nations had developed the requisite industrial base to engage in the production of arms; and (6) the production of arms became an integral part of the recipient nations' industrialization policy.

Figure 4.3 Deliveries of Military Equipment to Recipients (billions of U.S.$, 1989 constant)

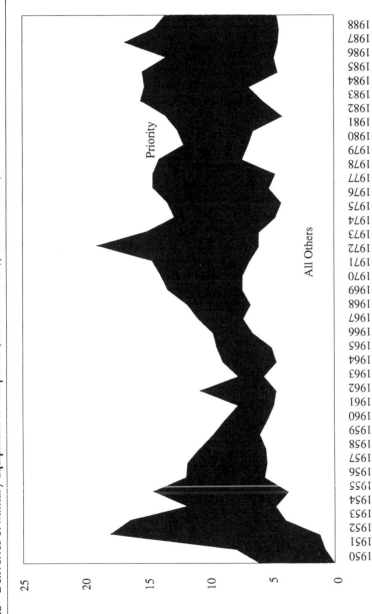

Source: U.S. DSAA; calculations by David J. Louscher.

The acquisition patterns of many arms recipients also reflected their ability to finance their weapons acquisitions. In the first three decades of the Cold War, the U.S. arms assistance programs and the limited concessionary financing by the Soviet Union shaped arms acquisitions patterns. However, the acquisition of arms or technology from other suppliers has been and remains highly dependent upon recipient hard currency reserves or ability to earn foreign exchange. Ironically, the relative depoliticization of the international arms transfer system beginning in the late 1970s has had the perverse effect of making weapons less, rather than more, available: Recipient procurement has become increasingly dependent upon the ability to pay in the coin of a convertible currency rather than with the "coin" of conforming to the foreign policy agenda of the supplier state.

The intersection of recipient and supplier motives has contributed to the creation of a four-tiered arms market: primary recipients that imported between $35 billion and $7.5 billion between 1983 and 1987, significant recipients that imported between $6.3 billion and $1 billion during that period, secondary recipients that imported between $981 million and $222 million, and minimal recipients that imported less than $199 million (see Table 4.3). The ten primary recipients received 49 percent of all arms deliveries, and the forty-four significant recipients received an additional 43 percent of all deliveries (see Figure 4.4). The remaining eighty-nine states account for 7 percent of all arms deliveries— less than either of the two largest arms importers, Iraq and Saudi Arabia, which account for 12.5 percent and 7.6 percent, respectively.

Modes of Transfer

The motives of recipient states in procuring arms remain security-oriented in the first instance but are increasingly shaped by developmental considerations. The ability to procure, however, has become increasingly dependent upon the ability to pay rather than upon the ability to offer political support in exchange for arms on concessionary terms. The modes of transfer have changed during the postwar period and have contributed to the evolution of the international arms transfer system. There are five modes of transfer: grants, or nonreimbursable aid, concessionary credit, cash, licensed production, and offsets. Each of these modes of transfer has existed since the 1950s; each has been used more extensively in one time period than in others. The change from the grant aid and concessionary credit employed extensively by the United States and the former Soviet Union in the 1950s and 1960s was significant in generating both the pressures for recipients to become producers and the demands for licensed production as well as offset agreements.

The predominant mode of the U.S. transfer of military equipment has been altered significantly since the 1950s. In the first decade of U.S. arms transfers, almost all equipment was provided to recipients with the help of grants (see Figure 4.5). When the European economies had fully recovered in the late 1950s, U.S. grants were phased out, and Europeans were pressed into assuming more

Table 4.3   Tiers of Arms Recipients, 1983–1987 (millions of U.S.$, 1989)

Country	Millions
Primary Recipients	
Iraq	34,932.23
Saudi Arabia	21,406.87
India	12,841.79
Syria	12,210.80
Iran	10,358.73
Vietnam	10,107.50
Cuba	7,792.01
Egypt	9,137.65
Libya	9,032.48
Angola	7,419.96
Significant Recipients	
Soviet Union	6,286.52
East Germany	5,638.00
Ethiopia	5,059.59
Japan	5,024.54
Poland	5,024.54
Israel	5,024.54
Bulgaria	4,931.06
Afghanistan	4,755.78
Czechoslovakia	4,709.04
Australia	3,873.57
Algeria	3,774.25
United Kingdom	3,634.03
Turkey	3,429.54
Netherlands	3,248.42
United States	3,078.99
Taiwan	2,932.93
Jordan	2,886.19
Switzerland	2,868.66
South Korea	2,734.28
West Germany	2,523.95
China	2,430.47
Nicaragua	2,301.94
Pakistan	2,243.51
Yemen (Aden)	2,231.83
Spain	1,986.45
Argentina	1,986.45
Nigeria	1,770.27
Belgium	1,694.32
North Korea	1,682.64
Yemen (Sanaa)	1,676.79
Greece	1,618.37
Mozambique	1,554.10
Kuwait	1,489.83
Malaysia	1,483.99
Thailand	1,372.98
Cambodia	1,297.03
Venezuela	1,273.66

(continues)

Table 4.3 (continued)

Country	Millions
Peru	1,238.61
Norway	1,226.92
Hungary	1,203.55
Canada	1,162.65
Italy	1,115.91
Singapore	1,063.33
Romania	1,010.75
Secondary Recipients	
Morocco	981.54
France	964.54
Colombia	917.27
Oman	917.27
Indonesia	864.69
United Arab Emirates	712.78
Yugoslavia	701.10
Tunisia	682.57
Laos	654.36
Qatar	648.52
Lebanon	619.30
Denmark	595.93
Brazil	537.51
Ecuador	537.51
Finland	519.98
Mexico	502.45
Sweden	496.61
Bahrain	496.61
Sudan	408.97
Portugal	408.97
El Salvador	397.29
Cyprus	373.92
Chile	368.08
Zimbabwe	350.55
Tanzania	315.49
New Zealand	292.12
Congo	274.60
Honduras	268.75
Guinea	262.91
Bangladesh	239.54
Cameroon	227.86
Somalia	227.86
Philippines	222.01
Minimal Recipients	
Gabon	198.64
Chad	192.80
Mali	186.96
Madagascar	151.90
Burma	140.22
Austria	134.38
Zaire	128.53

(continues)

Table 4.3   (continued)

Country	Millions
Guinea-Bissau	111.01
Sri Lanka	105.16
Uganda	105.16
Mongolia	93.48
Burkina Faso	93.48
Kenya	87.64
Guatemala	81.79
Ivory Coast	75.95
Benin	64.27
Ireland	58.42
Burundi	58.42
Ghana	58.42
Liberia	58.42
Paraguay	58.42
Panama	52.58
Papua New Guinea	46.74
Mauritania	35.05
Sao Tome and Principe	35.05
South Africa	35.05
Luxembourg	35.05
Costa Rica	35.05
Suriname	35.05
Bolivia	29.21
Equatorial Guinea	23.37
The Gambia	23.37
Niger	23.37
Zambia	23.37
Barbados	23.37
Dominican Republic	23.37
Guyana	23.37
Haiti	23.37
Malawi	17.53
Senegal	17.53
Cape Verde	11.68
Jamaica	11.68
Uruguay	11.68
Botswana	5.84
Lesotho	5.84
Sierra Leone	5.84
Togo	5.84
Iceland	5.84
Nepal	5.84
Central African Republic	0.00
Mauritius	0.00
Rwanda	0.00
Albania	0.00
Malta	0.00
Trinidad and Tobago	0.00
Fiji	0.00

Source: U.S. ACDA; calculations by David J. Louscher and Michael D. Salomone.

Figure 4.4   Tiers of Arms Recipients and Percentage of Total Arms Shipments Received, 1983–1987

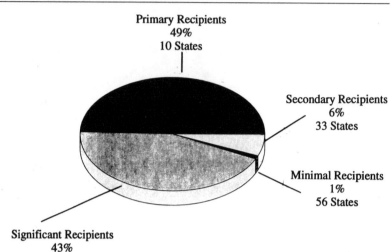

Source: U.S. ACDA; calculations by David J. Louscher.

of the cost of defense procurement. The war in Vietnam created another set of states receiving grants to pay for U.S. weapons; only after the decision to end the war in the late 1960s did U.S. arms transfers that were subsidized by credit expand in geopolitical scope.

Grant and concessionary credit was essentially limited to priority recipients, especially Israel and Egypt, and numerous base-rights recipients. The United States, in an effort to extend the Nixon Doctrine to its European allies and to lessen the pressures on the U.S. defense budget, encouraged and acceded to major license production agreements with the Europeans. This pattern of diffusion was spread to other U.S. arms recipients; by the late 1970s the U.S. government and U.S.-based firms were confronted with numerous demands for offsets in exchange for the acquisition of U.S. equipment. This change in the mode of transfer also contributed to the diffusion of weapons technology (see Figure 4.6).

Technology Proliferation

The level of technology requested by recipients and delivered by suppliers significantly changed in the 1970s and 1980s. In the first three decades of the postwar period, the weapons systems exported to the Third World had limited capabilities compared with the state-of-the-art equipment procured by the

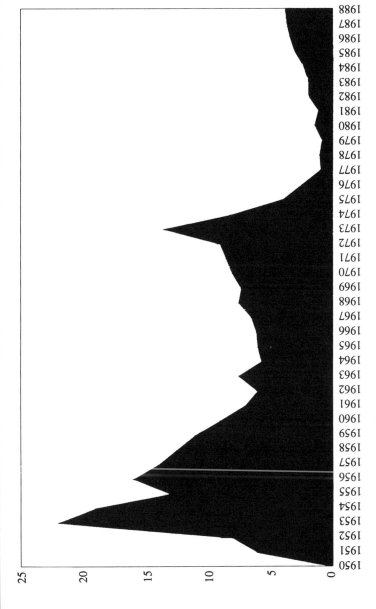

Figure 4.5 U.S. Military Grant Assistance, 1950–1988 (billions of U.S.$, 1989 constant)

Source: U.S. DSAA; calculations by David J. Louscher.

Figure 4.6 Suppliers of Major Systems Licenses, 1977–1983

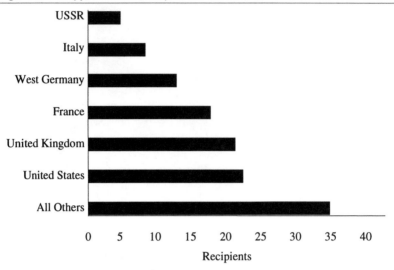

Source: SIPRI Yearbooks 1978–1984; calculations by David J. Louscher.

supplier. Both the United States and the former Soviet Union exported state-of-the-art equipment to their European and Northeast Asian allies. But the Military Assistance Program equipment exported by the United States in the 1950s, for example, was often surplus; this type of equipment formed the bulk of transfers at that time. The less privileged U.S. and Soviet grant recipient states were generally unsuccessful in purchasing anything other than surplus equipment, because they lacked any effective leverage with the supplier state. This relationship between the two superpowers and the states they supplied with weapons did not change until the early 1970s.

The Yom Kippur War demonstrated the commodity power of the oil-producing states of the Middle East; the oil price rise had the auxiliary effect of enriching those states. These two developments emboldened a financially powerful and important commercial constituency to demand state-of-the-art equipment and receive it. These nations now possess sufficient leverage over the supplier nations to obtain weapons systems that were once denied them. This change in the position of the recipient states was aided by a change in the number and nature of suppliers: The entry of the Europeans into the arms market, their weak market position, and their export orientation generated pressures for the transfer of state-of-the-art equipment by all suppliers to states with the financial wherewithal to pay for it. The efforts of the Carter administration to control the sale of such deliveries failed; today the United States and the Europeans are compelled to export weapons in their services' inventory. The Europeans must export their state-of-the-art products (for example, the Tornado and Mirage 2000 aircraft) in order to achieve the necessary economies of scale to sustain the defense sector of the economy. The United States is forced to sell such equipment because recipient states will accept nothing else (for example, Northrop could find not a market for the F-20, a plane designed specifically for the needs of the Third World).

Conclusion

The diffusion of weapons technology and the bid by Third World states to increase their share of the global arms market will only accelerate in the future. The changing nature of the global arms market, a market that is increasingly characterized by the export or licensing of weapons technologies rather than by the wholesale export of weapons systems, suggests that we must give closer consideration to the determinants of the effective demand these states will have for these technologies, the actual number of suppliers in the market, and the strength (or even the presence) of an international regime controlling the diffusion of weapons technologies.

The analysis of weapons technology transfer requires a more exacting definition of the motivations driving suppliers in order to determine the exact number of states (or firms) willing and able to supply state-of-the-art technologies. The effective number of suppliers, in turn, will define the market structure for that particular technology: The lower the number of effective suppliers, the more likely it will be that those nations can control the export of the technology and extract higher rents, be they financial or political in nature. It also leads to a reconsideration of the question of alignments, but the focus of the analysis changes. Rather than fixing upon the patterns of alignment between supplier and recipient, the critical dimension will be the alignment of suppliers: The more closely suppliers are aligned, the more likely it is that the proliferation of a technology will be controlled.

A final question revolves around the motivations driving suppliers to resist or acquiesce to the demand for state-of-the-art technologies. States will be driven by a complex of economic, political, military, and diplomatic considerations. Economic incentives to export state-of-the-art technology include defraying the cost of development or procurement or supporting a segment of the military-industrial complex; political incentives include strategic exports for political gain by an incumbent party; military incentives include the support of a favored weapons system or of a favored political ally to enhance military capabilities; and diplomatic incentives range from efforts to curry favor with a regime to those to sustain influence with a regional power.

Yet, diplomatic barriers to the transfer of technology exist, including the fear that the transfer could upset a delicate regional balance of power; political barriers are also found, such as domestic political opposition to supplying the target country; legal barriers flow from the prohibition of technology exports to strategic areas or target countries. There are also military grounds for resisting the transfer of technology: The net effect of the transfer could be a reduction in the effectiveness of the supplier's own armed forces. At this juncture the economic incentives appear to outweigh the political, military, and diplomatic barriers to supply. But the number of states possessing state-of-the-art technology fluctuates, and some suppliers are more sensitive than others to noneconomic variables.

The effective demand for state-of-the-art technology seeks to determine which states have the desire and the wherewithal to procure that technology. The effective demand for arms technology reflects a calculus of constraints on demand and incentives for procurement. The constraints on procurement will be largely economic in character: The ability to procure arms technology, rather than the will to do so, will be the sole barrier to the demand for technology. A secondary constraint will reflect the ability to apply the technology, even if the financial wherewithal to purchase it exists. But there will be manifold incentives to procure such technology: The formation of a competitive arms industry can be viewed not only as a key element of a modernization strategy but also as a method to ensure that the national armed forces are not bettered on the battlefield because of second-rate arms technology. Moreover, the possession of state-of-the-art arms technology is an issue of international status and political stability for governments notoriously dependent upon the military and industry for their survival. Finally, the ability to procure this technology can be viewed as part of the diplomatic quid pro quo guaranteeing access to the markets or resources of many Third World states.

The balance between the supply of, and the demand for, state-of-the-art technologies will be determined, in the end, by the constraints offered by the international weapons technology diffusion regime. The level of control over the diffusion of technology may be highly regulated, loosely cooperative, or highly competitive. A highly competitive regime would imply an absence of a regime or of a very permissive environment. A loosely cooperative regime implies a set of framework laws controlling perhaps only the most deadly technologies— nuclear, biological, and chemical—but little else. A highly regulated regime would control state-of-the-art weapons technologies that would, in effect, institutionalize the technological superiority of the traditional suppliers of arms as well as the existing hierarchy of power.

This modified model of technology diffusion focuses on the number of suppliers (large or small), the level of effective demand (high or low), and the likely international environment (restrictive or permissive) for different levels of technology. These three variables, with the assigned values, generate eight potential technology diffusion scenarios for the twenty-first century (see Table 4.4). The question that remains, however, is which scenarios are appropriate for which technologies.

Table 4.4   Potential Technology Diffusion Scenarios

Type	International Environment	Number of Suppliers	Intensity of Demand
1	Restrictive	Large	High
2	Restrictive	Large	Low
3	Restrictive	Small	High
4	Restrictive	Small	Low
5	Permissive	Large	High
6	Permissive	Large	Low
7	Permissive	Small	High
8	Permissive	Small	Low

❖ FIVE ❖

Soviet and Russian Arms Transfers and Relations with the Third World: Legacy and Prospects

Warren Phillips & Linda Racioppi

Soviet involvement was an important component of Third World security in the post–World War II era, with the former USSR trying to promote a range of policy objectives—political, military, and economic. Unlike U.S. and especially European involvement in the Third World, however, the connection between economic and military interests in the Soviet case prior to Mikhail Gorbachev was often seen as less than clear-cut.

The literature on Soviet involvement in the Third World prior to Gorbachev often emphasized the primacy of political-military over economic consider-ations.[1] During the 1970s, as Soviet economic relations with the Third World rapidly expanded, the USSR (alternating and competing with the United States) became the leading arms supplier to the Third World. Through arms exports the USSR could attempt to spread its influence, compete with the United States, and affect the outcome of Third World conflicts while acquiring markets for its arms industry and much-needed hard currency.

Arms transfers also fueled a debate concerning the nature of Soviet involve-ment more generally in the Third World: Were economic relations following military ties or vice versa? At what costs was the USSR willing to pursue its political-military interests? What price was it willing to pay for socialist or any other kind of development in the Third World? And relatedly, but receiving less attention, what were the interests of the Third World countries in pursuing ties with the USSR? Under what conditions could those countries attract Soviet economic and military aid and trade? Was a close confluence of military and political interests a prerequisite?

With perestroika, the demands of the domestic economy forced a retraction in Soviet policy in the Third World, and by the mid-1980s there was clearly a telling nexus between political-military interest and economic need in the area of arms transfers. How would the Soviet Union and, after its demise, Russia, balance the necessity for reduced involvement in the Third World with the urge to export arms as a means to earn hard currency? What are the connections between past Soviet practice and contemporary Russian policy in arms transfers to the Third World?

In this chapter we develop an understanding of arms transfers as grounded in the historical relationship between military and economic interests. We want to understand how political and economic changes in the USSR under Gorbachev affected the Soviet Union's ability to conduct economic and military relations with the Third World and what the demise of the USSR is likely to portend for relations between Russia and the Third World. Gorbachev professed interest in resolving regional conflicts and converting parts of the Soviet military-industrial complex to manufacture for civilian purposes; the Boris Yeltsin government has continued to support those policies. Thus, when the Soviet Union collapsed in 1991, it not only left Russia and the other former republics to discover how to make the transition from communism; it also left a legacy of involvement and alliances in the Third World.

In that context, the question of Soviet and Russian arms transfers to, and involvement in, the Third World is still critical today. How will interest in transforming the Soviet-Russian economy affect post-Soviet policy in the Third World, particularly with regard to the highly volatile area of weapons transfers? Will the disintegration of the Soviet economy and the Soviet Union itself mean a drastic cutback in military transfers, or will arms transfers be a bright spot in an otherwise dismal Russian economy? Will the nature or patterns of involvement in the Third World change? What historical patterns of Soviet involvement in the Third World may influence Russian options today? These are some of the questions we address.

Our purpose, then, is to examine patterns of arms transfers from the USSR within the context of overall Soviet involvement in the Third World. We first examine contending positions in the literature with regard to Soviet economic and military relations with the Third World and then explore the historical context for economic aid and trade and arms transfers to the Third World, briefly reviewing Soviet policy from Nikita Khrushchev to Gorbachev. We then look specifically at patterns of arms transfers and licensing agreements from the Leonid Brezhnev era, a period most scholars characterize as one of expanded use of the military instrument in the Third World, through the Gorbachev years. We argue that historically, arms transfers have served both political-military and economic purposes for the Soviet Union and that economic rationales became increasingly important because of the transformation of the Soviet economy; for these reasons, examination of the linkages between economic and political-military policy objectives remains critical to a consideration of Soviet-Russian relations with the Third World. We conclude with some suggestions about the prospects for Russian policies in the Third World in light of domestic economic reform in the former Soviet Union.

Debates and Dilemmas

What was the prime motivation for Soviet involvement in the Third World? How did the Soviet Union pursue its interests there? What was the relationship between military and economic interests in Soviet foreign policy in the Third World? The literature on these questions, not surprisingly, reveals some differing opinions.

Many Western scholars have seen Soviet policy in the Third World as motivated largely by political-military considerations. According to this view, in the Brezhnev era increased Soviet military capabilities in production and deployment led the USSR to rely increasingly on arms transfers and military assistance in its dealings with the Third World. The military instrument was critical in the USSR's foreign policy instrument arsenal. On economic matters, these scholars have argued that Soviet trade with the Third World could be explained as following the USSR's political and strategic interests (and, to a lesser extent, those of the particular Third World country). However, another argument stated that Soviet–Third World economic relations had more to do with the disadvantages of trading with the neocolonialist West than with any grand strategic scheme of the USSR. The first view saw a convergence of Soviet and Third World military-security interests (which were usually seen as directly contrary to U.S.-Western security interests), whereas the second view emphasized a convergence of Soviet and Third World economic needs (brought together by the difficulties of economic development in the capitalist world economy). These two views raise some interesting questions, as Marvin Jackson has noted:

> If the Soviet sword is an efficient substitute for the attractions of an economic system in swinging trade of the South from the West to the East, then why has so little of it swung? And if the interests of the South have been so badly damaged by trading with the West according to conventional rules of international commerce, then why have East-South economic relations not prospered more? (Jackson, 1985: 6)

Some researchers have suggested that part of the reason for the relatively small amounts of trade between the East and the South had to do with structural limits of centrally planned economies and the relative similarity of production in those economies to that in the developing countries. As Marian Paszynski has noted,

> The similarities and differences stem from the fact that while the developed capitalist economies operate under conditions of structural excess of industrial capacities, both socialist and, to a great extent, also developing economies face productive capacities lagging behind the expanding domestic demand. . . . [Furthermore, the] central planner abhor[s] installation of surplus capacities or the growth of capacity outpacing the growth of demand. Surplus capacity has been always taboo in the socialist economy. (Paszynski, 1981, 38–39)

Socialist economies, not unlike many developing economies, tended to favor imports over exports:

> In the socialist economies imports perform an important function of catering to the needs of the national economy and are beneficial as they complement insufficient domestic supply. Exports, on the other hand, compete with domestic demand for the indigenous production under conditions of supply lagging behind the growth of demand. (Paszynski, 1981, 39)

Thus, if it was a mutual desire to minimize the disadvantages of trading with the capitalist West that drew the East and the South together, there may have been some structural limitations on their ability to expand trade, although such limitations could be overcome. First, political will on both sides could have overcome difficulties. (The "trade following the sword" perspective suggests that a commonality of politico-strategic interests drives the relationship.) Countries could also seek a complementarity of economic advantage (Kaminski and Janes, 1988).

It should not be surprising, therefore, that the Soviet arms industry largely escaped this conundrum: It minimized the supply-constraint dilemma common in centrally planned economies and exploited the opportunities of the international arms market. Its success, then, can be partly explained by the fact that military-related research and industry fell under the control of defense and other related ministries and were given preferential treatment with regard to capital, technical, and labor inputs—partly because of the willingness of the regime to encourage overproduction, and partly because of a seemingly insatiable demand for weapons in the Third World (particularly in the 1970s, when the USSR was expanding its economic and military contacts). However, the privileged position of the military-industrial sector again begs the question of military as opposed to economic interests. Melvin Goodman has noted:

> The past three decades have seen a concerted Soviet effort to improve the USSR's military position in all areas. Total military manpower has increased by about one-third to its present size of about five million. Weapons production capacity has expanded by nearly 60 percent, and research and development facilities have nearly doubled. . . .
> In the Third World the growth of Soviet military power has led to the increased use of military instruments to gain political ends. Soviet arms sales to the Third World have increased rapidly since their beginning in the 1950s, and the number of Soviet military advisers in Third World conflicts has grown in increasingly active and threatening stages during confrontations in the Third World. (Goodman, 1987, 62)

Arms transfers, thus, were a leading instrument in a policy that was motivated primarily by Soviet military interests (although Goodman and others recognize that arms sales often brought a hard currency bonus). This explanation seemed to clarify Soviet relations with some of its major Third World allies, such as Egypt, Syria, and India.

Other scholars argued that although political-military considerations could not be ignored, economic interests increasingly motivated Soviet arms transfers to the Third World: "There is little doubt that arms exports and related convertible-currency earnings provide a crucial source of foreign exchange for the Soviet economy. . . . Economic motivations are now crucial to arms transfers" (Deger, 1985, 160–161). We contend that both views hold some truth and, indeed, that they are not mutually exclusive. In the Brezhnev years, for some Third World countries political-military interests seemed to drive economic and military aid and trade, but for a growing number of countries, military and economic ties with the Soviet Union were dictated increasingly by economic considerations in Moscow. This situation was exacerbated in the 1980s; perestroika, in a sense, accelerated a phenomena whose roots were beginning to be established before Gorbachev entered office.

The legacy of the past has had important consequences for Soviet and post-Soviet policy in the Third World in two ways: first, in terms of converting Soviet military production for civilian use under circumstances in which weapons sales could earn the USSR, and now Russia, more hard currency than most civilian products; and second, in terms of maintaining and developing relations with the Third World in the post–Cold War era. It is, therefore, essential that we understand the evolution of the Soviet Union's economic and military aid and trade policy in the Third World.

Background on Soviet Involvement in the Third World

From 1955 until the late 1960s, the USSR's ties with the Third World increased dramatically.[2] During this period, Soviet trade with the Third World grew from a mere 271.8 million rubles in 1955 (less than 1 percent of total Soviet foreign trade) to 1,743.6 million rubles in 1965 (about 12 percent of total trade).[3]

In addition to the rapid expansion of economic aid and trade, a limited program of military assistance was begun. As Rajan Menon points out, "Prior to the mid-1960s, Moscow provided arms exclusively to nonaligned states. In essence, this was due to Khrushchev's belief that the nonaligned nations, as opponents of the American strategy of containment, were the ones most likely to respond favorably to Soviet overtures of friendship" (Menon, 1986, 190). Primary recipients of weaponry were those countries with which the USSR had close political ties, particularly Egypt and India.

The peaceful competition between the capitalist West and the socialist East that had been encouraged during Khrushchev's reign brought about increased economic cooperation between the USSR and certain Third World capitalist countries.[4] Khrushchev's goal was to delink the developing countries from world capitalism, thus enabling them to make the peaceful transition to socialism. Soviet aid and trade, both economic and military, with newly independent countries such as India would enable them to become independent from Western militarism and would encourage the development of state-sector industries and public control of foreign trade in an effort to lead the recipient country toward a socialist development path. But the strategy was not all outward-looking. The USSR under Khrushchev used aid to boost trade, with Soviet economic aid based substantially on providing machinery and equipment for assistance projects and with the recipients supplying traditional goods, such as raw materials and primary products, as repayment.

Despite early successes with the USSR's aid and trade program under Khrushchev—the expansion of trade relations, the visibility of major economic assistance projects, and the extension of arms sales to the Third World—the approach was eventually rejected because it did not produce the anticipated results. Indeed, setbacks in countries such as Indonesia and the failure of major aid recipients such as India and Egypt to make the transition to socialism proved that Khrushchev's view of the prospects for a quick, peaceful transition in the Third World was overly optimistic. With Khrushchev's ouster and the establishment of collective leadership, the USSR did not appear willing or able to finance a global transition, and the quality of the Soviet exports (such as machinery and equipment) often failed to impress Third World economic policymakers, who were also being wooed by Western aid donors.

Although rapid growth in Soviet trade with the Third World marked the Brezhnev era, more of that growth occurred in the 1970s than in the period 1980–1985. Between 1970 and 1975 alone, total trade turnover with less-developed countries (LDCs) nearly tripled, increasing from 2,981.3 million rubles in 1970 to 6,308.8 million rubles in 1975. As a percentage of total Soviet trade, however, the Third World accounted for just 13.5 percent in 1970 and 13.2 percent in 1975. Trade continued to expand in the period 1975–1985, but much more slowly. Total turnover in 1980 was 11,961.6 million rubles, less than double that of 1975; by 1985, total trade amounted to just 17,225.1 million rubles. Furthermore, Third World trade as a percentage of total Soviet trade remained virtually unchanged, at 12.5 percent in 1975 and 12.7 percent in 1980 and dropping slightly to 12 percent in 1985.[5] Thus, despite dramatic increases in Soviet trade with the Third World, particularly in the early 1970s, the significance of that trade to the USSR remained relatively stable.

The same could not be said for arms transfers. During the 1970s, the USSR became the top arms exporter to the Third World, surpassing even the United States. It increased its weapons exports from $1,136 million in 1970 to $3,774 million in 1980 (constant 1975 dollars) (Deger, 1986c, 159; see also Chapter 4 in this volume). Furthermore, by the late 1960s, as Menon notes, the USSR had become more flexible in its choice of partners for arms shipments. Arms deals were "concluded with conservative states having strong ties to the West: Iran in 1967 and 1973, Pakistan in 1968, Kuwait in 1967 and 1984, and Jordan in 1981" (Menon, 1986, 190). Thus, at a time when Soviet trade with the Third World was increasing, the significance of the arms sales portion of that trade was outstripping other types of exports.

Furthermore, three major shifts in the Soviet approach to the Third World occurred in this period. First, there was a recognition of a single world economic system, albeit one with two critically important subsystems. As Brezhnev noted,

> We are not setting a course toward the isolation of our country from the outside world. On the contrary, we start from the position that it will develop under conditions of growing universal cooperation with the outside world, and therewith not only with socialist countries, but also in significant degree with states of an opposing social system. (*Pravda*, March 22, 1973, 1)

Having acknowledged the importance of global cooperation, the USSR needed to mesh the Third World economies with the socialist economies in an evolving pattern of widening global interdependence. This also contributed to the second policy shift under Brezhnev: the notion that the USSR could best serve the cause of world socialism by developing its own economy. As Brezhnev noted, "The more quickly our country moves forward in building the new society, the more successfully will our international tasks be resolved" (quoted in Valkenier, 1983, 13).

The free-and-easy aid and trade that characterized the Khrushchev period would be modified under Brezhnev: Economic relations would be for the *mutual* economic benefit of the USSR and the Third World recipient (Valkenier, 1986). More "rational" economic relations (including military and economic aid and, to a lesser extent, trade) were concentrated in particular countries (for example, Afghanistan, Cuba, Egypt, India, Mongolia, and Vietnam). Some scholars have argued that under Brezhnev a shift occurred from long-term economic program aid to short-term project aid and commercial venture assistance (Valkenier, 1983; Dawisha, 1979); these ventures were aimed primarily at the impact the projects were likely to have on Soviet economic conditions.

The USSR was becoming increasingly interested in the international division of labor and its implications for the USSR obtaining a better economic deal in the world economy. The USSR attempted to manage its relations with the Third World in such a manner that it acquired the primary products and natural resources it needed while using trade relations as a vehicle for sales of fuels, heavy equipment, industrialization technology, and, especially, arms.

During this period foreign trade was also used for the aggregation of hard currency. There was a dramatic shift from long-term intergovernmental agreements, which provided for the exchange of goods at predetermined prices, and the settlement of payments in nonconvertible currency. The USSR began to renegotiate many old agreements to require the settlement of payments in accordance with world prices and in hard currencies. Thus, an expansion of Soviet activities occurred, with aid still being used to boost trade, but aid and trade were targeted more carefully, with closer consideration of the economic benefits that would accrue to the USSR. The third innovation in policy during this period contributed to these efforts: The key ingredient of Brezhnev's new outreach was to support the establishment and succor of military regimes whose potential had previously been underestimated (Mirskii, 1972) and the expanded use of military assistance programs, as shown in Table 5.1. As the table shows, in the early Brezhnev era the ratio of military assistance to economic aid was three to one, but in the late 1970s it increased to four to one.

Whereas Table 5.1 demonstrates the expansion of military aid during the Brezhnev period, there was also a significant increase in the sale of arms and armament technologies. The USSR was frequently unable to compete directly with the West in economic terms but was able to use arms sales and aid to achieve early successes in the Third World, which could then be leveraged into increased sales opportunities that focused upon both commodities sales and acquisition of hard currency for use in foreign trade (mainly with the West).

Since Brezhnev's demise and the discrediting of his regime, some major changes were implemented in regard to the USSR's Third World policy, but some themes suggested under the Brezhnev regime were also extended and developed. Continued interest in global interdependence and economic pragmatism reflected the Soviet, and now Russian, inability to finance Third World development as well as interest in developing relations with East Asian newly industrialized countries (NICs).

To these strictly economic concerns, however, Gorbachev added those of regional conflict and conflict management. Military conflicts in the Third World were viewed as an area of potential superpower conflict, a major economic drain, and something to be avoided. The Soviet withdrawal from Afghanistan (and its admission that the intervention was a mistake), and its interest in finding negotiated settlements to the conflicts in Latin America, the Middle East, and Southern Africa demonstrated its reduced willingness and capacity to use direct intervention and large-scale military grants to protosocialist regimes as a central part of its Third World policy. However, any reduction in arms sales would have a significant impact on Soviet shares of hard currency and possibly on its future ability to gain access to other sectors of Third World markets. These concerns become even more acute in the context of the restructuring of the Soviet economy under Gorbachev (and the transition from communism under Yeltsin).

Table 5.1   Soviet Economic and Military Aid to the Third World, 1965–1979 (millions of U.S.$)

Agreements	Economic Aid		Military Aid	
	1965–1974	1975–1979	1965–1974	1975–1979
Middle East	2,227	3,354	10,763	12,465
South Asia	2,101	1,105	2,150	3,080
Africa	483	2,528	3,487	12,075
East Asia	3	180	—	—
Latin America	781	101	—	765
Total	5,595	7,268	16,400	28,385

Source: Gu Guan-fu, 1983, 74. Reprinted with permission.

If we examine the available foreign trade data, the dilemma becomes more apparent. In 1985 Soviet trade with the Third World stood at 17,225.1 million rubles (about 12 percent of Soviet trade), but by 1987 it had decreased to 14,504 million rubles (about 11 percent of total foreign trade). There was a small increase in trade in 1988 to 14,911.1 million rubles (about 11 percent of total foreign trade) and an even larger one in 1989 (the last year for which data are available) to 17,108.2 million rubles (12 percent of total foreign trade).[6]

Many analysts predicted that Soviet trade with the Third World would slowly diminish in the late 1980s and 1990s, based on the deteriorating condition of the Soviet economy, Gorbachev's interest in limiting Third World conflicts (and, therefore, presumably limiting arms exports), and the reduced capacity of the USSR to fund Third World development. Regardless of whether the 1989 and 1990 figures are simply anomalies, it is interesting that for those years, the only category of countries in which the USSR did not have a balance-of-payments deficit was the Third World (*Vneshnie ekonomicheskie sviazi SSSR* 1989g, 8).

Thus, this was a period of difficulty for Soviet foreign trade and the Soviet economy—a period in which the need for hard currency was increasing but the ability to earn hard currency through exports was decreasing. For around twenty years, however, weapons exports had been a bright spot in Soviet exports. What were the nature and extent of Soviet weapons sales to the Third World in the 1970s and 1980s? How would arms transfers fit into late and post-Soviet relations with the Third World?

Arms Transfers to the Third World: Patterns and Problems

Evaluating the extent and impact of arms transfers to the Third World is not simple, and assessing Soviet transfers and their relationship to economic policies is even more complex. Data problems are legion (for example, with both U.S. Arms Control and Disarmament Agency [ACDA] and Stockholm International Peace Research Institute [SIPRI] data).[7] Furthermore, arms sales and nonmilitary trade have become interconnected in the Soviet foreign trade data (indeed, most would argue that the USSR purposefully disguised arms sales in nonmilitary foreign trade statistics), and disaggregating the components of the so-called unspecified residual in Soviet trade data has occupied many scholars (see Smith, 1987). Thus, trying to understand patterns of aid and trade even in the relatively stable Brezhnev era is a formidable task; doing so under conditions of a transitional economy and a destabilized political system is even more onerous.

Despite these difficulties, some persistent patterns emerge in any consideration of Soviet arms transfers to the Third World, no matter what data set one uses.[8] Our task here is to lay out those patterns and to try to understand how the legacy of past military sales may influence future Soviet arms transfers to the Third World. We thus focus our review on the Brezhnev through Gorbachev periods—that is, the periods in which the USSR became the leading arms exporter to the Third World and, under Gorbachev, in which it lost that position.

Soviet Arms in the World Arms Market

During the 1970s the USSR expanded its arms sales to the Third World. It was able to compete effectively with the United States and to easily surpass the other major arms exporters—France, Great Britain, Germany, Italy, and China—in the world arms market (Chapter 4 in this volume). During the Brezhnev years, except for the period 1973–1977, the USSR secured a greater market share for arms delivered to the Third World than did its main rival, the United States, except for 1969, 1972, and 1975–1977, when the United States led (Menon, 1986, 185). Moreover, the United States and the USSR were responsible for up to 80 percent of arms supplied to the Third World throughout the 1970s and 1980s. Table 5.2 depicts both the competition between the United States and the USSR in arms transfers to the Third World and the predominance of the superpowers in the world market up to 1985, the pre-Gorbachev era.

Despite year-to-year fluctuations, Table 5.2 demonstrates the general expansion in arms trade across the board in the 1970s and early 1980s.[9] The data also indicate that in an increasingly competitive environment, the USSR maintained a strong position. For example, the USSR's share of weapons transfers to the Third World in 1971 was about 42 percent, dropped to 30 percent in 1975, increased to 45 percent in 1980, and dropped to about 38 percent in 1985. During the 1970s, Soviet arms exports increases outpaced those of the United States, more than doubling in value between 1970 and 1980. (China, which was one of the main USSR concerns in Asia, also nearly quadrupled arms sales during this period, although its market share never threatened that of either the Soviet Union or the United States.) Furthermore, although such increases could not be sustained into the 1980s, the USSR still held its place among arms exporters. Combined with the United States, the USSR retained more than 60 percent of the Third World arms market, compared with approximately 75 percent in 1975 and approximately 70 percent in 1980. Although the superpowers' share declined in the 1980s, they still formed the first tier of arms suppliers.

If we examine the trends during the Gorbachev years, a slightly different pattern emerges. As Table 5.3 indicates, a general downturn occurred in the world arms market in the second half of the 1980s. The Soviet number-one position is retained in the 1985–1990 period; however, by the end of the 1980s, Soviet exports to the Third World began to taper off in response to (1) Gorbachev's policy of relieving conflicts through political means, (2) the increasing demand that arms be purchased for hard currency, and (3) the impact these policies had on the prospects for arms sales in a sluggish international market. Indeed, from 1990 to 1991, the dollar value of Soviet arms agreements with the Third World was halved,[10] dropping the USSR almost 10 percentage points in terms of its share of the Third World arms market.[11]

Table 5.2 Arms Transfers to the Third World, by Major Suppliers, 1965–1985 (millions of U.S.$, constant 1985 prices)

Country	1965	1966	1967	1968	1969	1970	1971	1972	1973	1974	1975	1976	1977	1978	1979	1980	1981	1982	1983	1984	1985
USSR	1,356	2,597	4,317	3,787	2,164	4,110	4,956	5,874	7,025	4,732	2,874	4,875	7,231	9,035	10,118	9,085	7,992	7,777	7,164	8,382	7,315
United States	1,424	1,511	1,816	2,215	3,118	3,551	3,830	5,924	6,264	4,481	7,074	7,257	9,465	6,852	4,052	5,664	6,131	7,121	6,346	5,108	4,380
France	189	345	274	580	274	693	677	786	1,643	1,263	1,144	1,398	2147	2,406	3,264	2,356	3,134	2,892	2,771	3,476	3,531
Britain	338	315	478	518	1,038	472	1,212	1,195	1,307	1,071	1,196	834	1,641	1,200	773	703	1,161	1,648	900	1,434	888
Germany	43	60	66	36	56	3	86	108	—	408	261	166	204	258	162	283	931	320	1,169	1,819	479
Italy	26	37	96	121	85	37	95	137	148	268	139	163	294	323	975	653	1,332	1,347	1,000	1,068	987
China	74	233	214	162	86	101	321	417	232	382	320	211	114	459	412	484	328	675	878	1,296	767

Source: Adapted from Brzoska and Ohlson, 1987, 324–327.

Table 5.3 Arms Transfers to the Third World by Major Supplier, 1985–1990 (millions of U.S.$, constant 1985 prices)

Country	1985	1986	1987	1988	1989	1990
USSR	9,106	10,440	10,936	8,658	8,862	4,273
United States	4,114	4,981	6,328	3,939	3,465	3,048
France	3,588	3,446	2,659	1,413	1,642	1,330
Britain	1,050	10,091	1,681	1,281	1,187	971
Germany	395	661	254	367	168	496
Italy	579	399	320	363	49	39
China	1,217	1,463	2,553	1,810	817	926

Source: Adapted from SIPRI, 1991, 230–231.

Regional Distribution of Weapons Sales

Historically, the Soviet Union has concentrated its arms exports in certain areas (and to an even greater extent, as is discussed in the following section, in certain countries). Table 5.4 shows the relative share of markets by region from 1966 to 1985. The data clearly indicate the complete absence of Soviet arms exports to South Africa and a virtual absence of exports to South America. Except in the period 1966–1970, when it held a 46 percent share of the arms trade, the USSR also did not lead the market in the Far East. However, Soviet arms predominance was marked in South Asia and in North and Central Africa, and it shared the leading position with the United States in the Middle East.

Table 5.4 reveals that the USSR was a major supplier of weapons to regions with some of the most intransigent, protracted conflicts during these two decades. Further, the Middle East and South Asia were responsible for the bulk of Soviet arms transfers to the Third World. In the period 1981–1985, for example, the USSR was responsible for approximately $25,424 million (in U.S. dollars) in arms transfers to the Middle East and South Asia, whereas its transfers to all other areas of the Third World combined were only about half that amount.[12]

Table 5.4 Soviet Share in Arms Trade by Region, 1966–1985 (as percentage of total)

Region	1966–1970	1971–1975	1976–1980	1981–1985
Middle East	49	45	27	33
South Asia	58	54	63	54
Far East	46	23	33	25
North Africa	46	62	70	46
Sub-Saharan Africa[a]	44	27	59	40
Central America	54	57	69	66
South America	—	0	11	1

Source: Adapted from Brzoska and Ohlson, 1987, 338–339.
Note: a. Excluding South Africa.

An examination of data from the Gorbachev era shows that many of the trends shown in Table 5.4 persisted. The Middle East and South Asia remained the two most favored regions for Soviet arms exports. Although there was a definite reduction in arms supplied to regions with ongoing conflicts, the general pattern of Soviet arms exports persisted, demonstrating that old ties were not easily disrupted even by a regime intent on reducing regional conflicts and seeking political rather than military solutions to regional security.

Major Recipients of Soviet Arms

The patterns are even more striking when examined for country recipients of arms. Although the USSR had close military relations with a number of the top Third World arms importers, the USSR's arms exports portfolio was not particularly diverse. As Michael Brzoska and Thomas Ohlson point out, the vast majority of Soviet arms deliveries were to countries with which the USSR has signed a treaty of friendship and cooperation (Afghanistan, Angola, Ethiopia, India, Iraq, Mozambique, North Korea, Syria, Vietnam, South Yemen).[13] For the period 1981–1985, the ten countries listed in Table 5.5 received over 90 percent of all Soviet arms transfers.

Indeed, just four of those countries (India, Iraq, Libya, and Syria) accounted for over 70 percent of all Soviet arms exports to the Third World. From 1970 to 1990, these countries received some of the USSR's most advanced military technology, ranging from missiles (for example, SA-11, AT-5, SSN-2 Styx, AA-2 Atoll) to tanks (for example, the T-72) to naval ships (for example, the Tarantul Class Corvette, Kilo Class Submarine) to aircraft (for example, the Mi-26 Halo helicopter, MiG-29 fighter), and others. Although these four countries continued to receive large numbers of major weapons systems deliveries throughout this period, by the late 1980s India and Syria were clearly receiving far more in arms transfers than Iraq or Libya. Table 5.5 shows the top ten Soviet arms importers in 1981–1985 and the percentage share of Soviet arms in that country's market.

Table 5.5   Top Ten Soviet Arms Recipients, 1981–1985 (millions of U.S.$, constant 1985 prices)

Country	Amount	%
Syria	9,729	97
Iraq	8,343	55
India	5,887	68
Libya	3,490	61
Cuba	2,084	99
Vietnam	1,801	100
Angola	1,602	98
Algeria	1,080	52
Afghanistan	964	98
North Korea	927	82

Source: Calculated from Brzoska and Ohlson,1987, 339–350.

An examination of the USSR's top trade partners in the period 1987–1991 gives similar results, with India topping the list, followed by Afghanistan, Iraq, North Korea, Angola, and Syria—all with arms trade over U.S.$3 billion.[14] Also notable, six of the countries in Table 5.5 (Cuba, India, Iraq, Libya, Syria, Vietnam) had consistently been in the top ten since the early 1970s, and Algeria had joined those ranks in the mid-1970s. Thus, a constant group of countries had been the main recipients of Soviet arms for a substantial period of time.

This situation had important repercussions. First, some Third World countries became dependent on the USSR for their arms, and this dependence transcended political-economic orientation—that is, not just Communist Party–led states exhibited a high degree of dependence on Soviet arms but also countries such as India and Iraq. This led India, for example, to undertake a diversification of arms suppliers, a move that actually decreased the Soviet share of the Indian market.[15]

Second, the Soviet Union also became accustomed to relying on exports to a limited number of Third World partners. Indeed, Saadat Deger has pointed out that "about 63 per cent of the trade deficit in non-defense goods and services was financed by hard currency earnings from international sales of armaments" (Deger, 1986c, 167). Given that the USSR had come to count on arms transfers as an important component of its exports during the 1970s and early 1980s, the concentration of arms exports to a small number of countries was not insignificant. As the USSR moved further from bartering and other arrangements advantageous to Third World buyers in the 1980s (particularly in the second half of the decade), it was questionable whether its traditional major arms partners would be willing or able to purchase Soviet arms on less favorable terms.

The situation was exacerbated when, as occurred in the late 1980s, there was a general decline in the world armaments trade, because the USSR's own pool of buyers was not diverse. Perhaps in response to this situation, in 1990 and 1991 the USSR undertook sales of weapons to buyers with which it had not had close relations, selling the MiG-29, T-72 tank, and Kilo Class submarines to Iran and the SU-27 fighter to China.[16] This attempt to attract new purchasers continued in the post-Soviet period as Russia tried to win arms contracts in one of the few areas that was increasing its purchases, Southeast Asia.

Licensing Agreements

An additional dimension of Soviet military policy warrants mention, and that is the granting of licensing agreements to certain Third World countries. The licensing of arms production, although it was not used as pervasively as arms transfers, was a part of Soviet military policy in the Third World. The USSR used licensing arrangements to help cement relations with certain Third World allies such as India. For the Third World partner, licensing agreements can be an effective way to build a domestic arms industry and to earn currency on the re-export of goods. Re-export, however, required the permission of the USSR, but historically, the Soviet Union was reluctant to veto sales to third parties.[17] Thus, both sides had motivations to enter into agreements.

The USSR, however, was hardly extravagant in awarding licenses in the Third World: Indeed, only three countries received licenses—India, Iraq, and North Korea.[18] According to SIPRI, Iraq received one license in 1989–1990 for the production of the Saddam 122 mm towed howitzer.[19] North Korea held a variety of licenses for production of tanks (T-54 and T-55),[20] fighter aircraft (for example, the MiG-29, Su-25 Frogfoot), and missiles.

India was by far the most fortunate. It received a license to produce the MiG-21 in the 1960s; since that time it was granted a range of other licenses from Moscow, including those for updated versions of the MiG-21 in the 1970s and 1980s, followed by licenses to produce the An-32 Cline transport aircraft and the T-72 battle tank. In the last half of the 1980s, India was allowed to produce the MiG-29 and the Tarantul Class Corvette. Although these licenses were not representative of Soviet military policy in the Third World in general, they did mark the importance of Soviet arms trade with certain major arms partners.

The Arms-Economy Link

A review of Soviet economic and military involvement in the Third World reveals some interesting facts. First, despite a period of rapid expansion of foreign economic assistance and trade with the Third World, by the time Gorbachev took office the USSR had shifted its policy away from the free-and-easy aid of the Khrushchev period and had begun to move toward economic relations that would be of mutual economic benefit. It is interesting that in spite of a large increase in Third World trade in the 1970s, the USSR could not substantially increase the significance of its trade with the Third World. Indeed, there are indications that the importance of Third World trade to the Soviet economy actually declined during the Brezhnev era.

Furthermore, the Soviet economy began to rely on a few exports to subsidize imports, one of the most important of which was arms.[21] As the Soviet economy went into a downturn in the 1970s and 1980s, the arms production industry continued to post promising growth rates. Arms sales became increasingly important in the overall USSR export picture. Even at less advantageous prices, Soviet arms were usually cheaper than most Western arms, and Soviet delivery time was less than that of the United States.

The general trade picture with the Third World, however, did not improve (in a trade following the sword scenario), in part because of the limited numbers of major arms recipients and in part because other than arms and oil, Soviet exports faced the same limitations as exports of nations elsewhere in the world. Soviet weapons could compete on the world market in a way many of its other exports could not. However, the end of the Cold War, the demise of the Soviet

Union and the radical transformation of the post-Soviet economy, and an international economic downturn introduced conditions dramatically different from those of the past.

The Russian enterprises that were involved in the production of military equipment and services are facing severe shortages of finances for continuing the enterprises, converting their production from military to civilian products, and training their personnel in market-oriented strategies of survival. For instance, budget-funded orders for aviation hardware amounted to a mere 10 percent of the 1990 level in 1993 (*We*, May 31–June 13, 1993, 2, No. 11, 1). This has led to three major goals in cooperating with the West on conversion: (1) immediate acquisition of hard currency, (2) integration into the international economy, and (3) long-term growth.

If we look at indicators of the success of the Gaidar strategy in conversion, we can find quantitative surrogates to evaluate the progress. Prime Minister Yegor Gaidar's last economic presentation to the Supreme Soviet suggested that the process was not going well. If we take national income and capital expenditures as reasonable measures of the cash made available for conversion, national income was down 17 percent from 1992, and capital expenditure was down 44 percent from 1991 (Gaidar, March 1993, 3). The availability of cash from the system was almost nonexistent.

Capital from the West must rely on viable business plans for conversion. Export-import balances offer a first-cut approximation of Russian involvement in the international economy. Here, exports were off by 30 percent and imports were up by 18 percent (Gaidar, March 1993, 4). This underscores the fact that the debt situation was worsening, making it harder for cash flows from the government to enterprises in the military-industrial sector to be enhanced domestically in the near future. Finally, industrial production and retail turnover are indicators of the long-term growth potential of the economy; however, industrial production was down 13.2 percent, and retail turnover was off by 44 percent (Gaidar, March 1993, 4).

This situation was compounded by the government's being forced to cover the debt of inter-enterprise purchases, because the enterprises are not prepared to pay for intermediate products delivered from other enterprises. The industrial debt between enterprises in the first three months of 1992 exceeded 1992 GNP: It is now at 3 trillion rubles. This staggering figure is one of the major causes of inflation today. Personal incomes rose 600 percent in 1993, but the price index rose 1,170 percent (Gaidar, March 1993, 4).

In order to address these issues, several programs must be adopted under the rubric of conversion: (1) Liberalization of the economy—There must be a rationalization of intersectoral relations that allows for self-adjustment. (2) Restoration of the national economy—The productive levels of the past must be regained in civilian markets rather than in military sectors. (3) Economic growth—Growth is needed based upon a market economy with full recognition of customers' desires, purchasing power, and investment potential. Furthermore, the reduction of military expenditures had been accomplished, but no real adjustment had been forthcoming in the structure, size, or operational behavior of the military enterprise system.

The change from a state-owned enterprise system to a market mechanism requires a psychological as much as a structural adjustment. The move from the Western "cost plus fixed fee" concept for pricing the military industrial sector's products and services to a "firm fixed price" method of delivering products and services entails profit but more often involves risk, deferred reward, and client support. Further, in order to attract Western business partners, an adequate system of legal protections must be established.

Yeltsin's government must face these very real domestic problems while at the same time coming to grips with an increasingly demanding foreign economic environment. To solve this puzzle without the continued sale of arms means real integration into the international economy using the most value-added products in the Russian economy; however, most, if not all, of these products come from military production facilities.

Prospects for the Future

As the previous discussion has suggested, any consideration of the future of Russian arms transfers to the Third World must consider the economic and political pressures within Russia in the transition from communism. The states of the former Soviet Union, particularly Russia, face a dilemma: The Soviet Union had been a major arms supplier to the Third World. Arms sales were one of the few exports with which the Soviet Union could compete on the international market and earn badly needed hard currency.

However, the transition to a market economy requires the development of civilian and light industry and services, the ability to attract foreign investment, and the necessity of maintaining friendly relations with the West in order to decrease military spending. As the economy collapses and rebuilds, the need for imports is more acute than ever; however, hard currency is in ever shorter supply. Thus, the question becomes whether the established pattern of paying for imports with the sale of a limited number of exports—particularly arms—will continue into the post-Soviet era: "Russian President Boris Yeltsin on February 22, 1992, told *Izvestia* that arms exports were a 'buffer' that could reduce the blow to the Russian defense industry suffering from sharp cutbacks in domestic defense spending" (Grimmett, 1992, 2). As this statement demonstrates, there are powerful domestic pressures to stay with a formula that works.

The ultimate position of the military sector in the decentralized post–Soviet Union is still unclear. Many in the military industrial complex are staunchly opposed to decentralization and rapid transformation of the economy; however, many see the writing on the wall. Under Prime Minister Gaidar, the military industrial complex did not fare as well as it had hoped. Russian defense spending continued the downward spiral begun by Gorbachev in the late 1980s; moreover, within the limitations placed upon it, the Gaidar government seemed intent on promoting military conversion.

It is too early to tell whether Prime Minister Viktor Chernomyrdin's policies will change the course of conversion; however, there have been some indications that Gaidar's policies have been retracted.[22] Yeltsin has attempted to appease the military by allowing it to take the lead, particularly on Soviet military policy in areas along Russia's border and on technical dimensions of policymaking (Zisk, 1993). However, even if conversion is slowed, the military industrial complex will clearly not be favored as it was in the past. Will past successes in production for export continue, or will production capabilities diminish as protected status is withdrawn?

For some time the USSR relied on the military sector for production of high-tech and consumer goods (for example, radios, televisions, and VCRs were all produced under the auspices of defense-related ministries), and some argue that plans to resuscitate the Soviet economy have relied too heavily on conversion of military industries for civilian purposes. The military industrial complex, then, may be asked to fill several bills at once. Thus, the conversion process becomes an important part of any assessment of the prospects for future arms transfers and foreign trade.

The demise of the Soviet Union and the deterioration of the economy also generate another military threat: that of the proliferation of nuclear material and nuclear weapons technology. Some leaders in the Ukraine have hinted they may play the nuclear card if additional economic assistance is not forthcoming; however, there are real dangers in doing so with Russia and the West. A more pressing concern is the sale of nuclear knowledge through Third World countries' hiring unemployed nuclear scientists who have worked on the USSR's nuclear weapons programs. Although this potential problem seems to have been contained, it may emerge in the future as a more serious threat than conventional arms transfers.

The appeasement of some sectors of the military industrial complex and the potential for hard currency earnings are powerful motivators, but not all forces are pushing Russia and the other successor states to resume active policies of arms exports. First, as implied earlier, Russia's defense production has dropped precipitously since 1988. As Alexei Kireyev points out,

> In the period 1988–91, the production of aircraft declined by 44 per cent, tanks by 52 per cent, strategic missiles by 58 per cent, ammunition by 64 per cent, self-propelled and towed artillery by 66 per cent, and fighting landing craft and armored carriers by 76 per cent. Production of all medium and short-range missiles was completely stopped. (Kireyev, 1992, 383)

Second, for political and economic reasons, Russia will want to avoid antagonizing the United States and the states of Western Europe by increasing Third World arms trade, and an upturn could spoil relations, first, by demonstrating that

Russia is not serious about commitments to solve regional conflicts by peaceful means and, second, by entering an already crowded arms market that Western firms are trying to exploit. Finally, the international arms market itself will cause Russian arms sales to the Third World to be more difficult in the 1990s. Russia has few arms partners in the Third World, and some of those with which the USSR had close relations cannot afford to expend hard currency for arms. A variety of factors seem to limit the prospects of an expanded arms sales program.

No matter how much Russia wants to sell or export arms, one fact remains: With a few exceptions, the arms market has been stagnant for several years, and it is likely to remain that way for some time. Although at the moment Russia has much new equipment it could sell cheaply, problems exist in spare parts and in training and maintenance facilities. Potential buyers are not prepared for the long delays and added costs that accompany new facilities and training. The Russian government or enterprises will not be in a good position to extend credits or to otherwise defer payments. It will need cash as working capital, and competing suppliers in the market are much better equipped to provide these services.

Offering prices that do not reflect the true costs of production will be defeating in the long term, but this is likely to occur in the short term. In many small towns and even in a number of large cities, a defense enterprise is not only the chief provider of employment but is also the principal political influence. Leaders are most interested in selling their goods for hard currency (or in bartering for goods). Arms are one of the few commodities these Russian communities can offer. Further, the tens of thousands of servicemen, advisers, technical specialists, and similar groups who have benefited from arms sales are very interested in the hard currency implications of arms trade.

An estimated 40 percent of the arms produced in Russia are competitive in the international market (*Business World* [television program], May 28, 1992). Thus, the Russians continually attempt to bid systems and engines in international competition. The first export licenses for two Tula gun and ordnance plants were given in May 1992 (Warren Phillips's interview with Gennadiy Kochetkov of the USA-Canada Institute, January 10–12, 1993).

This has set the stage for a reorganization of the export of arms trade, which is set up under the Ministry of Foreign Economic Relations. Yeltsin called for the creation of a state company, called Oboronexport, for arms and equipment sales, and other organizations have also been established.[23] Thus, a new mechanism for movement into arms trade is being developed, and these institutions are also creating pressures on the government to allow increased access to arms markets. For example, at the urging of the Russian Ministry of Industry, a new advocate for military enterprises, Yeltsin signed a decree permitting enterprises in the Tula region to have free access to foreign arms markets (Warren Phillips's interview with Sergei Koulik of the USA-Canada Institute, January 10, 1993).

Obviously, these semigovernmental organizations are set up in the old monopolist principles the former Soviet Union employed. They will control information and, as much as possible, finances. But they cannot be as successful as their predecessors were because of the privatization movement.

A growing number of independent actors are also willing and able to sell weapons (despite the presence of the State Commission for Military-Technical Cooperation, which oversees weapons transfers). A recent example of the vigorous rivalry among Russian military enterprises and firms for overseas contracts occurred in Malaysia. According to the Ministry of Foreign Economic Relations, approximately eighteen different firms arrived in Malaysia in 1992, trying to curry favor with the government there (Glebova and Arkhangelskaya, 1993, 6). A $500 million contract was developed with two of those organizations—MAPO and Oboronexport. Whether Russia will be effective in competing with other arms suppliers in Malaysia and elsewhere remains to be seen, although as we have suggested, in today's buyer's market the Soviet legacy and current instability do not indicate a positive outlook for Russian arms exports.

Nevertheless, in order to attempt to control a weapons sales free-for-all, three mechanisms have been developed:

1. Export lists will be maintained. This is a holdover from the previous regime, under which lists of countries to which weapons could not be shipped were maintained and strictly enforced.
2. The license system will be maintained under the Ministry of Foreign Economic Relations.
3. The system has been streamlined and placed under a single ministry, and actors such as the KGB have been removed.

Another factor that could help to limit arms sales is the fact that the West is able to allow avenues for hard currency development by the very same industries, only in acceptable areas, of which there are three. First, the Nunn-Lugar funds to the Department of Defense (approximately $800 million to date) are to be used to help employ military weapons production scientists in either arms reduction efforts associated with arms treaties or in the creation of new civilian industries. Second, Russia has requested that its quota for export of nuclear materials be increased from 7 percent to 25 percent (Warren Phillips's interviews at the USA-Canada Institute, January 10–12, 1993); there are strong indications that this will be approved. In addition, the United States has signed an agreement with Russia to allow seven heavy missile launches for commercial purposes through the year 2000, allowing the missile industry to finance a significant proportion of their operations (Woolf, 1993, 4).

This leaves two other potential areas of counterproductive weapons sales, in addition to attempted sales to countries previously unassociated with Soviet weapons such as Malaysia. The first is to former friends such as Serbia (Yugoslavia) or India, and the second is to splinter groups within the former Soviet Union. Although these areas will likely continue to add to the current instability and to world tension, neither is likely to add significant hard currency to the enterprise system. Arms shipments to these areas, however, may demonstrate the persistence of long-established relationships and their continuing importance in post-Soviet policy.

Notes

1. See, for example, Menon, 1986.
2. In 1955, Khrushchev made a highly publicized trip to Afghanistan, Burma, and India, which was designed to demonstrate his government's budding interest in the developing countries.
3. See *Vneshniaia torgovlia SSSR*, 1955–1965.
4. That cooperation was identified by one Soviet scholar as a specific form of the struggle between capitalism and socialism (Prokhorov, 1972, 17).
5. *Vneshniaia torgovlia SSSR*, 1965–1985.
6. Ibid, various years.
7. For an excellent discussion of the problems of analysis using available arms trade data, see Chapter 2 of Laurance, 1992.
8. We have used SIPRI data for three reasons: (1) They focus only on major arms transfers; (2) they provide information into actual arms deals; and (3) the other prominent data set, WMEAT, significantly revised upward its figures on Soviet arms transfers during the period under examination here and, therefore, may suffer from more comparability problems across time for the USSR.
9. Examination of five-year moving averages, a more stable measure of the basic trends in arms transfers than year-to-year figures, for the 1971–1988 period also reveals the USSR predominance in world arms trade to the Third World. See SIPRI, 1991, 230–231.
10. See SIPRI, 1992, 272.
11. Grimmett, 8.
12. Calculated from data in Brzoska and Ohlson, 1987, 338–339.
13. Brzoska and Ohlson note that for the period 1981–1985, about 80 percent of Soviet deliveries went to these countries. See ibid, 44.
14. According to SIPRI, 1992, India imported $13,871 million in this period, Afghanistan imported more than $8,125 million, Iraq imported $7,049 million, North Korea imported $4,217 million, and Angola imported $3,544 million. It is interesting that the next five purchasers all imported arms valued at less than $1,000 million. Cuba, which had purchased over $2,000 million in arms in the preceding period, imported only $510 million in 1987–1991; Iran purchased more in this period ($715 million).
15. The Soviet Union could claim about 80 percent of Indian arms imports in the second half of the 1970s, but by the mid-1980s, it held approximately 68 percent. For a discussion of Indian arms purchasing, see Gupta, Chapter 6 in this volume.
16. Grimmett, 1992, 9.
17. Krause, 1988, 98.
18. See SIPRI, various years, for reports on licenses extended.
19. SIPRI, 1991, 258.
20. Listed as unconfirmed by SIPRI.
21. The other was oil.
22. For example, Chernomyrdin "took a contract to develop the Shtockman gas field in the Arctic Sea away from a consortium of foreign firms, led by Norsk Hydro, and

gave it instead to 19 Russian defense contractors. One of the main aims of this switch was to provide work for the giant nuclear submarine plant in Severodvinsk . . . and to keep the huge Kirov tank plant in St. Petersburg busy" (*Economist,* January 16, 1993, 52).

    23.   Another state company has assumed the responsibilities of the Main Engineering Directorate, the old Main Directorate for Collaboration and Cooperation has been split into two state companies, and the government has also created a Directorate for Military-Technical Cooperation (Warren Phillips's interview with Sergei Koulik, USA-Canada Institute, January 10, 1993).

SIX

Building an Arsenal: The Indian Experience

Amit Gupta

In the aftermath of the 1991 Gulf War, Western security analysts have begun to pay greater attention to the possibility of further North-South conflicts. The likely proliferation of high-tech weapons systems, particularly weapons of mass destruction, to the southern countries has created the fear that the West will be increasingly engaged in combating new military powers. The problem with this approach is that it is somewhat mechanistic: It looks at what systems are being produced or acquired by a particular country, then uses the likely existence of these systems to ascribe military capabilities to the possessor, and, finally, presents this "capability" as a threat that must be countered.

This approach has limited value, because it does not capture the complexity of the arms acquisition and weapons production processes in Third World countries. First, it does not explain why the military force structures in Third World countries tend to be lopsided. Some countries have strong missile programs, whereas others have strong tanks or artillery, but no country has the kind of viable and complete military system found in the major military powers. Second, the approach does not take into account the constraints that limit arms acquisition and production programs in the Third World. Efforts at military modernization in Third World countries tend to have an on-again-off-again character, because of such constraints as the lack of financial resources, the unavailability of technology, the feasibility of producing a particular weapons system, and the crucial role individuals (soldiers, scientists, and politicians) play in shaping decisions on force expansion. Overlooking these factors leads the West to paint an exaggerated picture of the capabilities of Third World countries. It also distorts attempts to understand the nature of the arms acquisition process in the Third World and what future trends may emerge. This lack of understanding has crucial policy implications, because it creates a world of rising military powers that may have to be contained through the use of force.

These factors are not adequately covered in discussions of the Third World armament process; therefore, my purpose here is to examine some of these questions by focusing on India. In the 1980s India embarked on a major military modernization program, under which it acquired state-of-the-art weaponry from both the former Soviet Union and the West. India was to acquire a second aircraft carrier and lease a nuclear submarine from the Soviet Union. A program was also initiated for the indigenous design and production of a nuclear submarine. Additionally, the Indian government agreed to the indigenous production of a light combat aircraft (LCA), a main battle tank (the Arjun), an advanced light helicopter (ALH), and an entire series of missiles under the Integrated Guided Missile Development Program (IGMDP), through which India was able to test its first short-range (Prithvi) and intermediate-range (Agni) ballistic missiles.

The combination of large-scale arms imports and the institution of major weapons production programs has caused India to be spoken of as the next superpower or, at the least, as a regional power with a very long extraregional arm. India, therefore, is a good case to study in order to understand both the nature of the arms acquisition and production processes in a major Third World nation and the limitations these processes impose on the eventual force structure a country creates.

The Indian Case

The Indian government argues that from the mid-1950s, when Pakistan began to receive arms from the United States, to the present, India has faced a fairly high level of threat. Since its independence in 1947 it has fought three wars with Pakistan—in 1947–1948, 1965, and 1971—and one war with China in 1962. It has also faced major insurgencies in its northeastern states since the early days of independence and, more recently, in the northwestern states of Punjab and Kashmir.

But in spite of the threat environment, India's major arms acquisitions have been only partially related to threats. India's recent, and most ambitious, military buildup began in the late 1970s when, by its own admission, it faced a low threat environment (Gupta, 1988, 6). Similarly, since independence the procurement of certain types of weapons systems and the modernization programs of specific services—particularly the navy—have not matched the existence of concrete threats. Therefore, what other factors have driven the arms acquisition process?

A large body of literature exists on Indian efforts at arms acquisition and production. Edited volumes by Michael Brzoska and Thomas Ohlson (1986) and James Everett Katz (1984, 1986) examine the success of Third World nations—including India—in arms production efforts and the global impact of Third World military industrialization. Ron Matthews (1989) has done a detailed study of the Indian arms industry. But these volumes have focused largely on the success attained in arms production and its implications for the international system; they only partially address why lopsided forces have emerged—or, the failure of weapons production efforts.

Another set of writings (Kavic, 1967; Thomas, 1978; and Kolodziej and Harkavy, 1982) discusses the development of national security policy in India. These volumes show primarily how threats have shaped the buildup of the Indian armed forces. Raju Thomas also discusses the bureaucratic agendas of the different branches of the armed forces and the crucial role resource availability plays in weapons acquisition.

Finally, there is the general literature on armament dynamics. Mary Kaldor (1982) argues that the transfer of weapons systems by the North leads to replication of military institutions and cultures around the world. Kaldor's argument is valid in that such replication creates a culture lag among Third World militaries as they aspire to become like their parent organizations.

But there is a gap between aspirations and eventual outcomes that cannot be explained using Kaldor's analysis. Edward Kolodziej (1987b, 216–220) has discussed the development of Military Industrial Scientific Technological complexes (MISTs), which are created to provide autonomy in weapons production but which, once in place, "tend to make claims on internal investment resources that progressively enlarge their impact on their national economies and the world economy" (Kolodziej, 1987b, 217). Within the Indian decisionmaking system the MIST is divided into military and industrial-scientific camps, which often compete with each other for scarce resources. Barry Posen (1984) uses balance-of-power and organizational pressures as the determinants of military doctrine.

Although both categories are useful to explain the evolution of military forces, factors such as bureaucratic competition, culture lags, and the role of technological constraints must be added in any discussion of the Indian process. Further, because India's military buildup—like that of a number of other Third World countries—has involved dependent militarization, we must include the role of external suppliers and—as Thomas (1978) has done—the availability of financial resources. I, therefore, examine the Indian arms acquisition and weapons production processes by taking into account (1) the role of the political leadership, (2) bureaucratic politics and perceived missions, (3) culture lags, (4) the role of individuals, (5) technological constraints, (6) the impact of external suppliers, and (7) the availability of resources.

The Role of the Political Leadership

One key factor in India's arms acquisition and weapons production processes has been the role played by the political leadership. The Indian nationalist leadership, which took over the reins of power from the British, believed that defense and development were competing claims, with military expenditure taking badly needed funds from development projects. Thus, India's first prime minister, Jawaharlal Nehru, sought to contain military expenditure in the 1940s and the 1950s; even after Pakistan began to receive U.S. arms, there was no rapid escalation in India's weapons procurement policy. Only after India's defeat in the 1962 Sino-Indian border conflict was Nehru forced to build up the Indian armed forces to meet the challenge from the North. Even then the official governmental policy was that increased military expenditure was a necessary evil given the changed threat environment.

During Indira Gandhi's second term (1980–1984), the perception of the Indian leadership underwent a fundamental change. As had past Indian leaders, Gandhi saw India as the most important state in the region and sought to insulate the South Asian region from intervention by the superpowers. Nehru had attempted insulation through the use of diplomacy, but by Gandhi's era the instrument to deter superpower involvement had become the acquisition of military capability. This change in policy was espoused in the so-called South Asian Monroe Doctrine, or, as it was better known, the Indira Doctrine.

This new doctrine sought to keep South Asia free from external influences, much as the original Monroe Doctrine had kept external powers out of the Americas in the nineteenth century. It rested on the following planks: India's relationship with its neighbors would be based on bilateralism, there should be no foreign bases in the region, the Indian Ocean should be demilitarized, and India should be consulted first by any regional nation on an issue in which Indian interests were involved (Nations, 1984, 26; Hagerty, 1991, 351–352). A failure to consult India on such an issue would be seen as an unfriendly act. The doctrine further sought to use Indian military capability to protect and promote India's interests in the region. Such a doctrine was possible because the modernization of the Indian armed forces, which began in the late 1970s, built up the country's military forces to the point where India could project power extraregionally, as well as make it difficult for an external power to intervene in South Asia. With such a shift in the political outlook, in the early 1980s, there was both an added impetus for procuring new weapons systems and a shift in military doctrine so as to better utilize the country's new military capability. But the will to use military power to achieve foreign policy objectives reached its zenith during Rajiv Gandhi's term as prime minister.

More than any Indian prime minister, Rajiv Gandhi was willing to use India's military might to achieve political ends. During his term India was involved in two near–border wars with Pakistan and China, became entangled in the bloody Sri Lankan civil war, and sent troops to the Maldives to crush a coup attempt. This link between foreign policy and military capability provided additional momentum to the military buildup in the 1980s.

Bureaucratic Pressures

The second factor driving arms acquisition has been the bureaucratic pressures exerted by both the Indian armed services and the domestic arms industry. One obvious reason armed forces require weapons is to handle the threat environment in which they are expected to operate. But a second reason, which operates at times quite independent of threats, is the perceived role the armed service sees itself as playing, which is a military role that is commensurate with its status, as well as with that of its country. Thus, the Indian navy has viewed itself as a blue water navy; the Indian air force (IAF) has always wanted to carry out long-range interdiction; and in recent years the Indian army has sought to become a mobile army that can conduct deep thrusts into enemy territory, including that beyond the Himalayas. For these operational roles to be pursued, however, the services require a particular force structure, and this becomes a driving force in arms acquisition.

Such desired roles, however, may not match what is needed to meet existing threats; therefore, the armed services' chances of developing the necessary force structures are dependent upon their ability to push their agenda through the bureaucratic process and also upon the availability of funds. In tight financial circumstances, funding for force development will likely be used to meet immediate threats. Only when the funding situation is highly favorable can resources be committed to procure systems needed to fulfill the perceived future roles of the different armed services. Conversely, when finances are unavailable, the acquisition of such systems has been put on hold until financial prosperity recurs.

Because force expansion is dependent upon funding, so are the creation of an operational doctrine and the identification of threats. When funds are available, the military force structure expands, and a new operational doctrine emerges. Justification for the new structure and doctrine is provided in a new set of threats. When funds are unavailable, plans for force expansion are cancelled, and the doctrine is adjusted accordingly. More important threats are defused or minimized. A good example of this philosophy can be seen in the development of the Indian navy.

The Indian navy, following its predecessor the Royal Indian Navy, has traditionally seen itself as a blue water navy, which has involved acquiring aircraft carriers. Yet in the immediate years after independence, India did not face a major naval threat; its main enemy, Pakistan, had an even smaller navy than India's. Also Britain, which was considered a friendly power, still had a substantial naval presence in the Indian Ocean. The lack of a real naval threat was reflected in the 1948 P.M.S. Blackett report to Nehru on the development of the Indian force structure. Blackett did recommend that the navy acquire a light carrier for escort purposes (Blackett, 1948, 9–15), but the low threat environment and the lack of funds caused the political leadership to delay the decision to purchase the carrier until the late 1950s.[1] The carrier, *INS Vikrant*, was purchased from Britain in 1961, before the 1962 Sino-Indian War forced the expansion of the Indian armed services. The purchase was possible because the Indian government had the necessary hard currency reserves to pay for it and other weaponry.

In the 1960s, despite two wars, the Indian navy did not play a major role in India's defenses. In fact, when the 1965 India-Pakistan War broke out, the *Vikrant* was in dry dock in Bombay harbor. Yet in 1968, when the British announced their pullout from east of the Suez, the Indian navy called for an expanded naval force to replace the British in the Indian Ocean (Thomas, 1978, 204). This would have involved two carrier fleets with a total of four carriers. The navy's belief that it could fill the vacuum left by the British withdrawal was considered neocolonialist by Indian observers, and the proposal was rejected by the Indian government (Thomas, 1978, 212).

The basic obstacle to the navy's demands for force expansion lay in the continuing lack of a credible naval threat. Pakistan still had a small navy; therefore, attempts were made to play up future Chinese and Indonesian threats. When this approach did not work, the argument was refined and presented along two lines: First, not just naval power but the country's entire maritime capability had to be strengthened to contribute to the nation's prosperity. The navy would serve as the guardian of this maritime capability. Second, such a naval force could not be built up overnight, and despite the lack of immediate threats, major steps in force acquisition should be taken immediately (Thomas, 1978, 213). The navy's demand for a larger role was backed increasingly by politicians and the media, and the government agreed to purchase new destroyers and attack patrol boats for the navy. Further, in response to Pakistan's acquisition of a U.S. submarine, the Indian navy acquired four Foxtrot-class submarines from the Soviet Union. But the proposed expansion of the carrier force did not come about.

The 1971 India-Pakistan War changed the fortunes of the navy. The *Vikrant* was used effectively in the Bangladesh campaign, which strengthened the navy's case for the retention and possible future expansion of the carrier force. In 1972 the navy flight-tested the British Sea Harrier aircraft aboard the *Vikrant* with the intention of purchasing it as a replacement for its aging Sea Hawks. The deal, however, could not be finalized because of a shortage of hard currency (Gupta, 1988, 6), at which time the navy agreed to continue to use the *Vikrant* as a helicopter carrier until its service life ended.

Little was said about building the carrier force the navy had wanted in the 1960s. With the financial upswing of the late 1970s, however, the navy was able to acquire the Sea Harriers, and the idea of a carrier fleet was revived. India acquired a second carrier in the 1980s and generally expanded its naval forces by purchasing new submarines and surface vessels (including the leasing of a nuclear submarine). Indian naval doctrine, which in the 1970s had been based on sea denial, now shifted to one of sea control (Tellis, 1990, 25) within its inner circle of defense (the peninsular region extending from Pakistan in the West to Burma and Indonesia in the East).

The Indian army's plans for expansion in the 1980s provide another example of bureaucratic pressures in the arms acquisition process. In the 1970s the Indian army sought to develop a force structure that would deter the enemy (Pakistan or China). In operational terms, this meant the Indian army should have a force advantage of two corps (six divisions) over Pakistan (the existing balance of forces with China was considered sufficient to deter a Chinese threat).[2] Further, the tank regiments were to be doubled, from twenty-seven to fifty-eight, and two mechanized divisions were to be added. By the early 1980s, however, these plans had changed, because opportunities arose for greater expansion.

The availability of hard currency to purchase weapons from the West, and the procurement of weapons from the Soviet Union on rupee terms, led to greater mechanization of the Indian army, which emerged as a force that could project power over long distances with the help of the growing transport arm of the IAF. Greater mechanization also led to a shift in doctrine. Prior to the 1980s the army had been restricted by its force structure to a doctrine that emphasized using the infantry and fighting from positional defenses. In the 1980s, that doctrine was rewritten to enable India to use its new mechanized strength to carry out deep thrusts into enemy territory, where its forces were expected to seize large areas of territory and fight the enemy on grounds of their choice.

To successfully carry out this new doctrine, a further expansion of the army was envisaged. In 1987 then Chief of Staff General Krishnaswami Sundarji made public the Army 2000 perspective plan for future force development, according to which by the year 2000, the army was to build up to a force level of forty-five divisions, including four tank divisions, eight mechanized divisions, seven Reorganized Plains Infantry Divisions (RAPIDS), and two air assault divisions. The RAPIDS were essentially infantry divisions with one mechanized brigade, which would provide greater mobility and allow a division to be used for either defense or offense (Rikhye, 1989, 77; 1990, 75). (To put this proposed expansion in perspective, in 1987 India had only two tank divisions, one mechanized infantry division, and no RAPIDS or air assault divisions.)

The Army 2000 plan could not be put in place because financial constraints ate into the army's modernization plans. By the late 1980s a rapidly growing foreign debt and lower hard currency reserves brought about a resource crunch that hurt all of the armed forces. Sundarji's Army 2000 plan ground to a halt, and the plan to create two assault divisions was also shelved, because it would have involved creating a huge helicopter force for which the necessary funding was unavailable.[3] With the shelving of these plans, doctrine was reviewed and the army returned to its focus on deterrence.

Another set of forces that drive the sort of weapons that are procured comes from the nature and traditions of organizations. The Indian armed forces were created by Britain, and their training, organization of units, and operational doctrine still reflect the British influence, resulting in a pro-British attitude. More recently, the easy availability of Soviet weapons systems created a pro-Soviet influence as well. The impact of such attitudes on weapons procurement has been that armed services prefer systems produced in these two countries.

Finally, in the context of organizational pressures, pressure is exerted by the domestic arms industry. Before the 1962 Sino-Indian War, India had sixteen ordnance factories and two defense public-sector undertakings. In the expansion that followed that war, these increased to thirty and eight, respectively. Yet, despite such a large infrastructure, the Indian arms industry supplies only a small portion of the weapons for the Indian armed services,[4] which have preferred to buy weapons from abroad because they do not trust the quality of Indian-made weaponry. The traditional ties of the armed forces to Western defense establishments have reinforced this tendency.

When the Indian armed forces have bought major systems from the Indian arms industry, it has been by force of circumstance—usually a lack of financial resources—rather than by choice. Thus, the navy invested in an indigenous ship-building program because it was allocated less than 15 percent of the defense budget. The air force, similarly, strongly resisted the Indian government's decision to license-produce the MiG-21, stating that it would prefer to have the U.S. Starfighter. But by the early 1970s, the IAF was depending on the indigenously produced MiG, because financial constraints precluded purchasing another aircraft.

By the 1980s, not only was the Indian arms industry one of the largest in the Third World, but, for a number of reasons, it had also begun to acquire political influence. Defense research and development again led the political leadership to believe it could achieve self-reliance. The fact that certain systems such as ballistic missiles could not be procured from abroad led to the birth of indigenous programs. Sheer organizational pressures also applied. So much capital had been invested in this industry, and such a large pool of scientific manpower had been assembled, that a few projects had to be given to these units. This was particularly the case with Hindustan Aeronautics Limited (HAL), which had not designed a new combat aircraft since the mid-1960s (and it had been a failure). In this period programs such as the Arjun tank and the ALH were also revived by the government. The existence of a large defense industry with growing political influence may press India to procure more weaponry indigenously in the 1990s.

Culture Lag

Another determinant in acquiring arms from abroad is the presence of a culture lag in the weapons acquisition process. The notion of a culture lag first emerged during the U.S.-USSR arms race (Evangelista, 1988). In the early 1960s the Soviets began copying U.S. design trends with little regard for their own operational needs. Thus, when the United States developed vertical geometry aircraft with the F-111, the Soviets responded with their own vertical geometry aircraft—the Su-24, the MiG-23, and MiG-27. The U.S. B-1 bomber was a large vertical geometry aircraft, so the Soviets built an even larger vertical geometry aircraft, the Blackjack.[5] Similarly, when the United States produced a slow-flying ground attack aircraft, the A-10, the Soviets came up with their own counterpart, in the Su-25 Frogfoot, which bore a striking resemblance to the Northrop A-9—an aircraft that had lost the U.S. air force competition to the A-10.

A similar situation exists in the Indian defense establishment, where the domestic arms industry tries to copy the latest technologies of the West without considering either the utility of these weapons in India's combat environment or the technological feasibility of the project. This is best exemplified by the LCA project. The initial specifications for the LCA—as a lightweight fighter optimized for air superiority with fly-by-wire technology—matched those presented in the U.S. Light Weight Fighter project of the mid-1970s, which led to the development of the F-16.

Although all of these factors serve to generate demands for acquiring weapons, they do not automatically lead to the procurement of the new systems the services want to have or the arms industry wants to produce. The navy's drive for a blue water fleet was put on hold in the late 1980s, as was the army's plan for large-scale expansion. Therefore, another set of factors, which can act as either constraints or opportunities, shapes the eventual force structure.

The Role of Individuals

One of the factors shaping acquisition and, more particularly, indigenous production has been the role of key individuals in the armament process. First, the existence of such individuals in power shapes the technological programs that are undertaken and those that are rejected. In most Third World countries, the scientific-industrial base is so small that weapons production programs are based around the availability of trained individuals rather than on specific military or scientific needs.

India, unlike other Third World countries, had a fairly large scientific community at the time it attained independence, but a number of its programs were also shaped by the presence of key individuals. Thus, India was one of the first Third World nations to have a systematically developed nuclear program, because a young Cambridge-trained scientist, Homi Bhabha, had both the vision and the personal contacts, including frequent access to Jawaharlal Nehru, to set it up. Similarly, India was an early entrant into the production of jet combat aircraft, because an Indian design engineer, V. M. Ghatge, was a former student of the German aircraft designer Kurt Tank and persuaded him to come to India to head the HF-24 Marut fighter jet project.

A more recent example is that of A.P.J. Kalam, who is called the "father of India's missile program." In the 1970s India's defense research units tried unsuccessfully to design, develop, and produce both ballistic and guided missiles. At the same time, India's civilian space program successfully put a rocket, the SLV-3, into space. In the early 1980s Kalam left the Indian Space Research Organization and joined the Defense Research and Development Organization (DRDO); he transformed DRDO's missile program, which had been close to being closed down in 1983, into one of the more successful weapons projects in the industry's history. Kalam was put in charge of the Integrated Guided Missile Development Program (IGMDP), which was to build an entire series of ballistic and guided missiles. It was from this program that India's short-range missile—Prithvi—and intermediate-range missile—Agni— were developed.

A second role played by key individuals has been in making decisions that fundamentally changed the Indian arms acquisition and weapons production process. The best example is Krishna Menon, the first Indian defense minister to have significant political input into decisionmaking on weaponry. Menon believed India should develop its indigenous arms industry so that it would one day be able to produce advanced systems that would satisfy the requirements of the Indian armed forces (Singh, 1977, 275). He thus encouraged the domestic arms industry and, more important, pushed for setting up the military relationship with the former Soviet Union.

As the Indian government was considering the purchase of the MiG-21, it was offered the F-104 Starfighter by the United States. The IAF did not favor the MiG, because it lacked an internal gun, had inferior avionics, and was not an all-weather fighter (Singh, 1977, 276). But Menon argued that the Soviets were willing to transfer the MiG technology, which would serve as the basis for a future Indian aircraft industry. Menon's will prevailed, and the Soviet military-technology link was established.

The role of individuals seems to serve as both an opportunity and a constraint. Menon, Bhabha, and Kalam all contributed to the growth of Indian military capability, but this growth was restricted to spheres in which their own skills or influence could shape matters. In contrast, where such dominant personalities have not existed, indigenous weapons programs have not fared as well.

The Role of Technology

If any lesson is to be learned from the Gulf War, it is that a missile program does not make a nation a military power. Iraq lacked the capability to produce a range of military systems that could counter the U.S. forces and avoid the impact of an arms embargo. Most Third World arms industries face similar problems. Developing systems across-the-board has not been possible because some technologies are easier to absorb than others. Today, for example, twenty-four nations have ongoing missile programs, but only two—India and Taiwan—have supersonic combat aircraft programs, because it is difficult to build state-of-the-art combat aircraft. No Third World nation has been able to develop its own high-performance jet engines or the advanced radars and avionics that go into modern fighter jets. Basic missile technology, however, dates back to World War II and the German V-2 rocket and is, therefore, much easier to develop.

Second, many Third World successes have been based not on the development of new systems but on the improvement of older ones. The Chinese F-6 is a reverse-engineered copy of the Soviet MiG-19, and the Brazilian Xavante is an improved version of the Italian MB 326. Because improvement rather than invention is being pursued, it is difficult even conceptually to move to the next technological step. No country can make the technological jump from producing piston engines to modern jet engines without going through the range of technologies that come between these two extremes.

As a consequence, no Third World nation has successfully developed follow-on systems to the weapons they have license-produced or reverse-engineered. The Israelis, for example, stole the blueprints for the Mirage III from Switzerland and reverse-engineered them to make the Kfir. When it came to a follow-on, the Lavi, the Israelis had to go to the United States for both critical technologies and design assistance (Reiser, 1989, 171–184). Similarly, India, despite license-producing the MiG-21 for nearly two decades and making improvements in the plane, was unable to build a follow-on; instead, it is now license-producing the MiG-27. This means that the most successful programs have been based on building what is feasible rather than on what is state-of-the-art. The Brazilian success with armored cars is a good example of this. In the Indian context, the Indian navy's successful frigate program involved mating the Leander-class vessels with new sensors and weaponry—something that was within the capability of the naval shipbuilders. But these shipbuilders ran into prolonged delays and quality problems when it came to building the hull of the two license-produced German-designed HDW T-1500 209 submarines.

The Indian arms industry tried to rectify this problem in the late 1970s and early 1980s by trying to produce indigenously an entire range of systems—tanks, helicopters, aircraft, and ships. The efforts so far have been less than promising. All of these systems depend heavily on imported components, and many doubt whether some of them can even enter service (Gupta, 1990, 850–853). Of particular concern is the LCA, which not only has heavy developmental costs but, with a production total of only four hundred planes, is uneconomical. The ability to produce only particular systems rather than weapons across-the-board, therefore, is the key reason the arms industries of Third World countries are so lopsided. India is no exception, because although it has one of the largest arms industries in the Third World, it remains largely a licensed producer of weapons and is also one of the largest importers of weaponry.

Hard Currency and the Soviet Link

Perhaps the two most crucial factors shaping acquisition are the availability of hard currency to pay for weapons systems and India's military relationship with the former Soviet Union. Despite a large and versatile arms industry, the bulk of India's weapons systems are still purchased outright or license-produced. Thus, the availability of financial resources becomes a key factor in the attempts to acquire weapons systems. If we look at the patterns of weapons procurement in India, the availability of hard currency has clearly played a central role in determining the suppliers of weapons technology and the amount and kinds of weaponry procured. When hard currency was available, India could purchase arms from the Western nations in substantial quantities; when it was unavailable, such transfers were put on hold. I should also point out that the desire for weapons from the West stems not just from the preferences of the armed services; it is also the case because certain advanced technologies—particularly electronics—are available only in Western countries.

India's first major acquisition of weapons from the West took place in the middle and late 1950s, when the Korean War boom and sterling balances from World War II left it with favorable hard currency reserves (Thomas, 1978, 104–105). The second major increase in Indian force levels took place as a result of the 1962 Sino-Indian War. Defense spending was doubled in the 1963–1964 budget, and ambitious plans were laid for the expansion of the Indian armed forces.

But this expansion could only take place by imposing a heavier burden on the Indian people in the form of a direct defense tax. The nation's economic health deteriorated rapidly because of two famines. The 1960s, unlike the 1950s, were marked by a persistent shortage of hard currency, and this affected Indian programs (Thomas, 1978, 110). Few deals were signed with Western nations, and these, too, involved license-production agreements. But India faced a severe threat environment and needed to build up its armed forces; this attempt was eased by the beginning of the military relationship with the former Soviet Union in the early 1960s.

In 1962 India entered into an agreement to license-produce Soviet MiG-21 fighter aircraft. This was the first time the Soviets had allowed licensed production by a non-Communist country, and it became the foundation of one of the major arms transfer relationships of the post–World War II era. The major advantage of the arms link with the Soviets was that it had a cushioning effect on Indian weapons procurement, because, at a time when India faced a severe shortage of hard currency, the link allowed it to import large numbers of aircraft, tanks, and ships and thereby build up its armed forces. This was possible because of the generous Soviet terms: The weapons were to be paid for in Indian rupees rather than with scarce hard currency; there was a seven-year grace period before payments began and a total repayment period of seventeen years; and the Soviets charged a low interest rate of 2.5 percent (Smith and George, 1985, 369).

Additionally, Soviet arms were always cheaper than comparable Western systems. Further, in later years, the Soviet Union provided India with its state-of-the-art technology.

The cushioning effect of the Soviet arms connection can be seen in the procurement that occurred in the 1960s. The IAF's only outright purchase of a combat aircraft in that decade was the rupee purchase of the Su-7 ground attack aircraft from the Soviet Union (Thomas, 1978, 178). India also undertook licensed production of the MiG, and by the 1971 war, it had approximately 140 MiGs and 100 Su-7s in its inventory. There were also two license-production agreements with Western nations, as India agreed to produce the British HS-748 Avro and the French Alouette III helicopters. But the major deals remained those for which India could pay in rupees.

The naval program, similarly, was hit by the lack of available funding. The navy, although still lacking a credible threat in the mid-1960s, had convinced the government to agree to an expansion program, claiming that the country needed to build up its general maritime capability, which required long-term planning (there was also some attempt to promote the threat posed by Soviet and U.S. warships in the Indian Ocean). India acquired of frigates, submarines, missile boats, and destroyers between 1965 and 1971. But the only deal worked out with the West was for the purchase of Leander-class frigates from Britain; the rest of the equipment came from the Soviet Union.

Finally, the Indian arms industry started to expand in this period, with an increase in the number of ordnance factories and defense public-sector undertakings. But the production units of the 1960s could not aid in the defense expansion effort, because they were too far away from indigenously producing major weapons systems. HAL was the only unit that had an ongoing major indigenous weapons program—the HF-24 Marut fighter. But the project was plagued with technical problems, and the Marut never became a realistic alternative to imported aircraft (Graham, 1984, 170). Thus India's expansion of its military forces in the 1960s was possible only because of the opening up of the arms relationship with the Soviets; otherwise, the shortage of hard currency and the inability of the arms industry to satisfy the demands of the armed services would have slowed down the expansion program, if not halted it completely.

In the early 1970s, the situation deteriorated further. The adverse financial situation continued, whiech ended procurement from the West. The IAF, for example, had test-flown the Jaguar in 1968, but by 1973 the deal had to be shelved because of the shortage of hard currency (Gupta, 1988, 6). A similar problem with the Sea Harriers was mentioned earlier. Worse, the relationship with the Soviets, after reaching a crescendo during the 1971 war—when the Soviets gave India considerable diplomatic support and secured it from potential military pressure from the Chinese—began to encounter difficulties. The Soviets wanted India to endorse their Asian Collective Security proposal, something India refused to do because it perceived the proposal to be anti-Chinese, and because doing so identified India as a member of the Soviet camp. Further, the

Soviets wanted a naval base either in the Andaman Islands or at Vishakhapatnam. India again refused, because its nonaligned status would be jeopardized. The Soviets then refused outright to sell certain types of weaponry to India (Gupta, 1988). India, thus, was caught in an unenviable position—it was unable to buy arms from the West for financial reasons and was finding it difficult to procure them from the Soviet Union for political ones.

In this "double jeopardy" situation, the armed forces asked the domestic arms industry to procure weapons systems. The air force continued to buy MiGs from HAL and initiated a project for modifying the license-produced Folland Gnat. The navy set up a follow-on program to the Leander frigates. Also, in the hope of saving hard currency and attaining self-sufficiency, two major indigenous projects were launched—the ALH and the Arjun tank.

This situation was reversed by the improved economic situation of the late 1970s. Indian hard currency reserves rose from about rs 500 crores (approximately $700 million) in 1975–1976 to about rs 5,500 crores (approximately $5 billion in 1979–1980).[6] This availability of hard currency allowed the Indian government to conclude the Jaguar and the Harrier deals in 1978 and 1979 and to sign a billion-dollar deal with Germany in 1980 for the purchase and eventual licensed production of HDW submarines. In the mid-1980s India concluded two more billion-dollar deals: one with France for the supply of 40 Mirage 2000 fighters, and one with Sweden for 1,500 howitzers.

Coupled with the renewed availability of hard currency was a change in the Soviet attitude. The Soviets viewed India's procurement from the West with alarm and, eager to retain their hold over the Indian market, devised several tempting offers for new weapons systems. Further, the Soviets invaded Afghanistan, after which, concerned about retaining the support of an influential nonaligned nation, they opened their arms cupboard to India. It was here that the Soviet military connection became important, because it allowed India to maintain a large military force despite the rapid escalation in weapons costs in the 1970s and 1980s.

India's frontline fighter in the early 1970s was the MiG-21, which cost $4–5 million. By the early 1980s its new frontline fighter, the Mirage 2000, cost over $30 million—a sixfold increase in the cost of the system. Such rapid cost escalations have taken place with virtually every new weapons system, which has created problems for countries that want to modernize their armed forces. In the West, prosperous countries such as Germany have been forced to scale down their purchase of new aircraft and retain older aircraft in their inventories. The problem is even more acute in the Third World, where financially strapped nations have either reduced their force levels or proceeded with outdated weapons systems. The Soviet military link, thus, proved vital to India, because it allowed it to retain and in some cases even expand and modernize its force structures. This would not have been possible if the Indian armed forces could have procured only Western weaponry.

The benefit India has enjoyed from the Soviet link becomes even more significant when we consider that the global availability of security assistance programs has declined. For the financially starved Third World, the supply of subsidized or often free weaponry from both the Eastern and Western blocs helped these nations build up their military forces to a level they otherwise could not have attained. In the 1950s and 1960s, the United States armed its various alliance partners with surplus weaponry. This provided a cheap way for countries such as Pakistan to attain significant military capability and challenge militarily stronger nations such as India. Raju Thomas cites figures, for example, to show that the U.S. security assistance program provided Paksitan with about $1.5 billion in arms between 1954 and 1965 (Thomas, 1978, 58). India also received some security assistance from Western nations after the 1962 Sino-Indian War. Such security assistance programs had dried up globally by the 1970s, however, and in the 1980s only a few states—primarily Israel, Cuba, Syria, and Vietnam—received subsidized arms from either superpower.

With security assistance programs no longer available, the next-best alternative was the type of arrangement India has had with the former Soviet Union. In the 1980s the IAF alone purchased 80 MiG-23 BNs and 80 MiG-29s and undertook the licensed production of 200 MiG-27s. Thus, India was able to obtain roughly twice the number of aircraft it purchased from the West (around 150 Jaguars and 40 Mirage 2000s) from the Soviet Union.[7] The Indian army got 700 T-72 tanks (of which 600 were to be license-produced) and eventually, through licensed production, over 1,000 BMP-2 infantry combat vehicles. The navy bought two submarines from the West (another two were to be license-produced) but purchased eight from the Soviet Union.

Had the price of such a large arsenal been paid in hard currency or lacked the favorable terms the Soviets offered, India could not have carried out this large-scale modernization of its force structure. Further, the Soviets provided their state-of-the-art weaponry to India. India received MiG-29s and Kilo-class submarines before any of the Warsaw Pact countries had them. In contrast, Pakistan, although it enjoyed a similar arms supply relationship with the Chinese, had to make do with 1950s vintage Soviet-designed weaponry (which had been reverse-engineered by the Chinese) for the bulk of its armed forces.

In India in the late 1970s and the early to mid-1980s, therefore, critical factors came together to facilitate large-scale armament. By the late 1980s, however, the situation again began to change drastically. India's hard currency reserves remained low as its external debt mounted and its access to soft loans began to decline. Worse, India's external debt more than trebled during the 1980s rising from $20 billion to $70 billion (Table 6.1).

India will have to pay $5–6 billion annually from 1992 to 1997 as debt repayments (Bhimal and Jain, 1992, 91). The debt is expected to increase by an additional $15 billion over the next three years (Bhimal and Jain, 1992, 91). The drop in hard currency reserves and the mounting external debt have created a crisis in weapons procurement. Indian analysts realistically expect that only a fraction of the country's Soviet weapons will be replaced with Western systems because of the continuing resource crisis (Bedi, 1993, 19).

Table 6.1   India's External Debt in the 1980s (millions of U.S.$)

	1980	1983	1984	1985	1986	1987	1988	1989	1990
Total debt	20,610	32,025	34,048	41,210	48,538	55,856	58,524	64,374	70,115
International reserves	11,924	9,126	8,804	9,730	10,814	11,449	9,246	11,610	5,637
Current account balance	−2,268	−2,640	−2,945	−5,536	−5,588	−5,987	−8,509	−7,940	−9,281

Source: World Bank Debt Tables, 1991–1992. Information for 1981 and 1982 was not available.

Coupled with the decline in hard currency reserves are the changes in the military relationship caused by the breakup of the former Soviet Union. In 1990 the Soviets first suggested that India pay for its weapons purchases in hard currency. By 1992, India was forced to end the rupee-ruble trade arrangement, because each of the newly independent republics wanted trade to be conducted in hard currency (Gidadhubli, 1992, 1120–1123). This could impose a major repayment burden on India, although now both the Russian and Ukrainian governments have extended the rupee purchase of defense equipment for another two years (Bedi, 1993, 18).

The continuation of the soft currency arrangement will eventually depend upon the extent to which the former Soviet republics are able to restructure their economies. Given the weak state of most of these economies and the fact that they are going through a painful restructuring process, it is recognized that weapons exports will continue to be a major source of hard currency for some time. There is also a growing feeling in the former republics that the arms industries must be retained for political, strategic, and technological reasons.[8]

At the same time, it is recognized that because of the adverse economic climate, these industries will have to seek external investments and partnerships to continue the research and development of new systems. This may work to India's advantage. The Ukrainian arms industry, for example, sees defense collaboration with the Indian arms industry as a means to reduce developmental and production costs. Under a proposed defense agreement, India will obtain weaponry through barter, and the Ukrainians hope eventually to have joint development of systems with India (Hummel, 1992, 35).

Conclusion

This discussion has shown first, that the availability of hard currency and the Soviet link created a pattern in Indian arms acquisition and weapons production. Even for a large developing country such as India, the task of building up its armed forces has been difficult. It has been possible primarily when either hard currency or a favorable political relationship with the former Soviet Union was in place. The most spectacular growth of the armed forces took place when these two determinants operated side by side in the late 1970s and early 1980s. The worst situation arose when both factors were not fully in operation in the early 1970s.

The importance of both factors working in unison should also be pointed out, because each factor by itself imposes limitations on the arms acquisition process. When hard currency is available, India has been able to approach the West and obtain advanced technologies. But these technologies are so expensive that India has only been able to procure them in limited numbers. Soviet arms, however, removed the need for hard currency and provided the numbers India needed to retain its force structure. But simply acquiring arms from the Soviets had its own limitations, because it restricted the technologies that could be procured and left India militarily dependent on that country. The operation of these two factors in unison, therefore, allowed for diversifying weapons supplies, acquiring critical technologies, retaining sheer numbers, and making the acquisition process affordable.

Second, when external sources of weaponry are available, the armed forces have preferred to use them over domestic systems. When external options have not been available, the domestic arms industry has been used to meet the demand.

Third, I should also point out that what the arms industry can provide has been limited in both systems and levels of technology. In the 1960s it was ordnance and obsolete fighter aircraft. In the 1970s it was license-produced tanks, ships, and aircraft of an earlier vintage. In the 1980s some programs such as the IGMDP produced results, but licensed production remained the main function of the arms industry. Thus, the arms industry has never been able to supply systems across-the-board, and crucial gaps have always remained in the force structure. Given these patterns, what future trends are likely in India's future militarization efforts?

First, there will obviously be gaps in the force structure that cannot be filled because of inadequate funds, because a supplier state is unwilling to part with a particular technology, or because India's arms industry lacks the technological knowledge to build the required system. India, therefore, cannot emerge as a complete military power. Financial and technological constraints will keep it from developing critical sections of its force structure that would allow it to both launch offensive operations against major powers and resist intervention by them. It is more likely that a few high-profile programs such as missiles or naval vessels may emerge; although these will give the illusion of military power, they will not dramatically change the course of a confrontation.

Second, modern systems will continue to become more technologically complex, and this will increase India's reliance on external suppliers. Even if weapons are produced indigenously, the reliance on key imported components such as engines, radars, and electronics will continue. Two consequences of this are that India will continue to depend on the West for weapons technology, and it will continue to produce weapons that are at least one generation behind, which, again, will hinder military capability.

Third, the gaps in the force structure will lead to a change in doctrines. When particular systems become available, doctrine will be molded to utilize them. Additionally, as force levels grow, the threats they are supposed to counter will be magnified so as to justify further expansion. When such systems or follow-on systems are unavailable, doctrine may revert to an older version or be put on hold until the next opportunity arises. In turn, the threats the systems were meant to counter would be defused or minimized. Thus, India's plans for a mobile army conducting deep thrusts into enemy territory have been put on hold, and the old focus on deterrence has been revived. Similarly, it will be interesting to see how the Chinese decision not to build an aircraft carrier for cost reasons will affect India's threat perceptions and doctrines. Put simply, when there is no money, there are fewer threats.

Notes

1. Interview with Vice-Admiral M. K. Roy (ret.), Urbana, Illinois, September 23, 1989.

2. Interview with Lt. General M. L. Chibber (ret.), Urbana, Illinois, September 13, 1990.

3. *India Today*, February 28, 1989, 43. Even if the financial situation had not been so grave, it is doubtful than an entire air assault division could have been raised. Rikhye estimates that it would have cost the army more than an entire year's budget to create one; Rikhye, 1990, 76.

4. For a detailed discussion of why the Indian arms industry has had a mixed track record, see Gupta, 1990.

5. Both aircraft have been plagued with technological problems.

6. *Reserve Bank of India Annual Report 1979–80*. Bombay: Reserve Bank of India, p. 20.

7. Figures obtained from SIPRI Yearbooks. London: Taylor and Francis, 1980–1990.

8. For a discussion of the future of the former Soviet arms industry, see Almquist and Bacon, 1992.

SEVEN

Modeling the Expansion of Military Spending: A Case Study of Taiwan, 1953–1988

John Hartman & Wey Hsiao

The literature on the determinants of military spending has revolved around three positions: arms race models of the Richardson variety, political-business-cycle models, and a variety of Marxist models. The first argues that military spending is determined by the state's response to various perceived external (or possibly internal) threats. The second contends that the state uses military spending to (1) stimulate the economy in anticipation of electoral benefits, (2) compensate for shortfalls in private consumption and investment, and (3) respond to the pressures of institutional-constituency demand (Nincic and Cusack, 1979, 112). Those employing Marxist models perceive military spending to be determined largely by the systemic needs of an advanced but moribund capitalist economy (see, for example, Sweezy, 1970; Mandel, 1975; Baran and Sweezy, 1966).

Recent studies by R. P. Smith (1987, 1989) and Larry Griffin and associates (1982a, 1982b) have sought to assess the balance among external threat variables, alliance behavior, and domestic political and economic concerns as potential determinants of military spending for the advanced capitalist nations. A much smaller literature exists for poorer nations, despite their massive and rising levels of military spending. Here we describe the determinants of military expansion in Taiwan and clarify the theoretical context of such events. In particular, we attempt to discern the extent to which military spending was based on forces exogenous to the nation versus the extent to which internal forces determined military outlays.

Literature Review

Explanations of Military Spending

We noted earlier that efforts to explain military spending generally fall into three camps, which we discuss here. Modern research on arms races generally traces its roots to the pioneering work by Lewis F. Richardson (1960), whose basic equation system was the familiar model:

(1) $dx/dt = ay(t) - bx(t) + g$
(2) $dy/dt = cx(t) - dy(t) + h$

The first equation asserts that the rate at which a nation changes its armaments level (dx/dt) is positively related to its fear of an external threat (y), is negatively related to the burden of its present military spending (x), and is positively related to an enduring hostility or grievance (g). Equation 2 is the mirror image of Equation 1; the second nation of the pair engages in military outlays (y) and has a persistent grievance (h).[1]

In both cases (t) is time.

Overall, such formal models of U.S. military spending have not yielded the desired results.[2] Studies by Stephen Majeski (1983), Majeski and David Jones (1981), John Freeman (1983), and Miroslav Nincic and Thomas Cusack (1979) have failed to detect significant reactivity. Cusack and Michael Ward (1981, 448) summarize the overall findings when they write that "little compelling evidence [exists] that an 'arms race' embodies the primary dynamic underlying U.S. defense expenditures." The same summation is echoed by Christian Schmidt:

> Most of the empirical tests to which it [an arms race] has been subjected during the present period have proved disappointing. Empirical studies over recent years seem to establish:
> (1) That far from being the rule, Richardson behavior seems rather to be the exception . . .
> (2) That the explanatory power of the internal models, drawing on bureaucratic analyses, generally proves superior to that of international inter-actional models. (1987b, 141–142)

In response to these perceived weaknesses in the arms race models, Charles Ostrom (1978) proposed a "synthetic" model of military spending, which brings in some elements of budgetary politics theory. For Ostrom, the defense budgetary process is thought to be initiated by actual or perceived "defense needs"; these determine the armed services' requests for defense appropriations. Ostrom describes the balance of the process:

> The initial policy-making rule (i.e., services' request for funds) can be viewed as a reaction to the changing conditions in the international and domestic environments which is then filtered through the remaining organizations (i.e., president, Congress, Department of Defense) to determine the magnitude, scale and timing of the reaction. (1978, 943)

Ostrom's effort to include a narrow segment of the "domestic context" of the arms race framework found little empirical support over the eight years following its publication. In a 1986 article, Ostrom and R. F. Marra cite both Caspar Weinberger and Ronald Reagan to the effect that Soviet military outlays were the primary concern: "You've got to build your budget on the Russian budget" (Weinberger as quoted by Ostrom and Marra [1986]). Ostrom contends that the key limitation with the various studies' failure to find reactivity, the central element in his 1978 article, was their use of Soviet data of poor quality. A reanalysis of the U.S. defense outlays finds that U.S. policymakers' responses to their own *estimates* of Soviet spending lagged by three time periods.

A recent effort by Michael McGinnis and John Williams (1989) to find a more convincing arms race structure in the U.S. time series relies on each nation's expectation of the other's action. Their model is a simple application of the familiar rational expectations formulation found in monetarist economics:

> Under sophisticated reaction, the military budgets of rival states should approximate the optimal allocations of two unitary rational actors capable of forming unbiased forecasts of each other's behavior. . . . We argue that intense and pervasive competition to influence policy will induce actors to gather and make effective use of such a wide range of information as to approximate efficient competition over policy. (1989, 1106)

In their empirical analysis, McGinnis and Williams find that the effect of an increase in the military spending on the part of one of the superpowers leads to an increase in the other's spending. Although none of the evidence contradicts their model, much of it would seem to fit one that is much less complicated. Overall, however, they find that economic variables and hostility variables play a larger role than argued for in the simplest arms race models.

At the same time the arms race models were experiencing severe difficulties in explaining military spending, Paul Baran and Paul Sweezy's work (1966) focused direct attention on military spending as a means for capitalist economies to avert a variety of crises endemic to capitalism: "If military spending were reduced to pre–Second World War proportions, the nation's economy would return to a state of profound depression, characterized by unemployment rates 15 per cent and up" (1966, 53). Military spending is, then, a tool of crisis avoidance.

Albert Szymanski provided one of the first empirical tests of the Baran-Sweezy thesis using a simple cross-sectional design for eighteen mostly affluent nations (Szymanski, 1973a). Although he examined the impact of military spending on economic stagnation, the simple measures of association computed by Szymanski are symmetric in nature, most being percentages. Szymanski concludes:

> The Baran-Sweezy theory of the role of military expenditure on economic stagnation has been shown to have serious deficiencies. Military spending does not generally appear to have the role attributed to it of reducing stagnation, although it clearly does, in most cases, reduce unemployment. (1973a, 11)

Szymanski's test can be faulted in many areas, including sample selection, design, measurement, and specification, but it did focus attention on domestic determinants of military spending.

Ron Smith's key articles in the *Cambridge Journal of Economics* (1977, 1978) are based on a kindred theoretical underpinning; however, he applies a more rigorous test to the Baran-Sweezy thesis. Using a cross-national model, Smith found little support for the use of military spending as a measure to forestall economic crisis. His later work (Smith, 1980a, 1987, 1989) uses a more traditional economic demand framework, looking primarily at the standard array of military price versus civilian price variables along with threat and alliance variables.

Working within the same theoretical framework as Smith's early articles, Griffin and his coauthors (Griffin, Wallace, and Devine 1982a, 1982b) contend that Smith erred in his empirical analysis by testing "an essentially dynamic and historical argument" using a static cross-sectional design. They also criticize Smith for extending the Baran and Sweezy model to other nations: "Other capitalist nations either had less economic and strategic need to resort to military expenditure or were actually barred from massive re-armament" (1982a, 2).[3] In their empirical analysis they find that military outlays, as a percentage of gross national product (GNP), are unrelated to various geopolitical, strategic, and crisis variables. They are, however, used as a countercyclical fiscal instrument by the state:

> Their use seems to be affected predominantly by economic fluctuations and trends in politically and economically dominant sectors of labor and capital and much less so by real or perceived threats from political opponents or by "legitimate" defence "needs." (1982a, 8)

Griffin and his coauthors (1982b) go on to note that increasing levels of aggregate concentration and centralization of capital tend to lead to increased military spending, and that state managers use defense budgets in an attempt to ensure their incumbency in positions of power in state apparatuses. Writing in response to Griffin's article (1982b), Christopher Jencks (1985) argued that (1) the Vietnam and Korean wars were major sources of variation in military spending; (2) public opinion is a potential constraint on military spending; (3) GNP should be considered to be a potential determinant of military spending; and (4) civilian spending, revenues, and deficits are endogenous, not exogenous (that is, the model needs to be estimated as a system of equations).

Griffin and his coauthors essentially responded to these criticisms by noting that they did perform many of the statistical analyses suggested by Jencks and that their conclusions from such analyses were largely unchanged. Regarding the public opinion analysis, they noted that the translation of constituent preferences into expenditure policy is constrained by the "embeddedness" of elite actors. They go on to state:

> Public opinion is often manufactured and then manipulated by state managers seeking to rationalize actions that are already a matter of policy. We think this

particularly likely in the case of military spending, where appeals to jingoism, patriotism, or fear may excite popular approval for bloated defense budgets at home and military adventures abroad. (1985, 385)

Alex Mintz and Alex Hicks (1984) have provided a slightly disaggregated model of U.S. military expenditures and somewhat modify the analysis of Griffin and colleagues. They conclude:

> Overall, our disaggregation . . . suggests three important modifications of Griffin, et al.'s conclusions. First, only military spending for the *procurement* of military equipment and the remuneration of military personnel are used as countercyclical tools to regulate the rate of growth or monopoly sector profits, and procurement expenditures are used to regulate unemployment among organized labor as well. Second, increasing levels of aggregate industrial concentration increase military procurement and personnel spending. . . . Third, elected state officials apparently used defense spending on the remuneration of military and civilian personnel of the U.S. Department of Defense to insure their reelection. (1984, 417)

Mintz and Hicks essentially confirm the results of Griffin and colleagues, with an emphasis on procurement and personnel.[4]

⟨Military Spending in the Third World⟩

When we turn to the peripheral economies, we find works by J. R. Lotz (1970), Saadet Deger and Somnath Sen (1983), Deger (1986a), Alfred Maizels and Machiko Nissanke (1986), Wayne Joerding (1986), Kwabena Gyimah-Brempong (1989), Robert Looney (1989c), Gary Zuk and W. R. Thompson (1982), and Paula de Masi and Henri Lorie (1989). These studies employ widely different samples, designs, and methods.

Lotz (1970) examined components of government spending for thirty-seven developing countries in the mid-1960s. Lotz's method was a cross-national regression analysis design, with military spending as a percentage of GNP as the dependent variable. He explained his findings by arguing that there is a certain absolute, technical minimum size for a modern military establishment, and that low-income nations would have to be able to counter threats from higher-income nations. Lotz does not control for simultanity in his analyses.

Later studies by Saadet Deger (Deger and Smith, 1983; Deger, 1986a) estimated military expenditure as part of a systems of equations model. The 1983 Deger and Smith study used a three equation model with endogenous savings, military spending, and economic growth variables. The determinants of military spending in the model were oil exports and war. The model was estimated over the 1965–1973 time period for about fifty less developed countries (LDCs). This same pool was used in Deger 1986, with an equation added for trade balance. The same variables—oil and war—dominated the explanation. Deger's analysis does have a number of problems: It tends to lean too heavily on a few significant cases, and it fails to include a number of political variables of interest.

Maizels and Nissanke (1986) provide a useful review of the existing literature on the determinants of military spending in the LDCs while estimating a model for eighty-three nations in the 1978–1980 time period. Their approach is interesting methodologically inasmuch as they attempt to isolate the impact of political, economic, and military factors given a regional or global context. The method is similar to the analysis of covariance approach.

The study by Looney (1989) is a simplistic systems of equations model for thirty-seven less developed nations. For some reason Looney employed a sample splitting method—running separate regressions for arms producers and arms consumers—which has the undesirable effect of reducing variation within each pool. Typically, simple analyses of covariance designs—such as Chow tests— are considered a more desirable approach. Looney's major finding is that economic factors are critical determinants of Third World military outlays.

Joerding's (1986) study used a Granger Causality framework to analyze the connection between military spending and economic growth for a large number of poorer nations for a fairly long sample period. He finds that military spending has little impact on economic growth, but that economic growth has a positive effect on military outlays.

Gyimah-Brempong (1989) estimated an interesting systems of equations model for the sub-Saharan African nations, in which military spending is determined by the level of economic activity, threat, Organization of Petroleum Exporting Countries (OPEC) membership, Soviet military ties, war, and the force ratio. In his estimation, measures of threat and OPEC membership are insignificant, but measures of war, economic activity, Soviet ties, and the force ratio are significant.

Two International Monetary Fund (IMF)–based economists (de Masi and Lorie, 1989) specifically examined the impact of IMF-supported programs on military expenditure for a fairly large number of countries. The analysis is limited to an examination of the percentage of nations that increased or decreased military outlays as a percentage of both gross domestic product (GDP) and total government expenditures. The authors find that in nations undergoing fiscal tightening, military spending tended to displace other forms of government spending, thus increasing its overall share. In nations characterized by fiscal accommodation, military spending would simply rise as a percentage of GDP. These findings highlight the resilience of military expenditures in the Third World.

Models for Taiwan

There have been two efforts to analyze quantitatively the connection between economic expansion and military spending in Taiwan, both undertaken by Steve Chan (1988a, 1988b). Chan (1988a) estimates around twenty different equations in an effort to assess the impact of military spending on development. These "models" include an odd assortment of dependent and independent variables in a rather haphazard model-building strategy.

Chan (1988b) utilizes the same approach to model construction. Using data covering the period 1961–1984, he estimates an equation with an odd assortment of regressors. In this mix he finds that People's Republic of China (PRC) military outlays are a determinant of Taiwanese outlays, along with a slew of macro-economy measures. Overall, these articles do not appear to provide a sure footing for future research in this area.

The Military and Economic Development in Taiwan

On October 25, 1945, after fifty years of Japanese occupation, the Nationalist government of mainland China took over the administration of Taiwan. The island became a new province.[5] Taiwanese soldiers who served in the Japanese military were returned to the island, and mainland officials arrived to replace the repatriated Japanese administration. The departing Japanese population included not only many soldiers but also numerous entrepreneurs and technicians. The rapid changes created a number of severe problems: conflict between the mainlanders and the Taiwanese, shortages of technical personnel, widespread economic dislocations, and general government neglect and incompetence. Accentuating these problems were the often clumsy efforts by the Nationalist officials to consolidate their authority.

As the mainlanders replaced the Japanese, the status of the Taiwanese people was unchanged—they continued to be the subordinate class. In the new administration, almost all key positions were given to the newly arrived main-landers, who in many cases were military personnel.[6] Because of the massive repatriation of Japanese technical and managerial workers, Taiwan was unable to expand or even repair the existing infrastructure. Under the Japanese, only 31 percent of technicians were Taiwanese.[7] New administrators and technicians from the mainland were needed.

In many ways a clear colonial division of labor existed between Japan and Taiwan: Rice, sugar, and other raw materials were exported to Japan, whereas Taiwan imported almost all of its agricultural inputs and manufactured goods from Japan. Taiwan was "an economic asset to Japan" or "an agricultural appendage of Japan" (Ho, 1978). After the war, economic relations were severed, and the problems of unbalanced growth became obvious: Postwar Taiwan lost the industrial imports from Japan and could not sell its agricultural products to Japan. Trade with the mainland was impossible because of the ongoing conflict, in which the Nationalist forces continued the battle against Mao's insurgents and paid little attention to Taiwan. The new government had little interest in the problems and grievances of the Taiwanese war veterans, who suffered from a combination of unemployment and readjustment to civilian life. For the Nationalists, Taiwan was viewed simply as a source of revenue from state monopolies on tobacco and liquor. The tax policies compounded the mainland's resentment.

The economic situation deteriorated and divided mainlanders and

Taiwanese. Finally, on February 28, 1947, rioting broke out in Taipei following an incident between the police and a street peddler who had violated the state's tobacco monopoly. The rebellion spread throughout Taiwan, and on March 8, large numbers of troops arrived from the mainland to put down the uprising. The organizers of the rebellion were either arrested or fled to the mainland. Order was restored by the end of March.

The failed rebellion had important consequences for Taiwan's development. First, it increased the depth and breadth of Nationalist control over Taiwan, which was evident in the Nationalists' ability to move directly to the island without resistance following their defeat on the mainland. Second, it permitted the Nationalist government to be perceived as a neutral arbiter in internal disputes. Without this political resource, it would have been difficult or even impossible for the Nationalist government to successfully conduct its extensive land reform.[8] Third, the rebellion gave the government a high degree of autonomy from the domestic power base and aligned the state closely with the military, thus further reducing any need to meet the claims of the traditionalist landlord class.

The History of Conflict

Following their defeat in 1949, the Nationalists, under President Chiang Kai-shek, fled to Taiwan and attempted to use Taiwan as a base for the recovery of the mainland. On October 25, 1949, the People's Republic sent tens of thousands of troops against Kinmen (Quemoy), a strategic island in the Straits, but the attack failed. This event locked the current boundaries in place.

During the first six months of 1950, Taiwan tried to survive under both attacks from the mainland and international political pressure. Nationalist troops continued their evacuation from the mainland while launching air and sea operations along the coast. Taiwan had a huge financial deficit, largely because of the enormous maintenance cost of the army. Many international observers thought Taiwan could not survive.

Virtually all active military conflict between Taiwan and the mainland during the next two decades revolved around the two small but strategic islands of Kinmen and Matsu, which were located very near the mainland. Held by the Nationalist government, they are viewed as important for the defense of Taiwan and Penghu. The largest battle for control of the Taiwan Straits started on August 23, 1958, when mainland forces fired 41,000 rounds on the Kinmen Islands in two hours. In the following 43 days, mainland forces fired about 500,000 rounds on Kinmen. Taiwan's air force shot down about twenty-seven MiG-17s and probably damaged ten more off the mainland coast. Taiwan's navy sank three Communist torpedo boats.

In June 1960, when Dwight Eisenhower visited Taiwan, tension in the Straits rose. The mainland forces hit Kinmen with more than 175,000 shells, and the Nationalists responded by destroying eight coastal guns, seven fortifications, and four ammunition depots. These events were followed by a few minor acts of military confrontation during the next five years.

Several military incidents occurred between 1965 and 1967, centering again on the Straits. In particular, 1965 was an active year for the Taiwanese navy, as it sank four Communist gunboats and damaged two others near Matsu in May. Two months later two Taiwanese gunboats sank five mainland vessels and damaged two others near Kinmen; in November the navy sank another four gunboats near the Chinese mainland. These events were followed in January 1967 by the Taiwanese air force shooting down two MiG-19s near Kinmen. Since then, no military activity has been reported.

· For a variety of reasons, 1967 was the last year in which Taiwan and the mainland had a major military confrontation. Clearly, one key reason was the mainland government's preoccupation with its own internal transformation. The implementation of the Cultural Revolution was its top priority, and it had little time for Taiwan.[9]

In spite of the apparent calm, considerable tension exists between the two sides. Some of Taiwan's security concerns are the deployment by the mainland of more numerous military forces, the unwillingness of mainland leaders to rule out a military option for the unification of China, and the apparent willingness of the People's Republic to proceed with a military solution without regard for world opinion (Gregor, 1986; Liu, 1988).

The Economy and Export Promotion

Under the protection of the Mutual Defense Treaty, Taiwan was able to pay more attention to economic development than to its military expansion. During the 1950s, Taiwan followed a policy of import substitution for three sound reasons (Lin, 1973; Ho, 1978).

First, the continuing military threats from the mainland dissuaded potential foreign investors. Given the obvious risks associated with an unstable Taiwan, the market was simply too small. Consequently, the government had to use the few policy levers at its disposal to encourage domestic production: protectionism through foreign exchange policy and high tariffs, along with a domestic capital formation strategy.

Second, "numerous small businesses had started up business immediately after the war, partly by acquiring old Japanese facilities and producing simple manufactures of poor quality but at high cost" (Ho, 1978, 297). These small businesses could not compete with Japanese and U.S. companies in the domestic market or the world market. Thus, import-substitution policies were adopted to protect domestic enterprises and to encourage domestic production of substitutes for import goods.

Third, in 1951 Taiwan was confronted with a sizable trade deficit, which continued throughout the 1950s (Kuo, 1983). Consequently, the government used high tariffs to restrict imports and an exchange depreciation to improve the trade balance.

However, a currency depreciation and high tariffs raised the domestic currency price of imports and actually worsened the terms of trade. In 1960 the government abandoned import-substitution policies and moved to a strategy of export promotion. The Statute for Encouragement of Investment was enacted, which provided investment incentives for foreign investors. Export processing zones were set up to integrate foreign capital with cheap domestic labor. In addition, the United States ceased economic aid to Taiwan but, starting in 1965, encouraged its companies to invest there. Since then, overseas investment has replaced U.S. economic aid and it has increasingly gone to the island. Economic growth has continued without U.S. economic aid.

From this discussion, it is clear that the trade-oriented economic policies enacted in 1960 had a major impact on the rate and composition of national economic growth. By the late 1960s exports had become a very large component of Taiwan's GNP, and the expansion of the economy was tied to other nations' demand for its products. The increase in domestic demand and technological change were somewhat less important in accounting for growth, although the Nationalist government carried out an extensive infrastructure development agenda in the 1980s.

Alliances

A number of countries quickly extended diplomatic ties to the mainland and severed relations with the government in Taiwan.[10] Although the United States recognized the Nationalist government as the only legal government of China, it distanced itself from the island but continued economic aid (Fairbank, 1983).[11]

With the outbreak of the Korean War on June 25, 1950, Taiwan's political situation changed dramatically. Two days after the start of the war, Harry Truman ordered the Seventh Fleet to patrol the Taiwan Straits to prevent a mainland attack. He then asked the Nationalist government to cease air and sea operations against the mainland in return for massive military and economic aid. Taiwan accepted his terms. When the People's Republic of China took part in the Korean War and fought with UN forces supported by the United States, Taiwan's status gained geopolitical importance. A key diplomatic event for Taiwan was the signing of the Sino-American Mutual Defense Treaty in 1954;[12] this document provided Taiwan with U.S. military protection.

In the late 1950s Taiwan received a number of items of advanced technology. In July 1959, the Nationalist army received advanced surface-to-air missiles from the United States.[13] The Vietnam War served to consolidate U.S.-Taiwan relations, as Taiwan allowed the United States to establish military resupply bases on the island. Somewhat emblematic of the close relations was the U.S. provision of advanced F-5A fighters to Taiwan in 1965.

The 1970s brought a reversal of the close relations of the mid-1960s. Richard Nixon signed the Shanghai Communiqué in 1972, which signaled the eventual normalization of diplomatic relations and the progressive withdrawal of U.S. military forces. The United States agreed that the future of Taiwan would be an internal Chinese matter. In October 1972, in the absence of strong U.S. support, Taiwan was forced to withdraw from the United Nations.[14] The 1970s brought other diplomatic reversals: the withdrawal of recognition by many non-Communist countries from 1971 to 1973, the U.S. recognition of Communist China in 1978, the death of President Chiang Kai-shek in 1975, and the removal of the few remaining U.S. military forces in 1979.

Foreign Policy and the Military Industries

As pointed out by Alice Amsden (1985), military industries are central to the Taiwanese economy. Although her primary concern in her short essay, "The State and Taiwan's Economic Development," is the economic effect of the Kuomintang (KMT) state, she notes the reciprocal effect of the military institutions and economic expansion:

> The important role of public enterprises, like the early economic self-sufficiency promoted by the state, is quite consistent with what can be presumed to be the interests of the military. . . . Export-led growth . . . appears to contradict the policies that the military could be expected to favor. . . . It must be emphasized that the increased reliance on international markets . . . did not extend to defense production. The military ran its own production facilities, supplied with basic inputs by state enterprises. (1985, 99)

The military's power gradually waned, and civilian technocrats came to the fore. Amsden's tale is one of unintended consequences. However, much of Taiwan's domestic arms industry *expanded* precisely when Amsden contends its power had diminished. A few items in this area should be noted.

In response to the geopolitical shifts of the early 1970s, Taiwan expanded its domestic arms industry, becoming more self-reliant and actively seeking out alternative suppliers of weapons and military technology (Gregor et al., 1986). At that time, however, Taiwan's military was tied financially to both the U.S. government and U.S. military contractors.[15]

In December 1978, the United States established formal relations with the People's Republic of China and terminated the Mutual Defense Treaty with Taiwan. All military assistance ceased, and the remaining U.S. troops were withdrawn in 1979. Since the normalization, Taiwan's sense of insecurity has increased, as mainland China modernizes its military with newly available Western technology.[16] In response to these concerns, the U.S. Congress passed the Taiwan Relations Act (TRA), which provides articles and services necessary to maintain a sufficient self-defense capability. This act provides a measure of security, but it is clearly of a different order of magnitude than the Mutual Defense Treaty.

The 1980s brought new challenges, as the PRC continued to protest any arms sales to Taiwan and made renewed military threats. In 1982 the United States decided ultimately to cease all arms sales to Taiwan. In the joint Washington-Beijing Communiqué, the United States said it would not increase arms sales to Taipei in quantitative or qualitative terms in the interim (Hickey, 1986). And so, during the period 1981–1986, U.S. arm sales to Taiwan decreased from $1.4 billion to $720 million.

Given the massive change in its geopolitical position over the past twenty years, Taiwan has found it difficult to purchase sophisticated weapons systems from major arms-producing nations that have close diplomatic or commercial ties to the mainland.[17] In the context of the feudalized advanced weapons market, Taiwan must rely on its own resources to produce weapons, even though the economies of scale are far below those needed for optimal efficiency (Gregor, 1986). In the 1980s defense budgets increased, and provisions were made for a special fund to develop a domestic high-technology weapons industry.

Taiwan has maintained a substantial arms industry since 1950, as James Gregor writes:

> The arms industry on Taiwan commenced with the local assembly of foreign arms, and progressed to the domestic production of weapons and weapon platform components. By the late 1960s and early 1970s, it was producing complete weapon systems that were relatively unsophisticated. By the early 1970s, it was redesigning and modifying foreign weapon systems for local production. Some of those systems . . . were the products of reverse engineering and local redesign. (1986, 110)

Under government efforts (for example, tax incentives), many private firms are involved in defense programs.[18]

Taiwan's Internal Reforms

The late 1970s and early 1980s saw a number of events of internal conflict, particularly the riots in 1977 (the Chung-Li Event) and in 1979 (the Kaoshiung Crackdown). The second half of the 1980s was marked by a number of political and economic reforms in Taiwan. Martial law, imposed four decades earlier, was finally abandoned in 1986. Various opposition groups formed the Democratic Progressive Party the same year. The party's influence increased, especially during election years, and a two-party system was established. Inside the KMT, political power went through a generational transfer (Chang, 1983, 1984).

In the late 1980s there were a number of signs of improved relations between

Taiwan and the PRC: increasing frequency of visits between relatives and friends; a marked increase in indirect trade, mainly through Hong Kong; an increasing number of Taiwanese businesspeople traveling to the mainland in search of investment opportunities; and the PRC's allowing Taiwan, under the name "Chinese Taipei," to participate in some international activities (for example, the meetings of the Asian Development Bank and the Asian Olympics). "The warming of relations" was Taiwan's rationale for a substantial reduction in its defense budget for fiscal year 1990 (Dreyer, 1990).[19]

Measuring Taiwan's Military

Taiwan has been relatively secretive about the size of its army, as well as its defense outlays. Here we examine several of the alternative measures and assess their merits.

Size of the Armed Forces

The Nationalist government has never officially disclosed the size of its armed forces. Based on estimates made by the U.S. Arms Control and Disarmament Agency (ACDA) in its *World Military Expenditures and Arms Transfers*, Taiwan's armed forces decreased from 544,000 troops in 1966 to around 365,000 in 1987. Armed forces personnel per 1,000 population also decreased, from 40.7 in 1966 to 18.5 in 1987. This represents a 32.9 percent decrease in armed forces and a 54.6 percent decrease in armed forces per 1,000 people (see Figure 7.1). In comparative terms, Taiwan has one of the world's largest military organizations (Ho, 1978).

Military Spending and Military Aid

Taiwan has never provided exact numbers on its level of military spending; it is always mixed with "general administration cost, police expenditure, and spending on foreign affairs." Table 7.1 lists defense expenditures as a percentage of total government expenditures and as a percentage of gross national product (GNP) from 1950 through 1988. The middle column of the table reflects the degree to which national output is absorbed by defense spending, whereas the right-hand column measures the burden of defense spending on the government's budget.[20]

Defense expenditures as a percentage of net expenditures of all levels of government decreased from 74.3 percent in 1950 to 53.8 percent in 1965. In 1966 the percentage jumped to 61.3; 1965 was the last fiscal year of U.S. economic aid to Taiwan. Government nonmilitary spending also dropped dramatically in 1966. Since 1967, overall, there has been a steady decrease in military spending. This tended to flatten out in the early 1980s. In 1988 only about one third

Figure 7.1 Size of Taiwan's Armed Forces, 1966–1987

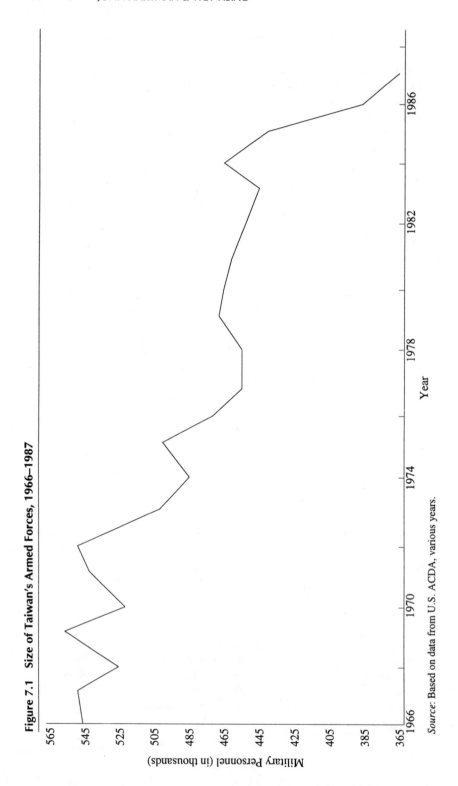

Source: Based on data from U.S. ACDA, various years.

(32.0 percent) of all government expenditures were for defense and administration.

As a percentage of GNP, defense spending exhibited a downward trend. In 1952, 12.3 percent of national output was absorbed by defense. Over time the

Table 7.1 Defense and Administration Spending

Year	Defense and Administration as % of Total Government Spending	Defense Spending as % of GNP
1950	74.3	—
1951	66.8	—
1952	59.3	12.3
1953	62.9	10.3
1954	60.8	12.9
1955	63.6	13.9
1956	59.2	13.0
1957	61.8	13.7
1958	62.4	14.9
1959	61.4	13.6
1960	60.5	11.8
1961	60.9	12.2
1962	59.0	11.8
1963	59.3	11.2
1964	58.4	11.0
1965	53.8	10.7
1966	61.3	11.6
1967	51.0	10.8
1968	54.4	10.6
1969	48.7	10.4
1970	48.8	10.6
1971	47.7	9.9
1972	43.3	8.7
1973	41.4	8.1
1974	41.0	6.7
1975	39.2	8.5
1976	36.6	7.8
1977	36.1	8.4
1978	37.1	8.5
1979	37.5	8.0
1980	39.1	9.1
1981	33.9	8.3
1982	34.4	9.0
1983	37.9	9.1
1984	34.1	7.7
1985	35.0	8.1
1986	35.4	8.0
1987	33.4	7.0
1988	32.0	7.0

Source: Taiwan Statistical Data Book, various years, Council for Economic Planning and Development, Republic of China.

amount of national output absorbed by defense becomes smaller; in 1988 defense expenditures accounted for 7.0 percent of GNP.

The U.S. Arms Control and Disarmament Agency has also sought to estimate Taiwan's military spending over the past two decades. Because the ACDA constantly revises its price-deflated data, we have converted the military expenditure series using 1987 prices as a deflator. Table 7.2 lists the ACDA military expenditure series in constant 1987 U.S. dollars, military expenditures as a percentage of central government expenditures (CGE), and military expenditures as a percentage of GNP.

Once again, these numbers have substantively different meanings. Military expenditures as a percentage of GNP reflects the degree to which national output is absorbed by military expenditures. Military expenditures as a percentage of central government expenditures measures the burden of military expenditures on the budget of the central government.

Military expenditures in constant 1987 prices increased from $1.896 billion in 1966 to $6.372 billion in 1986. The annual rate of increase during this period

Table 7.2   ACDA Estimates of Taiwan's Military Expenditures (millions of U.S.$)

Year	Military Expenditures (in constant 1987 prices)	Military Expenditures as % of	
		GNP	CGE
1966	1,896	—	—
1967	1,942	—	—
1968	2,067	10.5	48.6
1969	2,227	10.4	51.4
1970	2,507	10.6	50.8
1971	2,647	10.0	50.4
1972	2,633	8.8	45.8
1973	2,751	8.1	43.9
1974	2,321	6.8	39.8
1975	2,603	7.3	33.1
1976	2,739	6.8	31.4
1977	3,323	7.4	33.4
1978	3,816	7.5	32.3
1979	3,708	6.7	29.9
1980	3,884	6.6	28.0
1981	4,056	6.5	—
1982	5,046	7.8	46.8
1983	5,573	8.0	48.4
1984	5,099	6.6	46.8
1985	6,130	7.6	50.0
1986	6,372	7.0	50.0
1987	4,701	4.6	41.5

Source: U.S. ACDA, various years.

was 11.8 percent. The most significant single-year increase occurred between 1981 and 1982, the year after the United States normalized its relations with mainland China and ceased all military assistance to Taiwan. By 1987 the defense budget had decreased significantly to $4.701 billion because of improved relations with mainland China.

Military expenditures as a percentage of GNP decreased from 10.5 percent in 1968 to 6.5 percent in 1981, rose to 7.8 percent in 1982, then fell to 4.6 percent in 1987. The increase in the percentage during the period 1981–1983 was caused by the cessation of U.S. military aid and the development of a domestic arms industry.

As a percentage of central government expenditures, military spending exhibited an overall downward trend from 1968 to 1980, at which point the defense burden on the government rose rather rapidly to consume half of all central government outlays in 1985 and 1986. Three factors led to this state of affairs: first, the general resilience of military spending programs (de Masi and Lorie, 1989); second, the termination of U.S. military aid in 1979; and third, the sharply increased funding for the special high-technology weapons fund. Additionally, Taiwan's arms imports had increased fivefold from 1973 to 1988. The most significant increase occurred in 1981, the year after the United States severed its relations with Taiwan.

As military outlays accounted for nearly one-half of the government budget, other government functions were left underfunded (for example, social welfare and education) (Ho, 1978; Hsiao, 1990; see also Hickey, 1986; Dreyer, 1990). If the United States had not given Taiwan huge amounts of economic and military aid, the Nationalist government would have been in serious financial trouble. The military aid to Taiwan before 1979 reduced the conflict between the development of national defense and that of other sectors (Ho, 1978, 108). The economic aid before 1965 assisted Nationalist efforts in conducting land reform, encouraging agricultural production, improving the trade balance, and developing the island's infrastructure.

From 1949 through 1967, the United States gave Taiwan a total of $2.4 billion in direct military assistance—about $123 million a year.[21] In other words, almost half of Taiwan's military spending during this interval was underwritten by direct military grants from the United States (Gregor et al., 1986). From 1949 through 1967, Taiwan received $4.1 billion (in U.S. dollars) in U.S. aid, of which $2.4 billion was U.S. military assistance (see Table 7.3). In per capita terms, each person in Taiwan received $425 (in U.S. dollars) during the period 1949–1967; $187 of this was economic aid. The balance between grants and loans shifted in about 1962, with most of the grant monies for economic aid coming in the earlier period.

Military spending has cost Taiwan, on an annual average, about 10 percent of GNP—a sum that escalated from $187 million in 1956 to over $2 billion in 1982 (Gregor et al., 1986).

Table 7.3　U.S. Economic and Military Aid, 1949–1967 (millions of U.S. $)

	1949–1952	1953–1957	1958–1962	1963–1967	Total
Economic aid	467.8	529.5	502.3	269.0	1,768.6
loans	—	60.0	161.0	168.0	389.0
grants	467.8	469.5	341.3	101.0	1,379.6
Military assistance	48.0	1,178.9	720.4	436.9	2,384.2
loans	—	—	—	0.9	0.9
grants	48.0	1,178.9	720.4	436.0	2,383.3
Total aid	515.8	1,708.4	1,222.7	705.8	4,152.7
loans	—	60.0	161.0	168.9	389.9
grants	515.8	1,648.4	1,061.7	536.9	3,762.8
Assistance per capita	66.7	188.4	113.4	56.4	424.9
economic	60.5	58.4	46.6	21.5	187.0
military	6.2	130.0	66.8	34.9	237.9

Source: Ho, 1978, Table 7.2, 110. Reprinted with permission.

Measures of Threat and Alliance Behavior

In the previous discussion we noted how various fluctuations in the aggregate size of defense outlays tended to move with such putative causal agents as external threats, changes in alliances, fluctuations in foreign aid, and so forth. Although a particular year's jump in outlays might plausibly be linked to the fluctuation in another variable, the narrative approach tends to lack rigor, because it leaves out the concomitant variation in the other factors that form the balance of the array of theoretically significant factors.

As part of the effort to isolate the causes of military outlays, we perform a multiple regression analysis in which we attempt to fit a regression equation composed of several macroeconomic time series, threat series, and alliance series, and several controls. The analysis of the residuals from the regression equation will also provide us with some sense of where the equation falls short and what additional factors need to be taken into account.

We will look at two measures of threat: (1) an event-based measure from the New York Times Index (NYT-THRT), and (2) a dummy variable for years of greatest conflict (THREAT1). Event-based measures are problematic because of the very large number of stories filed for the years of greatest conflict and the absence of events for the remaining years. For example, in 1959 dozens of stories were filed on Kinmen and Matsu. In an effort to control for the exponential filing of stories, various transformations were used in regressions not reported here: logs, lags, moving averages, and decay terms. None worked better than the measures presently employed.

In the realm of alliances, the key positive events are the onset of the Korean War, which occurred prior to our sample; the Sino-American Mutual Defense Treaty of 1954 (MUT-DEF); and the Vietnam War (VIETNAM). Alliance reversals include Nixon's visit to the PRC (NIXON) and the withdrawal of U.S. recognition (USA-DERG).

In the realm of military spending, we opted for the numbers provided by the Taiwanese government, inasmuch as the ACDA data have at least as dubious an origin—there is little reason to choose one over the other.[22] Also, ACDA only has data for a much later date when little conflict existed between the mainland and Taiwan. Choosing ACDA data eliminates the years of greatest conflict for no tangible gain in credibility. These numbers were taken as a ratio: defense spending over GNP (DEF-GNP).

The control variables in the equation are a lag term (DEF-GNP1), thus setting up the stochastic difference equation. We also have a measure of U.S. aid to Taiwan (USAID), total government revenues (REVENUE), gross national product (GNPCU), and wholesale prices (WHOPRICE).

The design used in the estimation is a stochastic difference equation in which the dependent variable is lagged one time period—in this case, one year. This design enables us to determine the cause of a shift in the percentage of economic activity going to the military from one time point to the next.

Results

In Table 7.4, we present the results for the model outlined in the previous section. Equation 1 is the saturated model with four alliance interventions, two measures of threat, and four control variables. In the equation-building strategy, we found that the wholesale price control variable (WHOPRICE) was deleted first; Vietnam-era relations was deleted second (VIETNAM); the U.S. withdrawal of recognition was deleted third (USA-DERG); *New York Times* threat events was deleted fourth (NYT-THRT); and the threat dummy was deleted fifth (THREAT1). Note that the elimination of the five variables decreased the R-square by only .01, from .91 to .899.

Of the remaining variables in the equation, we have the lag variable, DEF-GNP1; two macroeconomic controls, GNPCU and REVENUE; and three alliance variables, MUT-DEF, NIXON, and USAID. The controls show that as the economy expanded, less of a percentage of the economy was devoted to military spending. Given that the size of the government expanded with the size of the economy, two of the control variables—GNPCU and REVENUE—compete for sources of variance. The weaker of the two terms, REVENUE, is positive and significant when entered into the equation by itself. When GNPCU is entered into the equation, REVENUE's sign changes, and it is reduced to an insignificant effect. Clearly, the determining factor is simply the aggregate size of the economy.

One of the alliance variables, USAID, is in the anticipated direction; a net addition of financial resources for military spending permits a greater percentage of GNP to be used for the military. The other two variables are more problematic. The coefficient for MUT-DEF indicates that the signing of the treaty in 1954 led to

Table 7.4 Determinants of Military Spending, OLS Equations (1953–1988)

Equation 1—Modeling DEF-GNP by OLS

Variable	Coefficient	Std Error	HCSE	t-Value
Constant	.0512342	.02140	.04318	2.39359
DEF-GNP1	.3204422	.15671	.25299	2.04484
USA-DERG	.0086994	.00796	.00993	1.09347
NYT-THRT	.0000917	.00011	.00034	.86084
VIETNAM	−.0029444	.00597	.01124	−.49280
MUT-DEF	.0267805	.00845	.02174	3.16933
NIXON	−.0163096	.00912	.01804	−1.78819
THREAT1	−.0065870	.00553	.00886	−1.19201
REVENUE	.000000134	.000000095	.00000	1.41096
USAID	.000000164	.000000078	.00000	2.09901
WHOPRICE	−.0000135	.00003	.00008	−.45515
GNPCU	−.000000035	.000000022	.00000	−1.62746

$R^2 = .91$
F-test $(11, 24) = 23.96$ [.0000]
Test for autocorrelation of orders up to 5

Lag	1	2	3	4	5
Coeff.	−.0825	−.1251	−.0348	−.0974	−.0134
S.E.s	.2717	2685	.2686	.2659	.2671

Chi-square test (df=5) = .784 with F (5, 14) = .07 [.9955]

Equation 2—Modeling DEF-GNP by OLS

Variable	Coefficient	Std Error	HCSE	t-Value
DEF-GNP1	.3263183	.15368	.16155	2.12339
Constant	.0483193	.02010	.01959	2.40421
USA-DERG	.0067353	.00658	.00548	1.02409
NYT-THRT	.0000916	.00010	.00020	.87330
VIETNAM	−.0030440	.00588	.00591	−.51809
MUT-DEF	.0262348	.00823	.00297	3.18743
NIXON	−.0180355	.00816	.00831	−2.20954
THREAT1	−.0070821	.00533	.00505	−1.32843
REVENUE	.000000125	.000000091	.00000	1.36755
USAID	.000000173	.000000075	.00000	2.31603
GNPCU	−.000000034	.000000021	.00000	−1.60328

$R^2 = .91$
F-test $(10, 25) = 27.19$ [.0000]

(continues)

Table 7.4 **(continued)**

Equation 3—Modeling DEF-GNP by OLS

Variable	Coefficient	Std Error	HCSE	t-Value
DEF-GNP1	.3561053	.14050	.16494	2.53458
Constant	.0429520	.01698	.01786	2.52989
USA-DERG	.0064148	.00645	.00544	.99379
NYT-THRT	.0001055	.00010	.00019	1.05642
MUT-DEF	.0261218	.00811	.00296	3.22045
NIXON	−.0151153	.00582	.00505	−2.59694
THREAT1	−.0085497	.00445	.00467	−1.92024
REVENUE	.000000127	.000000090	.00000	1.41265
USAID	.000000193	.000000063	.00000	3.08408
GNPCU	−.000000034	.000000021	.00000	−1.64248

$R^2 = .91$
F-test (9, 26) = 31.06 [.0000]

Equation 4—Modeling DEF-GNP by OLS

Variable	Coefficient	Std Error	HCSE	t-Value
DEF-GNP1	.3863055	.13714	.15614	2.81684
Constant	.0395021	.01662	.01678	2.37745
NYT-THRT	.0001028	.00010	.00019	1.03001
MUT-DEF	.0259869	.00811	.00302	3.20500
NIXON	−.0138423	.00568	.00491	−2.43857
THREAT1	−.0084816	.00445	.00450	−1.90561
REVENUE	.000000155	.000000085	.00000	1.81438
USAID	.000000190	.000000063	.00000	3.03689
GNPCU	−.000000038	.000000020	.00000	−1.87821

$R^2 = .91$
F-test (8, 27) = 34.83 [.0000]

Equation 5—Modeling DEF-GNP by OLS

Variable	Coefficient	Std Error	HCSE	t-Value
DEF-GNP1	.3969328	.13690	.18056	2.89941
Constant	.0368983	.01644	.38169	2.24445
MUT-DEF	.0264977	.00810	.38118	3.27058
NIXON	−.0126771	.00557	.00597	−2.27653
THREAT1	−.0058438	.00364	.00395	−1.60357
REVENUE	.000000156	.000000085	.00000	1.82987
USAID	.000000206	.000000061	.00000	3.37927
GNPCU	−.000000039	.000000020	.00000	−1.89198

$R^2 = .90$
F-test (7, 28) = 39.57 [.0000]
Test for autocorrelation of orders up to 5

Lag	1	2	3	4	5
Coeff.	-.0834	-.1537	.0469	.0002	.0195
S.E.s	.2422	.2392	.2400	.2364	.2358

Chi-square test (df=5) = .959
F-test (5,18) = .11 [.9875]

(continues)

Table 7.4 (continued)

Equation 6—Modeling DEF-GNP by OLS

Variable	Coefficient	Std Error	HCSE	t-Value
DEF-GNP1	.3795360	.14012	.18816	2.70866
Constant	.0395165	.01680	.23113	2.35276
MUT-DEF	.0227379	.00796	.23029	2.85562
NIXON	−.0100403	.00546	.00535	−1.83804
REVENUE	.000000162	.000000088	.00000	1.84467
USAID	.000000200	.000000062	.00000	3.20670
GNPCU	−.000000040	.000000021	.00000	−1.90642

$R^2 = .899$

F-test (6, 29) = 43.39 [.0000]

Test for autocorrelation of orders up to 5

Lag	1	2	3	4	5
Coeff.	.0568	−.0376	.1361	.0175	−.0511
S.E.s	.235	.2343	.2256	.2237	.2245

Chi-square test (df=5) = .518

F-test (5, 19) = .06 [.9967]

a jump in the percentage of GNP used for the military. It is, in effect, a dummy variable for 1953. The NIXON coefficient is negative in all equations rather than in the anticipated direction. This is likely caused by the nature of the transfer function used—it assumes an immediate impact of Nixon's visit rather than a complex and delayed effect.

It is evident from the ordinary least squares (OLS) regressions that none of the threat variables was remotely significant. It is also clear that the alliance measures fail to work where they do not have an economic basis. We can conclude that economic factors, rather than threat or alliance situations, determine military spending.

Figure 7.2 presents the unstandardized residuals, by year, for Equation 1 of Table 7.4. Note that there is only one substantial outlier, a large positive residual for the year 1958; this was the first year of massive military action against Kinmen and Matsu.[23]

Although the various autoregressive diagnostics detect no signs of pathologies, the equations were re-estimated using an iterative nonlinear least squares procedure. Table 7.5 displays the results for the same regressions when estimated using autoregressive least squares. The findings are substantively unchanged. The nonsignificant autoregressive parameter absorbs the effect for the constant and the mutual defense treaty. The three economic variables have essentially the same interpretation as before: REVENUE is determined by GNPCU, whereas USAID is in the anticipated direction and is borderline significant. Given that the autoregressive parameter has a t-value of .08, it would be wise to choose the parameterization in Table 7.4, Equation 6, instead.

Figure 7.2   Residuals from Equation 1, Table 7.4

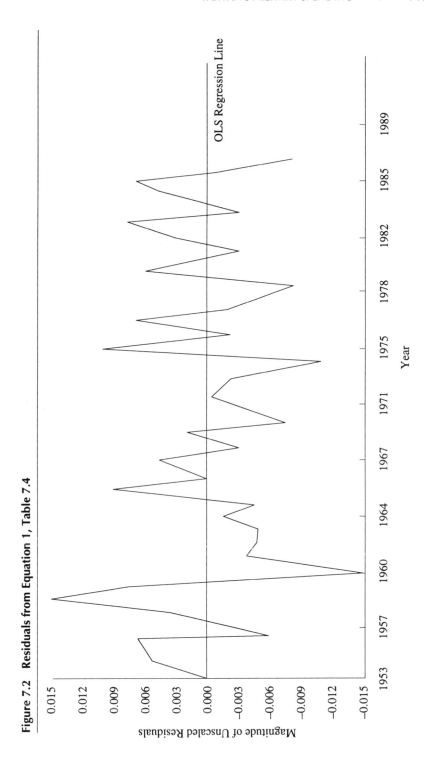

Table 7.5   Determinants of Military Spending with ALS Estimates Modeling DEF-GNP by Recursive Autoregressive Least Squares (RALS) (1953–1988)

Variable	Autoregressive Least Squares Estimates		
	Coefficient	Standard Error	t-Value
Constant	−.53326	6.62942	.0804
DEF-GNP1	.48329	.23852	2.0262
MUT-DEF	.58501	6.61019	.0885
NIXON	−.00848	.00618	1.3722
REVENUE	.000000161	.000000087	1.8394
USAID	.000000155	.000000082	1.8945
GNPCU	−.000000040	.000000021	1.8813
AR(1) process estimates			
Rho 1	.02531	.28885	.0876

Residual Diagnostics: 35 observations, 7 variables
Residual Autoregression of Order 5

Lag	1	2	3	4	5
Coeff.	−.0506	−.0799	.1228	−.0995	−.0347
S.E.s	.2319	.2297	.2219	.2264	.2294

Chi-square test (df=5) = 1.165
F-test (5, 19) = .15 [.9781]

It is also interesting that even with the alternative parameterization, the alliance and threat measures fail to work. We are left with a simple macroeconomic explanation based on the carrying capacity of the economy.

Discussion

As with much of the recent scholarly literature outlined in the first part of this chapter, we fail to find any evidence that military spending takes place in response to a perceived threat. Rather, military spending seems to be based on the levels of economic activity and of foreign support for the military. The Baran-Sweezy model, which has received a good deal of support for the United States, is clearly not applicable for Taiwan—a small, dependent economy that for four decades has been governed by martial law. In addition, the particular variant of the Baran-Sweezy model used by Griffin for the United States cannot be applied to Taiwan because of its emphasis on dual labor market theory and political business cycles; it is obvious that Taiwan's politico-military leadership was not concerned about electoral recall. In short, we found that military spending is based simply on the level of economic activity.

Notes

1. Good reviews of the then voluminous literature on arms race models are presented by Intriligator (1982) and Isard and Anderton (1985). A useful bibliography is provided by Anderton (1985).

2. For an interesting exchange on arms race modeling, see Desai and Blake (1981) and the response by McGuire (1977, 1981).

3. This is essentially the same issue discussed in the exchange between Sweezy (1973) and Szymanski (1973b).

4. Within the field of sociology, the analysis by these writers does not seem to have been picked up on.

5. Taiwan was retroceded to the Republic of China in accordance with the terms of the 1943 Cairo Declaration and the 1945 Potsdam Proclamation.

6. This could be rationalized by the history of the Taiwanese serving the now defeated Japanese colonial power, but these "servants of power" were few in number. Under the Japanese colonial administration, only 27 percent of the government employees were Taiwanese (Ho, 1978). The absence of native Taiwanese in the new administration clearly was largely because of the Nationalist government's distrust of the Taiwanese: They had been controlled by Japan for fifty years.

7. Within this group more than one third were physicians or pharmacists (Ho, 1978); few were engineers or electricians.

8. Much has been written about land reform in Taiwan; see Koo (1968) and Christensen (1968).

9. There is also a possible geopolitical element at work. The People's Republic supported North Vietnam in the Vietnam War and did not want to intensify the Vietnam conflict, given that the United States had a military base in Taiwan.

10. Two prominent nations that did so were the Soviet Union and Great Britain.

11. This contained no military aid at that time.

12. Economic aid was later approved by the U.S. House.

13. These were of the Nike-Hercules model.

14. The withdrawal of U.S. ground forces from Vietnam was connected to these events—Taiwan was no longer needed as a resupply center or as a rest and recreation base for military personnel.

15. Most of the weapon systems and spare parts were from the United States, paid for in part through congressional grant provisions advanced to Taiwan until 1974 and thereafter with the assistance of military credit, which continued until 1978 (Gregor et al., 1986).

16. Clearly, one element of this concern is the People's Republic's increased ability to impose a naval blockade on Taiwan.

17. This category of sophisticated weapons would include advanced fighter aircraft, air-to-air missiles, longer-range antiship missiles, antisubmarine warfare weapons, and airborne early warning systems.

18. For a detailed description of Taiwan's weapons systems and arms production, see Gregor et al., 1986; Gregor, 1986.

19. It should be noted that this warming of relations was interrupted temporarily by the 1989 events in Tiananmen Square and the nationwide repression that followed.

20. The figures on defense and administration may understate the actual military expenditures, because the military in Taiwan enjoys a number of subsidies that are not included in the military budget (e.g., rice, transportation services, and electrical power at subsidized prices) (Ho, 1978, 108).

21. These numbers are the procurement cost to the U.S. Department of Defense, not the lower market prices.

22. We discuss this at greater length elsewhere (Hartman and Hsiao, 1992).

23. In Studentized form, this residual has a value greater than two and may indicate that a more elaborate transfer function is required to model the sudden onset of active hostilities.

PART III

The Impact of Military Spending and Military Regimes on Development

❖ EIGHT ❖

Military Expenditures, Investment Funds, and Economic Growth

Jonas Zoninsein

The end of the Cold War brought the control and reduction of military expenditures to the top of the international agenda. Since the early 1980s, the world economy has been in a phase of profound structural adjustment in which public-sector reform has been the crucial instrument. The demand for investment funds in the United States, Eastern Europe, the former Soviet Union, and the developing countries of Africa, Asia, and Latin America has been increasing steadily since the late 1980s. The International Monetary Fund estimates that the additional demand for investment funding exceeded U.S.\$100 billion in 1991 and subsequent years. Cuts in unproductive public spending by the governments in these regions represent the most accessible and immediate means to generate additional noninflationary resources for financing immediate programs in the areas of infrastructure, science and research, education, and health.

The significant reduction in East-West tensions and the careful management and settlement of regional conflicts create a special opportunity to reallocate resources throughout the international system. Control and reduction of military expenditures not only satisfy the domestic goal of financial and fiscal austerity but also—given their positive effect on the security of other countries—have a multiplying effect that can create an international chain reaction and lead to a new phase of world economic growth.[1]

In this chapter I formalize an argument about the adverse effect of military expenditures on economic development and quantify the losses in the rate of economic growth generated by military expenditures during the 1980s. I then briefly discuss alternative approaches to world affairs that would favor the control and reduction of military expenditures.[2]

Military Expenditures and Losses in the Growth Rate of Output: The Experience of Latin America and the Caribbean

In those Third World countries that want to become regional hegemons, development policies were adopted primarily to promote the accumulation of capital and military power. These approaches to national development had two self-defeating characteristics: (1) the absolute disregard for the effects of these policies on the intensification of external threats and insecurity resulting from regional arms races, and (2) the underestimation of the effects of these policies on the reproduction of social inequities and internal insecurity resulting from authoritarian or centralized approaches to economic development. Resources available during the 1970s were unwisely channeled into military buildup and investment projects, with few positive effects on the international competitiveness of the economies.[3] The second oil shock (1979) and the sharp increases in interest rates ended economic growth and, with it, the local elites' dreams of regional hegemony, as well as whatever political legitimacy could be derived from these nationalistic goals.

The end of the Cold War offers the nations of the world a unique opportunity to cut their military expenditures, thereby freeing resources for productive investment. The Eastern European countries seem to be considering significant decreases in military expenditures. However, the situation in the industrialized and the developing countries, as well as the former Soviet Union, appears unclear (Hewitt, 1991; McNamara, 1991; United Nations, 1991).

In absolute terms, world military expenditures fell slightly in 1988 for the first time since 1971 (to a level of U.S. $ 1,032.4 million, equivalent to 4.5 percent of world gross domestic product [GDP]). Similar minor reductions in real terms took place in 1989 and 1990, reflecting the end of the phase of rapid increases characteristic of the early 1980s (United Nations, 1991). In spite of the international system's move toward limiting both nuclear and conventional forces, significant reductions in military expenditures are not yet part of the global scenario. At this juncture in world history, what are the obstacles to the demilitarization of the international system? Why is it so difficult to obtain the peace dividend?[4]

Obstacles to Demilitarization

One key obstacle is the special manner in which many Third World elites conceive of their security and developmental goals. These groups still see their countries as experiencing an early phase of political and economic development, in which state-building and nation-building must be based on authoritarian and coercive institutions, including the military. In this primary phase, such institutions provide the external and internal security required to generate political stability, orderly economic policies, and high rates of saving. Accordingly, excessive allocation of resources to military ends, although a short-term hindrance to economic growth, constitutes a rational choice for Third World ruling elites. In the long run, central state power accumulation would increase these elites' overall ability to promote economic growth and social welfare (Ayoob, 1991a).

The obstacles to demilitarization reinforce each other and produce a course for the international system in which continual political instability, regional imbalances, potential or real wars, and increasing domestic economic and social inequalities restrict public-sector reform and structural adjustment. Before further exploring this point and the alternatives in dealing with the obstacles to demilitarization, I explore some estimates of the loss of economic growth generated by excessive military expenditures. First, I delineate the economic consequences of the political choices regarding the volume of military expenditures. Subsequently, I utilize the classical framework of the Harrod-Domar growth model to estimate the reduction in the equilibrium growth rate of the economy generated by military expenditures.

The dominant view in economic theory is that military expenditures reduce the rate of economic growth, which results from their adverse influence on the volume of investment funds and, thereby, on the rate of capital accumulation.[5] In spite of the clear-cut conclusion of the theoretical debate that has taken place during the 1970s and 1980s, some confusion still exists surrounding this issue, as revealed by empiricist efforts to allow the (necessarily) imperfect quantification of the positive and negative effects of military expenditures in order to form the final answer to a question that is intrinsically theoretical. This confusion derives from a lack of questioning on a conceptual level of the relationship between the benefits and the costs to be expected from government decisions.[6]

Benefits of Military Expenditures

Whatever economic benefits could be expected from military expenditures, these benefits should be compared to their costs, in terms of the losses of the current and future stream of investment and consumption goods that would have been produced and then consumed, invested, or exported. Whatever benefits military expenditures might generate, these must be compared to their cost in terms of crowding out public and private reproductive investment.

In addition, when analyzing investment in the military,[7] attention is commonly concentrated on only one aspect of the expenditure process. Investment expenditures, however, have a dual effect on the economy. Investment is not merely an instrument for generating effective demand, employment, and income; it also increases the productive capacity of the economy and, therefore, has a long-term, dynamic effect upon it.[8] The assessment of the opportunity costs of military expenditures should concentrate on this second aspect.

Military expenditures, like any other investment expenditures, create employment and income. From this point of view, they cannot be differentiated from other components of effective demand.[9] What can be evaluated, from the point of view of economic dynamics, is, therefore, the nature of the product generated in the military facilities and its impact on the reproductive capacity of the economy.

The product generated by the military sector is, in general, barren and unproductive. Only a minuscule proportion of military-sector services can be used to produce other goods and services and, therefore, to support the material reproduction of society. Some authors (Benoit, 1973; Deger, 1986b; among others) argue, however, that military expenditures, despite absorbing investable resources, have favorable effects on economic growth: (1) The training, discipline, and skills of military personnel can be transferred to the civilian sector after demobilization; (2) military expenditures may accelerate the modernization of administration infrastructure and improve human capital; (3) military infrastructure (roads, airports, naval bases, mapping, meteorological services), can be used in part by the civilian sector; (4) military research and development have civilian spinoffs that increase the productivity of the economy; (5) the military might produce security services more inexpensively than the private sector can; and (6) in addition to this cost effect is the quantity effect in terms of the essential security required for economic progress.

The existence of effects (1) through (5) cannot be denied. However, in all of these cases, the favorable effects exist only as by-products of military expenditures and only because resources have been available to finance the expenditures. Similar or even more favorable effects on growth could have been produced by alternative expenditures. That is, in all of these cases, what prevailed was the political decision to allocate resources to the military. Effects (1) through (5) could have been created indirectly by military expenditures or by alternative civilian programs and expenditures without incurring the dominant unproductive component of military expenditures and thereby depressing the amount of resources available for productive investment.

Effect (6) is of a different nature. One political option of the security policy of any country is to dispense with a military force, thereby reducing significantly the amount of "hardware" security expenditures. Resources could be devoted instead to developing social and economic goals, to strengthening democratic institutions, and, thereby, to expanding the "software" components of security: legitimacy, integration, and policy capacity (see Ayoob, 1991a). I am using the option of not having an army, as adopted by Costa Rica, and that country's low military expenditures–GDP ratio as a proxy for defining and quantifying the amount of military expenditures that could be reallocated to the civilian sector of the economy of developing countries without producing a gap in the essential supply of security required for economic progress.

At this point, I quantify the reduction in the rate of economic growth that is produced by military expenditures.[10] I chose the period 1980–1989 for this quantitative assessment, a time when most of the developing countries were adversely affected by the international debt crisis, the short supply of foreign loanable funds, and the very high interest rates on the huge external debt that had accumulated since 1974. During the 1980s, the scarcity of investment funds in the public sectors of developing countries was the critical causal component of economic stagnation, mainly because of their servicing of the foreign debt. In those years, a significant reduction of military expenditures would have constituted a very positive factor in the recovery of developing economies.

From the quasi-identity

(1) $I_i^* = I_i + M_i$

where I_i is actual investment, I_i^* is potential investment, and M_i is military expenditures, we can easily derive the equilibrium growth rate of the i economy with an exogenously imposed military expenditures percentage of GDP

(2) $g_i = c_i/v_i - M_i/v_iY_i$

where g_i is equilibrium growth rate, c_i is potential investment ratio, v_i is marginal capital–output ratio, and Y_i is GDP.

This result shows that the growth rate of the economy is reduced proportionately to the share of military expenditures to GDP, with a coefficient equal to the marginal capital–output ratio. I use this expression to estimate the loss of economic growth (L_i) produced by the allocation of investment resources to military ends

(3) $L_i = M_i/v_iY_i - m_{CR}/v_{CR}Y_{CR}$

where m_{CR} is military expenditures in Costa Rica, v_{CR} is the marginal capital–output of Costa Rica, and Y_{CR} is the GDP of Costa Rica.

Table 8.1 shows the average marginal output–capital ratio for the period 1980–1988 [$1/(\Sigma v_i/n)$], the adjusted average military expenditures–GDP ratio [$\Sigma(M_i/Y_i)/n - \Sigma(M_{CR}/Y_{CR})/n$] for the period 1980–1988, the estimated loss of economic growth (L_i) produced by military expenditures for the period 1981–1989, the actual average rate of economic growth (g_i) for the period 1981–1989, and the potential average rate of economic growth ($g_i^* = g_i + L_i$) for the period 1981–1989 for all countries of Latin America and the Caribbean (except the Bahamas, Cuba, and Suriname).

Although Latin America and the Caribbean is the region of the world with the lowest percentage of central government expenditure devoted to military costs, the data in Table 8.1 suggest that for some countries—Argentina, Bolivia, Chile, El Salvador, Guatemala, Guyana, Honduras, Nicaragua, Peru, and Uruguay—the loss produced by allocating investment resources to the military significantly affected the growth rate of the economy during the 1980s. The proportional effect of this loss on the growth rates is particularly striking (columns 4 and 5).

Notwithstanding this significant loss, it is important to realize that the

Table 8.1 Loss in Economic Growth Produced by Military Expenditures, Latin America and the Caribbean, 1980–1988

Country	$1/(\Sigma v_i/n)$ (1)	$\Sigma(M_i/Y_i)/n$ $-\Sigma(M_{CR}/Y_{CR})/n$ (%) (2)	L_i (%) (3)[c]	g_i (%) (4)[c]	$g_i{}^* = g_i + L_i$ (%) (5)[c]
Argentina	0.239	4.0	1.0	–1.9	–0.9
Barbados	0.153	0.1	0.03	1.0	1.0
Bolivia	0.224	3.0	0.7	–0.8	–0.1
Brazil	0.282	0.1	0.03	2.1	2.1
Chile	0.431	7.2	3.1	2.9	6.0
Colombia	0.178	1.6	0.3	3.5	3.8
Costa Rica[b]	0.187	—	—	2.2	2.2
Dominican Republic	0.191	0.8	0.2	2.6	2.8
Ecuador	0.224	1.0	0.2	2.0	2.2
El Salvador	0.197	3.4	0.7	–0.9	–0.2
Guatemala	0.264	1.8	0.5	0.6	1.1
Guyana	0.080	8.0	0.7	–3.2	–2.5
Haiti	0.225	0.6	0.1	–0.8	–0.7
Honduras	0.213	3.2	0.7	2.3	3.0
Jamaica	0.165	0.7	0.1	1.9	2.0
Mexico[b]	0.168	—	—	1.2	1.2
Nicaragua	0.216	14.2	3.1	–1.7	1.4
Panama	0.234	0.9	0.2	0.0	0.2
Paraguay	0.207	0.6	0.1	3.1	3.2
Peru	0.246	7.0	1.7	–0.6	1.1
Trinidad and Tobago	0.154	1.9	0.3	–3.9	–3.6
Uruguay	0.325	2.1	0.7	0.0	0.7
Venezuela	0.187	1.9	0.4	0.1	0.5

Sources: The primary information for the military expenditures–GDP ratio is from SIPRI, 1989; data on GDP growth rates and investment coefficients are from the *Inter-American Development Bank 1990 Report: Economic and Social Progress in Latin America* (Washington, D.C.: Johns Hopkins University Press, 1990).

Notes: a. The marginal output-capital ratio for each of the n years is $[(dGDP_i/GDP_i)_t/(dK_i/GDP_i)_{t-1}]$, where dK = investment.

b. The average military expenditures–GDP ratio for Costa Rica in the period 1980–1988 was 0.7 percent. For Mexico it was 0.6 percent.

c. Columns 3, 4, and 5 also include 1989 data.

estimates of these losses reflect the low marginal output–capital ratios calculated on the basis of a very poor macroeconomic performance of this region. The value of the ratios has been influenced decisively by the debt crisis of these economies and the outward transfer of resources that took place during the 1980s. It should also be noted that the procedure used in these calculations does not account for the compound effect over many years of the crowding out of investment and the reduction of the growth rate produced by military expenditures. For comparison purposes, Table 8.2 presents the losses in the growth rate of the economies of

Table 8.2   Loss in Economic Growth Produced by Military Expenditures, Selected Countries, 1980–1988

Country	$1/(\Sigma v_i/n)$	$\Sigma(M_i/Y_i)/n$ $-\Sigma(M_{CR}/Y_{CR})/n$ (%)	L_i (%)
United States	0.230	5.5	1.3
Hungary	0.100	2.5	0.2
Turkey	0.270	4.2	1.1
Egypt	0.337	5.6	1.9
India	0.246	2.5	0.6
Pakistan	0.342	5.7	1.9
Ethiopia	0.289	7.9	2.3
Tanzania	0.226	3.3	0.7

Sources: SIPRI, 1989; IMF, 1990.

selected developing countries in Africa, Asia, and the Middle East, plus those of the United States and Hungary.

∠Adverse Effects of Military Expenditures ＞

As noted previously, the outward transfer of resources constituted one of the main causes of the growth slowdown in the developing countries, particularly in Latin America and the Caribbean.[11] The aggregate rate of growth in this region decreased from an average of 5.9 percent per annum during the 1970s to an average of 1.1 percent per annum during the 1980s. During the 1970s, the net resource transfer continually favored Latin American economies. During the period 1981–1989, because of very high interest rates and the short supply of external funds, the net resource transfer became a net outflow. This outflow of funds, together with the drop in the gross domestic savings rate (resulting from recession and, later, slow economic growth, high rates of inflation, and government financial exhaustion) produced a decrease in the investment coefficient throughout the 1980s. In this specific sense, the outward transfer of resources represents a drag on economic growth, which can be compared to military expenditures. The figures presented in Table 8.3 show that for those countries in which the loss in the growth rate produced by military expenditures is significant (Table 8.1), the amount of excessive military expenditures is similar to, or even larger than, the outflow of resources produced by the international debt crisis.

A further indicator of the adverse effect of military expenditures on the investment coefficient can be obtained by comparing the shares of total investment and military expenditures to the total central government expenditures. One of the main characteristics of the economic slowdown of the developing countries during the 1980s was the financial exhaustion of the public sector and the reduction of the public-sector share in gross domestic investment.

Table 8.3 Military Expenditures and Net Transfer of Resources (NTR), Latin America and the Caribbean, 1980–1989

	1980	1981	1982	1983	1984	1985	1986	1987	1988	1989[a]
$M_i/Y_i - \Sigma(M_{CR}/Y_{CR})/n$ (%)										
Argentina	5.7	6.4	6.9	3.9	3.8	2.8	3.0	2.7	2.3	
Bolivia	3.3	4.4	3.8	3.2	2.7	2.7	2.1	2.2	2.4	
Chile	6.0	6.7	8.8	7.3	8.9	6.9	7.2	6.1	7.1	
El Salvador	2.1	3.0	3.7	3.7	3.9	3.7	4.2	3.1	—	
Guatemala	1.1	1.2	1.7	1.9	2.2	2.9	—	—	—	
Guyana	5.8	5.3	6.8	9.0	8.5	9.2	11.7	—	—	
Honduras	1.7	1.6	2.1	3.3	4.5	5.7	—	—	—	
Nicaragua	3.7	4.6	5.7	9.7	10.2	21.5	43.4	—	—	
Peru	4.6	5.3	9.7	8.9	5.8	6.8	7.9	—	—	
Uruguay	2.2	3.2	3.3	2.5	1.9	1.7	1.6	1.4	1.4	
NTR/GDP (%)										
Argentina	6.9	5.6	–0.7	–1.8	–1.2	–3.8	–1.6	–1.0	–4.2	–6.4
Bolivia	4.2	6.5	1.8	4.0	1.6	6.3	4.8	6.6	3.1	3.3
Chile	4.7	10.8	–1.9	–5.7	–3.9	–7.9	–8.2	–6.9	–5.6	–4.0
El Salvador	4.4	6.0	3.7	2.8	4.2	5.0	6.7	4.6	6.1	8.5
Guatemala	5.7	8.0	3.8	1.2	3.2	–0.1	–0.2	6.2	6.0	5.0
Guyana	19.0	22.6	13.1	15.5	0.9	6.5	12.9	5.5	4.2	4.9
Honduras	9.0	4.3	–0.8	0.9	4.6	3.9	2.3	2.8	2.3	1.3
Nicaragua	23.3	17.7	9.1	12.0	16.0	18.9	17.0	18.5	20.4	11.5
Peru	–11.0	–2.3	0.3	2.1	–3.3	–5.8	–6.6	–6.9	–6.8	–10.3
Uruguay	4.3	3.5	2.7	–3.7	–6.3	–7.1	–6.0	–2.5	–3.6	–4.0

Sources: SIPRI, 1989; *Inter-American Development Bank 1990 Report.*
Note: a. Data available only for NTR/GDP calculation.

Until the early 1980s, the public sector in late-developing economies commanded the process of capital accumulation by investing directly in infrastructure and basic raw materials and, indirectly, through subsidies and credit allocation. These actions created the opportunities, incentives, and resources required to support profitable private investment in new competitive activities.

This crowding-in effect of public-sector expenditures collapsed, however, as a result of the international debt crisis that began in the early 1980s. Inflationary effects on public-sector revenues, subsidies, and expenditures, as well as the direct burden of the increased debt service, exhausted the finances of the public sector in most highly indebted developing countries.[12] Because of the lack of resources, public investment was cut sharply, and economic growth was interrupted. The figures presented in Table 8.4 illustrate the extent to which military expenditures constituted a constraint on the productive investment of the public sector and, therefore, on economic growth during the 1980s.

Table 8.4 Central Government Investment and Military Expenditures, Latin America and the Caribbean, 1980–1989

	1980	1981	1982	1983	1984	1985	1986	1987	1988	1989
Central government investment as % of GDP										
Argentina	8.9	8.2	7.9	8.8	7.2	6.5	6.9	7.0	7.9	5.7
Bolivia	1.2	0.9	0.4	0.7	0.7	1.8	2.0	1.3	2.7	—
Chile	2.6	2.8	2.2	2.4	2.6	3.1	3.2	3.0	3.5	2.9
El Salvador	4.3	4.4	3.4	3.9	3.0	2.6	2.5	2.3	1.7	2.0
Guatemala	2.7	3.6	2.4	1.8	1.8	1.1	0.8	1.0	1.6	2.1
Guyana	12.2	18.1	15.0	11.8	12.1	18.3	12.8	15.0	10.2	11.4
Honduras	10.0	8.3	9.1	10.7	11.6	8.6	6.0	6.1	6.1	5.8
Nicaragua	4.7	5.6	6.2	10.9	8.9	3.0	5.8	3.5	3.7	1.1
Peru	3.0	3.3	3.1	2.9	2.9	2.3	2.3	1.1	0.5	0.6
Uruguay	1.6	1.6	1.8	1.6	0.9	0.7	0.7	1.1	1.6	1.6
Central government investment as % of total central government expenditures										
Argentina	15.9	15.5	16.1	12.0	10.6	5.6	7.4	7.8	12.1	8.4
Bolivia	6.6	6.1	2.4	3.5	3.4	12.9	24.6	12.1	23.3	—
Chile	8.4	8.4	5.6	6.8	7.4	9.2	9.6	9.6	10.1	10.4
El Salvador	23.6	21.2	16.8	18.3	15.6	15.0	14.1	14.8	12.7	15.5
Guatemala	18.4	22.4	18.1	15.3	15.6	11.2	7.8	8.5	12.3	15.5
Guyana	19.9	23.6	20.6	14.8	14.0	19.3	12.3	16.7	12.5	12.2
Honduras	16.7	11.4	11.5	11.3	11.4	11.7	11.0	14.0	14.7	15.4
Nicaragua	14.0	15.6	15.0	17.1	15.1	5.4	12.0	7.9	8.0	5.2
Peru	15.3	18.1	17.7	15.1	16.2	13.4	13.8	6.4	3.5	4.8
Uruguay	9.6	8.9	7.4	7.9	4.7	3.9	4.0	6.8	8.7	9.0
Military expenditures as % of total central government expenditures										
Argentina	16.9	14.8	25.9	14.9	17.2	10.7	8.4	6.0	—	—
Bolivia	18.0	22.7	7.4	10.7	5.4	—	22.8	26.0	28.1	—
Chile	17.2	16.7	17.3	17.4	16.8	15.9	15.3	19.0	16.3	—
El Salvador	15.5	17.3	20.4	22.8	31.0	29.1	35.2	35.4	34.9	—
Guatemala	9.9	8.0	12.6	15.5	17.5	17.0	12.3	15.6	13.4	—
Guyana	5.7	5.6	—	—	—	—	—	—	—	—
Honduras	9.0	7.8	8.2	10.9	14.7	14.0	15.8	16.7	14.5	—
Nicaragua	18.8	17.6	21.4	15.7	20.9	26.2	—	—	—	—
Peru	24.4	22.3	39.0	24.7	30.6	36.8	40.7	34.2	—	—
Uruguay	13.1	15.4	13.2	12.4	10.9	10.6	10.1	—	12.0	—

Sources: Inter-American Development Bank 1990 Report; ACDA, 1990.

Conclusion

Removing the obstacles to demilitarization is a highly difficult and complex process that involves a long-term approach to multilevel negotiations on economic, political, and security matters. At this point, however, many important participants in the international affairs arena are clearly not willing to embark on such a process or to accept the removal of military power as an instrument of international supremacy.

In spite of this obvious limitation on the control and reduction of military expenditures, I explore here logical inferences from the analysis of the obstacles to demilitarization discussed in this chapter. Global military overstretch and the end of the Cold War, reinforced by the coalition's victory in the Gulf War, open the space for a re-examination of global security affairs. In order to enhance ⟨collective security,⟩ a feasible alternative approach to the continuation of a general struggle for power, defined primarily in military terms, does exist. In this alternative approach, security is conceived as a function of the ratio between threats and capacities. This means that nation-states, and, thereby, collective security, can be expanded not only through additional military capacity but also by reducing perceived threats (Nelson, 1991). Arms control, trade, and other sorts of agreements and unilateral initiatives are the instruments used to reduce perceived threats.

This alternative approach has a special appeal for developing countries. Overcoming economic stagnation, policy paralysis, and increasing social unrest requires economic modernization, state reform, the dismantling of authoritarian and coercive institutions, and an unrestricted process of political liberalization and civil society participation.

These processes are under way in many countries. Within them, the control and reduction of military expenditures will need to occupy a central role in order to liberalize funds for productive and social investments. Although determining the role of the military is the prerogative of each government, the international community should explore ways to limit military expenditures. One powerful mechanism would be to link financial assistance from international organizations and donors to the reduction of military expenditures to certain predetermined levels.

Notes

1. Camdessus (1991) estimates that if all countries had reduced their military expenditures in 1991 to the worldwide average level of 4.5 percent of GDP in 1988, U.S. $140 million in savings would have been generated.

2. In this chapter I attempt to explore further the conceptual approach I used in Ruiz and Zoninsein (1979), which was presented at the 1979 Congress of the International Political Science Association. The core of this approach is the notion that military expenditures affect economic development primarily through their effect on the investment coefficient.

The methodology adopted in the 1979 article had the purpose of evaluating the long-term effects of military expenditures reduction; the mathematical simulation covered a period of several decades (from 1960 to 2000). The Latin American World Model (LAWM) was originally developed in the 1970s to demonstrate that the main problems facing humanity are not those of physical limitations. The deterioration of the physical environment was seen as a result of social organizations that are based on destructive values. In the 1979 article I used the conceptual and mathematical framework of the LAWM for dealing quantitatively with the question of disarmament. I examined the impact of reduction of military expenditures, the redirection of liberated resources in the period of time needed, and the conditions under which economic and social development in different regions of the world could satisfy the basic needs (in terms of calories and protein intake, number of dwellings, and places available for the first twelve years of formal education) of their populations.

The LAWM characterizes socioeconomic policymaking as a problem of optimal allocation of capital and labor resources. The objective is to establish how and over what time period basic needs can be satisfied. The target of satisfaction of basic needs is represented in the model by the maximization of life expectancy at birth, subject to a set of constraints. The policy I tested in 1979 differs from the standard run of the LAWM in that a reduction of military expenditures is enforced. Starting in 1980, this reduction is performed at an annual rate, and the minimal level of military expenditures is set at 10 percent of the 1980 values. When comparing the standard run of the LAWM with the run of military expenditures reduction, the desirability of this second scenario is shown by the fact that the satisfaction of basic needs is obtained in a significantly shorter period of time. A second simulation of military expenditures reduction—including economic aid financed by resources liberated from military expenditures in industrialized countries— produced the best result. In this scenario basic needs are fully satisfied for the populations of Africa and Asia before the year 2000.

3. The World Bank estimates that one-third of the debt of some major developing countries accounted for the financing of arms imports (SIPRI, 1990, 210). In this case, the opportunity cost of purchasing security through military expenditures is the loss in the creation of productive assets that could have produced the means to repay the loans.

4. Mead (1990) argues that the main threat to the U.S. financial leadership comes from an eventual shift by OPEC countries to hold their liquid assets in yen, marks, or European Currency Units (ECU) instead of the dollar. The U.S. security relationship with the oil states of the Middle East is, therefore, the key variable in maintaining its hegemony.

5. This point of view is based on a review of economic theory and research literature on the subject. See Benoit (1973); Smith (1977, 1980b); Ruiz and Zoninsein (1979); Ball (1983a); Deger and Sen (1983); Lim (1983); Faini, Annez, and Taylor (1984); Biswas and Ram (1986); Deger (1986b); and Grobar and Porter (1987). I explore here the theoretical argument found in this literature by emphasizing the concepts of *dual effect of investment expenditures* and *opportunity costs* associated with military expenditures. Both concepts are crucial for distinguishing the favorable and adverse effects (from the point of view of economic variables) of military expenditures on economic growth. They are also useful to demonstrate that the favorable effects are necessarily secondary when compared with the negative dominant effects of military expenditures on economic growth.

6. Regarding the importance of the opportunity costs and the economic value of time, from an economic-liberal point of view, see the seminal article by Johnson (1971). His basic point is that any project or program in the public and private sectors uses goods and services and, consequently, denies these to other possible projects. For society as a whole, the opportunity cost of undertaking a project is the value of resources used to invest and operate the new facilities, which is measured in terms of the net benefits the resources would have provided if used in some alternative project or program. These net benefits are, therefore, the opportunity costs of the project or program undertaken (see Little and Mirrlees, 1974). Most econometric studies, particularly those with more complex structures, illustrate the point of view of the predominance of adverse effects of military expenditures on economic growth. Also, those few exercises oriented toward illustrating the dominance of favorable effects of military expenditures do not show robust results (for a review of the econometric work on the subject, see Grobar and Porter, 1987). Nevertheless, these quantitative studies do not prove anything; they simply constitute

illustrations of theoretical arguments that are expressed in the specification of econometric models.

7. Military expenditures generate facilities to produce security services and, therefore, can be considered a special category of macroeconomic investment.

8. For a discussion of the dual nature of investment, see Domar (1957). For a more recent treatment of the role of capital investment in the process of economic growth, see Jorgensen and Landau (1990).

9. A common view in economic theory is that in capitalist economies, military expenditures must compensate for the lack of private investment and consumption and, consequently, must be conceptually differentiated from other expenditure components. According to this view, the end of the laissez-faire phase of capitalism produced a tendency to underinvest and underconsume. Full employment would require state intervention to generate compensatory demand. This reasoning, however, is incomplete. What produces the underinvestment and depresses aggregate demand is the expected low profitability of planned investment. Accordingly, military expenditures are promoted with a view to maintain political stability, create a safe environment for business activities, and, thereby, improve profit expectations in the economy as a whole.

10. Benoit (1973) distinguishes three channels through which military expenditures have an adverse influence on economic growth: (1) income effect—increases in the military expenditures–GDP ratio produce a one-period reallocation of investment funds toward the military sector; (2) investment effect—as a consequence of the income effect, increases in the military expenditures–GDP ratio lower the future production of investment and consumption goods; (3) productivity effect—the reduction in the supply of production of capital goods produces a decrease in the intensity of capital in the civilian sector and, therefore, in the productivity component of economic growth.

11. The outward transfer of resources corresponds to the nonfactor current account surplus, which is equivalent to the excess of gross domestic savings over gross investment.

12. The original sources of these inflationary effects were the policies oriented toward aggressively promoting exports and supporting the service of the foreign debt, as well as toward the outward transfer of resources.

NINE

The Political Economy of Military Expenditures in Developing Countries: Establishing Some Empirical Norms

Lewis W. Snider

The question of military spending and its effect on the economic growth of developing countries is bound to remain a serious issue in the emerging post–Cold War world, as the problems of economic adjustment in the developing world continue without prospects for significant improvement and as the living standards of some Third World populations continue to decline. The charge is often leveled that the economic stabilization and adjustment targets of many economically troubled developing countries would be more attainable if the share of government budget allocated to military spending were cut back drastically.[1]

The argument appears valid at first glance. The problem is that it overlooks a critical difference between what constitutes "national security" in the developing world and how that notion is understood in the West, where it is externally oriented toward defending against threats beyond a state's national boundaries. In the developing world, perceived threats to state security often emanate from within national boundaries, and national security often boils down to the regime's political survival, often in the face of domestic opposition that can quickly turn violent. When external threats do exist, they often attain saliency primarily because of the political tensions and social conflicts that usually abound within Third World states (Ayoob, 1991a, 261).

This critical difference in the orientations of national security concerns implies that military spending patterns in the Third World cannot be well understood simply by evaluating the size of the military budget against the existence or severity of external threats. To the extent that national security is equated with fending off domestic challenges to the leadership's political survival, military expenditures are linked closely to distributive issues and to the fine-tuning of political support from key members of the regime's support coalition. One such constituency is the military. The distributive aspects of

159

military spending might be most noticeable in those Third World countries in which domestic military production is viewed as a critical sector of the industrialization program. We cannot infer that some Third World countries are "overspending" without taking into account the domestic political orientation of their security policy.

The question is, how can we know if a government is spending more than it "should" on its military establishment? Any answer is highly subjective: *Should* in relation to *what*—the budget shares devoted to social welfare, the country's need for investment in civilian infrastructure, or the gravity of its internal and external security threats? Even if we could be certain that a Third World government is devoting about what it should to military spending, how do we know if the country's economy can sustain that level of expenditure?

We do not have to agree on which set of norms to use in evaluating Third World military expenditures. What matters is that we can select a set of empirically based criteria to suit the purpose of our analysis. These can be used to generate an "expected" share of government budget or national product devoted to the military, compared with what other countries with similar rankings on these criteria would be predicted to spend on the average. A ratio of actual military spending to expected military spending provides a reasonably exact assessment of whether the military's share of the government budget or consumption of national product is too high or about right, given the evaluation criteria posited. The approach also provides sufficient flexibility to enable us to take into account some of the real-world political, economic, or structural complexities that may affect the shares of national resources devoted to the military but that are hard to incorporate systematically into more conventional analyses.

Military Spending and the Politics of Adjustment

Stabilization Versus Structural Adjustment

Gaining an understanding of the impact of military spending on the politics of economic adjustment becomes easier when we remember that long-term structural adjustment involves an uneasy merging of austerity, which is a by-product of short-term stabilization packages, with economic liberalization, which is associated with long-term structural change. This is a politically combustible combination. The politics of stabilization may not impinge directly upon the interests of the military, but the politics of structural adjustment will, particularly if building a domestic weapons production capability is part of the country's industrialization strategy and if the civilian government depends upon the military for political support against domestic threats to the regime.

Economic stabilization is essentially a short-term quick-fix package of measures designed to remedy a foreign exchange shortage, which is essentially a problem of liquidity. The standard set of instruments includes fiscal austerity, credit ceilings, and increased domestic interest rates—remedies that basically involve the manipulation of prices. More drastic measures include currency devaluations and the reduction of subsidies or price supports, which have the advantage of being largely within the control of the central government's economic authorities (ministry of finance or the central bank) and of yielding a high degree of compliance.

The politics of stabilization is relatively easy to manage, the outbreak of public protests over wage freezes or reduced food and fuel subsidies notwithstanding. Determined governments with average political capacity can usually contain or ride out such protests and proceed with the stabilization program. Because stabilization measures are "temporary," political strategies designed to neutralize opposition are not too costly. These include persuading the public to undergo short-term sacrifices for their own longer-term benefit and for that of the country as a whole and obfuscating which groups or classes may have to bear most of the burden of austerity. Most important, they require no institution-building.

Military spending is not likely to be affected by stabilization programs. Spending on weapons and equipment is usually a capital expenditure involving a multiyear commitment. Forces are not demobilized, because doing so would release more young people and intensify the competition for jobs in the civilian sector. Lifting or reducing price supports and subsidies is usually confined to civilian consumption items, not to state-owned enterprises and other industries, so domestic military production is not affected. Further, most governments prudently realize that they may need the armed forces to quell large-scale public disturbances if mass protests get out of hand.

By contrast, the politics of structural adjustment involves the politics of the long term and addresses the more fundamental issue of solvency. Adjustment measures include privatization of state-owned enterprises, liberalization of trade restrictions, deregulation of commerce, and tax reform. Emphasis is on altering patterns of domestic investment (usually shifting investment from the "nontradeables" sector to "tradeables"), making production more efficient (cutting costs and payrolls), and revising development strategies. In effect, this means shifting domestic investment from import-substituting industries to export-oriented industries, thereby changing the distribution of political winners and losers in a society. The ultimate long-term objective is to achieve sustained economic growth, and for many Third World countries, making economic growth the centerpiece of macroeconomic policy may be a politically hazardous undertaking.

Most important, structural adjustment involves altering the role of the state in society and in the economy. Adjustment policies are not largely or even partially under the control of the central government. In countries that have parliaments, most adjustment measures—such as trade liberalization, deregulation of commerce, the privatization of public-sector enterprises, and tax reform—require legislative approval. Implementing these reforms requires the cooperation of a number of government agencies whose directors and staffs may not understand, or may fundamentally oppose, the reforms. Successful implementation usually requires the active cooperation of elements of the private sector that, based on past experience, distrust the government and prefer to do nothing. Moreover, because the adjustment process is protracted, opportunities abound for those who stand to lose—inside and outside the government—to organize and to form coalitions to block change. Prospective coalition partners can include disgruntled elements in the military as occurred in Argentina in 1990 and in Venezuela in 1992.

Military Expenditures, Economic Structures, and the Political Objectives of Macroeconomic Policy

The belief that military expenditures must be detrimental to economic growth fails to consider the possibility that the political aims of macroeconomic policy in many developing countries often nullify the objective of economic growth, no matter how little or how much the government spends on the military.[2] The politicization of macroeconomic policy, however, is one of degree. Political leaders generally tend to view public expenditures as key policy instruments, but economic growth usually remains an overriding, if not the primary, objective of macroeconomic policy. Politically weak governments, however, may use public expenditures for direct fine-tuning of the polity rather than for promotion of economic growth.[3] The targets of this fine-tuning can include social classes, specific regions, party activists, or specific political elites—any group in a position to contribute to the political survival of the incumbent leadership.

In many developing countries the military is one such constituency. The share of the budget allocated to military spending may serve as an indication of the importance of the military in a country's politics. By contrast, military expenditures as a percentage of gross national product (GNP) reflect the share of national resources being absorbed by the military, which may be offset by the value of military production in relation to GNP and foreign currency earned from arms exports. Other indicators of government attempts at political fine-tuning are the budget shares allocated to subsidies and to wages and salaries of government employees.

Government expenditures on subsidies are usually aimed at keeping the prices of essential goods and services within the means of the ordinary citizen, particularly during periods of high inflation. In countries in which bureaucrats compose an important fraction of the politically active population, the active expansion of civil service positions may coincide directly with increases in the share of public expenditures allocated to government consumption. When the military plays a political role unrelated to its formally declared mission of external defense, its share of central government expenditures may be noticeably higher than expected, particularly if the country is not facing a serious external security threat. [In many developing countries the government's ability to mobilize and direct the human and material resources under its nominal control in pursuit of national objectives is weak. In such polities, the military, along with civil servants and parastatal managers, constitute powerful and privileged constituencies that are able to influence government policy in their own interests, not through the channels prescribed in constitutional documents but by the incorporation of their interests into the government itself.]

[Politically weak governments may show unexpectedly high levels of military spending and external debt, particularly if part of their foreign borrowing was used to finance the purchase of weapons abroad.[4] Levels of defense spending may not be related to any urgent external threat to these countries' national security but may result from problems of domestic political insecurity. Politically weak governments with high levels of military spending may also characterize countries in which real political authority does not reside where it is formally declared to rest—with the civilian government. In such cases the military may be both an important political player in a country's domestic politics and an important source of political stability and support for the regime. Therefore, higher than expected levels of military spending may reflect government efforts to ensure the loyalty of the military. [This is not uncommon, because the principal threats to national security in the developing world often originate within national boundaries rather than coming from external sources.]

Domestic Arms Production and the Civilian Economy

Even when macroeconomic policy promotes growth, uncovering the relationships between economic structure and military expenditures is complicated by the fact that military spending serves several purposes [Investment in domestic military production, for example, may produce results similar to those of other kinds of industrialization if domestic defense industries have an impact on increasing the availability of foreign exchange that can be used for other purposes. Increased exchange availability can come about through increases in foreign exchange earned through the export of domestically produced military equipment. Arms exports may also improve a country's terms of trade by increasing the share of total exports that are manufactures as opposed to primary commodities. Foreign exchange availability can also improve as a result of declines in the amount of foreign currency spent on imported weapons.[5]

Countries with a domestic arms production capability should be less dependent upon imports of some classes of weapons and other military equipment to maintain a given level of military expenditure. The lower import content per dollar of military spending should also give Third World arms-producing countries a stronger military expenditure income multiplier and, hence, have a more positive impact on growth (Looney, 1989c, 36). However, defense industrialization itself depends upon the state of technological expertise in the civilian industrial sectors (Ball, 1988, 357–361).

Reducing dependence on arms imports or increasing arms exports may have a negative net impact on economic growth and may worsen a developing country's external debt situation if its arms industry is limited to assembling imported components in turnkey plants erected by foreign suppliers.[6] Absent the requisite civilian industrial infrastructure to support domestic military production, the net effect of increasing arms exports as a percentage of total exports may be the same as increasing arms imports in relation to total imports. As a rule, this sort of capital import produces no earning stream of its own.

Defense industrialization may also affect expenditures in nonmilitary categories. Robert Looney reports significant differences between arms-producing and nonarms-producing countries in the way military expenditures interact with expenditures allocated for social and economic purposes. The very existence of a domestic arms industry apparently affects the budgetary process in arms-producing countries in a manner that does not occur in nonarms-producing countries (Looney, 1988a, 159–168). In a later study, Looney (1989c) reported that the possession of an indigenous arms industry exerts political pressure to maintain relatively high and stable levels of military spending. Hence, defense spending in these countries is less susceptible to reductions in the absence of any serious external security threat than are the spending levels in nonarms-producing countries. The latter do not appear to face the same political pressures to maintain high levels of defense expenditures in the absence of external threats simply to maintain employment in defense plants (Looney, 1989c, 33–46). A critical link between domestic arms production and levels of military spending is the subsidies absorbed by domestic arms industries.

Domestic military production and structural adjustment. Domestic arms industries almost always depend upon direct government subsidies, without which they would be unable to operate. The effect is to enlarge the share of the economy in which prices are controlled and not driven by market forces. The larger the size of this controlled price sector (as measured by direct subsidies as a percentage of gross domestic product [GDP]), the greater the barrier it poses to successful adjustment.[7]

Subsidies are not only a drain on public finances and an engine of fiscal deficits. Generally, the larger the percentage of GDP absorbed by subsidies, the larger the share of public resources that cannot be reallocated from the nontradeable goods sector to promote the tradeable goods sector. Hence, subsides are also a serious barrier to successful structural adjustment. To the extent that domestic arms production consumes a large share of government subsidies, any attempt to reduce or remove such subsidies will likely be actively opposed by the military and its civilian supporters. Further, there is no reason to expect that direct subsidies will decline as domestic arms industries expand both their capabilities and the domestic content of the equipment they produce.

Classifying military production capabilities. One index that ranks developing countries' military production capabilities is the classification scheme developed by Herbert Wulf (1983, 232–328).[8] It is based on indices of a country's industrial capacity (based on six key industries that are needed to support arms production) and a "manpower base" (the number of people employed in these key industries and the total number of scientists, engineers, and technicians engaged in research and development). "Minimal" producers are those that are engaged in some arms production but whose civilian industrial capacity and technological skills are insufficient to develop an effective arms industry. The net effect of these countries' production on their military budgets is probably minor. Countries whose industrial capacity and manpower skills are adequate for the simple assembly of weapons but that are not capable of more extensive production are classified as "assembly" producers. The net effect of these countries' military production and arms exports on their military spending could be about the same as increasing their arms imports as a percentage of total imports. Hence, an "assembly" capability would also be expected to increase the military's share of the central government budget.

"Diversified" arms producers have the industrial capacity and the manpower base, including the ability to incorporate new technologies and to apply research and development, to engage in extensive and diversified weapons production. This capability ranges from the capacity to produce basic components of a weapons system designed by a foreign supplier to the ability to engage in final assembly of the end item. It includes, at a minimum, a capacity to indigenously design and manufacture weapons using all domestic components. Very few countries possess this capacity for more than a few types of major military weapons. The military and arms exports of this group of producers could conceivably produce a significant offsetting effect on a country's external debt or debt-service burden.

The top ten Third World arms exporters for the period 1982–1986 are diversified arms-producing countries that are ranked based on the value of their arms exports in constant (1985) prices.[9] Increasing these countries' arms exports in relation to total exports may not produce a significant net offsetting effect on their military expenditures or on the dollar value of their arms imports. All are engaged in ambitious weapons production programs that involve importing specialized components or advanced technologies, and many require heavy government subsidies to continue operation.[10]

Political Strength, Military Expenditures, and Economic Adjustment

The links between Third World countries' defense expenditures and domestic insecurity, on the one hand, and the ability of these governments to implement structural adjustment policies, on the other, originate in their political performance as reflected in (1) the level of the government's political capacity—the ability to extract resources from society and to redirect them for state purposes; (2) the share of government expenditures allocated to subsidies and government consumption, mentioned earlier; and (3) the equality with which the burdens and benefits of society are distributed, as reflected in tax structures. Political inability to extract more revenues from society to meet the demands placed upon government by elites and various social groups is one reason many Third World governments resorted to extensive foreign borrowing in the 1970s and 1980s. Political constraints on a government's capacity to reallocate and redirect public resources are one major impediment to its ability to sustain stabilization measures and adjustment policies and to achieve economic growth.

Threat, Growth, and Politics: A Missing Link?

The existence of an external or internal security threat undoubtedly exerts a decisive influence on increasing the average share of central government expenditures allocated to the military sector. Yet, increases in military expenditures in response to national emergencies may increase the resources available for civilian spending. This can occur if a national emergency triggered by an external or internal security threat prompts the government to strengthen its tax system. Nicole Ball (1988) suggests that such threats may stimulate the government to be more efficient in mobilizing the country's resources through more effective taxation in its eagerness to supplement the armed forces' budget. In times of crisis, the population may be more disposed to accept changes in the tax system it would normally resist in the absence of a security threat (Ball, 1988, 207–210). The government may be able to take advantage of such circumstances to raise additional revenue to finance projects in the civilian sector, particularly if the level of taxation does not return to the precrisis level when the emergency has ended and military expenditures may have declined or leveled off. If so, the increased tax effort may improve the political strength of the government with respect to the elites and other organized constituencies that form the basis for its political power. However, if a politically weak government is heavily dependent upon the military to defend it against *internal* challenges, the military could easily become another political constituency with its own agenda.

The Politics of Adjustment and Military Expenditures

The question of who will bear how much of the burden of putting the country's economic house in order is politically threatening to debtor governments. Political strength is often a prerequisite to successful stabilization and adjustment programs. The weaker the government is politically, the more likely it will be to take the position that the existing winners and losers represent the only possible political equilibrium. Hence, the impact of imperatives of adjustment on the size of defense budgets is not clear-cut.

When a developing country faces a serious external threat, the exigency of national security may override the pressures of adjustment. However, the most serious threats to national security originate within the country and sometimes within the armed forces themselves. The series of attempts by military units in 1988 and 1989 to overthrow the government of Corazon Aquino in the Philippines while fighting the New People's Army and armed Muslim guerrillas (the Bangsa Moro Army) underscores this point. A similar problem confronted the government of Carlos Andrés Pérez in Venezuela twice during 1992.[1] The less the central government is able to mobilize and direct the human and material resources under its nominal control, the more it may have to rely on a proliferation of state security and military agencies, not only to check domestic unrest but also to act as a counterweight to the regular military forces.

In states with limited abilities to mobilize society's resources or to logistically implement government decisions, the proliferation of government agencies serves a security purpose in addition to that of expanding the number of appointments and additional conduits for channeling patronage. Creating agencies with overlapping functions limits the prerogatives of any single arm of the state; however, the regime relies upon these same state agencies to enforce security, perform essential services, and implement government policy. Therefore, national leaders cannot impair these mechanisms too severely, or they will be unable to perform the tasks necessary for the state's and the regime's survival.

One way to cope with this problem is to extend state influence over large businesses and other large organizations whose products earn badly needed foreign currency or whose products and services directly benefit the regime. These groups can be bought off with subsidies, discriminatory tax policies, and protection against foreign competition. Thus, it is possible that the more a weak government depends upon the military to ensure its political security, and the larger the share of GNP absorbed by the military, the more such a government will need to subsidize nonstate organizations to counterbalance an essential but potentially threatening state security apparatus. The cumulative effect, however, is to expand the controlled price sector and, thus, to undermine the objectives of economic adjustment.

Political Strength and Tax Structures

The ability of the central government to extract human and material resources from society is measured by its relative political capacity based on its tax collections. The government's ability to mobilize and allocate the nation's resources is reflected in the country's tax structures. Differentials in tax structures based on ease of collection reflect an important distinction between strong and weak states: the ability of governments to implement domestic adjustments to external economic shocks and how the burden of that adjustment may be distributed. Tax structures reflect a government's ability to penetrate society, in the sense of establishing its presence throughout the territory under its nominal control to the exclusion of competing authorities, and to coordinate society's activities through its own infrastructure.[12] If a government cannot effectively utilize and redirect society's resources to achieve national objectives, it will concentrate on mobilizing whatever resources it does control, which are generally those that directly affect the fewest domestic groups.

Many Third World governments face severe political constraints against altering current tax structures, which usually favor the wealthy at the expense of those with earned incomes. Political leaders understandably want to avoid antagonizing those groups that are the foundation of their political support. Hence, many governments rely disproportionately on taxes on foreign trade, which generally impinge upon the fewest domestic political groups. Trade taxes are relatively easy to collect, because imports and exports are channeled through centralized port facilities. Therefore, even with smuggling, corruption, or physical insecurity, tariffs and export taxes are much easier to collect than are direct taxes on personal incomes, profits, and capital gains. Politically weak governments rely heavily on trade taxes precisely because they do not have to be very effective in establishing their authority throughout the country. The more effectively the government has penetrated society, the larger its "mobilization ratio": the share of government revenue extracted in the form of direct taxes versus the proportion of revenue realized from trade taxes.

Heavy reliance upon trade taxes as a source of revenue creates a vicious circle. The greater the share of tax revenues collected from the foreign trade sector, the more the government's revenues are susceptible to shocks and unfavorable changes in the international economy. These include falling world commodity prices, rapidly rising interest rates in the Eurocurrency market, or the drying up of credit in foreign capital markets. Heavily indebted developing countries that depend upon trade taxes will be severely hampered in undertaking any sort of structural adjustment. Dependence upon trade taxes reflects a narrow tax base; the narrower the tax base the less able the government is to mobilize society's resources, and the more it may have to rely upon the military as an instrument of political survival.

Political Capacity, Tax Structures, and Military Expenditures

The lower the mobilization ratio, the higher the share of the central government budget allocated to the military. Generally, the relative size of Third World military budgets is a function of past domestic insurgencies and international conflicts. Weak governments must weigh their need for effectiveness of the state apparatus and national security against the risks to their own political survival through creating agencies that can become power centers capable of impeding government initiatives. In weak states the military is often needed to support the government against domestic challenges to its authority. Yet, it is military and security agencies that have often posed the most serious challenges to political leaders.

One option in checking this threat is to create two or more military forces to serve as counterweights to one another. Competing security agencies may take the form of special elite units, "people's militias," "home guards," or special border security units. Thus, political weakness may compound the problems of external debt service and economic adjustment. The government is constrained from reallocating public resources to address the pressures of economic adjustment; further, the military budget may be difficult to pare back if it is related more to the regime's political survival than to a serious external threat to national security.

Economic Constraints on Military Expenditures

Apart from political survival, increases in the defense budget's share of government expenditures would be expected to be driven by the amount spent on arms imports, the costs of which are related to the presence of an external threat to national security when such a threat is perceived to exist. If developing countries have built up domestic arms industries and export part of their military production, the size of the defense budget may be partly offset by (1) the value of military production in relation to GDP if this production contributes to military import substitution and (2) the foreign exchange earned by arms exports.[13] In such cases, the value of military production and arms exports may in effect represent an additional subsidy to the military and would actually contribute to increasing the size of the defense budget.

Modeling the Political Economy of Military Expenditures

To summarize, understanding the political economy of military expenditures in developing countries is not the same as accounting for variation in the share of the central government budget absorbed by military spending.[14] Rather, it involves looking at how political weakness, distributive politics, and domestic and external security concerns combine to affect military spending in relation to total central government budget and GNP. Hence, the model must include a *political* dimension, an *economic* or *structural* dimension, and a *security* dimension.

The Dependent Variables

The share of government spending devoted to military spending usually shows much wider variation over time and across countries than the share of GNP absorbed by the military. The military's share of the total budget is undoubtedly more sensitive to episodic internal security problems such as insurgencies and mild forms of domestic political violence. It can also be expected to be affected by distributive issues such as competing claims by the civilian sector for scarce public resources.

By contrast, military expenditures as a percentage of GNP should reflect longer-term structural characteristics. The share of government expenditures allocated to the military may be increasing in relation to the size of total government spending; but if the economy is experiencing steady, sustained economic growth, an expanding military budget will not likely have the same social impact as would be the case if GNP were experiencing zero or negative growth. Military spending as a percentage of GNP should also be more responsive to structural characteristics, such as the level of economic development and the share of GDP generated by military production, and to the legacy of a country's involvement in interstate wars and less to bouts of domestic political violence than the military's share of total government spending.

Causal Variables: The Political Dimension

The political dimension addresses the perennial political problem facing most Third World governments: that of balancing the simultaneous demands for political legitimation and economic development, on the one hand, with a low capacity for extracting resources from society in the face of domestic resistance in order to finance those demands, on the other. This was one of the principal motivations for much Third World borrowing in international capital markets. Countries that are the most highly indebted are usually the weakest politically.

The average external debt of countries the World Bank classifies as "severely indebted" countries (SICs) is significantly *lower* than that of other Third World borrowers in relation to exports of goods and services and as a percentage of GNP. What makes these countries severely indebted is their considerably higher debt-service ratios in general and their interest payments as a percentage of export earnings in particular.[15] As a group, their average political capacity is lower than that of other heavily indebted developing countries. The SICs generally devote more public spending to subsidies and to government consumption, wages, and salaries. These traits suggest that underlying structural conditions, not external debt levels, may distinguish the SICs from other debtors.[16] None of the SICs fought an interstate war during the 1974–1986 period.[17] As a group, the SICs allocate a significantly higher share of their government budget to the military than do the non-SICs. Because the SICs' mobilization capacity-cum-tax structure appears to be significantly different from that of the other debtor countries, this subset serves as a comparison group with the entire thirty-five-country population (see note 15 at end of this chapter).

The political dimension addresses the possibility that the primary mission of many Third World military forces is that of supporting the government against potential domestic threats including insurgencies and coups d'état. These requirements are met by including two indicators of the government's political strength: relative political capacity (RPC), reflecting the state's extractive capability,[18] and tax structure, representing the state's mobilization capability. The latter is the ratio of the share of total government revenue from direct taxes on income and profits divided by the share from taxes on trade and international transactions.[19] It is referred to hereafter as the mobilization ratio.

The combination of governmental political weakness and a sense of insecurity with respect to the country's armed forces is often expressed by having two or more military forces serve as counterweights to one another. The greater the number of competing security agencies—such as special elite units, people's militias, "home guards," or special paramilitary and border security units—the more precarious the government may view its position with respect to the armed forces. The severely indebted countries, for example, have a significantly higher number of such forces than the other countries in this study. Further, these forces are noticeably larger relative to the regular military. The larger the number of competing military units, the greater the military's share of central government expenditures.[20] This variable underscores how national security may equate with political survival in many developing countries.

To the extent that political weakness and arms imports contribute to increasing foreign borrowing, political weakness compounds the problems of external debt service and adjustment by raising the shares of government budget and national product allocated to military spending.[21] Thus, arms imports are logically included in the security dimension, but as with the proliferation of security organizations outside the control of the defense ministry, they often contribute to the political security of the government.

The politicization of macroeconomic policy is crudely reflected in a government's spending priorities in the form of the budget shares devoted to salaries and wages of government employees and to subsidies. Government consumption and expenditures on government employees' salaries are concentrated in the civilian sector. If government bureaucracies must compete with the military for scarce resources, the competition should be reflected in a strong inverse relationship between the share of government budget devoted to government salaries and the military's share of public resources in relation to total government spending.[22] Subsidies not only include price supports for staples such as food, fuel, and transportation; they also reflect the size of the controlled price sector, which can include a country's domestic arms industries. If so, the larger the amount of public resources allocated to subsidies as a percentage of GDP, the larger the military budget's share of central government expenditures. The relationship, however, is indirect; it is mediated by the value of military production as a percentage of GDP.

Causal Variables: The Economic Dimension

As earlier discussion suggests, military spending is shaped in part by a country's arms production capability based on its level of industrialization. These structural characteristics must be included in the models tested here. The level of industrialization affects the size of the national resource base that could be made available for military purposes. The level of arms production capability can make a difference in whether the military industrial sector is just one more "white elephant" parastatal operation that provides employment to the country's work force or whether it is capable of contributing positively to the country's foreign exchange reserves and growth in the civilian economy.

Similarly, the share of GNP absorbed by the military (through subsidies and direct military spending) is conditioned by the general level of economic development. Per capita income is an adequate indicator of economic development levels in industrial societies, because it reflects differences in the resources a government can mobilize. It is an inadequate measure for developing nations, many of which still depend heavily on subsistence farming and are barely semi-industrialized and in which market and nonmarket economies often exist side by side. In such countries the real productivity of the population is higher than national accounts register. Therefore, the agricultural share of GDP is a more accurate indicator of economic development levels when working with the differentiated collection of countries that constitute the developing world.

Causal Variables: The Security Dimension

The security dimension of military spending cannot be considered in isolation from the political economy of military expenditures. From the point of view of the government, political survival often cuts to the heart of security in the Third World. The political and security dimensions should not be considered mutually exclusive on either empirical or theoretical grounds. Hence, the number of paramilitary organizations can represent the security, as well as the political, dimension. Because there is reason to suspect that the presence of an external threat may help strengthen a government vis-à-vis society by improving its extractive capabilities, it is reasonable to believe that the higher a government's political capacity, the larger the percentage of national resources (GNP) devoted to military spending. This would certainly be expected for countries such as Israel, India, Egypt, and Korea, which have faced continuing external threats and have fought severe interstate wars. Domestic insurgencies should exert upward pressures on the size of the military budget for similar reasons.

The cumulative frequency of involvement in interstate wars, and the presence or absence of a domestic insurgency and the frequency of various forms of domestic political instability (political protest demonstrations, political strikes, riots, or deaths from domestic political violence) are used to represent the magnitude of external and domestic security problems. In times of national emergency—real or contrived—populations are more disposed to accept changes in the tax system that they would normally resist in the absence of a security threat. The government becomes more efficient in mobilizing the country's resources, initially in order to supplement the armed forces' budget. Taxes seldom return to their precrisis levels, even when the emergency has passed and military expenditures have declined or leveled off. In other words, the national emergencies on which the government acts create a ratchet effect in the government's extractive and mobilization capabilities. Therefore, the more often a country becomes involved in an interstate war, the higher should be the share of GNP devoted to military spending. The more often the government confronts a domestic insurgency and other forms of domestic political violence, the greater should be the percentage of central government expenditures commanded by the military.

Another area in which the political, economic, and security dimensions overlap concerns the volume of arms imports as a percentage of total imports.[23] Arms imports must be paid for in hard currency. The fact that a country has a domestic arms production capability does not mean that arms imports will automatically decrease as a percentage of total imports, for at least two reasons. First, domestic arms production is unlikely to meet all of a country's weapons needs, particularly when advanced combat aircraft, missiles, and armored fighting vehicles are concerned. Second, a domestic arms industry may be a white elephant if the civilian economy lacks the technological infrastructure to support it. In that case, some countries would switch from importing finished military products to assembling various components and kits domestically. This would still require a substantial outlay of foreign exchange for military imports.

The Structure of the Model

The combination of exogenous and endogenous causal variables requires a two-stage least squares model to capture the immediate political, structural, and security determinants of military spending while simultaneously taking into account the effects of autonomous security imperatives and the degree of arms production capability within each country. To this list must be added the distributive attributes of public spending that may be an important source of domestic social conflict. The first stage specifies the exogenous and endogenous political, economic, and national security determinants of military spending. These are represented by variables such as the size of the government deficit as a percentage of GDP the previous year $(_{t-1})$, previous commitments to subsidies and to government salaries, the level of industrialization, and the number of interstate wars fought since independence. The second stage specifies the immediate determinants of military spending. It incorporates the direct effects of government patronage (budget shares devoted to government salaries) and the direct and indirect effects of governments' political capacity, their mobilization capabilities, the military industrial complex, and security imperatives.

Assessing the cumulative impact of political capacity, structural attributes, and internal and external security pressures on military expenditures cannot be limited to one regression equation; rather, a system of equations using a combination of variables is needed to model the political, economic, and security relationships discussed earlier. Some of the causal variables are determined by forces outside of (exogenous to) the model. Other explanatory variables are at least partly determined by causal factors incorporated in (endogenous to) the model. Two such variables are arms imports as a percentage of total imports and the value of military production as a percentage of GDP. These must be estimated separately, because some of the variables that help to explain their behavior also account for much of the variation in military spending.

Endogenous Causal Factors: Arms Imports and Military Production

Apart from the frequency with which a developing country has been involved in war, the value of arms imports as a percentage of total imports may be a response to domestic security concerns and political instability reflected in the frequency of various forms of domestic violence. If so, politically weak governments may be the heaviest importers. Additionally, such governments were often those that borrowed from abroad the most heavily in the 1970s and 1980s. Military imports are thought to have contributed significantly to some developing countries' economic problems, particularly if they resorted to foreign borrowing to pay for those imports. In such cases, arms imports would increase as a percentage of total imports in response to external borrowing.

A large share of the military imports of countries with domestic arms industries may consist of weapons components and subassemblies. We cannot make any inferences concerning the content of a country's military from its monetary value. However, when Third World arms industries are well established, those countries usually export a large volume of what they produce, because few indigenous military establishments can absorb all of what is produced. If a significant share of a country's military imports is used in its own domestic arms industries, the value of military imports should be driven by the value its arms exports add to the total volume of exported manufactured goods. The arms imports of countries that are diversified arms producers or that are among the top ten Third World arms exporters should constitute a significantly smaller share of total imports compared with countries with minimal or no military production capabilities.

The impact of domestic arms production on military spending, and on the prospects for long-term economic adjustment in turn, is also conditioned by a variety of factors, some of which also affect military spending directly. Among the more prominent of these is the role military industries play in a country's industrialization plans, as reflected in the value of military spending as a percentage of gross domestic investment and in its aggregate level of economic development. In addition, the actual and intended effects of policy are often very different. If military expenditures are used to achieve domestic political objectives, they can also contribute to the perverse outcomes of policy. An example is the degree to which prior military expenditures and prior gross domestic investment may complement each other or work at cross-purposes to produce unforeseen effects on the economy. When military spending is part of the warp and woof of a country's industrial strategy, the higher the ratio of military spending to gross domestic investment (as percentages of GDP), the greater could be the drag military spending produces on the economy. Such would be the case if military production absorbs an important share of domestic savings that would otherwise be devoted to investment in the civilian sector.

Presumably, the level of production capability not only generates distributive political pressures on government policies, but the volume of domestic military production (as a percentage of GDP) may be used by the military to justify larger shares of public spending. These pressures may be reflected not only in the military budget but in the amount of public expenditures devoted to direct subsidies. Military production usually depends heavily upon direct subsidies. Subsidies, along with the value of whatever share of gross domestic savings may be diverted to military industrialization, are two manifestations of a potential clash between the politics of national security and that of economic adjustment.

Research Design

The research design is a cross-section pooled time series design, which permits valid generalizations concerning a large, representative sample of countries (space) across time (several years for each country). This is the only way to generate a valid measure based on the comparative extractive performance of a large number of countries across a wide variety of resource bases (space) across several years for each country. The data set consists of thirty-five countries covering the period 1974–1986.

The pooled time series structure, however, creates statistical problems arising from the possibility of autocorrelated error terms within each country and heteroscedastic disturbances (unequal variances) across a group of countries at any one point in time.[24] Ordinary least squares regression is not suited to a pooled time series data set, because it cannot simultaneously control for heteroscedastic disturbances in the cross-sectional analysis and control for autocorrelation in the error terms in the time series. Consequently, tests for serial correlation such as the Durbin-Watson d statistic often yield unreliable results. In addition, the d statistic is not appropriate when lagged values of the dependent variable are included as an independent variable, as is the case here. The most serious problem concerns the ambiguous definition of "degrees of freedom" in the cross-sectional pooled time series structure.[25] The possible confounding effects of serial correlation (trend) on military spending can be isolated by including time (year of observation) as a variable. However, this does not address the problem of multicolinearity and heteroscedastic disturbances in the cross-sectional analysis.

One straightforward way to address this problem is to include a version of the dependent variable, Y, at the previous time period (Y_{t-1}), which is correlated with the current value of Y (Y_t) but uncorrelated with current and prior values of X. The variable is called an instrumental variable (Y^*_{t-1}). It is generated by regressing the dependent variable on the causal variables in the current time period and in the previous year $(X_{1t}, X_{1t-1} \ldots X_{nt}, X_{nt-1})$. This yields a predicted value of Y, Y^*_t. The latter variable is then lagged by one year to provide Y^*_{t-1}. It is inserted in the regression in place of the original Y_{t-1}. The resultant instrumental variable will yield consistent parameter estimates, because both Y^*_{t-1} and the other explanatory variables are uncorrelated with the error term.[26] This is the case because the explanatory variables (X_t and Y^*_t) are now uncorrelated with the contemporaneous error terms ($\hat{e}_t$). The method is commonly referred to as "pseudo-generalized least squares" or "estimated generalized least squares" (EGLS).

This approach is based on the assumption that X_{t-1} is not correlated with the error term in the ordinary least squares (OLS) regression and is likely to be correlated Y_{t-1}. The problem is that the effects of trend can be distributed over more than the time point immediately preceding the current period. In addition, states have generally increased the share of national product they have been able to extract over time. As this share has increased, so has the size of the public sector. Therefore, the variable "Year" was added to control for these cumulative trend effects.

Data Analysis

The main purpose of the data analysis is not to account for as much variation as possible in military expenditures but to explain as much variation as possible using a particular set of criteria to establish a benchmark of "normal" military spending. The next step is to use the predicted values derived from the data analysis to determine if the military expenditures of particular Third World countries are close to this norm or are much higher. This is a straightforward way of assessing the degree to which countries may be overspending on the military, given the mix of political, economic, and security constraints and pressures we would expect to account for a significant amount of military expenditures in relation to total government spending or GNP.

Because the effects of political strength, economic performance, and social structure must be analyzed within the context of previous spending commitments, autonomous economic forces and history of external warfare, and the endogenous effects of arms imports and military production, the coefficients for the equations are estimated using two-stage least squares.[27] The data analysis begins by estimating the parameters for the endogenous causal variables.

Arms Imports as a Percentage of Total Imports

Table 9.1 shows the impact of political weakness, external security problems, and military production on arms imports in relation to total imports. The regression constant is usually interpreted as the average value of the arms imports as a percentage of central government expenditures if the values of the causal variables were equal to zero. The coefficient for the constant indicates that military imports would average 1.6 percent of total imports if the influence of the causal variables specified in Table 9.1 were zero. This compares to an actual mean of 3.97 percent. The variable "Y-Hat Arms Imports . . ." is the instrumental variable Y^*_{t-1} described under "Research Design."

The t-ratios in Table 9.1 support the proposition that the political weakness of governments helps drive military imports. A 1 percent decrease in a government's mobilization ratio can increase arms imports about one-half of 1 percent in relation to total imports.[28] Some indirect effects of political weakness on arms imports are evident in the resort to foreign borrowing to pay for a portion of military imports.

Arms imports are responsive to both internal and external security problems, as well as to the political weakness of the government. For every war the country has fought since independence, arms imports increase by an average of 1.8 percent (b = 1.834). Arms imports are almost equally responsive to increases in domestic political violence, as indicated by the magnitude of the beta coefficient for the natural log of political strikes and the t-ratio.

The import-substitution effect of military production emerges from the coefficients for the dichotomous variables grouped under domestic arms production capability. The regression coefficients and the t-ratios of the dichotomous variables are interpreted in terms of their relationship to the comparison group, represented by the "(dropped)" category. The military imports of countries that either possess a "diversified" arms production capability or are among the "top ten" arms exporters are significantly lower in relation to their total imports than countries with minimal or no domestic military production capability.

Nevertheless, the net import-substitution effect of arms exports may be ephemeral for most Third World producers. Every 1 percent increase in arms exports, in relation to the value of all exported manufactures, produces an average 1.3 percent increase in military imports. The net effect may be the content, rather than the value, of what is imported.

Military Production as a Percentage of GDP

The results in Table 9.2 indicate that to the extent that the expansion of military production requires the mobilization of gross domestic savings and support through direct subsidies, the state's capacity to mobilize and reallocate public resources for this purpose is critical. The results support the argument that the "true" share of national product absorbed by military spending exceeds the total military budget as a percentage of GNP.

Additional resources are consumed by direct subsidies earmarked for military industries. The strength and direction of this relationship bolster the prima facie assumption that the military is often an essential source of political support to the regime. It suggests one way the size of the military budget may be

Table 9.1 Estimating the Endogenous Effect on Arms Imports as a Percentage of Total Imports, 1974–1986

Variable	Coefficient	Beta	t-Ratio	Signif. of t
Constant	1.5896	0.006	1.325	0.186
Log Mobilization Ratio	−0.501	−0.302	−2.448	0.000
Number of Wars	1.834	0.321	2.985	0.003
Log Political Strikes	1.421	0.228	3.595	0.000
Domestic Arms Production Capability				
Assembly Only	0.485	0.001	0.994	0.221
Diversified	−1.632	−0.085	−2.326	0.020
Top Ten	−1.977	−0.033	−2.076	0.038
Minimal/No Capability	(dropped)			
Military Production as % of GDP$_{t-1}$	0.076	0.003	0.548	0.584
Arms Exports as % of Mfg.	1.334	0.165	3.117	0.002
External Debt as % of Exports	0.433	0.215	2.849	0.005
Y-Hat Arms Imports as % Total Imports*$_{t-1}$	−0.800	−0.008	−1.318	0.188

Notes: $R^2 = .34$ $F (10, 44) = 16.55$
Adj. $R^2 = .33$ Prob > F = 0.0000
N of Obs. = 455

R^2	The coefficient of multiple determination.
Adj. R^2	The coefficient of multiple determination adjusted for the degrees of freedom (number of causal variables) and number of observations ("N of Obs.").
$F (10, 444)$	The ratio of the variance accounted for by the linear regression (using 10 degrees of freedom in the numerator) divided by the unexplained variance (444 degrees of freedom in the denominator).
Prob > F	The probability of obtaining a higher F-statistic with the same degrees of freedom by chance (here, less than 1 in 1,000).
Coefficient	The unstandardized regression coefficient.
Beta	The standardized regression coefficient.
t-Ratio	The ratio of the regression coefficient to its standard error.
Signif. of t	The statistical significance level of the t-ratio, using a two-tailed test criterion.
Constant	The constant for the linear regression.
Log Mobilization Ratio	The ratio of revenues from direct taxes (on income and profits) to revenues from taxes on trade and international transactions, both as percentages of total central government revenues.
Number of Wars	Cumulative number of interstate wars fought since year of independence or since 1947 if the country was independent before World War II.
Log Political Strikes	Natural logatrithm of yearly frequency of political strikes.
Domestic Arms Production Capability	Country rank on domestic arms production capability index created by Herbert Wulf, based on six key industries and human technical skills needed to support domestic arms production, compared to developing countries with only minimal or no indigenous capability.

(*continues*)

Table 9.1   (continued)

Military Production as % of GDP$_{t-1}$	The value of domestic production as a percentage of current gross domestic product (GDP) in the previous time period (year).
Arms Exports as % of Mfg. Exports	The value of arms exports as a percentage of the value of total value of exports of manufactured products.
External Debt as % of Exports	Total public and publicly guaranteed external debt as a percentage of exports of goods and services.
Y-Hat Arms Imports as % of Total Imports$_{t-1}$	Instrumental variable for arms imports as a percentage of total imports the previous year.

Table 9.2   Estimating the Endogenous Effect of Military Production as a Percentage of Gross Domestic Product, 1974–1986

Variable	Coefficient	Beta	t-Ratio	Signif. of t
Constant	8.632	0.006	1.440	0.150
Mobilization Ratio$_{t-1}$	0.092	0.105	3.002	0.003
Subsidies as % of GDP	0.081	0.077	2.009	0.045
Gross Domestic Savings as % of GDP	−0.066	−0.086	3.118	0.002
Domestic Arms Production Capability				
Minimal Capability	0.941	0.066	1.643	0.101
Assembly Only	0.027	0.026	1.841	0.066
Diversified	0.307	0.185	1.454	0.147
Top Ten	2.655	0.307	3.749	0.000
No Capability	(dropped)			
Arms Exports as % of Total Exports$_{t-1}$	0.045	0.067	2.748	0.006
Y-Hat Military Production as % of GDP$^{*}_{t-1}$	−0.044	−0.005	−1.472	0.142

Notes: $R^2 = .43$ $F (9, 445) = 41.32$
          Adj. $R^2 = .42$ Prob > F = 0.0000
          N of Obs. = 455

Mobilization Ratio$_{t-1}$	The ratio of revenues from direct taxes (on income and profits) to revenues from taxes on trade and international transactions, both as percentages of total central government revenues in the previous time period (one year).
Subsidies as % of GDP	Direct government subsidies as a percentage of GDP.
Gross Domestic Savings as % of GDP	Gross domestic savings as a percentage of GDP.
Arms Exports as % of Total Exports$_{t-1}$	The previous year's value of arms exports as a percentage of the value of total exports.
Y-Hat Military Production as % of GDP$^{*}_{t-1}$	Instrumental variable for domestic military production as a percentage of GDP the previous year.

linked to other social and economic allocations noted by Looney (1989c).[29] If this is the case, it is useful to ponder how this might work.

We recall that states with a limited capacity to mobilize and direct the population's or society's resources in pursuit of national objectives will tend to counterbalance one state agency with another. This prevents any one arm of the state from becoming an independent power center and forestalls further fragmentation of state social control and possibly a military takeover. The negative relationship between the share of central government expenditures earmarked for the bureaucracy's salaries and the share allocated to military spending probably reflects the competition between two powerful state institutions for public resources (see Migdal, 1988, 209–213). The commitments of larger shares of GDP to the controlled price sector may also reflect governments' ideological predisposition toward state-led industrialization in which domestic arms industries constitute an important part. This is implied in the strength and direction of the relationship between defense spending and military production as a percentage of GDP (Table 9.4).

Domestic military production is also supported by the value of the previous year's arms exports. However, the bulk of Third World military production appears to be concentrated in the top ten Third World arms exporters and, to a lesser extent, in countries with an "assembly only" production capability. Military production appears to absorb an important share of gross domestic savings. A 1 percent increase in gross domestic savings with respect to GDP yields an average drop in military production of around one-half of 1 percent. If, indeed, a tradeoff exists between generating additional domestic savings and expanding domestic military production, the imperatives of adjustment may pose a serious political challenge to any regime that depends upon the military establishment for its political survival.

Military Expenditures as a Percentage of Central Government Expenditures

The results in Table 9.3 suggest that the military's share of total government spending may be more responsive to domestic political and security pressures than to the threat of war from foreign adversaries. In many respects it appears to be an instrument for staving off domestic catastrophe. Involvement in interstate war is felt indirectly through the impact of arms imports on military spending.

The cumulative impact of political strength on military spending is most clearly indicated by the relationships between the mobilization ratio and relative political capacity and military spending. The lower a state's mobilization capability, the larger the military's share of total government budget. Particularly intriguing is the difference in the direction of the relationship between relative political capacity for the entire sample (which is positive) and the subset of SICs, which is negative: The lower a state's political capacity, the larger the share of government spending earmarked for the military. Given the relation-

Table 9.3 Political, Economic, and Security Determinants of Military Expenditures as a Percentage of Central Government Spending, 1974–1986

Variable	Coefficient	Beta	t-Ratio	Signif. of t
Constant	17.584	0.001	0.677	0.499
Mobilization ratio	−0.632	0.145	−2.663	0.008
RPC_{t-1}	1.061	0.241	3.395	0.000
$RPC \times SICs_{t-1}$	−4.238	−0.292	−3.053	0.002
Govt. Wages and Salaries as % of Central Govt. Expenditures	−1.132	−0.046	−2.107	0.036
Number of Paramilitary Organizations	1.722	0.409	3.474	0.000
Log Deaths from Domestic Political Violence	0.483	0.335	2.175	0.030
Insurgency	3.636	0.168	2.454	0.014
Domestic Arms Production Capability				
Assembly Only	0.006	0.005	0.479	0.632
Diversified	0.800	0.372	2.590	0.010
Top Ten	0.230	0.058	1.121	0.263
Minimal/No Capability	(dropped)			
Arms Exports as % of Total Exports$_{t-1}$	1.192	0.233	3.087	0.002
Arms Imports as % of Total Imports$_{t-1}$	0.581	0.275	3.443	0.000
Y-Hat Military Spending as % of Central Govt. Expenditures*$_{t-1}$	0.056	0.003	0.262	0.794

Notes: $R^2 = .45$ $F (13, 441) = 31.19$
Adj. $R^2 = .44$ $Prob > F = 0.0000$
N of Obs. $= 455$

RPC_{t-1} — Relative political capacity (RPC) the previous year.
$RPC \times SICs_{t-1}$ — Relative political capacity (RPC) the previous year for the severely indebted countries (SICs) the previous year.

Govt. Wages and Salaries as % of Central Govt. Expenditures — Government expenditures on wages and salaries as a percentage of central government expenditures.

Number of Paramilitary Organizations — Number of different paramilitary or internal security organizations controlled by the central government.

Log Deaths from Domestic Political Violence — Natural log of annual total number of deaths from all forms of domestic political violence.

Insurgency — Dichotomous variable indicating the years (if any) a country is fighting an insurgency (1 = yes, 0 = no).

Arms Imports as % of Total Imports$_{t-1}$ — The previous year's value of arms imports as a percentage of the value of total imports.

Y-Hat Military Spending as % of Central Govt. Expenditures*$_{t-1}$ — Instrumental variable military expenditures as a percentage of total government expenditures the previous year.

ships between military expenditures and most of the other causal variables, this is easy to understand.

Military spending is strongly and positively related to the proliferation of paramilitary organizations outside of the control of the ministry of defense, to the intensity of domestic political turmoil (represented by the frequency of deaths from political violence), and to the occurrence of domestic insurgencies. The strong connection between the number of security and paramilitary organizations (outside ministry of defense control) and the size of military budgets supports earlier speculation about the political role such formations play in a country's national security structure. Every additional security organization means an average increase of 1.7 percent in the military's budget share. The political role of these organizations appears to address a different type of internal security problem in the severely indebted countries than in other Third World nations. For the entire sample, the higher a country's previous relative political capacity, the greater the current number of competing security organizations. For the severely indebted subset, however, $RPC_{(t-1)}$ is strongly and inversely related to the number of autonomous security and paramilitary organizations.

The severely indebted countries, RPC, and military spending. The relationship of the SICs' RPC to military expenditures suggests that the roles of the state in society and in the economy are significantly different in this subgroup of countries than in other Third World states. If so, the SICs' distributive politics may be much different from those of other developing countries on certain critical attributes. The SICs are characterized by a lower average political capacity than other developing countries. Hence, the imperatives of political survival may prompt politically weak governments such as the SICs to use public expenditures more relentlessly than other governments as a source of patronage. The targets of such patronage can include social classes, specific regions, party activists, or specific organized groups that are in a position to contribute to the political survival of the regime.

The budget shares allocated to subsidies, to government consumption, and to wages and salaries can be considered crude indicators of sources of such patronage. The SICs allocate a significantly higher percentage of public expenditures to subsidies ($t = 5.133$, $N = 455$, $p \leq 0.000$), to government consumption ($t = 4.377$, $N = 455$, $p \leq 0.000$), and to government expenditures on wages and salaries ($t = 4.233$, $N = 440$, $p \leq 0.000$) than do other developing nations. They also devote significantly larger shares of central government to military spending ($t = 6.231$, $N = 455$, $p < 0.000$). The higher budget shares devoted to subsidies are one indication that elements of the public sector or a highly protected private sector may be important sources of political support for the governing coalitions in many of these countries.

The budget shares absorbed by government consumption, subsidies, and military spending may reflect a peculiar role of the state in the economy. These expenditure categories represent sources of state patronage, particularly when the government plays an active role in the economy through public-sector enterprises. In such cases the state becomes an arbiter of social relations and a godfather of public favors through the dispensing of licenses, contracts, jobs, university scholarships, protection against foreign or domestic competition, and other forms of patronage. When spending on government consumption constitutes an important form of patronage, government leaders can be expected to resist cutting these outlays because of the kind of commitments they represent. These expenditures often constitute one of the few effective instruments available to weak governments for maintaining a modicum of social control.

In this regard, domestic insurgencies and deaths from domestic political violence are also inversely related to low political capacity and add significantly to military spending. For example, every year a Third World government is fighting an insurgency means increasing the military's share of government spending, on average, by over 3.6 percent (b = 3.636). An increase in the intensity of domestic political violence adds an average of 1.6 percent to the military's share of central government expenditures.

The percentage of government budget spent on wages and salaries and its negative association with military spending are indications that the ruling coalition's political survival depends in part on the recruitment of bureaucrats. This is a common survival strategy in countries in which civil servants compose an important fraction of the politically active population.[30] In times of crisis, leaders can create new government jobs and increase wages to prevent inflation from eroding bureaucratic salaries. Launching more public works projects, by contrast, entails too long a gestation period before any political benefits can be realized.

However, as Table 9.3 indicates, the share of central government budget allocated to civilian government jobs means a decline in what can be earmarked for the military. Every percentage increase in government spending on civilian wages and salaries means an average decrease of 1.13 percent available for military spending. If this diagnosis is correct, many of the SICs have created a plethora of interest groups within the state agencies and enterprises upon which they must rely to carry out structural reforms.

The actual impact of domestic military production on military spending is unevenly distributed. Countries classified as "diversified" producers and exporters appear to allocate almost 1 percent, on average, more to military spending than do other countries with a domestic military production capability. The impact of arms exports is difficult to interpret in this context. It is possible that the money earned from the previous year's arms exports provides additional resources to the military that it might not otherwise have. However, given the numerous connections between political weakness and higher levels of military spending, the impact of domestic military production capabilities and arms exports on military spending probably reflects political pressures to maintain relatively high and stable levels of such spending. This can be expected to persist in the absence of external threats simply to maintain employment in defense plants.

Military Expenditures as a Percentage of GNP

Table 9.4 presents the results of the analysis of the model of military expenditures as a percentage of GNP. As expected, military spending as a percentage of national product is more responsive to external influences than is the case when it is evaluated as a share of total government expenditures. The exception is the number of autonomous security and paramilitary organizations. Each additional security agency adds an average of four-tenths of 1 percent to military spending. Interstate war involvement does not account directly for a significant increase in the amount of GNP consumed by the military. Its direct impact is mediated through arms imports as a percentage of total imports. Prior war involvement is also mediated through the previous year's military production as a percentage of GDP.[31]

The influence of prior war involvement is further understated, because such involvement in interstate war usually leads to an increase in relative political capacity. The effects of previous external security threats associated with previous war experience and the value of arms imports as a percentage of total imports significantly increase the share of GNP allocated to defense. This finding lends support to the proposition that the effects of previous wars have at least an indirect ratchet effect on the military budget and possibly on a postwar government's political strength. The latter effect is implied in the positive relationship between RPC and military spending.

The impact of RPC on military spending is probably understated as well. High political capacity levels are strongly related to achieving sustained levels of economic growth and to defining the number of autonomous security and paramilitary organizations and their size in relation to the size of the regular armed forces.

The domestic arms production ranking indicates that countries with a "minimal" capability devote 1.78 percent more of their GNPs to military spending than Third World countries that lack a domestic arms production capability. The revenues generated by arms exports as a percentage of total manufactures have no direct effect on military spending. If they affect military spending decisively, the impact appears to be mediated through arms imports as a percentage of total exports.

Generating Military Spending Benchmarks

The predicted values of military expenditures as percentages of central government expenditures (MILEX % CGE) and GNP (MILEX % GNP) enable us to address the question raised at the beginning of this chapter: Do the resources some of the economically troubled Third World countries spend on the military appear excessive in light of what might be expected given their internal and external security situation and their political capacity to reallocate public spending?

Table 9.4   Political, Economic, and Security Determinants of Military Expenditures as a Percentage of Gross National Product, 1974–1986

Variable	Coefficient	Beta	t-Ratio	Signif. of t
Constant	−3.854	−0.001	−2.075	0.039
RPC	0.410	0.391	2.653	0.003
Number of Wars	0.072	0.002	0.112	0.911
Number of Paramilitary Organizations	0.401	0.659	2.611	0.009
Level of Economic Development	−0.021	−0.077	−1.040	0.299
Military Production as % of GDP$_{t-1}$	0.633	0.715	3.531	0.000
Domestic Arms Production Capability				
Minimal Capability	1.783	0.300	2.115	0.035
Assembly Only	0.031	0.075	0.053	0.958
Diversified	2.588	0.118	1.735	0.083
Top Ten	1.816	0.126	1.444	0.150
No Capability	(dropped)			
Arms Exports as % of Mfg. Exports	0.035	0.021	0.739	0.461
Arms Imports as % of Total Imports	0.541	0.341	2.735	0.006
Y-Hat Military Spending as % of GNP*$_{t-1}$	−0.016	−0.019	−0.093	0.926

Notes: $R^2 = .50$ $F (12, 442) = 43.22$
       Adj. $R^2 = .48$ Prob $> F = 0.0000$
       N of Obs. = 455

RPC	Relative political capacity.
Level of Economic Development	Level of economic development as represented by the value of agricultural production as a percentage of GDP. The *lower* the value of agricultural production as a percentage of GDP, the *higher* the level of economic development.
Arms Imports as % of Total Imports	The value of arms imports as a percentage of total imports.
Y-Hat Military Spending as % of GNP*$_{t-1}$	Instrumental variable military expenditures as a percentage of GNP the previous year.

If a country's military expenditures are very close to what would be predicted given the variables in their respective equations, their ratios should be close to one.[32] This is about what a country "should" be spending on the military compared with countries with similar characteristics and attributes that were specified in the regression equations. A ratio of, say .505 indicates that a country is spending about half as much as might be expected compared with other countries with similar political capacities, economic attributes, and security imperatives. Mexico and Turkey are examples of such countries. A ratio of, say 2.50 or greater suggests just the opposite: A country is spending noticeably more (about two and a half times more) than would be expected (that is, than it "should") compared with other countries with similar characteristics and circumstances. The military expenditures of Bolivia and the Philippines fit this pattern.

The maximum values in the summary table (see endnote 32) indicate that some countries are spending over nine times more of their total budget or their GNP on the military than they "should." An inspection of the actual ratios indicates that these extreme scores are few and episodic. Twenty-one of 455 cases (4.6 percent) are devoting more than two and a half times the amount of government expenditures to the military than would be expected given the combination of security, political, and economic variables used in this study. The average "overexpenditure" for this subset is 4.1. In 65 cases (14.3 percent of the total) military expenditures absorb more than two and a half times as much GNP than the amount seen as expected in the model in Table 9.4. Again, the average "overexpenditure" is 4.1.

A comparison of the military expenditure variables with their benchmarks raises some interesting implications for evaluating progress in economic adjustment. The first implication is that very few countries consistently "overspend" on the military in relation to their central government budget or with respect to GNP. The exceptions are Bolivia (central government expenditures and GNP), Liberia (GNP), Nigeria (GNP), the Philippines (GNP), Uruguay (GNP), Venezuela (central government expenditures), and Zambia (central government expenditures and GNP).

Second, a country can appear to be "overspending" in terms of the share of national product absorbed by military expenditures but not in terms of central government expenditures. This is an indication that even if a country is not "overspending" with respect to the share of central government budget devoted to the military, that level of expenditure may not be sustainable by the country's resource base. This condition implies that even if the share of government spending devoted to military spending is about what it "should" be, that amount may be much more than the country's economy can sustain for any length of time.

This raises the question of whether these two benchmarks are of equal importance in understanding the relationships between military spending and economic adjustment. *MILEX % CGE NORM* should add the most information in this regard. Percentages of government budget allocated for various purposes often reflect competing claims among various political constituencies—in and out of government—for shares of public resources. The relative political strength of these contending interests undoubtedly has some impact on the absolute spending levels that finally emerge. Political strength accounts for a larger share of the variance in military spending as a percentage of central government expenditures than do military expenditures with respect to GNP.

Hence, predicted *MILEX % CGE* should match observed military spending more closely than is the case in the equation for military spending as a share of GNP. This is not surprising, because three political strength variables (mobilization ratio, RPC_{t-1}, and $RPC \times SICs_{t-1}$) are included in the equation for *MILEX % CGE* in Table 9.3. Only one explicit political variable, RPC, is included in the equation for estimating military expenditures as a percentage of GNP (Table 9.4). Further, the share of GNP consumed by the military may be a by-product of the budgetary competition. In that sense the share of central government budget allocated to the military is more "political" than the percentage of GNP it absorbs.

Third, the benchmark for military spending as a percentage of total government expenditures is unrelated to trend. Therefore, notwithstanding the imperative of stabilization and structural change, "overspending" on the military in terms of total government outlays did not decline during the years 1974–1986. However, "overspending" in terms of the share of national product consumed by the military declined significantly over the same period. What is not clear is whether this decline is attributable to the pressures of adjustment.

Fourth, these benchmarks can be used as either outcome variables or causal variables in further research. For example, the explanatory factors used as causal variables have accounted for all of the variation in military spending they can. Therefore, regressing the benchmarks on relative political capacity should yield no strong relationships. Yet, prior and current levels of RPC are related to these spending norms: The higher the previous year's RPC, the lower a country's spending norms in relation to GNP.[33] This suggests that the political strength of nations operates indirectly through a variety of public expenditure decisions and other agencies. For example, the shares of government spending allocated to wages and salaries, subsidies, and government consumption are inversely related to RPC.[34] The larger the share of central government expenditures absorbed by subsidies, government employment, and government consumption, the more frequently the military budget spending norm will be exceeded. The larger the share of government expenditures committed to salaries and wages, the more frequently military spending will exceed the norm in relation to consumption of GNP.

The consequences of exceeding military spending norms can seriously undermine efforts at adjustment. For example, the more frequently military spending exceeds the norm for share of central government expenditures, the greater the dampening effect on the growth of gross domestic investment as a percentage of GDP.[35]

Finally, these military spending ratios permit a limited "apples-and-oranges" comparison between countries that may spend more than 25 percent of their budgets on defense (for example, Israel and Egypt) and countries that devote 5 percent or less to the military (for example, Bolivia, Brazil, and Venezuela). Egypt and Israel have been spending an average of over 30 percent of their budgets on their armed forces, but this is about what they "should" be spending, because they exist in a high-risk environment. Venezuela spends an average of less than 5 percent of its budget on the military. Yet, for half of the years covered in this study, Venezuela appeared to be spending more than twice what it should on its armed forces.

Conclusion

The results of this exploratory analysis suggest that most developing countries are not spending much more of their government budgets or larger shares of their GNPs on their armed forces than they "should," given the political, economic, and security criteria specified earlier. An alternative set of criteria could yield much different findings. This analysis casts doubt on the argument that many Third World countries' external debt or structural adjustment problems could be easily remedied simply by cutting military spending. Nevertheless, the approach spotlights directions for further research that can increase our understanding of the linkages among military expenditures, national security, distributive politics, and the imperatives of structural adjustment.

Some of these countries, however, appear to be spending a much larger share of their GNP on the military than they "should" compared with other countries facing similar security problems, levels of development, and industrialization. This suggests that even if the budget share devoted to military spending is about what it "should" be, it is doubtful that many Third World countries' economies can long sustain that share of national product being devoted to the military without adversely affecting economic performance.

Notes

1. For example, see Bandow (1988, A34), Tullberg (1985, 453), and George (1988, 22).

2. Studies exhibiting this orientation include Benoit (1973), and George (1988).

3. Discussions of politically weak Third World governments manipulating macroeconomic policy to ensure political survival are found in Ames (1987), Haggard (1985), and Jackson and Rosberg (1982, especially 33–43).

4. The relationships between political weakness and high debt-service ratios and military spending are discussed in more detail in Snider (1991, 167–190).

5. Looney and Frederiksen (1986) compared the effects of per capita military expenditures on growth in real gross domestic product (GDP) of a sample of Third World arms-producing countries with a group of developing countries that lacked a domestic defense industry, for the years 1972–1980. The results of their multiple regression analysis showed that military expenditures per capita exerted a strong negative impact on economic growth in the nonarms-producing group but had a strong positive effect on the arms-producing group. They concluded that capital inflows associated with domestic weapons production have an effect similar to that of foreign aid (Looney and Frederiksen, 1986, 329–338).

6. See, for example, Brzoska and Ohlson (1986, 281), Ball (1988, Chapter 9), and Louscher and Salomone (1987, 167–170).

7. Indirect subsidies via preferred tax rates and credit terms are excluded from this expenditure category.

8. The rankings have been refined and updated by Ball (1988, 341–363).

9. Rankings are derived from SIPRI (1987, 198). See also Brzoska and Ohlson (1986, 31).

10. Israel's Merkava main battle tank (which includes foreign components such as its Teledyne Continental engine) is reputed to be one of the most lethal such tanks in the world, but the substantial costs of producing it have not been recouped by export orders. Meanwhile, the cost of subsidizing Israel's substantial military industries is causing serious economic difficulties. Brazil has a number of missile projects under way for its own armed forces and, eventually, for the export market, but progress is currently hampered by a shortage of government funding. See Foss (1989, 1009).

11. However, two critical differences between the military revolts in Venezuela in 1992 and the Philippines examples should be mentioned. First, the Venezuelan armed forces were not fighting a domestic insurgency. Second, the principal motivations for both coup attempts concerned the corruption associated with the way stabilization and adjustment policies were being implemented rather than the rigors of adjustment per se.

12. More detailed discussions of this ability are found in Snider (1987), and Mann (1984).

13. Political and strategic considerations, however, undoubtedly provide the overriding rationale for building a domestic arms industry or opting for a policy of military-led industrialization in most developing countries.

14. Given the purpose of this research, a model that accounted for, say, more than 75 percent of the variance in military spending might be self-defeating. In that case the ratios of actual to expected military spending would almost always be very close to one. Therefore, every country's spending would be scored as "normal" or "just about right."

15. The countries the World Bank *World Development Report* (1991) defines as "severely indebted" are those in which three of the four key ratios are above critical levels: external debt to GNP (50 percent), debt to exports of goods and services (275 percent), accrued debt service to exports (30 percent), and accrued interest to exports (20 percent) (World Bank, 1991, xi). The severely indebted countries included in this study (circa 1989) are Argentina, Bolivia, Brazil, Chile, Costa Rica, Côte d'Ivoire, Ecuador, Egypt, Mexico, Morocco, Peru, the Philippines, Uruguay, Venezuela, and Yugoslavia. The other countries are Algeria, Ghana, India, Indonesia, Israel, Jamaica, Liberia, Malaysia, Nigeria, Pakistan, South Africa, South Korea, Sudan, Tanzania, Thailand, Turkey, Uganda, Zaire, and Zambia.

16. The SICs' mean relative political capacity is significantly lower than the average RPC of other highly indebted Third World countries (t = –2.553, N = 455, $p \leq$ 0.011). This suggests that SICs allocate a significantly higher percentage of public expenditures to subsidies (t = 2.946, N = 455, $p \leq$ 0.003), to government consumption (t = 2.247, N = 455, $p \leq$ 0.025), and to government expenditures on wages and salaries (t = 3.453, N = 455, $p \leq$ 0.001) than do other Third World borrowers. These differences in allocations of public expenditures suggest that a different view of the role of the state's participation in the economy may prevail in the SICs than is the case in other Third World countries. The SICs have suspended payments on their external debt and sought rescheduling far more frequently (t = 3.529, N = 455, $p \leq$ 0.000) than other debtor countries. The SICs have had to accept a significantly higher average number of IMF-supported stabilization programs (t = 4.917, N = 455 $p \leq$ 0.000) than the other debtor countries in this analysis.

17. Some of these countries, such as Morocco, the Philippines, and Peru, are facing serious internal security threats. However, the kind of hardware required to deal with internal insurgencies seldom involves expenditures on expensive imported weapons such as main battle tanks, sophisticated fighter aircraft, battlefield support missiles, elaborate

air defense systems, or major surface combatants. Acquisition of these classes of weapons can dramatically increase military budgets and the amount spent on arms imports. For the thirty-five-country sample here, the average size of the military budget for countries not facing an external threat is 13.5 percent of central government expenditures; this is about half the average budget share of the Third World debtors facing an external threat (25 percent). The average value of arms imports as a percentage of total imports for debtor countries facing an external threat is twice as high (6.6 percent) as the corresponding share for countries not confronting such a threat (3.3 percent).

18. The concept of political capacity as fiscal extraction is represented as a ratio of actual tax revenues gathered by the government over the predicted tax revenues given the productivity of the population, natural resources, and reliance on the foreign trade sector. It is based on establishing two reference points:

$$\text{Political Capacity} = \frac{\text{Actual Extraction}}{\text{Predicted Extractive Capacity}}$$

The actual revenue extracted is measured with respect to a country's resource base, which is usually a government's tax revenues as a percentage of GDP. It is much more challenging to obtain an accurate approximation of predicted revenue extraction given the tremendous variations in the populations, natural resource endowments, and levels of economic development among the developing nations used in this study. How this is achieved is discussed at length in Snider (1990b, 1269–1270). The regression model used to estimate taxable capacity is found in Snider (1988).

19. Data for the tax structure variable are taken from International Monetary Fund (various years).

20. The principal data sources for this variable are IISS, (various years); Chris Cook (ed.), *The Facts on File Political Almanac*; John Keegan, *World Armies* (various editions); Robert C. Sellers (ed.), *Armed Forces of the World* (various editions); and Trevor N. Dupuy et al. (eds.), *Almanac of World Military Power* (various editions).

21. The effects of political weakness and arms imports as a percentage of total imports on increases in foreign borrowing and debt-service burden are reported in Snider (1990a, 292–301; 1991, 181–186).

22. Data on subsidies and government wages and salaries are from International Monetary Fund (various years).

23. Data on arms imports and military expenditures are taken from United States Arms Control and Disarmament Agency (ACDA) (various editions).

24. In plain English, unequal variances across countries are an indication that the observations are not equally valid for every country in the sample. The same problem can arise within a country over time. It is a problem that must be confronted whenever one is working with data on Third World countries.

25. For example, the pooled time series data set used in subsequent chapters consists of 455 observations, 13 years for each of 35 countries. Strictly speaking, only 35 cases (countries) are truly independent of one another. The 13 observations for each of these countries are independent of the 13 observations for any other country in the sample. However, some of the causal variables how a strong linear dependence with one another (multicolinearity). For example, certain measures of public expenditures could not be used as causal variables with one of the measures of political capacity in the same regression equation, because the prior and simultaneous impact the political capacity variable had on the other measures was stronger than the effects of these causal variables on the outcome. Within each country the 13 observations can exhibit serial correlation (the effects of trend) and multicolinearity. Consequently, tests for serial correlation such as the Durbin-Watson d statistic often yield unreliable results, because they are based on

the assumption that the 455 observations have the same independence from one another as the 35 countries have from each other.

26. This approach assumes that X_{t-1} is not correlated with the error term in the OLS regression but will likely be correlated with Y_{t-1}. It is commonly referred to as a first-order auto regressive structure. See Johnston (1972, 318), and Ostrom (1990, 32–33, 67–68). The surest way to ascertain whether the OLS results are significantly affected by autocorrelation is to adopt the following procedure: (1) Estimate the relationship using OLS; (2) compute the residuals $\hat{e}_t$ and $\hat{e}_{t-1}$; (3) regress $\hat{e}_{t-1}$; (4) test the significance of the coefficient $\hat{e}_{t-1}$ in the regression in step 3. This procedure was used with all of the regressions in the study. No significant correlations between $\hat{e}_t$ and $\hat{e}_{t-1}$ emerged.

27. This estimation method involves (1) computing the least squares estimates of the reduced form equations for the jointly endogenous variables using all of the exogenous variables in the model, replacing the observed data for the jointly determined endogenous variables by their calculated values from the reduced form (the first stage); and (2) computing the least squares regression of the dependent variable on all of the variables consisting of the *calculated* values of the jointly determined variables and the observed values of the predetermined variables (the second stage).

28. The mobilization ratio is the ratio of the percentage of government revenue from direct taxes to the percentage of revenue from trade taxes. The higher the ratio, the more able the government is to penetrate society. A 1 percent decrease means a 1 percent decrease in direct tax revenues (the most difficult to extract) in relation to revenues from taxes on customs and trends, which are the easiest to collect.

29. The main implication of Looney's analysis is that reduction in Third World arms production would probably result in lower aggregate levels of military expenditures in developing countries.

30. See, for example, Ames (1987, 212–215).

31. Cumulative involvement in war accounts for 35 percent of the variance in military production as a percentage of GDP.

32. The summary statistics for the military expenditure (MILEX) variables and their respective benchmark variables are:

Variable Name	N. of Obs.	Mean	Std. Dev.	Min. Val.	Max. Val.
MILEX % CGE	455	15.68	10.65	1.525	61.12
MILEX % CGE NORM	455	1.10	0.81	0.122	9.56
MILEX % GNP	455	4.06	5.04	0.292	33.75
MILEX % GNP NORM	455	1.36	0.92	0.050	9.56

33. The adjusted R^2 is .04, $t = -3.113$, $p < .002$.

34. Direct subsidies and government consumption as percentages of central government expenditures were not used as causal variables in the regression analyses.

35. The dependent variable is the percentage change in gross domestic investment as a percentage of current GDP. Adjusted $R^2 = 12$, $b = -1.926$, $t = -7092$, $p < 0.000$.

❖ TEN ❖

The Military and Development in Thailand and Indonesia: Patrimonialism Versus the Market

Donald Crone

The proclivity toward a central role for the military in their regimes has made the question of the impact of the military on security and development a central concern in the analysis of Third World countries. Mohammed Ayoob (1991a) has noted that the internal vulnerability of a state or regime composes an important dimension of the security concerns of its military. This vulnerability, or weakness, of Third World states frequently brings the military directly into the wider range of political, economic, and social policy in the quest for security (Buzan, 1989). For all practical purposes, the range of professional roles of a Third World military has few specific boundaries, because development is a major component of security. This boundary problem is compounded by the tendency of Third World regimes and states, military and otherwise, to gain legitimacy through their developmental performance.

But what is the impact of the military on development? Are specific consequences to be expected from the intrusion of the military into the political, economic, and social domains otherwise run by civilian elements of the elite? The overall effects on aggregate economic growth have been the subject of considerable contention, with some arguing that military expenditure has stimulating effects and others finding that the military burden negatively affects growth (Benoit, 1978a; Ball, 1988). Some Latin American analysts point to authoritarian, military rule as necessary if a country is to move beyond the "easy," import-substitution phase of industrialization, whereas others feel labor repression is the primary result of such rule.

At a more disaggregate level, some cross-national studies find that the military has no effect on basic human needs, whereas others find systematic negative effects on the quality of life for the masses (Dixon and Moon, 1986; Looney, 1990). Apparently, either the impact of the military on development is so subtle as to evade analysis, or it is so idiosyncratic that it has no systematic effects.

193

Subtle and idiosyncratic effects, however, do not defy analysis; they simply call for a different method. Here, I employ a comparative case method to explore the Thai and Indonesian experiences. One rather subtle variable, the degree of military predominance within the ruling regime, is related to another, the conception of development. The degree of military predominance in the regime can vary from a "pure" military government to military control of the most important ministries and the administrative structure of the state to equal inclusion of military and civilian elements in the cabinet and the administration to the predominance of civilians in a government that still includes military figures to the relegation of the military "to the barracks" and complete civilian control (neither extreme has characterized my two cases).

Conceptions of development are limited here to the manner of control over principal features of political and economic structures. A patrimonial structure is one in which both political and economic ties are channeled and controlled as essential elements of a patronage and benefices system that extends directly from the peaks of power downward through society. A more marketlike structure is one in which the choice of who participates in the organization of politics and business, and how they do so, is left largely to social and economic agents. The principle of such a structure, rather than specific aspects of a liberal economic order, is what is important here. A marketplace, for both economic and political purposes, assumes that entry is open to a wide array of actors and that competition will determine eventual success or failure. Perhaps as important, a market is a "bottom-up" structure (even though it may operate within the parameters of state regulation), whereas a patrimonial system is decidedly "top-down."

Both sets of variables are substantially judgmental, and they defy clear quantification or modeling. Furthermore, the correlation of a particular model of development with a particular compositional pattern of a regime cannot by itself establish causation, although the correspondence of shifts in the two may increase our confidence. And, although some direct evidence of a military preference for a certain sort of development does exist, much has to be inferred from the outcomes observed, because of the inaccessibility of most of the decisionmakers. The result, although it may persuade us, is still tentative and must be judged by whether it makes the best possible sense of the cases in the face of their subtlety and idiosyncratic richness.

I show here that a high degree of military predominance supports a patrimonial conception of development, whereas a reduction of such predominance has led to more marketlike models of development. The cases show that military predominance indeed has an effect on development, most directly on how it is structured and controlled and only indirectly on the measures of growth and social welfare more commonly tested. With a high degree of military predominance a security coalition governs the political economy, whereas lesser levels of military intrusion allow for the emergence of a growth coalition.

The Military Outlook

The issue of what are appropriate roles for military actors presumes some set of boundaries between behaviors presumed to correspond to those actors' professional knowledge and skills and behaviors beyond their training and legitimate interests. At the extreme is a Western conception of functional differentiation—military professionalism limited to combat—which occurs ideally under ultimate civilian direction. However, in many Third World settings, the "security problematic" is broader than threats from the international system (Ayoob, 1991a). Threats with an internal origin are far more frequent. Revolutionary insurgencies, ethnic secessions, regional rebellions, even militant peasant or labor organizations may pose a threat to the continuance of the established regime. Thus, the external focus of security issues is eroded, and Third World militaries may primarily perform what might be termed "police functions." Indeed, the growth of military organizations in the Third World is most often related to domestic, rather than international, challenges. Military professionalism expands correspondingly to encompass more than those skills required for an international role.

Simply from the domestic perspective, the behaviors relevant to the military role bloom beyond simple coercion. Straightforward maintenance of order may treat the symptom but not the cause of internal security threats. Especially in cases in which the government is heavily military, or the civilian regime is not addressing broader issues that result in security challenges, the attention of the military is likely to expand from the relatively simple maintenance of order to the more complex, and conceptually boundless, creation of a more orderly environment. This role expansion has been fostered and supported by Western counterinsurgency training—"hearts and minds," "civic action," and related doctrines that suggest that economic, social, and political issues must be treated simultaneously as intrinsic aspects of localized opposition to an established government and its regime if security is to prevail. Thus, their environment crafts a multifaceted security role for many Third World militaries.

It is this environment, rather than any particular cast of the military mind, that has been stressed in analyses of the Southeast Asian case. Muthiah Alagappa (1988) and Harold Crouch (1988) point to the role of the military in ensuring domestic stability, a prerequisite of development, as a central determinant of their expanded behavior. When the environment is one of developmental weakness and the military has a central political role in the regime, ensuring social order and the stability of the existing government naturally brings the military to emphasize economic development as a foundation for the legitimacy of the system. If military skills are not suited to elements of the task, such as economic management, technocratic elites may be co-opted. Political and economic instability account for an extended military role.

However, the way the military may pursue these tasks is still an unanswered question. The modern military, by its nature, stresses order, authority, hierarchy, discipline, efficiency, professionalism, and specialized expertise and often views itself as, therefore, superior to the contrasting civilian tendencies toward disorderliness, anarchy, wasteful competition, inefficiency, lack of professionalism, and corrupt behavior. These characteristics seem to provide a set of clues: Structures that ensure control and some degree of predictability of outcome are one key to military models of development.

The structure of a relatively open marketplace does not fit this aspect of the military mentality. Outcomes are difficult to predict or control; the process is frequently quite messy and inefficient; "better" or "worse" approaches are established only after the competitive fact rather than through standard operating procedures; and, in fact, confidence in the superiority of the ultimate outcome requires a considerable act of faith. The fundamental decentralization of a market does little to ensure control or predictability, in comparison to standard operating procedures.

In contrast, noncompetitive political and economic structures seem to fit more comfortably with military procedures. One possibility would be a single-party (or a no-party) socialist structure, which has resulted from military-led revolutions in many Third World states. This structure has not been attractive to Thailand or Indonesia, in part because of its existence in neighboring Southeast Asian states. Another possibility (with roots in Thai and Indonesian historical experience) is a patrimonial system. This loosely replicates a military structure in the political and economic realms, in that it is hierarchical and, therefore, relatively authoritative and orderly. Loyalty and benefits provide the exchange goods, decisionmaking is top-down, and control by the ultimate patron is emphasized.

In the following sections I provide, first, an overview of the patterns of development in Indonesia and Thailand. Then I examine periods of military predominance, with emphasis on the apparent conception of development being followed. In both cases, there have also been periods when the dominance of the military was eroded, which provide interesting analytic counterpoints. Throughout, I emphasize how the military pursued its "extended" roles of political and economic management.

Thai and Indonesian Development Patterns

The recent histories of Indonesia and Thailand are ones of militarily predominant governments that have exercised decisive influence over all aspects—political, economic, and social—of their countries' development. For Thailand, the 1932 coup against the monarchy brought the military, a central element of the coup group, to power. It exercised preponderant power until 1973, with minor interludes of nominally civilian governments, and again from 1976 to 1979; after

1980 the military role gradually declined to that of a more equal partner with civilian elements of the regime. The Indonesian anticolonial revolution established an important power base for its military, one that expanded to preponderance after the 1965 coups ended nominal civilian governments; it has remained preponderant, although the 1980s brought greater power to civilian elements.

The pattern of political development in Thailand has been one in which the military, during its predominance, occupied the pinnacles of power. The head of government has normally been the senior army figure who is next in line when the presiding general looses confidence or control, with replacement by a (usually) bloodless coup; this has occurred nine times since 1932. Senior cabinet positions—Defense, the Interior, frequently Foreign Affairs and Industry—have been occupied by members of the ruling military clique, although the civilian bureaucracy has as long and as independent a tradition as the military and rules the areas left to it with substantial autonomy. The elected branch of government, the assembly, has had little influence until recent years, because the appointed senate, dominated by military personnel, acted as a brake on its independence until the early 1980s; many of the political party leaders are retired, prestigious military officers.

The ruling military group is essentially an extended patronage structure. The senior officers are frequently drawn from a single cohort of the military academy, for whom long ties and similarity of professional experience form the basis of a firm, factional bond. They bring with them a network of junior officers who have gained promotions and positions by tying themselves to senior mentors. Critical positions at the peaks of military authority—in the cabinet, government, and the senate—go to members of this faction; nonfaction members are accorded less powerful and less desirable military and administrative appointments.

Increasingly since the late 1950s, the monarch has become the legitimator of the system, with considerable influence over forming new governments, dismissing the old, and setting norms for the allowable level of disharmony among political actors. This last function—regulating conflict—is the most important for my concerns, because the king has consistently supported a view of politics largely compatible with the military tendency to clamp down when protest and contestation become at all open.

The Thai political pattern, then, is essentially one in which politics takes place within a clientele structure effectively dominated by the ruling military group. Open disorder is minimized in favor of quiet, behind-the-scenes maneuvering among clique members. When one clique can no longer maintain control, it is displaced by one that can. Administration is the preferred method of governance, with the military ensuring that it proceeds relatively smoothly and without contest. Bangkok is the definitive center from which national and provincial rule emanates in an ordered fashion.

In Indonesia, the political system is likewise centered on the military, although in a manner institutionalized differently from the Thai pattern. Since 1967, when the military came decisively to power, the executive has been

General (now retired) Suharto. Although military figures were prominent in the cabinet prior to that time, critical portfolios—Defense, Education and Culture, Industries, Manpower, Home Affairs, and the coordinating ministries for Political Affairs and Security and for Public Welfare—have generally been in military hands since 1965. In addition, the autonomy of the civilian administration— never as strongly institutionalized as its Thai counterpart—was reduced by extensive cuts in the premilitary rule cohort, the creation of a parallel military structure down to the village level, appointments of active or recently retired military personnel to open positions, and military provincial governors. Representative bodies and political parties have no real influence and are co-opted by the military; the only partial exception is the government party, GOLKAR, which took a more independent role in the late 1980s. The only significant group not dominated by military appointments is a small circle of economic technocrats in the cabinet and select ministries, and these are frequently staffed by military appointments at the next lower level of authority.

Unlike the Thai case, the Indonesian military has developed a formal doctrine to support its wide involvement. Rooted in the constitution (Article 30), which states that "all national forces will be totally and integrally utilized with ABRI [the armed forces] as the core in order to defend the independence and sovereignty of the Republic of Indonesia, secure the integrity of the nation and safeguard efforts to attain Indonesia's national goal," this doctrine evolved from pursuing a "middle way" of influencing but not predominating to a "dual function" of defense and "an active part in all efforts and activities of the state and the nation in order to defend the Pancasila ideology, to give content to independence and to strive for the welfare of the whole Indonesian people" (Djiwandono, 1988, 79). The military is to act as dynamizer, stabilizer, and ideological vanguard in the development of the country and its social, political, and economic forces.

Even more so than in Thailand, the Indonesian model is one of administration, with open politics seen as far too disorderly and chaotic. Local-level activism by the closely circumscribed political parties is forbidden outside of the mandated pre-election "festival of democracy" period, in accordance with an official depoliticizing policy of the "floating mass" (Rogers, 1988). During elections, issues that may be raised are vetted, and approval is withdrawn if the support becomes too emotional. Opposition is defined broadly, and even prominent individuals seen as out of sympathy with the government are sanctioned by travel restrictions, surveillance, and termination of "facilities." The truly political discussion takes place in an extremely small circle around the president, is couched in language so obscure as to defy common interpretation, and is most commonly understood by the shifting group of individuals in the ruling circle. "Uncle" Suharto is the certain nexus of an all-encompassing clientele structure that maintains control and order until the wider population is mature enough to participate politically without disruption and chaos. In the interim, political stability is ensured by close military control, a firm hierarchy descending from the president, and virtual exclusion of actors outside the patrimonial system.

The pattern of political development established by these militarily predominant governments is one that reflects their corporate and professional preferences. The maintenance of control through a closely monitored hierarchy produces order and stability; the wide appointment of military figures transfers expertise, reliability, and efficiency to the government; actors outside the chain of command are not relevant or are kept that way by coercion; social forces are channeled through captive organizations into orderly expressions. The chaos of open politics is avoided.

In the economic realm, the indeterminate effect of military rule in Thailand and Indonesia can be seen in selected statistics (see Table 10.1). Growth for both countries has been determined largely by forces from outside, rather than within, each country. Thailand's growth was fueled by strong aid flows during the Indochina wars and, in the late 1980s, by large inflows of capital from East Asia into manufacturing ventures that increased exports. Military expenditures increased, partly because of the Vietnamese occupation of Cambodia, but this seems to have had little economic impact. Indonesian growth was simply a reflection of the international market for petroleum until the late 1980s. Economic development in Thailand has been stronger than that in Indonesia despite apparently larger allocations to the military, which produced larger gross domestic product (GDP) growth, lower poverty rates, and higher levels of GDP per capita. Military expenditures account for little economic variation in these cases.

However, aggregate figures for both countries must be taken rather lightly, because what goes into the military budget is both more and less than standard military expenditures. The Thai military, for example, controls a large, secret fund, allocated separately from the defense budget, and has used considerable resources—especially in the period after 1976—for development projects that are not military in nature. In Indonesia, government funding of the military does not reflect the resources actually used by the military but raised independently, or, as with petroleum revenues prior to 1976, off-budget. Compared with other countries in the region, Indonesia and Thailand grew at slower paces than Malaysia or Singapore, in which civilian, but relatively authoritarian, governments predominate but that also rely more on economic markets; both countries grew faster than the nominally civilian Philippines.

In both countries' economic systems, the pattern of control reflects that of the political structure and is more easily differentiated from nonmilitary systems of the region. Each economic system has different historical roots, but their overall structure during military predominance has been similar.

In Indonesia, the revolutionary struggle shaped an autonomous role for then-fragmented military units, in that because of the lack of central government resources, units had largely to forage for themselves, establishing enterprises to raise funds through such activities as the unauthorized export of natural resources under their control. Suharto himself was reprimanded or transferred

Table 10.1 Selected Statistics: Indonesia and Thailand

GDP Growth (%)		1960–1970	1970–1980	1980–1985	1985–1989
Indonesia		3.5	7.6	3.5	5.3
Thailand		8.2	7.2	5.1	7.0
Military Expenditure/Gross					
Domestic Product (%)		1965	1975	1985	1988
Indonesia		1.3	3.8	3.0	2.3
Thailand		2.3	3.7	5.0	4.0
Military Expenditure/Central					
Government Expenditures (%)			1975	1985	1988
Indonesia			19.1	10.6	8.3
Thailand			17.3	20.2	18.7
Export Growth (%)		1960–1970	1970–1975	1975–1980	1980–1988
Indonesia		1.7	54.7	25.5	–4.9
Thailand		5.9	31.8	21.8	9.7
GDP Per Capita ($)	1960	1970	1975	1980	1988
Indonesia	73	79	239	517	440
Thailand	96	198	360	688	1,000
Poverty Rate (%)	—	1970	—	—	1988
Indonesia	—	56	—	—	39
Thailand	—	34	—	—	30

Sources: GDP Growth—World Bank, *World Development Report* (1990); Military Expenditure/GDP—SIPRI, Yearbook; Military Expenditure/Central Government Expenditures—International Monetary Fund (IMF), *Government Finance Statistics Yearbook*; Export Growth—UNCTAD, *Handbook of International Trade and Development Statistics* (1990); GDP Per Capita—UN, *Yearbook of National Account Statistics*; Poverty Rate—UN, *Human Development Report* (1992).

several times during the 1950s for irregular economic activities (Emmerson, 1988, 120).

Cooperation between military units and local ethnic Chinese businesspersons emerged during that time, a pattern that has continued, grown in scale, and encompassed foreign investors, producing some of the country's largest business conglomerates (Crouch, 1978, Chapter 11). The essence of this cooperative relationship hinges on the "pariah minority" status of the Indonesian Chinese (and their predominant economic position, established during colonial times), which requires that they seek protection and assistance from those connected to government at local and national levels. This outsider status has been carefully preserved, a feature of Indonesia's ethnic politics that ensures that Chinese business activities operate only under the umbrella of official Chinese contacts. In this fashion, a pyramid of economic activities is established that is connected to the political pyramid and that is operated—at least loosely—under central control.

This entrepreneurial system easily lends itself to abuses, excesses, and corruption—topics that became increasingly difficult to suppress during the 1980s (when, for example, the Customs Service had to be hired out to a Swiss firm in order to establish some degree of regularity in its operations). Aside from commercial activities, the military inherited the operation of Dutch enter-prises—plantations, mines, oil wells—upon Dutch nationalization, which served as the base for state-owned corporations. Overall, the result was an economy closely controlled by the military, directly and indirectly, with few avenues left to the market.

The Thai economy during military predominance shows similar structural patterns but much less intensity of interpenetration. During the 1950s a set of concerns arose within military circles about "foreign" control of the economy, which stimulated a series of decrees designed to limit non-Thai influence and ownership. As with other Southeast Asian countries, the commercial and banking sectors of the Thai economy had become largely a preserve of the resident Chinese-Thai population, which, in the aftermath of the Chinese Revolution, was thought to be vulnerable to penetration and foreign control.

One of the mechanisms adopted to control this group was that of placing members of the governing group in corporate board positions. In a less intense manner than occurred in Indonesia, a network of personal relationships grew that was designed to protect Chinese entrepreneurs in exchange for income and perquisites to be given to Thai military figures (Girling, 1981). In an economy characterized by extensive use of state corporations that ensured indigenous ownership and control, this provided a measure of protection to Sino-Thai businesses, and the income derived was useful to military patrons in sustaining and expanding their entourage. This pattern provided an umbrella for the growth of large Sino-Thai businesses and ensured military control (at least in a nominal sense) within the political leadership.

These arrangements were pursued with such vigor during the 1950s that the accumulation of wealth by regime leaders caused strong political criticism. Only the collapse of military control in the early 1970s disrupted these networks, by which time the previous anti-Chinese sentiment had been replaced with asser-tions of assimilation, and at least some of the Chinese businesses had become large enough to be relatively independent. Other aspects of economic policy during this period were also linked to security concerns, especially rural development and transportation, which were funded largely by foreign aid (Muscat, 1990).

In Thailand and Indonesia, the manner in which economic development in the broadest sense was molded depended upon resource endowments. Indonesia had oil and other natural resources; Thailand had rice, rubber, and tin. The respective courses of their development varied, but the manner in which their economies were controlled was essentially the same: They were controlled through patronage linkages between the military leadership and the leading commercial enterprises, which in both cases were owned and operated by an ethnic group defined as nonindigenous. Rather than eject this group (as occurred, for example, in Burma and Uganda), the military leadership chose to control it by incorporating it into its own clientele structures.

Although in both cases the military (or, more properly, a few leaders within the military regimes) benefited financially, what is striking is the congruence in the way political and economic structures were organized. Both were incorporated into a patrimonial system that provided military leaders with direct and personal control while giving considerable rein to Chinese business acumen. In fact, the political and economic sides of the patrimonial system were mutually supporting: Military leaders derived finances from the economic relationships that funded their political ventures; Chinese businesspersons gained access to state-controlled licenses, contracts, and facilities; through their control of business, the political elite guaranteed stability and continuity.

An economic perspective might argue that the patrimonial system is inimical to rapid economic development. It inhibits competition; many different forms of corruption are fostered; resources are undoubtedly allocated with less than ideal efficiency; the economy is characterized in some sectors by extensive state ownership and in others by political monopolies. At the same time, behind the protection and control, fairly large-scale enterprises grew that provided the foundation for some firms' rapid expansion into extensive conglomerates and even into multinational firms, which strengthened their international competitiveness. However, the external dependence of both economies largely eliminated local economic factors, because growth resulted from changes in the international realm. Patrimonial structures produced sufficient, if not the maximum theoretically attainable, growth to sustain the regimes. This political advantage of the military became the core of civilian discontent in both countries.

Civilizing Influences

Although the general pattern of political and economic control in Indonesia and Thailand has been structured by the predominance of both countries' militaries and by the military outlook, in both cases there is some variation from that norm. More notably in Thailand than in Indonesia, the weight of the military within the ruling circle has varied. But even in Indonesia, the military faction's predominance is not always decisive, and recently it has visibly declined. These deviations from strong military predominance provide opportunities to observe how changing regime compositions affect the models of development. In both cases, we can see movement toward market models of political and economic management.

The Indonesian military has been important throughout that country's independent history, but it has only been predominant since the late 1960s. In fact, relevant aspects of the old order (pre-1965) were important in the rise of military power. The political and economic orders were more marketlike, but neither produced coherent outcomes. In particular, the chaos that resulted from greater political pluralism and poor economic planning was one stimulus for the formulation of the military doctrine of intrusion. The economy was not particularly "liberal"; the Sukarno years were ones of intense nationalism and nationalization, but there was little central control (Rudner, 1976). In fact, economic policy was chaotic, as various factions sought to capture relevant ministries; with little central control or direction, results were disastrous. In the political realm, a plethora of political parties competed for position and support and even votes, often creating confusion. Sukarno increasingly maneuvered to provide balance; the process was more open in the early years of the Sukarno era, but was never stable or predictable.

Stability and predictability were what the military sought to attain in redressing the structural defects of this era in the first years of its rule. Economic policy became centralized, and political parties were "rationalized." What existed of a marketlike structure was eliminated in favor of a patrimonial system centered on President Suharto.

By the early 1980s, that centralization was weakening. Some elements of the military, and a group of past notables, were pressing for more political openness. The "political vehicle" of military rule, GOLKAR, was given more rein. With its base in the bureaucracy and its connections to some indigenous economic elites, GOLKAR started to become modestly more independent. One aspect of this independence was visible in the 1987 elections, in which the degree of military coercion was reduced in favor of administration-controlled patronage as the means of electoral victory. Political repression was lessened, both on individuals formerly isolated for their opposition and on the secular political parties (although the Islamic Party structure came under increasing scrutiny and control). The possibility of more nonmilitary governors was discussed by the military commander, portending a shift in the military-civilian balance within the bureaucracy. Technocrats assumed more important roles at the government center. Questions were raised about the length of military tutelage and the concentration of political power.

Even such a modest shift in the predominant military role was accompanied by changes in the economic sphere. By the mid-1980s, Indonesia was engaged in a program of economic liberalization that opened opportunities for a wider array of actors, in some cases directly at the expense of monopoly holders and licensees who were a part of the larger patronage system. Import monopolies were trimmed to stimulate wider manufacturing activities; export of nontraditional manufactures was encouraged outside of the conglomerates associated with the political regime; access to bank credits was widened beyond those with political connections to these facilities. With uncertainty about continued privileged access to business, some of the large regime-associated economic groups moved to establish alternative bases of operations outside Indonesia. Corruption (political manipulation of the economy) was addressed more frequently. Monopolies drew more criticism when they were established, as, for example, the clove monopoly assigned to President Suharto's son. Although it would be an exaggeration to characterize the economy as a free market, more marketlike elements were allowed outside of the clientele structure, and important aspects of the economy were freed from the former close military control.

Part of the motivation for these changes is economic. The "easy" money from petroleum plummeted with price reductions, spurring a search for a wider-based economy. Outside pressures increased from such sources as the foreign aid consortium (the Intergovernmental Group on Indonesia) and the World Bank; because the majority of Indonesia's development budget was derived from foreign aid, these sources were important, and they enhanced the stature and clout of the technocratic faction in the regime. Part of the motivation is political: Criticism of growing visible inequalities and lack of social justice increased; the business empire created by members of President Suharto's family became a prime example of the abuse of the patrimonial system, and suppression of open discussion of this situation became more difficult; resentment of the overarching control by the regime increased among those excluded from its purview.

Although a patrimonial model of political and economic control is still as predominant as military rule, it is weakening. Modest political and economic liberalization is lessening the extent of control and increasing the competitive element of the development model. Unpredictability is increasing, and even the continuance of President Suharto's rule is being contested. The circle is widening, and the development model is shifting to favor marketlike structures over the widespread patrimonial ones.

The Thai experience is more dramatic. In 1973, students led a challenge against military rule that resulted in the king sending the military leaders into exile and appointing a civilian regime. The political and economic structure that accompanied this regime change, however, tolerated a higher degree of public protest and challenge than the king was ready to concede, and military rule was reimposed in 1976. However, important factional divisions had developed within the military that eroded its unity, and the degree of military predominance did not reach its former level. Beginning with the governments of General Prem in 1980, civilians and party politicians became more central in the cabinet, and the assembly became a more significant body. General Prem resigned and a nominal civilian, Chatchai Choonhavan, was appointed as the head of an elected civilian government in 1988.

The process of political change in Thailand has had several important effects. Even more so than in Indonesia, the influence of the technocratic elements of the bureaucracy increased during the 1980s. A strong cohort, frequently trained by or in the United States, became more central in planning and economic policy areas (Muscat, 1990). In part, this was a result of a new conception of development held by the faction of the military associated with General Prem, which redirected military attention toward broad political involvement and away from central control of the economy. This conception focuses on creating a political structure that more broadly encompasses rural areas into a loosely populist framework of quasipolitical organizations for democracy and development and that, not incidentally, enhances national security by bolstering the legitimacy of the king and the military by addressing issues of social justice and political alienation (Suchit, 1988; Saiyud, 1986). Some retrenchment from the patrimonial control of the economy may also have been forced when the network of senior military relationships with major enterprises was disrupted by the 1973–1976 ejection from power (Yos, 1989).

At the same time, the economic elite has grown strong enough to provide a basis of independence. Military figures continue to have significant economic involvements, such as in forestry concessions, but these exist more on an individual level than as part of a centralized patrimonial system.

By the late 1980s, a change from the former patrimonial pattern was clear. Many of the economic relationships had ended, along with some of the central governmental control of the economy, in favor of a more open, competitive structure that was not tied into one overarching control structure. In addition to the military and the bureaucracy, political parties had become important components of the regime, many with close ties to the business world. This greater political pluralism was symbolized by the resignation of General Prem, as a non-elected prime minister, to make way for a government composed of elected figures (albeit, many of them retired military personnel). The resulting political structure still had many economic links, but it included contesting factions rather than having a central patrimonial nature.

Marketlike structures assumed an important role in political and economic spheres. The government under Chatchai had fewer military ministers, especially in economic portfolios, which were hotly contested by civilian members of the coalition because of their value in providing large contracts and other resources to political party-based groups. Previous restrictions on business were largely lifted; the Board of Investments, which had exercised a restraining hand on foreign investment, came close to elimination at a time when—largely for external reasons—Thailand experienced a vast inflow of foreign investment. The economy boomed and was more capitalistic than it had ever been. Political parties competed for position, prestigious figures, financial support, and voter networks in a manner that altered their prior character as mere factions of the Bangkok elite.

However, the tension between a military vision of development and one of market structures was not resolved. Throughout the 1980s, central military figures had articulated an anticapitalist philosophy that to some degree motivated their alternative vision of Thai development. Corruption and links to criminal groups were part of what the military characterized as the "dark forces" associated with the Thai business and political elites. Only the military and the technocrats were seen as having sufficient integrity and commitment to national causes to justify rule.

This philosophical tension was increased by the rise to power of a new faction of the military (Class 5 of Chulachomklao Military Academy) and by interference by the civilian government in military affairs—especially in the appointment of military figures from outside this faction to defense posts. The result was something that had become unthinkable during the 1980s—a coup in early 1990 that dismissed the civilian government in favor of rule by a military junta through a governmental structure led by technocrats. The politicians' and businesspersons' "excessive behavior" quickly came under pressure. Syndicate leaders, frequently associated with political figures, were personally warned by the junta to curb their activities, and investigations of corruption on the part of leading cabinet figures were initiated—ultimately without dramatic result. The market had gone too far, and order was returned.

However, the military was no longer predominant within the evolving political system. Civilian pressure (supported by some elements of the military) to return to an elected government intensified. When the coup leader engineered his own appointment as prime minister, the resultant demonstrations, and their bloody repression, led to his removal and to the return to an elected, civilian government. The Chuan government continued the move toward a marketlike political economy, albeit with greater regard for order.

In Thailand, periods of decline in the degree of military predominance within the regime have produced development models more akin to market structures than to command and control structures. In the political sphere, other centers of power developed in competition with the military network, reducing the range and degree of military involvement. In the economic sphere, control over the national economy was considerably eroded. The patrimonial system, which was at its peak in the 1950s and 1960s, was only a weak shadow in the 1980s. The Thai case also provides hints about the limits of civilian transitions in regimes involving the military. The extent of market "messiness" seems critical to security issues.

Conclusion

Overall, as military regimes Thailand and Indonesia do provide some interesting lessons about the impact of the military on development. Large economic aggregates, as with those of other cases, are not revealing. However, a look at the manner in which a military influence within a government affects developmental structures is more revealing.

Military predominance shapes other aspects of the society in its own image. A system of close control, what we might call a "security coalition," pervades the polity and the economy. This is broadly patrimonial in form and is apparently concerned far more with stability and control than with other aspects of development. In contrast, when the regime is broadened to include significant civilian elements, something more akin to a "growth coalition" emerges, which decentralizes power in the political sphere and relies more on the economic market than on central control mechanisms. In Thailand and Indonesia, the fact that the civilian elements with which power has been shared are largely business interests has shaped this outcome.

The role of technocrats is particularly interesting in these cases. They have a critical position in Indonesia, as well as in Thailand during militarily predominant regimes; in Thailand's civilian regimes their influence has been reduced but is still important. As the traditional administrative professionals and possessors of technical knowledge, they were closely involved in, and largely compatible with, the Thai military regimes. More recently, however, as many have become advocates of the market, they have also provided support to alternate development models. Indonesian technocrats have become, in some senses, the major element within government that President Suharto uses to balance the military. Their technical training gives them legitimacy, which they lend to either form of government. One speculation is that by lending their weight to relatively modest changes in the balance of forces within the regime, they magnify the shifts between control and market philosophies.

The military does affect development, at least in these Third World societies. This is not visible in the aggregate economic effect, however, but rather is seen in the organizational and philosophical foundations. An economic perspective would point to negative effects on growth from such nonmarket structures, yet political economy perspectives increasingly link strong organizational features to economic development in the Third World in a more positive manner. The degree of integrity of such structures is more likely the major issue for developmental outcomes. Corruption, a significant feature of both Indonesian and Thai patrimonial structures, may be the single issue that erodes the security coalition. The fact that factions of both militaries are critical of this feature of their systems may have more positive implications for their countries' development than the move toward market structures.

Legitimacy itself is a key issue. All governments pursue it and fall with its erosion. What they pursue in the name of legitimacy varies, however. Military factions of the elite define legitimacy in terms of stability and control and pursue these values through their development philosophies; for them, growth may in fact be destabilizing. Civilian factions of the elite, in contrast, pursue growth as an outcome that will legitimate their regimes; stability and control, to the degree that they inhibit growth, are the destabilizing forces. These are the roots of contrasting—and sometimes conflicting—visions of the appropriate development model.

❖ ELEVEN ❖

Military Regimes, Military Spending, and Development: A Comparison of Brazil, Nigeria, Pakistan, and the Republic of Korea

Norman A. Graham & Peter M. Lewis

Under what circumstances do military regimes successfully implement projects of economic development? We seek to illuminate this issue by examining four countries attempting programs of state-led capitalist industrialization under military auspices: Brazil, Nigeria, Pakistan, and the Republic of Korea. The central period under comparison is 1965 through 1989, allowing for minor variations among cases. These countries reflected divergent performance during this period, and we attempt to clarify the differential role of military rule in helping to account for such disparities.

Debates over the developmental capabilities of Third World military regimes represent a lineage that extends almost four decades. Until the late 1960s, concern with the putative "modernizing" capacities of national militaries focused attention on the professional orientations of military leaders and the corporate and hierarchical characteristics of armed forces organizations. The experiences of numerous military regimes during the 1970s, reinforced by several cross-national studies, suggested that economic performance could *not* be closely associated with nominal regime type. Military regimes, as a category, did not possess any inherent proclivities toward economic development, nor did they necessarily reflect superior developmental capabilities. Nonetheless, some military governments have achieved notable developmental successes, and their military character was not irrelevant in assessing their efficacy.

The shift to state-centric analyses in the 1980s cast military regimes in a new light. A specific focus on state capacity made the distinction between "weak" and "strong," or "soft" and "hard," states more consequential than ideological or institutional identity. Although military governance gave a significant degree of nominal autonomy to state actors, there was no reason, a priori, to assume *effective* autonomy or the ability to gain a wide range of compliance. Weak authoritarianism was far more prevalent among Third World regimes than strong states of any variety. Yet, the ability of certain regimes to assert an effective and independent developmental role raised important questions about the relative capabilities of different leaders and governing structures.

We inquire whether specific characteristics or circumstances of these regimes qua military regimes help to account for their achievements. In posing this question, we acknowledge that military rule is not the sole determinant of developmental success. Obviously, developmental performance may be attributed to a number of causes including colonial legacies, resource endowments, elements of social structure, cultural attributes, and the strategic and policy choices of leaders. However, military rulers have clearly played a crucial leading role during strategic phases of growth and diversification in certain countries, and this comparison can help us to understand the sources of successful economic leadership by a military regime.

Functionalist assumptions about the developmental role of the military, such as those implied by the bureaucratic-authoritarian model, do not provide a satisfying explanation for military developmentalism (O'Donnell, 1973; Collier, 1979). The challenges of stagnant economic performance or structural deepening do not necessarily create "requisites" for military intervention or state-led industrialization. Indeed, these responses by military leaders are rather uncommon, and military motives are rarely focused primarily on economic change. Those leaders assuming a modernizing or developmental orientation are motivated by particular ideological and professional concerns.

Informed by this agenda, we address, in a preliminary manner, the following question: When does military rule enhance the developmental capacity of the state? The question of when or how military regimes can successfully implement a developmental program entails a number of subsidiary questions, which we note here. Proceeding from the distinction between weak and strong authoritarian regimes, we may inquire whether military rule can significantly strengthen the state. If so, we want to identify the ways in which military regimes enhance state capacity.

Moreover, it is useful to outline the circumstances in which military rulers have successfully undertaken strategies of productive accumulation. We need to ask what factors impel certain rulers toward a concerted developmental purpose. Presumably, the economic policies pursued by military leaders are not merely idiosyncratic; development strategy is linked with other professional concerns, notably security objectives and the professional doctrine of the military. This might lead us to relate certain types of security concerns with particular economic strategies.

The developmental task of the military is clearly affected by relations with other classes or groups in the political system. Although military rule may confer ostensible state autonomy, strategic and policy choices are affected or constrained by relations with strategic constituencies. We, then, need to assess the relative importance of factors internal to the military and the extent to which military rule may be seen as a dependent or an intervening variable in the process of development, constrained by additional exogenous factors.

In this light, it is also essential to bear in mind the broader international context in which regimes operate. The proximate regional security situation informs military perceptions of threat, which may induce military rulers to undertake state-building initiatives or efforts toward growth. Aid and sponsorship from major powers may also be critical in bolstering state capabilities or inducing particular policy directions. Moreover, global market forces and exogenous shocks will create pressures impinging upon certain choices (Haggard, 1990).

With these questions and caveats in mind, it is useful to elaborate the distinctive characteristics of military governance and the salient factors affecting the developmental roles of the military. Nearly all military-led regimes are, in fact, hybrids of military and civilian elements in which civilian technocrats, civil servants, and even politicians may play critical policy and linkage roles; consequently, we need to be sensitive about the variations in military governance. Within the range of civil-military relations, it is nonetheless clear that military-dominated regimes embody common characteristics. They are (almost by definition) authoritarian. They typically place constraints on popular participation (notably politicians, students, and labor), which confers the possibility of regime autonomy for these governments. Patterns of decisionmaking in such regimes tend to be closed, hierarchical, and collegial. These regimes are also motivated by distinctive professional and security concerns, including territorial integrity, international power and prestige, domestic stability, and the corporate integrity of the military itself. Such interests are reflected in perceptions of threat and proclivities of military spending.

A preliminary comparison of economic development in Brazil, Nigeria, Pakistan, and the Republic of Korea for the period 1965–1989 provides the empirical base for our analysis. During this period, Korea sustained a high rate of economic growth and industrial diversification, attended by relatively equitable income distribution and general economic stability (see Table 11.1). Brazil also experienced high growth rates and positive structural change, especially in the manufacturing sector; however, Brazilian development was burdened by wide income disparities, severe inflationary pressures, and increased indebtedness, and growth slowed in the late 1970s and the 1980s. Nigeria, whose growth was driven by petroleum wealth, reflected mediocre growth of the nonoil gross domestic product (GDP), minimal structural change in manufacturing, increased maldistribution of income, and severe fiscal instability. Pakistan enjoyed spurts of substantial growth and institutional development, but, constrained by resource limitations and political instability, it achieved little diversified or consistent development. In important respects, Pakistan has failed to move beyond initial stages of state-building.

Without providing a detailed assessment of the economic policies of each government, we venture four conclusions about the countries' developmental experiences. First, comparison of these cases suggests that a concerted developmental program is preceded by a distinct project of state-building and is accompanied by the further development of institutional capacity. The institutional context is essential to the creation of an effective state and the implementation of a project of accumulation. Given the nature of military governance, three factors appear especially salient in the developmental orientations of such regimes: the relative unity of senior leadership, the strength and coherence of developmental doctrine, and the technical and administrative support available to leadership.

A second conclusion is that the military's definition of national security animates the developmental orientations of military regimes. A proximate external threat, in the case of Korea, fostered a strong incentive to assume a mercantilist view of national economic power and equally provided a mantle of legitimacy to an authoritarian regime pursuing a concerted development push. External threats were strongly perceived by Pakistan's military rulers, although perhaps defined differently, but there was no real impetus toward consistent economic and industrial development comparable to Korea's. The definition of internal security, accompanied by class polarization, in Brazil bolstered guarantees to property and fostered an alliance between industrializing elites and military rulers. A nationalist orientation to security, unaccompanied by salient external threats—as seen in Nigeria—did not provide a distinctive inducement for economic development, although it did accentuate statist proclivities in development strategy.

There is scant basis for correlating the relative or absolute level of military expenditures with developmental performance in these four cases. Military expenditures have been burdensome in Brazil, Korea, and Pakistan at times, and some evidence exists of multiplier effects from domestic military procurement and technology transfer in the arms industry. Moreover, military rulers guarantee the military's entitlement to resources, and we can assume that certain levels of expenditure are higher under military governance than under a secure civilian regime. However, as discussed in Chapters 2 and 3 of this volume, levels of

Table 11.1 Growth in GDP and GNP in Brazil, Nigeria, Pakistan, and the Republic of Korea, 1965–1989

Country	Growth in GNP	Growth in GDP		
	1965–1989	1965–1973	1973–1984	1980–1989
Brazil	3.5	9.8	4.4	3.0
Nigeria	.2	9.7	.7	−0.4
Pakistan	2.5	5.4	5.6	6.4
Republic of Korea	7.0	10.0	7.2	9.7

Source: World Bank, *World Development Report* (1986–1991).

military expenditure are also strongly related to perceptions of threat and security definitions: Apprehension over security has been consistently high in Korea and Pakistan in response to external threats; these concerns were moderate and rising in Brazil in the 1960s, primarily in reaction to a perceived "subversive," or leftist, threat; and security was almost exclusively an internal problem in Nigeria, declining sharply in salience after federal victory in the civil war.

Finally, the policy choices and state capabilities of each regime have been influenced by their relative global positions. The role of U.S. economic aid, policy advice, market access, and military assistance to the Republic of Korea is indisputable. Such factors played an important role in fostering a strategy of export-led growth and contributed to its success. Conversely, the fortuitous changes in the world oil market clearly influenced Nigeria's turn toward an import-substitution strategy while also eliminating many incentives for efficient investment and the development of indigenous production.

The Cases

Brazil

Brazil offers a contradictory record of relative state autonomy and impressive economic growth combined with domestic constraints limiting the sustainability and depth of economic transformation. The military era in Brazil (1964–1985) began with a decade-long economic "miracle" characterized by rapid economic expansion and industrial diversification. The regime played a pivotal role in stemming inflation, breaking through political stalemate, and sustaining conditions for investment.

Nonetheless, the military in Brazil has had limited autonomy in resisting domestic consumption pressures and marshaling resources toward investment. This stems largely from the populist tradition in Brazilian politics and the relatively strong class forces confronted by the regime. The need to deal with more coherent corporate groups, including civilian politicians, presented constraints on economic policy. This political context affected the distributive impact of rapid development and contributed to reliance upon a debt-led strategy of growth.

An extended process of state-building yielded a stronger Brazilian state in the 1960s than was the case in Nigeria or Pakistan. The authoritarian regime of Getúlio Vargas (1930–1945) went a long way toward reducing regional autonomy and consolidating the authority of the central government. By reducing social and institutional barriers to accumulation on a national scale, the Estado Novo provided a legacy that strengthened subsequent development efforts.

The societal context was fractious and volatile. Relatively strong class politics had produced considerable polarization, increased violence, and a sense of threat among the middle and upper classes. The repression of the populist coalition, notably organized labor, was accompanied by a growing alliance between military elites and the industrial bourgeoisie. The reassertion of property rights was a leading concern in the early years of authoritarian rule, and this served to foster subsequent investment and expansion.

The João Goulart regime, beset by growing political instability and unable to manage a deepening economic crisis, was ousted by the military in 1964. The new regime targeted a deteriorating internal security situation and the worsening economy as central problems. Although intially professing a "caretaker" role, five successive military leaders ruled over the next twenty-one years.

The military regime enlisted a team of civilian technocrats as the architects of economic policy, an alliance that fostered a more coherent developmental focus within the state. The centralization of policymaking in the hands of a small economic team backed by the repressive power of the military created considerable license for economic reform. Upon taking power, the regime instituted a concerted anti-inflation program, which was followed by a concerted industrial push. The "Brazilian miracle" spanned nearly a decade, yielding impressive levels of economic growth and a considerable deepening and expanding of the industrial sector.

Despite intensifying authoritarianism, the military in Brazil manifests less autonomy than is the case in Korea. Although the regime instituted a widespread suppression of political mobilization, military leaders were still constrained by relations with corporate interests.

Between 1962 and 1973, we observe steadily rising defense spending, reflecting increasing military concerns with internal security, focusing especially on the threat from the left. After 1975, military expenditures stabilized and then declined (see Table 11.2).

Nigeria

Nigeria's experience illustrates the liabilities of a dirigiste strategy within the context of a weak authoritarian state. The fragmentation of government and private-sector elites provided a weak social foundation for state-led development. Political instability and factionalism inhibited the assertion of state autonomy, and key entrepreneurial groups were incorporated into rent-seeking alliances with state actors. Security challenges did influence the developmental orientation of the military, but authoritarian rulers proved incapable of sustaining a coherent policy direction, subordinating key social groups to the exigencies of accumulation, or fostering the administrative capacities necessary for economic management. Despite the windfall conferred by abundant export revenues, military governments in Nigeria have displayed scant success in promoting economic growth and transformation.

The colonial process of state formation bequeathed postindependence Nigeria a deeply divided society. The Nigerian political system has been dominated by three hegemonic ethnic groups—the Hausa-Fulani, the Yoruba, and the Ibo—alongside numerous adjacent minority groups. Initially, each of the

Table 11.2 Brazil: Military Expenditures, GNP, Central Government
Expenditures, and Development Assistance Receipts, 1967–1989

Year	Military Expenditures (ME) (millions of dollars) Current	Gross Nat. Prod. (GNP) (millions of dollars) Current	ME/GNP (%)	ME/CGE (%)	Official Development Assistance Receipts (millions of dollars)
1967	746	33,135	2.2	19.4	—
1968	765	37,907	2.0	17.8	—
1969	891	43,333	2.1	21.9	—
1970	1,160	50,664	2.3	23.8	—
1971	1,300	59,856	2.2	21.7	—
1972	1,420	69,580	2.0	19.4	—
1973	1,680	79,514	2.1	19.0	—
1974	954	76,660	1.2	6.7	—
1975	994	88,130	1.1	5.6	—
1976	1,222	102,700	1.2	5.8	—
1977	1,085	113,900	1.0	4.0	—
1978	1,381	158,300	.9	3.5	113
1979	1,385	183,900	.8	3.2	107
1980	1,559	217,800	.7	2.8	85
1981	1,665	229,100	.7	2.6	235
1982	2,382	243,400	1.0	3.2	208
1983	2,169	244,500	.9	2.8	101
1984	2,226	268,400	.8	2.8	161
1985	2,402	300,900	.8	2.1	123
1986	3,018	337,200	.9	2.5	178
1987	3,356	361,800	.9	2.1	289
1988	1,209	372,600	.3	NA	210
1989	—	—	—	—	189

Sources: U.S. ACDA (1967–1989); and World Bank, *World Development Report* (1986–1991).

major groups dominated one of the three semiautonomous regions. Through a number of subsequent subdivisions, the nation was divided into thirty states by 1992. Nonetheless, ethnic and regional divisions continue to pervade Nigerian politics and society, and invidious communal pressures are evident in all public institutions, including the military. Class politics and class identities tend to be weak, but ubiquitous ethno-regional factions exert strong clientalist pressures on the state.

For more than two-thirds of its postindependence history, Nigeria has been governed by military rulers. At independence, nationalist political leaders inherited a weak and fractious central state. The centripetal pulls of regional contention ultimately threatened the nation's existence. In 1966, Nigeria's First Republic was ousted by a group of southern officers, citing intractable corruption and corrosive ethnic antagonism as the rationale for intervention against the civilian regime. Within a year, the military government was in turn overthrown by rival officers, concerned with the preponderance of Ibos in the leadership and the centralizing initiatives of the regime.

The Gowon government quickly found itself embroiled in civil war, as ethnic pogroms erupted in the north and the Ibo states of the east attempted secession. Following the central government's victory in 1970, Yakubu Gowon presided over the incipient petroleum boom and promised a transition to civilian rule. Impatient with his slow progress, another military faction ousted Gowon in 1975. General Murtala Muhammed proceeded with a political transition and an ambitious program of state-led economic expansion. Murtala was assassinated in an abortive coup attempt after nine months in office, but his colleague, Olusegun Obasanjo, continued his central policies.

The transition to civilian rule was carried out in 1979, but the Second Republic quickly succumbed to massive corruption, political fraud, and violence; and a stern, "corrective" regime led by northern officers took power at the beginning of 1984. Within two years, policy drift and authoritarianism had eroded the legitimacy of the Buhari government, and General Ibrahim Babangida took power in a bloodless coup. President Babangida initiated a new transition to civilian rule, which was postponed several times to (and in) 1993, and implemented a broad program of economic liberalization.

Recurrent civil-military political cycles in Nigeria have yielded not only regime instability but also administrative weakness. Although Nigeria possesses the elements of a vigorous civil society, there have been few strong pressures from below to impel democratization. Nonetheless, each successive military regime has necessarily sought legitimacy through commitment to a democratic transition. Regimes that have eschewed or procrastinated in their caretaker roles have traditionally been ousted by other officers. Senior military leaders have continually evinced a concern with the corporate identity of their institution and have left power lest they be excessively politicized.

Successive leaders during the 1970s presided over a massive expansion in state activities, fueled by burgeoning petroleum revenues. The civil war accentuated nationalist feelings and statist proclivities among the senior leadership. The dirigiste tendency in development strategy was soon infused by abundant external resources, prompting an aggressive development drive led by the public sector. An ambitious program of state-led import-substituting industrialization was initiated, with the objective of converting Nigeria from a primary producer to a significant industrial power within a decade. The military implemented an expansive program of public investment without an attendant development of administrative capacity. Economic growth was driven by the fortuitous, yet unstable, petroleum windfall and was not paralleled by enhanced state capabilities or the foundations of an integrated productive infrastructure.

This episode yielded minimal growth in the nonoil sectors of the economy and ultimately failed to engender diversification or structural change. Changes in relative prices and the neglect of nonoil exports yielded stagnation in the agricultural and mineral sectors. A raft of expensive industrial capital projects were afflicted by planning problems, administrative disarray, corruption, and fiscal shortfalls. Domestic private investment gravitated toward trade, real estate, and services; and widespread capital flight depleted local financial markets. In consequence, an average annual GDP growth rate of 4.5 percent during the 1970s gave way to a negative average growth rate over the next decade, as petroleum receipts declined and other productive sectors remained moribund.

As the decade-long petroleum boom subsided in the early 1980s, new rulers grappled with the challenges of economic austerity and adjustment. Through these long cycles of development, Nigeria's military leaders have been relatively unsuccessful in fostering economic transformation. The boom era yielded a profligate and haphazard expansion of the state sector, accompanied by a proliferation of rent-seeking and illicit activities in the private sector. A decade of crisis impelled military leaders to impose stabilization measures, but the reforms of the 1980s yielded scant productive effects and did not engender greater discipline within the state sector.

The overwhelming security challenge since independence has been to maintain Nigeria's integrity as a federal entity. The secessionist threat, leading to civil war in 1967, stands as the preeminent military challenge in the nation's history. The victory of federal forces in 1970 largely allayed this danger, and the country has not faced a comparable internal security threat since the end of the war. Regionally, Nigeria has been engaged in minor border disputes and more recently has spearheaded regional peacekeeping efforts in Liberia. External security concerns have never been especially salient, facilitating a demobilization of the military soon after the civil war and decreasing defense expenditures thereafter. The absolute reduction in military spending during the oil-boom era resulted in a sharp decline in defense expenditure as a proportion of GDP.

Although security concerns have accentuated military concerns with economic development, threat perceptions have not impelled a concerted mercantilist drive. Military expenditures have carried scant direct growth effects. The external and domestic challenges that have emerged since 1970 have been met with existing resources and have not prompted military escalation. Low levels of spending have yielded few multiplier effects, and military leaders have lacked both the incentive and the technological capacities to erect a substantial domestic defense industry.

The pattern of military expenditure (Table 11.3) reflects this security context. Military expenditures rose sharply between 1966 and 1972, reflecting wartime expansion. Demobilization after the civil war prompted a leveling of expenditure between 1972 and 1974. After 1975, when Murtala Muhammed initiated a concerted reduction in the size of the military, expenditures gradually declined. The proportional weight of defense spending dwindled even more rapidly than absolute reductions amid general fiscal growth during the boom period.

In sum, the military has proven to be a weak developmental agent in Nigeria. Military rule has not resolved the fundamental dilemmas of state weakness and elite fragmentation, which hobble the capacity for effective intervention in economic affairs. Military regimes have been susceptible to the invidious ethnic rivalries and communal antagonisms that permeate Nigerian society, and authoritarian leaders have been unable or unwilling to assert autonomy from a multitude of distributive pressures exerted by strategic constituencies. Military leaders have been unable to rely upon a strong technocratic cadre, and perennial bureaucratic purges and reorganizations have engendered an unstable and corrupt administrative environment. The security context has provided few incentives to foster economic growth. Moreover, the availability of abundant external revenues has dampened concern for domestic productive growth and has tended to mask the consequences of inefficiency and fiscal profligacy. A

Table 11.3 Nigeria: Military Expenditures, GNP, Central Government Expenditures, and Development Assistance Receipts, 1967–1989

Year	Military Expenditures (ME) (millions of dollars) Current	Gross Nat. Prod. (GNP) (millions of dollars) Current	ME/GNP (%)	ME/CGE (%)	Official Development Assistance Receipts (millions of dollars)
1967	252	6,817	3.7	NA	—
1968	412	7,000	5.9	NA	—
1969	906	9,277	9.8	48.0	—
1970	732	12,495	5.9	36.6	—
1971	623	14,711	4.2	24.1	—
1972	814	15,601	5.2	25.4	—
1973	890	17,716	5.0	21.1	—
1974	1,136	38,680	2.9	13.7	—
1975	2,314	41,710	5.5	15.7	—
1976	1,894	48,970	3.9	11.6	—
1977	518	14,850	3.5	14.4	—
1978	520	16,900	3.1	18.3	43
1979	467	19,350	2.4	13.1	27
1980	505	21,350	2.4	13.5	36
1981	515	22,410	2.3	13.7	41
1982	449	24,100	1.9	11.9	37
1983	405	23,680	1.7	11.1	48
1984	377	22,600	1.7	11.3	33
1985	333	25,350	1.3	9.4	32
1986	279	27,150	1.0	5.4	59
1987	202	26,830	.8	2.7	69
1988	223	28,690	.8	2.6	120
1989	—	—	—	—	339

Sources: U.S. ACDA (1967–1989); and World Bank, *World Development Report* (1986–1991).

combination of internal social constraints, professional concerns, and global market conditions have framed the policy choices and political efficacy of Nigeria's military rulers.

Pakistan

Despite a rapidly growing and burdensome population, a literacy rate of less than 30 percent, and a substantial proportion (in excess of 50 percent) of the population dependent upon agricultural employment, Pakistan has enjoyed periods of substantial economic growth. Annual growth in the economy averaged slightly more than 6 percent during the 1980s, for example. But war, natural disasters, and political instability, with frequent changes in administration and policy, have seriously weakened the economy and set back growth and development for significant periods. Indeed, as indicated in Table 11.1, the average annual growth in GNP for the period 1965–1989 was a rather modest 2.5 percent.

The societal context has been rather chaotic and divided on regional, linguistic, religious, and partisan bases. Accordingly, political regimes have been unable to exercise consistent autonomy in the formulation and implementation of a coherent development plan.

In the first twenty-five years after independence from Britain and partition from India in 1947, Pakistan operated with seven different constitutions—clearly a country beset with persistent political instability and internal threats to, and discontent with, its numerous military, quasimilitary, and civilian regimes. The presidential system of government initiated by Field Marshal Mohammad Ayub Khan in June 1962 was replaced in August 1973 with a parliamentary system. In the wake of charges of corruption and fraud in the general election of March 1977, which was won handily by the ruling Pakistan People's Party (PPP), strikes and protests urged and organized by the opposition Pakistan National Alliance raised the threat of civil war. The army responded with a coup and a declaration of martial law under General Mohammad Zia ul-Haq. Prime Minister Zulfikar Ali Bhutto and several other leading politicians were arrested. General Zia assumed the presidency in September 1978 after the conclusion of President Fazal Elahi Chaudhry's constitutional term and began the development of a political system based upon Islamic values and law.

Former Prime Minister Bhutto was hanged in April 1979 after a controversial death sentence (for allegedly conspiring to murder a political opponent) was confirmed by the Supreme Court. Political turmoil and maneuvering ensued, as Zia struggled to redefine the political system on a nonpartisan basis with an enhanced presidency. His "Islamization" program received overwhelming approval in a referendum in 1984, but the voting was tainted by a boycott organized by the Movement for the Restoration of Democracy—composed of PPP leaders—and by charges of fraud. Parliamentary elections in February 1985 helped to confirm Zia's hold on the reins of government, and Mohammad Khan Junejo was designated prime minister.

The Junejo government was, however, dismissed by President Zia in May 1988 in a "constitutional coup." The following year Zia was killed, along with the U.S. ambassador, in the suspicious crash of a military transport plane. The military refrained from exerting renewed control, and Ghulam Ishaq Khan was named acting president of an Emergency National Council. The PPP received a plurality in the subsequent parliamentary elections.

Benazir Bhutto, daughter of the former prime minister, had returned to Pakistan from London to lead the PPP and was appointed prime minister by Khan. But her support soon faded in the face of concerted opposition from a coalition of conservative and religious-oriented political leaders. Charges of abuse of power and corruption led Khan to dismiss Bhutto in August 1990. The PPP was then soundly defeated in the November parliamentary elections, and Mian Mohammad Nawaz Sharif, of the anti-Bhutto Islamic Democratic Alliance, was named prime minister.

The security situation in Pakistan offers an almost perfect illustration of the "multilayered cake" concept developed by Mohammed Ayoob in Chapter 2 of this volume. Pakistan's external environment has been characterized by a continuing and significant perceived threat from India to the south and east. This, of course, is rooted in the long-term rivalry and conflict between Hindus and Muslims in the region—made abundantly clear by the communal rioting, large-scale migration, and loss of life and property set in motion at partition—but it also stems from persistent territorial and geopolitical disputes. At the base of the conflict are competing claims to the border territories of Jammu and Kashmir. The Kashmir dispute erupted into war with India in 1965 and has remained a source of hostility to the present.

Internal instability and violence in both India and Pakistan have been accentuated and drawn upon in the relations between the two countries. The most dramatic instance came with India's support for the Bengalis in the East Pakistan crisis, over which war between India and Pakistan broke out in 1971. The result was the independence of East Pakistan in the form of the state of Bangladesh. More recently, India has charged Pakistan with complicity in Sikh separatist moves in the Punjab and as a stimulus to growing Hindu-Muslim tensions in various regions of India. Ethnic-linguistic tensions in Sind, the Punjab, and Baluchistan have erupted into violence in Pakistan. Pressures to redraw provincial borders and increase autonomy have complicated the central government's state-building task (see Rizvi, 1991).

India's detonation of a nuclear device in the Rajasthan Desert near Pakistan in May 1974, not surprisingly, heightened Pakistani perceptions of threat, despite repeated Indian claims of the peaceful intent of its nuclear development program. This led Pakistan to embark upon a systematic effort to acquire nuclear weapons technology and production capability—much to the dismay of the United States, a primary source of Pakistan's foreign military and economic assistance.

U.S. and Soviet rivalry and competition in arms transfers, particularly during the periods of "bloc competition" and "bloc competition modified"—to use the terms developed by David Louscher and James Sperling in Chapter 4 of this volume—are well illustrated in South Asia, with India qualifying for the "primary recipient" category and Pakistan as a "significant recipient." U.S. military and economic support for Pakistan has been substantial, rather more than that provided to Brazil and Nigeria but less than that allocated to Korea in the 1950s and 1960s. But aid to Pakistan varied according to the salience of the U.S.-USSR Cold War struggle, with some emphasis, for example, on assisting Pakistan's pivotal role in supporting the struggle against Soviet influence in Afghanistan. It has also varied according to the depth of U.S.-Pakistan disagreement over Pakistan's nuclear development program. Total official development assistance receipts by Pakistan in recent years are fairly substantial in comparison with the other three countries we examine here, as Tables 11.2–11.5 suggest.

Pakistan has attempted to diversify its sources of military equipment supplies, relying at times on the People's Republic of China, for example. Military expenditures by the government of Pakistan have been substantial and consistent, as indicated in Table 11.4. Indeed, measured as a percentage of both central government expenditures and GNP, Pakistan has consistently outspent Brazil and Nigeria since the early 1970s and has frequently surpassed the military expenditures of the Republic of Korea. The burden of this expenditure may well be a significant drain on economic growth in Pakistan, but so are inconsistent development efforts and political fragmentation. Military rule in Pakistan has, to be generous, stabilized a divided and conflict-ridden political environment at times, but there is little evidence to suggest that it has "hardened" the state regarding economic development.

Republic of Korea

Since the early 1960s, Korean leaders have engendered the development of a relatively strong and effective state. In part, this success stems from prior state-building experience, including the development of institutional capacity under Japanese rule and the effects of U.S. sponsorship, aid, and policy advice, which bolstered technocratic roles and administrative capacity. The strong external sponsorship has included access to markets and technology, as well as technical and financial assistance, but the government has also faced hard choices, given resource constraints and the phasing out of prodigious U.S. assistance. Annual economic growth has varied, but, as shown in Table 11.1, it has averaged in excess of 7 percent since the 1960s.

The nature of the military role has varied substantially, but its influence has consistently been important. This of course derives in part from clear security concerns, external and internal (indeed, Ayoob's concept of a security "multi-layered cake" in Chapter 2 again seems appropriate here): The immediate, strong external threat from the north spurred a mercantilist development effort. National sacrifices were readily justified, and the embattled national circumstances

Table 11.4 Pakistan: Military Expenditures, GNP, Central Government
Expenditures, and Development Assistance Receipts, 1967–1989

Year	Military Expenditures (ME) (millions of dollars) Current	Gross Nat. Prod. (GNP) (millions of dollars) Current	ME/GNP (%)	ME/CGE (%)	Official Development Assistance Receipts (millions of dollars)
1967	274	4,600	6.0	20.5	—
1968	319	5,150	6.2	20.5	—
1969	339	5,709	5.9	29.1	—
1970	389	6,755	5.8	31.8	—
1971	456	7,159	6.4	43.6	—
1972	505	7,515	6.7	40.8	—
1973	572	8,633	6.6	39.7	—
1974	544	9,612	5.7	28.3	—
1975	664	10,890	6.1	26.5	—
1976	730	12,170	6.0	26.1	—
1977	537	9,788	5.5	23.8	—
1978	636	11,490	5.5	24.5	639
1979	701	12,950	5.4	21.6	684
1980	845	15,570	5.4	23.6	1,075
1981	1,019	18,460	5.5	23.7	768
1982	1,210	20,900	5.8	27.2	850
1983	1,581	23,100	6.8	29.0	735
1984	1,626	25,180	6.5	27.0	749
1985	1,905	27,840	6.8	28.1	801
1986	2,109	30,020	7.0	25.1	970
1987	2,287	32,940	6.9	25.7	879
1988	2,516	36,380	6.9	27.1	1,408
1989	—	—	—	—	1,119

Sources: U.S. ACDA (1967–1989); and World Bank, *World Development Report* (1986–1991).

enabled the military to assume a mantle of legitimacy. As Table 11.5 depicts, military expenditure has been fairly consistent and substantial. Because the security concerns of the Republic of Korea were clearly viewed within the context of the Cold War struggle, U.S. economic assistance was substantial, particularly in the 1950s and 1960s (Mason et al., 1980, 165–208). As noted in Chapter 4 of the present volume, the Republic of Korea remained a "significant recipient" of military equipment transfers in the 1980s. In part through capability developed with the assistance of licensed production arrangements with U.S. firms, it has also become a "significant supplier" of military equipment.

If we examine the societal context, the early period was marked by weak class formation and a high degree of regime autonomy, labor repression, and restrictions on participation. A relatively successful land reform program did help to improve income distribution, particularly in comparison with other

Table 11.5 Republic of Korea: Military Expenditures, GNP, Central
Government Expenditures, and Development Assistance Receipts,
1967–1989

Year	Military Expenditures (ME) (millions of dollars) Current	Gross Nat. Prod. (GNP) (millions of dollars) Current	ME/GNP (%)	ME/CGE (%)	Official Development Assistance Receipts (millions of dollars)
1967	207	5,315	3.9	22.9	—
1968	252	6,252	4.0	22.9	—
1969	302	7,544	4.0	22.5	—
1970	332	8,559	3.9	22.8	—
1971	442	9,804	4.5	25.7	—
1972	513	10,901	4.7	23.8	—
1973	501	13,372	3.7	24.5	—
1974	906	20,870	4.3	26.7	—
1975	1,144	24,450	4.7	26.4	—
1976	1,670	29,660	5.6	30.6	—
1977	1,873	32,930	5.7	30.8	—
1978	2,923	48,650	6.0	32.6	164
1979	2,943	56,640	5.2	26.7	134
1980	3,607	58,860	6.1	29.3	139
1981	4,249	68,330	6.3	27.8	331
1982	4,755	78,430	6.2	27.2	34
1983	4,979	90,240	5.8	27.9	8
1984	5,182	101,600	5.4	26.6	−37
1985	5,630	111,100	5.4	26.6	−9
1986	6,125	126,900	5.2	27.5	−18
1987	6,427	146,700	4.8	25.5	11
1988	7,202	168,010	4.3	25.2	10
1989	—	—	—	—	−9

Sources: U.S. ACDA (1967–1989); and World Bank, *World Development Report* (1986–1991).

developing countries. Industrial leaders gained greater leverage in the 1970s, however, and class formation has been evident in recent years, adding to growing pressures for democracy. During the transition to democracy, the regime has lost some autonomy and increased its distributive function.

The task of rebuilding the republic after the Korean War, both economically and politically, was enormous. Unfortunately, the early political leaders directed much of their efforts toward holding on to power (see Graham, 1991). Concern about the tide of political instability and the failure to act on evident corruption in the army finally led a group of young officers, headed by Major General Park Chung Hee, to seize power on May 19, 1961.

The Park military regime began with a sweeping effort to remove incompetent and corrupt army leaders—"military purification"—as well as politicians considered unfit for government service. Two principal institutions became dominant in the efforts of the junta, the newly created Korean Central Intelligence Agency (KCIA) and the Supreme Council for National Reconstruction. The National Assembly was dissolved, and military officers were appointed to prominent government posts.

Following earlier patterns, Park became concerned primarily with holding on to political power, to which end he instituted constitutional amendments and declarations of martial law. Park resigned from the army to run in the first election of the Third Republic on October 15, 1963. He won this and two subsequent elections and served for three terms after circumventing constitutional prohibitions on a third term.

President Park eliminated his legislative problems by proclaiming a state of national emergency on December 6, 1971, in response to what he perceived as an increasingly threatening international environment. Internal repression increased with the declaration of martial law on October 17, 1972. Park justified increasing repression as a response to security threats from North Korea and uncertainty about the reliability of U.S. support in light of the Nixon Doctrine and the fall of South Vietnam.

Economic development was important among Park's goals, and he implemented two five-year economic plans that achieved substantial economic growth. The plans were characterized by aggressive industrial-export expansion during the 1960s. In 1973, the regime inaugurated a campaign of industrial deepening and diversification of export markets. The period was characterized by sustained high growth, capital formation, and industrial diversification.

The Park regime began the export drive with a sharp increase in subsidies for exporters. This was gradually raised to the level of compulsion, as export targets were set for individual firms by planning officials, who offered financing in a multiple interest rate regime. Exports as a percentage of GNP grew from 5 percent in the 1950s to 35 percent in the 1980s. Foreign investment was not encouraged; Korean firms were driven to achieve international competitive success independently (Amsden, 1989, 66–72).

But Park's political fortunes changed in the late 1970s, as economic growth slowed, partly because of the rise in oil prices and the attendant global recession. Labor unrest grew, electoral support declined, and confrontations with students in Taegu, Seoul, and especially Pusan became more threatening. Calls for reduced repression went unheeded, which led to open conflict among Park's close political associates. Finally, on October 26, 1979, a strategy meeting involving Park, Kim Jae Gyu, the director of the KCIA, and Ch'a Ji Chol, chief of the Presidential Security Force, ended when Kim assassinated both Park and Ch'a.

In the wake of the assassination, Major General Chun Doo Hwan and a group of younger officers gained control of the military. Chun exercised considerable power behind the scenes, convincingly putting down political unrest—most notably in the Kwangju incident, which would haunt him later, at least politically.

The Fifth Republic was established on March 3, 1981, with the inauguration of Chun Doo Hwan (who had retired from the army) as president. Chun promised a period of "self-realization" for Korea and eliminated many of the repressive measures of the previous regime. He also promised democratization and a limitation of his tenure as president to one seven-year term. His stated goal was to build a democratic welfare state.

Economic growth and progress toward self-realization were substantial under Chun. GDP grew at a rate of more than 9 percent in the 1980s, but there was also considerable trade friction and concern about the growing dominance of the major industrial groupings, or Chaebol. There were also periods of stagnation and concern about trade imbalances and dependence upon foreign technology. External economic shocks, capital shortages, and inflation threatened growth early in the Chun regime; but economic leaders borrowed substantially, introduced austerity measures effectively, and increased labor productivity dramatically. The result, together with continued entrepreneurial drive in the private sector, was a decade of nearly 10 percent annual growth (see Table 11.1 and Amsden, 1989).

The president did make good on his promises to promote democracy and limit his own tenure. Direct presidential elections among retired General Roh Tae Woo, Chun's preferred candidate and two opposition leaders, Kim Dae Jung and Kim Young Sam, were conducted in December 1987. Roh narrowly defeated the split opposition and was inaugurated as president in February 1988. In December 1992, Kim Young Sam defeated Kim Dae Jung and Chung Ju Yung (founder of the Hyundai business group) for the presidency. Kim Young Sam had joined Roh's Democratic Liberal Party and thus added the regime's political (and military) support to his own political base. The election was not entirely free from regime-sponsored interference, but a relatively orderly transfer of democratic leadership was achieved. Certainly, no direct role of the military was evident.

Much of the development, policy, and political intervention of the military in the republic must be seen as a coherent and direct response, based on a broad internal consensus, to external military threats and concerns with internal subversion perceived as emanating from North Korea (not without substance, of course, given the war and the subsequent incursions and assassination attempts). These security concerns, together with some measure of the personal ambitions of key leaders—notably presidents Syngman Rhee and Park Chung Hee—have led to heavy military involvement, in a variety of forms, in the government of the Republic of Korea for most of its history. The military has also been an important tool of social mobility in the republic, and a strong commitment to national development as well as to national security has been evident in the officer corps (see Bunge, 1982, 188; Steinberg, 1988, 11).

As the economy has become more developed and complex, however, military or retired military bureaucrats have become increasingly inappropriate for key technical positions. Civilian bureaucrats with technical skills appeared increasingly indispensable during the Chun years. Moreover, elements of civil society have arisen to challenge the rationale of authoritarian rule. Disaffected students, long the conscience of the drive for democracy, have found it increasingly difficult to radicalize the emerging and prosperous middle class, particularly in an environment of government reform and military restraint. This, in turn, has lessened the continuing anxiety of military leaders over political instability and external threats. Substantial economic and industrial development, fostered by a successful mercantilist orientation and considerable external support, together with economic weakness in North Korea and a post–Cold War reduction in external political support for the North, have reinforced the confidence and strength of the South's civilian leadership.

Conclusion

In this chapter we have broadly compared the economic performance of four military regimes from the mid-1960s through the 1980s. We have observed considerable divergence in growth rates and structural change in the economies of Brazil, Nigeria, Pakistan, and the Republic of Korea, and we have looked to variations in the nature of military governance as a partial explanation for these differences. We find several broad qualitative features that can help to account for the developmental orientations of military regimes.

First, security concerns and professional interests may motivate a concerted developmental program. In all four countries, strong security challenges prompted a more statist and authoritarian direction in development strategy. The differences in performance resulted from an array of other factors.

Second, the military must work through a broader state apparatus. Military governance may strengthen the state, but it is equally likely that a weak state will constrain economic policy. In Korea and Brazil, the regimes inherited a relatively sound legacy of state-building and took additional measures to bolster state capabilities. In consequence, these governments were able to control domestic consumption, to channel investment and shape domestic incentives, and to implement a "labor-repressive" industrialization policy. In Nigeria and Pakistan, comparatively fragmented and unstable states proved too weak to manage the diverse political and technical requisites of economic growth.

Third, security challenges did not correspond in linear fashion with defense expenditure or economic growth. The link between military spending and development was generally indirect and rather tenuous.

Finally, the global context was a crucial element in the developmental performance of the military. Regional security concerns provided a proximate threat in two cases—Korea and Pakistan. External sponsorship and advantageous market position also provided crucial resources to some regimes, notably Korea (foreign aid and market access) and Nigeria (oil revenues). However, as we have seen, developmental doctrine, technocratic direction, and state strength proved decisive in the utilization of such resources and the realization of a successful transformational strategy. Table 11.6 provides a suggestive summary of the comparison.

Table 11.6 Summary Comparison

Country	Economic Growth	Military Spending	Definition of Threat	Societal Division	External Support
Brazil	High/medium	Medium	Strong/moderate (internal)	High (class)	Low
Nigeria	Medium/low	Low	Strong (internal; 1966–1970)	High (communal)	Low
Pakistan	Medium/ sporadic	High	Strong/moderate (external and internal)	Medium	Medium (but sporadic)
Republic of Korea	High	High	Strong (external); moderate/weak (internal)	Low/medium (ideolog.)	High

❖ TWELVE ❖

War, Military Spending, and Food Security in Africa

Marcus Cheatham

Famine is rarely a bolt from the blue, a wholly random and unpredictable occurrence that can be meaningfully considered in isolation from the economic, social, and political structures of a specific society.... The proximate cause of a famine might lie in some apparently unpredictable "natural disaster," like a flood or drought, or in a "man-made" calamity like a civil war or invasion; but these are often no more than the precipitating factors, intensifying or bringing to the fore a society's inner contradictions and inherent weaknesses, exposing an already extant vulnerability to food shortages and famine.

—*David Arnold*

During the past twenty years sub-Saharan Africa has become the hungriest region on earth. Although per capita food production rose during the period in all other regions, it declined by 20 percent in Africa. Africa must import nearly 10 billion tons of grain each year to feed its people, yet even with imports, food availability declined 5 percent (FAO, 1990; UNDP, 1989). The effects of hunger are manifest in high levels of infant and child mortality and high adult mortality from diseases such as measles and dysentery, which are not usually fatal unless the body is weakened by malnourishment.

It is readily evident that military activity is at least partly to blame for Africa's food crises. Discussing the African famines, Paul Pyschas and Pentti Malaska wrote: "The correlation between war and famine is quite plain to see. War diverts a nation's resources and distracts the attention of its leaders; fighting can disrupt planting and harvesting and drive people from their farms and into refugee camps; relief efforts can be delayed by the conflict or blocked altogether. War sows fear, confusion and hate, reaping harvests of hunger, homelessness and death" (1989, 114).

If such were necessary, empirical research has confirmed the association between war and hunger in Africa. For example, in their survey of Africa's food crises in the 1980s, John Borton and Edward Clay concluded, "Civil war and externally financed insurgency were primarily responsible for propelling a food crisis into a famine in five out of the six worst affected countries" (1986, 258). John Staatz found that between 1970 and 1980, average calorie availability declined by four-tenths of 1 percent per year in African countries affected by war, whereas it increased by two-tenths of 1 percent per year in African countries enjoying peace (1989, 3). In this chapter I use the term *military famine* to describe sharp increases in hunger that have primarily military origins.

The fact that the United States, the former Soviet Union, Cuba, and South Africa dramatically altered their strategic postures in Africa during the 1980s raised hopes that Africa's military famines would abate at last. The hegemonic powers pulled back troops and agents, reduced or eliminated arms exports to most African countries, and worked together to pressure combatants to reach negotiated settlements. Yet, as the case of Somalia dramatically confirms, military famines continue to plague Africa. Military famine has even reappeared in Europe in Bosnia.

The "multilayered cake" approach employed by Mohammed Ayoob in Chapter 2 of this volume to define the concept of security provides a useful framework within which to understand the durability of military famine in Africa. First, Ayoob's definition of the concept of security can embrace economic and ecological threats, such as famines, if these take on political dimensions. Although his major purpose in defining security was to narrow the concept sufficiently to be tractable for analytical purposes, he agreed that "famines . . . become part of the security calculus [when] they threaten to have political outcomes that affect the survivability of states, in either the territorial or institutional sense or both, or of governing elites within those states" (Ayoob, 1991a, 259).

Second, the layers of Ayoob's cake correspond to levels of analysis employed by scholars working in the area of war and hunger. The topmost layer, the international system, is the level of analysis favored by world systems theorists and students of the global arms trade (Ball, 1988; Shindo, 1985; see also Deger, 1986a; Nordlinger, 1970; Wolpin, 1986). The world systems theorists assert that hunger in Africa is caused by the *militarization* of African countries, a broad concept encompassing the growing influence of the military over political life. Militarization can be observed and measured by a country's military budget.

Prior to the rapprochement between the United States and the former Soviet Union and before the de-escalation of South Africa's total war, the world systems theorists saw militarization as the result of the rivalry between the hegemonic nations for influence in Africa. In pursuit of their strategic aims, the hegemons were said to supply weapons to proxy armies, encouraging them to destabilize governments backed by their rivals, thus creating or aggravating civil wars (Chege, 1987; Nzongola-Ntalaja, 1987).

But militarization also causes hunger by increasing spending on arms imports and military operations. To pay for the military, African governments distort their agricultural policies, establishing artificially low official producer prices so government can keep the difference between the farm gate and consumer prices. African governments also distort foreign exchange rates by overvaluing their currency to make both arms and food imports less expensive. Distorted exchange rates reduce the demand for domestically produced food by cutting exports and drawing in imported food. These distorted economic policies depress food production and, in the long run, slow overall economic growth as well.

The intermediate layer of Ayoob's analytical cake, regional conflict, is an appropriate level of analysis for military famine in Southern Africa. The erosion of white minority rule in the former Portuguese and British colonies created a legitimacy crisis in apartheid South Africa. Furthermore, the black majority states that came into power on the "front line" were disposed to aid antiapartheid efforts in South Africa. To secure itself, the South African government sought to tame neighboring black majority states or to embroil them in paralyzing internal wars. Two of the most intractable military famines in Africa, those in Angola and Mozambique, were the direct result of South African destabilization efforts. South Africa launched major attacks on Angola in 1985, 1987, and 1988 and made commando raids on Mozambique in 1984 and 1985 (Minter, 1989, 1990).

But the concept of regional conflict has applications even in cases in which interstate wars have not occurred. Ayoob says in Chapter 2, "Artificially drawn and arbitrarily imposed colonial boundaries provide much of the raw material for interstate conflict." Internal wars resulting from secessionism or irredentism can be interpreted as having their roots at the regional level. The internal wars that caused military famines in Nigeria-Biafra in 1968–1969, Uganda in 1985–1986, and Liberia in 1992 and that are now occurring in Sudan result at least in part from the imposition of state structures upon peoples who were not one political community (Bonner, 1989). The weapons circulating in Somalia were acquired by the government during the period in which populist rhetoric called for forging a greater nation embracing Somalis in Ethiopia, Kenya, and elsewhere.

The lower layer of the cake, the one I rely upon the most in my description of military famine, is the level of domestic politics. Ayoob's explication of the security problematic focuses upon "state-making [and] the lack of unconditional legitimacy of Third World states" and, thus, is particularly useful for understanding the causes of military famine in Africa.

In the jargon of political science, legitimacy refers not to whether a particular government is legitimate in an ethical sense but to how members of society perceive the state. A state is said to possess legitimacy when "most citizens have a predisposition to regard compliance with the officers of [the state] as appropriate and reasonable" (Jackman, 1992, 20). To establish its legitimacy a state must be able to perform two distinct types of functions. In the short run, the state must retain the raw military capacity to suppress challenges to its authority. In order to strengthen its position over the long run, it must be able to meet key demands placed upon it by other important segments of society, such as the bureaucracy, business, labor, and the military. The ability to meet political demands wins accord from society that the government in power should rule.

But African states have been singularly ineffectual at both tasks. Africanist social scientists have offered a variety of explanations for the failure of African states to establish their legitimacy. Authoritarian rule in Africa has been explained as originating from the primacy of ethnic identity coupled with the weakness of norms supporting bureaucratic neutrality (Lemarchand, 1987; Hyden, 1983); as resulting from the class background of political elites who have interests concentrated in urban, industrial, and parastatal activities as opposed to the interests of the peasantry and urban workers (Diamond, 1987; Fatton, 1988; Nafziger, 1988); or as stemming from conflict between clientelist political networks contending for control of the new state (Callaghy, 1987; Chazan et al., 1988; Kasfir, 1984; Lemarchand, 1987). Whatever their origin, authoritarian regimes stifle economic development, because the resources of the state are prone to be consumed by corruption: "Unconstrained by the hollow formalities of laws and constitutions, these networks use the state to appropriate its wealth (and that of other social groups and organizations) for their own enrichment. State office is awarded primarily as an entitlement to accumulate personal wealth" (Diamond, 1987, 581).

Inevitably, such regimes appear illegitimate to those outside the circle that has access to patronage. In ethnically heterogeneous societies, which predominate in Africa, state incapacity is doubly injurious. The impossibility of economic and social justice virtually guarantees vigorous challenges to the status quo by disaffected groups with separatist or irredentist sentiments. According to René Lemarchand, "The declining capacity of state institutions must be regarded as the critical element behind the rise of factions." Such groups are organized to "provide protection" for their members that the state cannot (1987, 156).

Illegitimacy was especially debilitating during the period of superpower rivalry. Nascent guerrilla movements found it relatively easy to turn their grievances into action because foreign hegemons were eager to influence political developments in African countries. "The mere existence of warring factions [was] enough to generate offers of external assistance" from the United States, the former Soviet Union, South Africa, Cuba, or Libya (Lemarchand, 1987, 160). "Why is Africa a 'crisis ridden continent' where perfectly normal situations of conflict do not remain in the realm of politics but so frequently turn to violence, proceed from violence to a search for allies, and from allies expand to a cold war battlefield? The single response is that current African conflict arises from the inchoate and developing nature of African states, both on the domestic and international levels" (Zartman, 1989, 12).

The relationship between the military security of the state and the economic security of society given in this description is *simultaneous*. The depredations of the military can depress economic security, engendering a backlash that threatens to topple the state. Ayoob rightly criticizes Nicole Ball for simplistically dichotimizing the choice Third World governments face between expenditure on security and expenditure on development and reminds us that development is an instrumental value, part of whose function is to enhance the political legitimacy of those who can claim credit for it.

Can this description be applied to the politics of food security? I believe it can. In this chapter, I have three major goals. First, I want to confirm that political violence has played a major role in causing hunger in Africa, even when other variables such as environmental conditions and economic policy are held constant. Second, I want to test whether military spending and political violence have significant effects on food security independent of each other, and I want to investigate the ways both types of military activity have their major impacts. Specifically, I want to know whether countries with larger military budgets distort their economic policies to pay for arms and armies and whether these policy distortions cause hunger. Finally, I want to take account of the possibility that a simultaneous relationship may exist between military activity and food security. Are countries with hungry populations at greater risk of internal war? When food security improves, is the likelihood of political violence reduced?

I first explore two case studies, Angola and Ethiopia, because in some respects they are "ideal-typical." They establish an inductive basis for the three main research goals developed above rather than test hypotheses (which is the purpose of the quantitative analysis). These two cases draw attention to the critical role food policy plays in the struggle for security. In Angola and Ethiopia, years of internal war devastated the economies and displaced hundreds of thousands of people. Insurgents capitalized on this situation by seeking access to international flows of food aid, which they used to stabilize their rural supporters in liberated zones. To shore up their crumbling legitimacy, the governments in each case responded by trying to convince donor nations to allow them to control relief supplies. In the case of Ethiopia, observers baldly stated that the government's successful famine relief efforts made it possible for the regime to survive longer than it would otherwise have (Giorgis, 1989, 227; Kaplan, 1988, 140–147). Ultimately, however, in both Angola and Ethiopia rebel movements were able to gain control of the flow of food aid and succeeded in toppling or stalemating the governments.

I then fit a pooled time series of data on fifteen African countries for the years 1964 through 1985 to a structural model of cereal production. The model takes account of the economic effects of military spending and of the simultaneous relationship between war and food security.

Such a model enables me to disentangle the separate effects of political violence, military spending, and economic policy distortions. The results of the quantitative analysis support the conclusion that the direct effects of fighting have a preponderant effect on food security. But they also show that military spending is an important cause of hunger, because part of its influence occurs through economic policy distortions. Furthermore, the results suggest that countries with lower levels of food security are indeed more likely to suffer outbreaks of political violence.

Angola

Since the splintering of the coalition government that was formed at independence from Portugal in 1975, Angola has suffered nearly continuous internal war. Three major forces have struggled for power: the Popular Movement for the Liberation of Angola (MPLA), the National Union for the Total Independence of Angola (UNITA), and the National Front for the Liberation of Angola (FNLA). The MPLA controlled the government of Angola from independence; its main rival was UNITA, the FNLA having lost influence among the peasantry. Whereas the MPLA was dominated by an urban-oriented and ideologically motivated leadership, UNITA represented rural, primarily ethnic Ovimbundu interests. During the course of the conflict 20 percent of Angola's population was displaced, and a quarter of a million people died. Half a million people were forced to flee to other countries. In May 1991 the government and UNITA finally signed a peace accord, although fighting flared up again in 1993 (USCR, 1991).

Overall, the government of Angola attached little importance to the development of peasant agriculture. In the 1970s precooperative organizations called *Estaçoes de Desenvolvimentos Agrarios* were set up in many villages with the goal of eventual nationwide collectivization, but they failed to deliver inputs or consumer goods to the countryside. The few resources available for agriculture were diverted to state farms. Until undertaking reforms in the late 1980s, Angola had highly distorted economic policies. In 1986 the Angolan kwacha was overvalued by a factor of 40. Although reliable price series are not available for Angola, it seems clear that producer prices were held artificially low (Galli, 1987, 29–31; *New York Times*, January 31, 1986).

The government of Angola placed primary emphasis on defeating UNITA and devoted most of its resources to this task. From 1984 to 1988, Angola earned $1–2 billion annually from its oil exports. But it imported an estimated $4 billion in arms from the Soviet Union and other Eastern bloc countries during the period and was assisted by tens of thousands of Cuban troops at a cost of nearly half a billion dollars per year.

Control of the civilian population was a critical part of the strategies of both sides, the effects of which were most evident in the strategically important planalto, the Ovimbundu heartland. Before the war, because of the planalto, a high plain straddling Huambo and Bié provinces, Angola was a major coffee exporter. To separate civilians from guerrillas, the government resettled people closer to towns. To prevent UNITA from receiving assistance covertly, people were not allowed to move outside their villages without obtaining passes, which dampened trade and made it difficult for people to gather wild foods, honey, firewood, or thatch. Reports of physical abuse of noncombatant civilians caught without passes were common. Furthermore, government forces in remote or besieged posts levied food taxes to sustain themselves (Marcum, 1988; Rone, 1989, 42).

Their ethnicity did not protect the people of the planalto from UNITA. UNITA fighters in the field often resorted to a form of terrorism they called "strangulation" in their battle against those thought to be MPLA collaborators. UNITA's strategy was to make the highlands ungovernable. It attacked government buildings and development projects associated with the state or with the dominant Kimbundu group. It also deliberately fostered hunger by burning crops, killing animals, and mining fields and foot paths. In a particularly pernicious tactic, UNITA fighters would warn farmers not to harvest their crops under penalty of death, returning later to take the food for themselves. The expressed goals of this tactic were to cause peasants to move to UNITA-controlled areas and to deprive government forces of food. Production of coffee and other cash crops nearly disappeared, because marketing became impossible (Galli, 1987, 31; *New York Times*, December 28, 1985; Rone, 1989, 87).

Foreign military assistance helped UNITA to maintain a secure liberated zone in the southeastern portion of the country centered around Jamba. South Africa entered Angola in 1981 to dislodge the South West African People's Organization (SWAPO), which was fighting for independence for neighboring Namibia. South Africa's ground and air forces repelled MPLA advances on Jamba in 1985 and 1987. In return, UNITA helped South Africa fight SWAPO. After 1985 TOW and stinger missiles from the United States made it dangerous for Angolan MiGs to attack UNITA positions, protecting Jamba after South Africa had withdrawn from the conflict.

UNITA attempted to make its liberated zone militarily secure and agriculturally productive by increasing its population. Over the years an estimated 600,000 Ovimbundu moved from their homes in the fertile highlands to the arid plains around Jamba (Africa Watch, 1991). Many went voluntarily or moved to escape the government. Some Angolans interviewed by Africa Watch in 1989 reported living with UNITA fighters, enjoying their protection, and receiving food aid from them. Others were clearly forced to move, and some were held against their will or compelled to work on UNITA farms. Whether they went voluntarily or under duress, once they reached UNITA territory they had to give its forces a portion of the food they grew (Rone, 1989, 87): "From the testimonies we were able to gather it is obvious . . . that UNITA has a political program designed to win over the population, and that they devote resources and trained personnel to this task" (Rone, 1989, 95).

During the war, per capita food production fell well below historical levels. By 1981 many highland households no longer grew enough food to last the entire year, and the highlands were gripped by a seasonal hunger cycle. Typically, food would run out during the fall months, and the shortage would last until the first harvest in January.

Drought exacerbated Angola's problems; rainfall was below normal in 1983 and 1984. But drought does not likely explain the food crisis. For example, nationwide cereal production fell from 447,000 tons in 1980 to only about 332,000 tons in 1985. But in the rainy years of 1986 and 1987, only 356,000 and 382,000 tons of cereals, respectively, were grown. Per capita food production was actually 3 percent lower in 1987 than in 1985 (FAO, 1989).

Food relief became a key element in the struggle for advantage during the peace negotiations. The government and UNITA campaigned vigorously to influence the distribution of food. Each wanted to stabilize the populations in areas it controlled. The United States clearly favored UNITA in its food allocations. Even though only 10 percent of the people affected lived in UNITA-controlled areas, the United States—the largest food donor—earmarked nearly half of its food for them. The United States complained to the United Nations when the government prevented food convoys from moving into the southeast, but it ignored UNITA attacks on convoys in government territory, even when the targets were U.S. volunteers. It also encouraged organizations such as World Vision and the International Medical Corps to make illegal overland and air deliveries of food to UNITA territory from Zambia and Zaire (USCR, 1991).

Ethiopia

Several insurgencies were active in Ethiopia. After the government occupied what had been the autonomous region of Eritrea in 1962, the Eritrean Liberation Front (ELF) and later the Eritrean People's Liberation Front (EPLF) fought for control of the province. The 1973 famine critically weakened support for Emperor Haile Selassie, enabling a group of young officers and Marxist intellectuals to seize control of the country in 1974. The new head of state, Colonel Mengistu Heili Mariam, did not alter the government's policies toward Eritrea, however. The next year a rival Marxist faction, the Tigray People's Liberation Front (TPLF), began to fight for autonomy for Tigray province as well.

Recently, the Oromo Liberation Front (OLF) has become active in areas disrupted by the government's agricultural policies. As of this writing, the EPLF is in complete control of Eritrea, and the TPLF is the most powerful faction of the Ethiopian People's Revolutionary Democratic Movement (EPRDM), which controls Addis Ababa.

The cost of Ethiopia's internal wars and the Soviet arms imported to fight them was tremendous. Although the Ethiopian economy grew only 24 percent from 1974 to 1984, annual military spending increased 420 percent, to half a billion dollars (United States ACDA, 1989).

In the 1980s the government adopted drastic policies toward the peasantry, which eroded their ability to feed themselves and created tremendous social instability. Six million people were moved into collective villages, in which agricultural land could be owned only by the state or peasant associations, which also allocated the inputs farmers used. Furthermore, farmers were required to sell half of their output to the Agricultural Marketing Corporation (AMC) at prices fixed at about half the free-market level. The AMC distributed food to the military and urban dwellers associations. The AMC had planned to stockpile 180,000 tons of grain against the country's frequent droughts, but when rains failed in 1983, the warehouses were nearly empty—the grain had gone to feed soldiers (Bulcha, 1988; Giorgis, 1989, 157).

The government also created hundreds of resettlement schemes and moved three-quarters of a million people. There were two types of schemes. Most took members of the ethnically dominant Amhara or related groups and settled them on Oromo and other people's land in the south. A smaller number of schemes moved Tigray people from their traditional northern homeland to the south. Occupied land sometimes was annexed to make way for settlers.

The motives for the resettlement schemes were complex. Officially, it was said resettlement was done to alleviate pressure on overused land. But the resettlement of Amharas duplicated a historical pattern of encroachment by this group into Oromo territory; thus, resettlement was also driven by and redoubled ethnic conflict. And at least some Ethiopian leaders, notably Worker's Party official Legesse Asfaw, undoubtedly hoped that removing some of the Tigray would weaken the TPLF (Clay and Holcomb, 1986, 28–31; Giorgis, 1989, 270; Woldemeskel, 1989).

In order to persevere, the insurgent movements had to counter the effects of the government's social and agricultural policies and maintain people on the land. In Tigray the TPLF fought a classic guerrilla war. Its fighters were organized into small, ostensibly democratic cells sheltered by villagers in Ethiopia's highlands, with rear bases in neighboring Sudan. From an early date, TPLF propaganda de-emphasized classical Marxist ideas and stressed economic and ethnic grievances against the state. The issue of food security appeared frequently. The TPLF redistributed land in its liberated zone and opened "people's shops," selling grain below market prices. These activities were to ensure that Tigray peasants would remain in Tigray and support the struggle and to establish work projects, such as weaving and sewing cooperatives for Tigray refugees at UN relief centers in Sudan. These work projects were designed to sustain refugees until they could be repatriated; the TPLF's relief arm, the Relief Society of Tigray (REST), frequently organized marches of peasants back into the hills (Clay and Holcomb, 1986, 58–66; Firebrace and Smith, 1982, 30, 75).

The EPLF, meanwhile, had carved out a liberated zone in the desert behind trenches and mine fields. Countless Eritreans lived underground in bomb shelters for years to escape the Ethiopian MiGs that controlled their skies. The hospital at Orota consisted of 5 miles of fully or partially underground wards (Cliffe, 1989, 386; Marando, 1987). The EPLF ran a centralized and technologically sophisticated enclave, with numerous factories producing everything from ball bearings to sanitary pads for female guerrillas. Because of relentless bombing and fluctuating battle lines, Eritrea faced chronic food deficits. Therefore, the Eritrean Relief Association (ERA) ran a continuous relief operation with World Food Program support, which met 50 percent of the enclave's food needs, and grew much of its own grain at the Rora Habab Development Project. Journalist Robert Kaplan called the ERA "the most effective locally-based famine relief agency in Africa" (1988, 57).

The TPLF and EPLF, however, were notorious for using hunger as a weapon. They regularly destroyed relief convoys, arguing that the food was destined for Ethiopian soldiers. During an attack on Korem, TPLF fighters kidnapped volunteers of the Save the Children Federation. The TPLF hit feeding centers at Bati, Mille, and Lalibela. The Afar minority group in Eritrea resisted incorporation into the enclave. In one incident one hundred Afar men were massacred for refusing to join the EPLF (Human Rights Watch, 1990, 22–25).

In its war of terror and hunger, the Ethiopian government outdid the rebels. Ethiopian MiGs bombed markets and farms during daylight, making work and travel dangerous. One air attack killed 1,800 people at the market in Hausein. Government soldiers pursuing rebels conducted search-and-destroy missions in Tigray, often torching entire villages along with their crops. The government deliberately used hunger against ethnic Tigray and Eritreans. It refused to permit relief organizations to bring food into areas that were not firmly under its control, and it withheld relief food from people arriving at feeding stations unless they had identity documents attainable only in government-held areas.

The war made it difficult for people to supplement their diets with purchased food. Laborers who had traditionally gone to work on plantations in Sudan and in the south found that fighting blocked their paths (Clark, 1988). Although rainfall was below average in 1983–1984, famine conditions developed in 1984–1985 because of people's inability to supplement their production shortfalls.

The famine thoroughly delegitimized the government, but the food policies of the insurgent groups boosted their legitimacy. Jason Clay and Bonnie Holcomb reported that by 1985, Tigray and Oromo refugees in the Sudan spoke approvingly of the TPLF and the OLF. Many people told them they would be willing to feed fighters, whereas others said they wanted to join the movements. Farmers indicated that they expected to receive assistance from the TPLF in the form of inputs for their farms when they returned to live in the liberated zone (1986, 76, 152).

By the end of 1989, the old regime's military situation had become completely untenable. The EPLF seized all of Eritrea except Asmara and Massawa, and the TPLF began to advance toward Addis Ababa through Gondar and Wollo provinces. The Soviet Union, which had not renewed agreements to provide Ethiopia with military assistance in 1988, pressed Mengistu for reforms. The government was forced to open negotiations with the rebels. In order to provision its remaining garrisons, the government had to permit ERA and REST to become the main conduits of World Food Program food into the north, using overland routes from Port Sudan, or face the cutoff of all food aid to Ethiopia. The EPLF wooed the inhabitants of Asmara by allowing two planeloads of grain to be landed per day, and 6,000 tons of grain were scheduled to dock at Massawa. Loss of control of the food policy was fatal to the government. The liberation movements had demonstrated their capacity. Peasants sacked their communal farms, and soldiers deserted in large numbers (*Keesings,* 37807, 37946).

The cases of Angola and Ethiopia provide some inductive evidence in support of the three assertions made thus far. First, it is evident that internal war had a devastating effect on food security in both Angola and Ethiopia. But the cases also suggest that the militarization of these two countries, specifically the explosive growth in the military and attendant economic policy distortions, may have substantially aggravated hunger. At a minimum, agricultural policies were clearly driven in part by the needs of the military, and the wartime economies were clearly austere. Finally, it seems that causality not only flowed from military activity to food security but that the reverse was also true. In each case, deteriorating food security appears to have redounded to the benefit of insurgents, inflaming warfare. Insurgents capitalized by using international relief food to ostensibly promote food security and stabilize civilians in more food-secure liberated zones.

Quantitative Analysis

Do systematic analyses of cross-national data support these conclusions? In my work on this subject I have found that the results one obtains when modeling the relationship between military activity and hunger depend entirely upon how a model is specified and how measurements and corrections are made. There is no clear basis for selecting among competing models. The fact that a given model explains a higher proportion of the variation in a selected group of endogenous variables given the number of exogenous variables is some evidence that the model is better than others, but it is far short of proof. I cope with this by making the simplest assumptions in modeling and employing broadly accepted techniques. When no simple and clear solution to a modeling problem presents itself, I eschew the use of methods (such as principal components) that yield only ambiguous or difficult-to-interpret results.

The model I want to estimate is presented in Figure 12.1. It is a food production model in which total production is a function of area harvested and yield. The independent variables must have their effects through the area harvested or the yield.

The model takes into account the issues raised in the theoretical literature and case studies. First, it assumes that the most important exogenous factors determining cereal production are demographic, environmental, and economic. Most important, the model assumes that direct political violence (armed attacks) reduces cereal production by depressing the area harvested and the yields. Next, in response to political violence, states can be expected to increase military spending (milex). To do this, the model predicts, economic policies that transfer

Figure 12.1   Model to Be Estimated

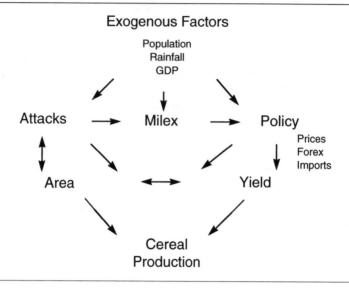

resources from agriculture will be implemented. States will lower producer prices (prices), overvalue foreign exchange rates (forex), and increase cereal imports (imports). Military spending is allowed to affect area harvested and yields directly to allow for the possibility that all of its impacts are not captured by the policy distortions I could measure.

The model also allows the area harvested and average yields to affect each other, because the two variables are inversely related to one another both across countries and within countries over time. Countries with larger areas harvested tend to be those with lower average yields; within countries in which the area harvested is lower, yields are often higher. I think this is true because marginal producers are the first ones affected by a drought or a war. The total effect of the causal variables on cereal production can be estimated by tracing the paths from those variables through the area harvested and the yields to cereal production. Finally, the model takes account of the possibility that the relationship between military activity and food security is simultaneous by allowing changes in the area harvested to influence the number of armed attacks. I believe that as the area harvested declines, more attacks are likely.

Definition and Measurement

The only variable in this model whose measurement I discuss at length is the primary dependent variable, food security. The other variables have received extensive treatment by other authors, and I refer the reader to appropriate sources throughout this section. However, I have devised an innovative way of measuring food security, and I want to explain it clearly.

Food security—reliable access to sufficient quantities of food to support normal bodily functioning and growth given an individual's basal metabolism and level of activity—is difficult to measure from a distance, especially in dispersed peasant communities such as those that predominate in Africa and during times of war. In order to do cross-national empirical work, it is necessary to identify suitable indirect measures. Economist Amartya Sen (1982) argued that this problem should be approached by explicating the relationship between food availability and food consumption. His insight is that different groups of people have different ways of obtaining food. Sen called these ways of obtaining food *exchange entitlements*, examples of which include home food production, working for cash wages to purchase food, or barter. He said that hunger occurs when a person can no longer "exchange" entitlements for sufficient food.

Data on an exchange entitlement, such as cash income or access to farm land, would be a valid proxy for food security if the measured exchange entitlement were the only one used to obtain food and if all of the entitlement were exchanged for food. These conditions never hold in reality; instead, it must be argued that the measured exchange entitlement is sufficiently correlated with food security to allow us to claim that it is a serviceable proxy. In the case of Africa, where the majority of the population consists of peasant smallholders, access to land is the single-most-important exchange entitlement. Furthermore, throughout Africa, cereal crops constitute the main source of food calories. Thus, I select cereal area harvested in hectares as a proxy for food security.

The area of cereal crops harvested should be highly correlated with changes in food consumption in most African countries for two reasons. First, most African farmers are largely self-provisioning. For example, the International Food Policy Research Institute (IFPRI) reports that Ethiopian peasants obtain 80 percent of their calories from domestic food production—that is, from the land they farm (IFPRI, 1989). Although many rural Africans supplement their diets with food purchased with cash from wage labor or crop sales, few buy all, or even the largest proportion, of their food.

Another reason the area harvested should be a good indicator of hunger is that agricultural land is not held collectively at the national level but is held by independent farming households—that is, it is a "lumpy" good. Each household is tied to its own parcels of land by legal or customary bonds, and the consequences of decisions about the area placed under production are borne by its members. Therefore, there should be a correspondence between the amount of land under production and the incidence of hunger affecting families. That is, if the area harvested declines, it does not mean every family in the country has reduced its area under production by a tiny amount. Rather, we can confidently infer that some families who were once farming are no longer doing so.

Of course, knowing how much the cereal area harvested declines during warfare does not tell us precisely how many people go hungry nor how hungry they are; it does not even tell us whether food production has increased or decreased. Thus, although the theory of exchange entitlements suggests that the area harvested is a good proxy for hunger in most African countries, we still want to know the final impact on food production. Therefore, I also include total cereal production and average cereal yields as dependent variables in my analysis.

Space does not permit detailed discussion of the other variables in the model. However, it is important to point out a difficulty with the variable used to measure political violence—the number of armed attacks in a country per year. These data are based on the *New York Times* and *Keesing's Contemporary Archives* and almost certainly underestimate the number of armed attacks. Underreporting biases estimation of a regression coefficient upward. However, as long as underreporting is random, other statistics—such as standard errors, t-ratios, correlation coefficients, and standardized coefficients—are not biased.

The variables in the model are shown in Table 12.1, although I cannot describe all of them in the text. Clearly, the factors having the most powerful effects on food production are demographic and environmental. Countries with the largest populations are the largest food producers. Environmental variables such as rainfall have an overwhelming influence on food security and must be taken into account. During the past twenty years, average rainfall in parts of Africa has been lower than at any time since record keeping began, and the downward trend may continue (Glantz, 1987). Data for these variables were taken from standard sources as indicated. Rainfall was estimated by averaging the reports from several stations in each country.

Methodology

The results of the quantitative analysis do not depend on the selection of "ideal typical" cases for success. Fifteen countries were selected for inclusion in the data set: Angola, Burkina Faso, Chad, Côte d'Ivoire, Ethiopia, Ghana, Kenya, Mali, Mozambique, Nigeria, Somalia, Sudan, Uganda, Zambia, and Zimbabwe. Observations were collected for the years 1964–1985. After lagging some of the variables the total pooled sample size is 315. The sample should be considered a stratified sample. Selection of countries was guided by a desire to achieve variation among the factors I have asserted are causes of hunger. I wanted to include cases in which there was warfare (Angola, Ethiopia) and cases in which there was peace (Mali, Zambia), cases in which economic policies were distorted (Ethiopia, Ghana) and cases that have been said to be less distorted (Côte d'Ivoire, Kenya), and cases of drought (Mozambique, Sudan) alongside cases of more regular rainfall (Côte d'Ivoire, Ghana).

The methodological issues involved in sorting through the causal relationships among political violence, military spending, and hunger—especially in a pooled time series—are all but insoluble. First, the fact that many countries are used together in one sample requires correction, both for the differing country variances and for the bias introduced by time trends. This necessitates the use of

Table 12.1 Variables in the Model

Variable	Source	Discussion
Cereal area harvested Average cereal yields Cereal production Cereal imports	Food and Agriculture Organization	Paulino & Tseng 1980
Armed attacks	World Handbook of Political and Social Indicators	Brocket 1992 Taylor 1983
Military spending (milex)[a] Gross domestic product (GDP)	Arms Control and Disarmament Agency United Nations International Comparison Project	Deger 1986a
Price distortion index (prices) Exchange rate distortion (forex)	International Monetary Fund United Nations International Comparison Project	Agarwala 1983 Jaeger 1987
Rainfall	National Oceanic and Atmospheric Administration	
Population Population density	The World Bank	

Note: a. Military spending and gross domestic product were deflated using data from the International Comparison Project of the World Bank.

generalized least squares (GLS).[1] Second, the variable I use to measure political violence and sometimes treat as dependent—the number of armed attacks—is a limited variable. The number of attacks can never be less than zero. A different method, tobit, must be used when armed attacks is a dependent variable.

Third, simultaneous relationships such as those modeled here bias GLS results and require correction by a two-stage least squares procedure. But high levels of political violence and military spending tend to occur together, with the overlap combined with economic policy distortions making it hard to separate the independent effects of each. That is, they are colinear, and multicolinearity reduces the efficiency of regression estimates—and two-stage least squares compounds this problem. Some of these paths could not be estimated. Certain variables, when incorporated into the two-stage GLS procedure, became colinear with exogenous variables and had to be dropped from the model, which is why cereal imports and military spending do not appear in some of the tables presented in "Results." All of these issues are discussed in detail in standard econometrics texts (see Greene, 1990).

Results

Let us start at the beginning of the cycle linking military activity and hunger, in the upper left-hand corner of the model illustrated in Figure 12.1. Did military spending in Africa increase during the period 1964–1985 in response to increases in armed attacks? Indeed, it did. Here, a simple lagged dependent variable model is used.[2] The model asserts that the best predictor of a given year's military budget is the previous year's budget plus an increment for each armed attack that occurred (see Table 12.2).

The model performs very well. Sixty-nine percent of the variance in military spending is accounted for by these two variables. The regression coefficient for armed attacks, 1,474,400, says that in these data military spending increases nearly $1.5 million for each reported attack the previous year. The t-ratio, 4.473, indicates that the probability of observing such a relationship randomly is less than .001. The partial correlation coefficient of armed attacks is .2271. Its square, .0516, indicates that about 5 percent of the variance in military spending not accounted for by the lagged dependent variable is accounted for by attacks. The standardized coefficient, .0590, means that a 1 standard deviation change in the number of attacks would cause roughly 6 percent of a standard deviation change in military spending. To illustrate, the standard deviation of armed attacks is 21, and the standard deviation of military spending is 500 million. Twenty-one times the regression coefficient, 1.47 million, is about 30 million, which is 6 percent of 500 million. The strength of these findings is not surprising, but it is reassuring in that the model is not yielding counterintuitive or difficult-to-interpret results.

What, then, are the effects of higher levels of military spending? Do countries with larger military budgets have more distorted economic policies? In these data that seems to be the case, as least insofar as measurement and estimation are possible. In Table 12.3 the dependent variable is a deflated index of agricultural price distortion set to 100 in the base year 1980.

Again, a lagged dependent variable model is used. Price distortion is modeled as a function of last year's distortion plus the effect of military spending. Sixty-three percent of the variance is accounted for in this way. The regression

Table 12.2 Dependent Variable: Military Spending

Variable Name	Estimated Coefficient	Standard Error	t-ratio 283 Degrees of Freedom	Partial Corr.	Standardized Coefficient
Lagmilex	.7544	.0331	22.755	.7646	.7901
Lagattacks	1,474,400	329,557	4.473	.2271	.0590

Note: Buse R-square = 0.692, F = 129.69.

coefficient for military expenditures is in millions—that is, for every additional $1 million budgeted for the military, the index of price distortion increases .002. The relationship is highly significant. The square of the partial correlation (.4203) coefficient, .1766, means military spending explains 17 percent of the unexplained variance in the index of price distortion. Moreover, a 1 standard deviation change in military spending (500 times .0021) would push the index up 1 point.

Military spending also aggravates distortion of the foreign exchange rate. The dependent variable in Table 12.4 is an index of exchange rate distortion. It is the ratio of the official exchange rate to purchasing power parity calculated using Ramgopal Agarwala's method (Agarwala, 1983).

The coefficient for the regression of this index on military spending is nearly the same as that for the index price distortions. A 1 standard deviation change in military spending would raise the index 1 point. The t-ratio, 2.36, is significant at the .02 level of confidence; however, the relationship is not strong. The partial correlation coefficient and standardized coefficients are small because the standard deviation of exchange rate distortion, 42, is large. These results suggest that military spending has more of an effect on pricing policy than on the exchange rate.

What are the effects of military activity and economic policy on food security? The best indicator of food security is the area harvested, because it measures variation in the peasantry's most important exchange entitlement. Table 12.5 includes all of the independent variables (see Figure 12.1) that were sufficiently uncorrelated with each other to be included together.

Table 12.3 Dependent Variable: Agricultural Price Distortion

Variable Name	Estimated Coefficient	Standard Error	t-ratio 283 Degrees of Freedom	Partial Corr.	Standardized Coefficient
Lagprices	.6094	.0386	15.749	.6746	.6383
Milex	.0021	.0002	7.983	.4203	.0327

Note: Buse R-square = 0.627, F = 249.78.

Table 12.4 Dependent Variable: Foreign Exchange Rate Distortion

Variable Name	Estimated Coefficient	Standard Error	t-ratio 283 Degrees of Freedom	Partial Corr.	Standardized Coefficient
Lagforex	.7373	.0319	23.045	.8008	.7012
Milex	.0020	.0008	2.360	.1355	.0131

Note: Buse R-square = 0.642, F = 266.18.

Only two variables in the model are statistically significant: armed attacks and the population density. The regression coefficient for armed attacks, –5,185, can be interpreted as meaning that each recorded armed attack was associated with an average decrease of over 5,000 hectares in cereal area harvested. A typical peasant family works a plot of 2 or 3 hectares. Even if undercounting inflates the coefficient by a factor of 10, a single attack is devastating to an agricultural community. The t-ratio, –3.27, indicates that the probability of observing such a relationship randomly is less than .005. Other statistics point toward the importance of armed attacks. First, the partial correlation of armed attacks, –.3062, is larger than any of the others except the population density. About 9 percent of the variance not explained by other factors is accounted for by armed attacks. Second, the area harvested changes by over .1 of a standard deviation for a 1 standard deviation change in armed attacks. By this criterion, only population density and the average yield have a larger effect.

It may seem surprising that rainfall does not have a greater impact on the area harvested; however, the area harvested responds slowly to drought. A higher order lagged model beyond the scope of this chapter would probably have some success predicting the area harvested. Other variables such as population and GDP could also be included to boost the R-square substantially. But, as mentioned before, after making the two-stage least squares corrections, these variables would be highly colinear with many of the others. This is also the reason it is not possible to test for a significant direct effect of military spending in this equation. At the minimum, it is apparent that economic policies do not have a discernible effect on the area harvested in the model as tested. This negative result is fairly robust. I believe economic policies have little effect on the area harvested because most land under cultivation in Africa is worked by self-provisioning peasants and not by commercial farmers attuned to changes in the marketplace.

Armed attacks likewise have a strong effect on average yields. In Table 12.6,

Table 12.5 Dependent Variable: Cereal Area Harvested

Variable Name	Estimated Coefficient	Standard Error	t-ratio 290 Degrees of Freedom	Partial Corr.	Standardized Coefficient
Attacks	–5,185	1,585	–3.271	–.3062	–.1270
Lagprices	610.92	598.97	1.019	.0600	.0129
Lagforex	–138.34	276.98	–.4994	–.0294	–.0075
Rainfall	10.453	95.296	.1096	.0065	.0040
Rainsqr	–.0117	.0640	–.1841	–.0108	–.0073
Density	3,098	232.08	13.349	.6181	.4121
Yield	–175.77	115.07	–1.527	–.0896	–.1620

Note: Buse R-square = 0.459 F = 27.45.

average yields are given in kilograms of cereal per hectare, so a recorded attack depresses yields by nearly 1 kilo per hectare nationwide. Because the average area harvested is 2.3 million hectares, the effect of a single attack would be to reduce the total harvest by nearly 2,000 metric tons.

When average yields are considered, economic policy variables now have a strong negative effect. A 1 point increase in the index of price distortion lowers average yields 2 kilos per hectare. A 1 standard deviation increase would lower yields 30 kilos per hectare, or nationwide by 70,000 metric tons on average. The t-ratio indicates that this variable is highly significant, and it explains nearly 8 percent of the unexplained variance in yields. Only the two variables for rainfall have larger standardized coefficients. Distortion in the foreign exchange rate has a somewhat weaker impact. It explains only 1 percent of the unexplained variance, but the relationship is significant at the .03 level of confidence. It seems reasonable that economic policy should have most of its effects through average yields. Policy distortions could cause farmers to forgo use of expensive yield-enhancing inputs.

Rainfall is overwhelmingly the most important influence on average yields. As indicated by the sign and the t-ratio of the square of average rainfall, the relationship between rainfall and yields is an inverted parabola. More rainfall tends to improve yields, but too much causes crop damage and drives yields back down.

The full effects of an armed attack or of changes in economic policy distortions on cereal production can now be estimated by tracing the paths from independent variables through the area harvested and average yields to cereal production. The regression coefficients along these paths can be multiplied together to estimate the total effect.

In Table 12.5 we saw that a recorded armed attack takes 5,185 hectares out of production. From Table 12.7 we can see that all other things being equal, 1,036 kilos of grain are produced on each hectare in the sampled countries. Multiplying

Table 12.6   Dependent Variable: Cereal Yield

Variable Name	Estimated Coefficient	Standard Error	t-ratio 304 Degrees of Freedom	Partial Corr.	Standardized Coefficient
Attacks	−.8995	.2439	−3.687	−.2113	−.0442
Lagprices	−2.148	.4185	−5.132	−.2881	−.1046
Lagforex	−.3660	.1634	−2.172	−.1114	−.0459
Rainfall	.7291	.0720	10.115	.5100	.6618
Rainsqr	−.0003	.00004	−8.247	−.4353	−.5012
Density	.2432	.1743	1.395	.0815	.0743
Hectares	−.00004	.00003	−1.394	−.0815	−.0519

Note: Buse R-square = 0.557, F = 32.415.

Table 12.7 Dependent Variable: Cereal Production

Variable Name	Estimated Coefficient	Standard Error	t-ratio 312 Degrees of Freedom	Partial Corr.	Standardized Coefficient
Hectares	1,036	64.177	16.186	.6847	.4838
Yield	1,113,000	76,664	14.517	.6443	.0949

Note: Buse R-square = 0.676, F = 310.107.

–5,185 times 1,036 indicates an effect of attacks on cereal production through the area harvested of –5,371,660 kilos. An attack also reduces the cereal yield by .8995 kilos. Holding other things equal, there are 1,113,000 hectares in the typical sampled country. The effect of an attack on yields is thus –1,001,143 kilos. Remember that in the model estimated here, changes in the area harvested are permitted to affect yields, and vice versa. These effects through these paths must also be added in. Looking back at Tables 12.5 and 12.6, we see that a 1 kilo increase in yields reduces the area harvested by 175.77 hectares, and a 1 hectare increase in the area harvested depresses yields .00004 kilo. The total reduction in cereal production attributable to a single measured attack is –5,978,170 kilos, or nearly 6,000 metric tons—enough food to feed 15,000 people for 1 year.

Consider the fact that the standard deviation of armed attacks is 21. A 1 standard deviation change in the number of recorded armed attacks would reduce cereal production 125,000 tons altogether. A sharp increase in the number of recorded attacks, say 50, such as was observed in Ethiopia or Angola, would reduce cereal production by 300,000 tons. In fact, these production shortfalls correspond closely to the food deficits reported by international relief agencies for these crises. Thus, the model yields predictions consistent with what has actually been observed, increasing confidence in the results.

What about the total effect of changes in economic policy? I begin with price policy. By adding the products of the four paths from the index of price distortion to total cereal production, we find that a 1 point increase in the index is associated with a decrease of 1,400 metric tons. The standard deviation of the distortion index is over 14 points, so a 1 standard deviation change would reduce cereal production by 20,000 tons. In the same way, a 1 point increase in the index of foreign exchange rate distortion decreases cereal production by 474 tons. The standard deviation of the foreign exchange rate index is 42 points. A 1 standard deviation change would also reduce production by about 20,000 tons. Economic incentives are vital to commercial food producers and, insofar as food security depends upon the availability of food in shops, to food security as well.

To complete the tour of the model we must close the circle. According to many Africanist writers, the relationship between military activity and hunger should be treated as simultaneous. How does the number of armed attacks respond to changes in food security? Are more food-secure countries also more politically secure?[3]

Once again the lagged dependent variable model is used; however, a tobit estimation procedure is employed, because the distribution of armed attacks is limited to zero or positive numbers (see Table 12.8). The model performs well, with a square correlation between observed and expected values of .488. The frequencies of predicted and observed armed attacks being greater than the limit of zero are similar.

In my sample the cereal area harvested has a strong effect on political violence. As the area harvested (measured in thousands of hectares) decreases, the number of attacks observed rises. For each thousand hectares out of production the number of attacks increased .02. If the area harvested declined by .25 of a standard deviation, which is 500,000 hectares, 11 additional attacks would be recorded.

Higher levels of military spending (in millions of dollars) depress the number of armed attacks. Thus, although military spending may reduce the area harvested, thereby stimulating attacks, the state can resist insurgency through spending on the military. GDP (in millions of dollars) also depresses armed attacks. Its regression coefficient is suspect, because GDP is colinear with population. However, its purpose is to control for military spending, which does not suffer from colinearity problems in this particular model. The finding that GDP and military spending have the same sign is interesting, and I return to this point shortly.

Taken together, these results support the idea that a simultaneous relationship exists between military activity and food security. Armed attacks and military spending both decrease food security. Armed attacks work mostly by displacing rural people from the land. Military spending distorts economic policies, eroding incentives to adopt improved methods. However, the process

Table 12.8 Dependent Variable: Armed Attacks, Tobit Model

Variable Name	Regression Coefficient	t-ratio 290 Degrees of Freedom	Normalized Coefficient
Lagattacks	.2148	2.431	.0102
Hectares	−.0215	−3.187	−.0008
Lagmilex	−.0176	−2.885	−.0008
LagGDP	−.0019	−3.240	−.0001
Population	1.391	2.372	.0658

Note: Log-likelihood function = −793.984
Mean-square error = 179.178
Squared correlation observed and expected values = .488
Predicted probability Y > limit = 0.4503
Observed frequency Y > limit = 0.5267

is self-reinforcing. As people become food-insecure, political violence increases, and military spending rises in response. Although growth of the military may temporarily suppress rebellion, a cycle of famine and violence may exist such as those in which some African countries have found themselves trapped. Hunger breeds rebellion, which drives the state to further deplete society's resources in its struggle for control.

As noted previously, military spending distorted agricultural policies, but the relationship was not very strong. Because of multicolinearity arising from the two-stage procedure, I was unable to calculate the total effect of military spending on food security, because I could not include the variable in the estimated equations. However, I believe there are additional negative effects of military spending on food security which I have not measured in the two indices I used. Consider Table 12.9, which contains the results of the GLS (not two-stage) regression of average yields on all of the variables in the original (unestimatable) model in Figure 12.1. This model suffers from a defect: It does not take into account the fact that some of the included variables may be products of each other. However, it has a virtue: Because no colinear second-stage instruments are included, we can estimate the partial effect of military spending beyond that accounted for by policy distortions while acknowledging that some bias may be present.

This table reveals several things about what happens when these variables are treated as part of a simultaneous system. First, by the R-square criterion, the simultaneous model does a better job with fewer variables. The R-square for yields in the simultaneous model was .55, but three fewer variables were employed. Second, armed attacks have a greater effect in the simultaneous

Table 12.9   Dependent Variable: Cereal Yield, GLS Model

Variable Name	Estimated Coefficient	Standard Error	t-ratio 304 Degrees of Freedom	Partial Corr.	Standardized Coefficient
Attacks	−.3632	.1845	−1.968	−.1122	−.0361
Lagmilex	−.0547	.0146	−3.737	−.2096	−.0758
Lagprices	−.9279	.2642	−3.511	−.1974	−.0681
Lagforex	−.4067	.1377	−2.952	−.1669	−.0672
Imports	−.1670	.0234	−7.116	−.3779	−.2095
LagGDP	.0058	.0015	3.697	.2075	.1443
Rainfall	.5621	.0707	7.950	.4149	.5092
Rainsqr	−.0002	.00001	−6.566	−.3524	−.3889
Density	.6334	.1185	5.343	.2930	.2019
Hectares	−.0327	.0092	−3.547	−.1994	−.0767

Note: Buse R-square = 0.501, F = 30.595.

model. Armed attacks "absorb" variance from other variables.[4] The economic policy variables, however, do well in both models, with price distortions doing slightly better in the simultaneous model, and foreign exchange distortions improving in the GLS model.

The difficulty encountered by not being able to control for military spending, GDP, and imports is revealed by the GLS model. These variables show strong results consistent with theory. Higher GDP is associated with higher yields, perhaps because high-GDP countries have more demand and more efficient production methods. Higher cereal imports are associated with lower yields, either because low-yielding countries require more imports, or because imports depress incentives for production, or both.

The importance of controlling for these various factors is made clear by the variable military spending, which has a substantial, significant negative impact on yields above and beyond that captured by the policy distortions I could measure. Military spending explains 4 percent of the unexplained variance—which is better than any of the political or economic variables except imports. Its standardized coefficient is larger than any of the other political or economic variables except imports and GDP. A $1 million increase in military spending decreases cereal production one-twentieth of a kilo per hectare. According to this model, a 1 standard deviation ($500,000,000) increase in military spending would depress production 25 kilos per hectare or 57,500 tons in the average case—enough food to feed 150,000 people for 1 year.

Remember that the area harvested, GDP, and military spending were all negatively related to armed attacks. This suggests that in countries with higher GDPs—particularly if the rural population enjoys food security—there are fewer attacks, or greater political security exists. It also suggests that, holding other things constant, security is enhanced by military preparedness. Unlike GDP, however, higher levels of military spending decrease the area harvested—food security. That is, one of the means of ensuring political security—military spending—undermines food security, with the consequence that hunger eventually leads to more violence anyway. This is the result predicted by the Africanists.

How much should we trust the GLS results? We know that if the correct model is structural, GLS alone without two-stage modeling is biased. But in practice the amount of bias can be fairly small. In general, GLS is preferable to other estimators known to be inefficient or biased. One clue to how much a coefficient would have changed had it been included in a structural equation is to look at the difference between the variance of the raw variable and the second-stage instrument. The standard deviation of the instrument for military spending is 85 percent the size of the original variable. The correlation between military spending and its instrument is .73. This suggests that if the instrument had been included in the second stage, it would have behaved similarly to the raw variable in the two-stage regression.

Conclusion

Famine chronicler David Arnold wrote that food is "fundamental to the structures of dominance and dependency that [arise] out of this most vital of all commodities" (1988, 3). Food is a political good; as such, understanding how control over and access to food are determined reveals much about the structure and nature of society. When political tensions grow, such as in time of war, the revelations of a political economy of hunger become increasingly stark.

Political security is a prerequisite for food security, and political security may well include some level of military spending. But in developing polities, such as those in my sample of African countries, excessive demands by the military can become inimical to food security. Militarization undermines political security when food security deteriorates to the point that insurgents can claim greater legitimacy for their cause and undermine the state. As the state struggles to hang on to power, its depredations only accelerate the cycle of famine and insurgency.

In the 1970s and 1980s, militarization—including distortion of the economy—driven by a combination of internal rebellion against domestic political failure and foreign interventionism, was a real phenomenon in Africa, and this caused the great military famines. More recently, the United States and the former Soviet Union, in cooperation with African governments, brought some African civil wars under control.

However, peace alone cannot ensure food security. Economic factors are also important. In fact, food insecurity caused by economic collapse is an important factor driving rebellion and instability. Conversely, price and policy reforms by themselves cannot be sufficient. Rather, important parts of pricing policy are driven by the need for security in countries convulsed by war.

If demilitarization is a prerequisite for policy reform, then other means of ensuring political security must be found. In some cases, democratic political reforms may be the best way to legitimize government and bring soldiers in from the bush. Furthermore, if policy reform is conceived of in terms of the harsh medicine of structural adjustment, it can be expected to exacerbate conflict and reignite the cycle of war and famine. Beyond providing security guarantees for combatants and encouraging democratization, the international community will be called upon to assist Africa by reducing its debt burden, lowering barriers to African products, and supporting income-maintenance programs during the period of economic reconstruction.

Notes

1. I used a random effects model with the data transformed into mean deviates to eliminate the possibility that the independent variables were correlated with the country cases. In some of the equations, a lagged dependent variable model is employed. In these

estimations the Dhrymes method is used to correct for serial correlation. I used the Akaike information criterion to determine the lag order.

2. If a variable is included in lagged form—that is, using data from the previous year to predict the value of the dependent variable for the present year—it is designated with the prefix "Lag" in the table.

3. As before, food security should be measured in terms of the area harvested. Of the measures of food security used here—area harvested, average yield, and total production—the area harvested is by far the best predictor of armed attacks. When armed attacks are regressed on the three variables at the same time, only the area harvested is significant.

4. This is not true for the area harvested, where in both the two-stage and GLS models armed attacks remain the only important variable with roughly the same impact as before.

❖ PART IV ❖

Conclusion

❖ THIRTEEN ❖

The Quest for Security
and Development

Norman A. Graham

The workshops that led to this volume began with several ambitious goals: (1) to address complex questions about the relationship among security, military expenditures, and economic development in the Third World; (2) to develop and test new approaches to research and analysis of these questions, with an eye particularly toward longitudinal, multidisciplinary, and comparative research designs; and (3) to comment on emerging trends and challenges in the search for order and stability in the international system. I think it is fair to say that the preceding chapters have made contributions to each of these goals. Because the goals were indeed ambitious and broad, however, we must conclude (not surprisingly) that more research is required. The workshops led to some promising directions of inquiry, considerable exchange on the relative merits of alternative data sources and methodologies, and useful collaboration among political scientists, economists, and sociologists. Unfortunately, these efforts may have been more successful in revealing the complexity and subtleties of the processes, determinants, and relationships at work than in resolving the principal controversies and conflicts among scholars in this area reviewed in Chapter 1 and in several of the subsequent empirical efforts.

Areas of consensus among the authors and other participants in the work-shops include the following. First, there is clearly considerable variability in the relevant structures, conditions, and political and economic processes in Third World countries. The cases assessed by Cheatham, Crone, Graham and Lewis, Gupta, Hartman and Hsiao, and Phillips and Racioppi help to illustrate variability in the determinants of military expenditures and in economic growth and development for a range of Third World countries, as well as in the security and domestic political contexts within which elites operate in each case. Ayoob's conception of the security problematic of the Third World as a "multilayered cake" composed of the power balances of the present international system, regional security challenges and balances, and the imperatives of the processes of state formation and legitimation in the internal dimension of security was found to have utility in helping to sort out this variability in the case study analyses, as well as in the quantitative modeling by Cheatham, Snider, and Zoninsein. Nutter's efforts then helped to make the concepts of security and threat concrete and more susceptible to future modeling efforts; and Louscher and Sperling, in a global sense, and Phillips and Racioppi, for the Soviet/Russian case, helped to flesh out the historical change and emerging trends of important aspects of the international security context facing Third World elites—particularly the role of, and influences on, military assistance and arms suppliers.

The domestic security and political context was found to be crucial in the explorations by Cheatham, Crone, Graham and Lewis, and Snider. Relatedly, Gupta, Snider, and Zoninsein stressed the relevance of economic and financial constraints and resources and, along with Hartman and Hsiao, the impact of military expenditures on economic growth and external debt. Second, and given this variability (and complexity), considerable consensus seemed to exist on the value of multidisciplinary and longitudinal studies. The workshops (and the resulting chapters), I think, can be characterized fairly as benefiting to an unusual degree from the synergy of economists, political scientists, and sociologists, as well as specialists in quantitative analysis on the one hand and in area studies and case study analysis on the other, working together on related questions and exchanging views on conceptualization, data problems, method, and interpretation. This synergy, of course, did not always come easily—indeed, the persistent commitment to analytical predispositions and key variable selection is still evident—but I think the volume does illustrate the fruits of a willingness to go beyond disciplinary boundaries and to accept guidance on how best to address the economic, political, and social complexity stressed earlier. Although, unfortunately, there were no formally trained historians among the participants, there was clearly a strong commitment to be sensitive to the dynamic elements of the cases under analysis and a strong effort to use longitudinal data sets in the research designs when possible. There was also some consensus that this remains an important challenge for future data collection and research.

Finally, the studies presented in this volume suggest continued growth in the military expenditures of many countries of the Third World. Beyond manpower training and support, significant portions of this expenditure are directed toward acquisition of highly sophisticated weapons systems from suppliers pressured to export for domestic economic, balance-of-payments, and employment considerations. Indeed, competition for Third World arms markets continues to grow among manufacturers in the United States, France, Germany, the United Kingdom, and other Western industrial countries. As Phillips and Racioppi suggest, there is increased evidence of Russian interest in expanding arms sales in light of domestic economic pressures and the need to earn foreign exchange credits. Moreover, as Louscher and Sperling, and to some extent Gupta, suggest, we have begun to see the impact of sophisticated production and export efforts by defense manufacturers in countries such as Brazil, India, Israel, South Korea, and Taiwan.

The implications of these trends for arms control and security in the Third World, and for an enhanced "buyers' market" for elites motivated toward increased military expenditures, suggest little reason for optimism about progress toward demilitarization. In addition, the authors and workshop participants are not sanguine about the prospects for a broadly based new world order.

This final point leads many of us to propose a future line of comparative inquiry into the prospects for industrial conversion in many of the national settings examined in this volume. What are the political, economic, and social constraints in operation as various industrial and developing countries begin to address seriously the prospects for converting some portion of their military production to economically competitive or at least viable consumer or civilian purposes? Such an inquiry must pay close attention to the implications of the external and internal security environments of the countries in question, as stressed in this volume.

❖ Bibliography ❖

Adekanye, J. Bayo. 1983. "Domestic Production of Arms and the Defense Industries Corporation of Nigeria." *Current Research on Peace and Violence.*

Adelman, Irma, and Sherman Robinson. 1978. *Income Distribution Policy in Developing Countries: A Case Study of Korea.* Palo Alto: Stanford University Press/World Bank.

Africa Watch. 1991. *Angola: Civilians Devastated by 15-Year War.* New York: Human Rights Watch.

Agarwala, Ramgopal. 1983. "Price Distortions and Growth in Developing Countries." World Bank Staff Working Paper, No. 575. Washington, D.C.: World Bank.

Agarwell, Rajesh. 1978. *Defense Production and Development.* New Delhi: Arnold-Heinemann.

Alagappa, Muthiah. 1988. "Military Professionalism and the Development Role of the Military in Southeast Asia." In J. Soedjati Djiwandono and Mun Cheong Yong (eds.), *Soldiers and Stability in Southeast Asia.* Singapore: Institute of Southeast Asian Studies.

Alexander, Arthur, et al. 1981. *Modeling the Production of International Trade of Arms: An Economic Framework for Analyzing Policy Alternatives.* Santa Monica: Rand Corporation.

Allan, Pierre. 1983. *Crisis Bargaining and the Arms Race.* Cambridge, Mass.: Ballinger Press.

Almquist, Peter, and Edwin Bacon. 1992. "Arms Exports in a Post-Soviet Market." *Arms Control Today* (July-August).

Ames, Barry. 1987. *Political Survival: Politicians and Public Policy in Latin America.* Berkeley: University of California Press.

Amsden, Alice H. 1985. "The State and Taiwan's Economic Development." In Peter B. Evans, Dietrich Rueschmeyer, and Theda Skocpol (eds.), *Bringing the State Back In.* New York: Cambridge University Press, pp. 78–106.

———. 1989. *Asia's Next Giant: South Korea and Late Industrialization.* New York: Oxford University Press.

Anderton, Charles H. 1985. "A Selected Bibliography of Arms Race Models and Related Subjects." *Conflict Management and Peace Science* 8 (2): 99–122.

Apter, David E. 1965. *The Politics of Modernization.* Chicago: University of Chicago Press.

261

Armer, J. Michael, and A. Schnaiberg. 1972. "Measuring Individual Modernity." *American Sociological Review* 37.

Armstrong, P., A. Glyn, and J. Harrison. 1991. *Capitalism Since 1945*. Oxford: Basil Blackwell.

Arnold, David. 1988. *Famine*. London: Basil Blackwell.

Ashley, Richard. 1980. *The Political Economy of War and Peace*. London: Pinter.

Ayoob, Mohammed. 1983–1984. "Security in the Third World: The Worm About to Turn?" *International Affairs* 60 (1): 41–51.

———. 1991a. "The Security Problematic of the Third World." *World Politics* 43 (January): 257–283.

———. 1991b. "India as Regional Hegemon: External Opportunities and Internal Constraints." *International Journal* 46 (3): 420–448.

———. 1991c. "State-Making, Democracy and the Security Problematic of the Indian State." Paper presented at the Twentieth Annual Conference of South Asian Studies, Madison, Wisconsin, October 31–November 1.

———. 1992. "The Security Predicament of the Third World State: Reflections on State-Making in a Comparative Perspective." In Brian Job (ed.), *The Insecurity Dilemma: National Security of Third World States*. Boulder: Lynne Rienner, pp. 63–80.

Bajusz, William D., and David J. Louscher. 1988. *Arms Sales and the U.S. Economy: The Impact of Restricting Military Exports*. Boulder: Westview Press.

Ball, Nicole. 1983a. "Defense and Development: A Critique of the Benoit Study." *Economic Development and Cultural Change* 31: 3. 330.5 E 198

———. 1983b. "Military Expenditure, Economic Growth, and Socioeconomic Development in the Third World." In Bo Huldt and Atis Lejins (eds.), *Militarism and Militarization*. Stockholm: Swedish Institute of International Affairs, pp. 37–66.

———. 1983c. "Military Expenditure and Socio-Economic Development." *International Social Science Journal* 35 (1). 305 I 611

———. 1985. "Defense Expenditures and Economic Growth." *Armed Forces and Society* 11 (2). 355.05 A 282

✓ ———. 1988. *Security and Economy in the Third World*. Princeton: Princeton University Press. HC 59.72 . D4 B35 1988

Ball, Nicole, and Milton Leitenberg (eds.). 1983. *The Structure of the Defense Industry: An International Survey*. New York: St. Martin's Press.

Bandow, Doug. 1988. "Aid Money That Just Buys Guns." *Wall Street Journal,* June 14, A34.

Baran, Paul, and Paul Sweezy. 1966. *Monopoly Capital*. New York: Monthly Review Press.

Bates, Robert H. 1981. *Markets and States in Tropical Africa: The Political Basis of Agricultural Policies*. Berkeley: University of California Press.

Baugh, William. 1984. *The Politics of Nuclear Balance*. New York: Longman.

Bedi, Rahul. 1993. "India's Westward Glance." *Jane's Defence Weekly* (January 9).

Bellamy, Chris. 1987. *The Future of Land Warfare*. London: Croom Helm.

✓Benoit, Emile. 1973. *Defense and Economic Growth in Developing Countries*. Lexington, Mass.: Lexington Books. HC 79 . D4 B45

———. 1978a. "Growth and Change in Developing Countries." *Economic Development and Cultural Change* 26: 277ff.

———. 1978b. "Growth and Defense in Developing Countries." *Economic Development and Cultural Change* 26: 2.

Bhimal, Shefali, and Sunil Jain. 1992. "In Deeper Trouble." *India Today* (November 30).

Bienen, Henry. 1981. "Armed Forces and National Modernization: Continuing the Debate." *Comparative Politics* 16: 1–16.

———. 1987. "Domestic Political Considerations for Food Policy." In John W. Mellor, Christopher L. Delgado, and Malcolm J. Blackie (eds.), *Accelerating Food Produc-*

tion in Sub-Saharan Africa. Baltimore: Johns Hopkins University Press, pp. 296–308.

———— (ed.). 1971. *The Military and Modernization*. Chicago: Aldine/Atherton.

Biswas, B., and R. Ram. 1986. "Military Expenditures and Economic Growth in Less Developed Countries: An Augmented Model and Further Evidence." *Economic Development and Cultural Change* 34 (January): 361–372.

Blackett, P.M.S. 1948. "The Scientific Problem of Defense in Relation to the Needs of the Indian Armed Forces." Unpublished report to the Honorable Defense Minister of India, New Delhi (September 10).

Blainey, Geoffrey. 1973. *The Causes of War*. New York: Free Press.

Bonner, Raymond. 1989. "A Reporter At Large: Famine." *New Yorker Magazine* (March 13): 85–101.

Booth, Ken. 1991. "Security and Emancipation." *Review of International Studies* 17 (4): 313–326.

Borrus, Michael, Wayne Sandholtz, Steve Weber, and John Zysman. 1992. "Epilogue." In Wayne Sandholtz et al. (eds.), *The Highest Stakes: The Economic Foundations of the Next Security System*. New York: Oxford University Press.

Borton, John, and Edward Clay. 1986. "The African Food Crisis of 1982–1986." *Disasters:* 258–272.

Boulding, Kenneth. 1962. *Conflict and Defense: A General Theory*. New York: Harper and Row.

Bread for the World. 1990. "Hunger 1990: A Report on the State of World Hunger." Washington, D.C.: Institute on Hunger and Development.

Bremer, Stuart. 1977. *Simulated Worlds: A Computer Model of National Decision-Making*. Princeton: Princeton University Press.

Brockett, Charles D. 1992. "Measuring Political Violence and Land Inequality in Central America." Department of Political Science, University of the South. Mimeo.

Brodie, Bernard. 1973. *War and Politics*. New York: Macmillan.

Brown, Seyom. 1987. *The Causes and Prevention of War*. New York: St. Martin's Press.

Bruno, M., and J. Sachs. 1985. *Economics of Worldwide Stagflation*. Cambridge: Harvard University Press.

Brzoska, Michael, and Thomas Ohlson (eds.). 1986. *Arms Production in the Third World*. Philadelphia: Taylor and Francis.

————. 1987. *Arms Transfers to the Third World, 1971–1985*. Oxford: Oxford University Press.

Bueno de Mesquita, Bruce. 1980. "Theories of Conflict: An Appraisal and Analysis." In Ted Robert Gurr (ed.), *Handbook of Political Conflict*. New York: Free Press.

————. 1981. *The War Trap*. New Haven: Yale University Press.

Bulcha, Mekuria. 1988. *Flight and Integration: Causes of Mass Exodus from Ethiopia and Problems of Integration in Sudan*. Uppsala: Scandinavian Institute of African Studies.

Bull, Hedley. 1977. *The Anarchical Society*. New York: Columbia University Press.

Bunge, Frederica (ed.). 1982. *South Korea: A Country Study*. Washington, D.C.: U.S. Government Printing Office.

Bush, Ray. 1988. "Hunger in Sudan: The Case of Darfur." *African Affairs* 87: 5–23.

Buzan, Barry. 1989. "The Concept of National Security for Developing Countries." In Mohammed Ayoob and Chai-Anan (eds.), *Leadership Perceptions and National Security: The Southeast Asian Experience*. Singapore: Institute of Southeast Asian Studies.

Callaghy, Thomas M. 1987. "The State as Lame Leviathan: The Patrimonial Administrative State In Africa." In Zaki Ergas (ed.), *The African State in Transition*. London: Macmillan, pp. 87–116.

Camdessus, M. 1991. "Global Investment Needs, Savings, and Military Spending:

Excerpt of Speech at the United Nations Economic and Social Council, July 1991." *Finance and Development* 28 (September): 28.

Carter, Nick. 1986. *Sudan: The Roots of Famine: A Report for Oxfam.* Oxford: Oxfam.

Center for Defense Information. 1980. "Soviet Geopolitical Momentum: Myth or Menace?" Washington, D.C.: Center for Defense Information.

Chan, Steve. 1984. *International Relations in Perspective: The Pursuit of Security, Welfare, and Justice.* New York: Macmillan.

———. 1987. "Military Expenditures and Economic Performance." *World Military Expenditures and Arms Transfers, 1986.* Washington, D.C.: United States Arms Control and Disarmament Agency.

———. 1988a. "Defense Burden and Economic Growth: Unraveling the Taiwanese Enigma." *American Political Science Review* 82 (3): 913–920.

———. 1988b. "Taiwan's Calculus on Military Spending." *International Interactions* 14 (3): 267–281.

Chang, Parris. 1983. "Taiwan in 1982: Diplomatic Setback Abroad and Demands for Reform at Home." *Asian Survey* 23 (1): 38–46.

———. 1984. "Taiwan in 1983: Setting the Stage for Power Transition." *Asian Survey* 24 (1): 122–126.

Chasin, Barbara. 1986. "The Sahel Famine: A Social Disaster." *Politics and the Life Sciences* 4 (2): 166–187.

Chazan, Naomi, Robert Mortimer, John Ravenhill, and Donald Rothchild. 1988. *Politics and Contemporary Society in Africa.* Boulder: Lynne Rienner.

Chege, Michael. 1987. "Conflict in the Horn of Africa." In Emmanuel Hansen (ed.), *Africa: Perspectives on Peace and Development.* London: Zed Press, pp. 87–100.

Chellaney, Brahma. 1991. "South Asia's Passage to Nuclear Power." *International Security* 16 (1): 43–72.

Cheung, Tai Ming, and Jonathan Friedland. 1991. "Peace and Insecurity: Asian Governments Resist Pressure to Cut Arms Budgets." *Far Eastern Economic Review* (November 7): 52–53.

Choucri, Nazli, and Robert North. 1975. *Nations in Conflict: National Growth and International Violence.* San Francisco: W. H. Freeman.

Christensen, R. P. 1968. *Taiwan's Agricultural Development.* Department of Agriculture. Economic Research Studies. Report No. 39. Washington, D.C.: U.S. Government Printing Office.

Chubin, Shahram, and Charles Tripp. 1988. *Iran and Iraq at War.* Boulder: Westview Press.

Clapham, Christopher, and George Philip (eds.). 1985. *The Political Dilemmas of Military Regimes.* London: Croom Helm.

Clark, Lance. 1988. *Study of Early Warning of Refugee Flows.* Washington, D.C.: Refugee Policy Group, Center for Policy Analysis and Research on Refugee Issues.

Clay, Jason E., and Bonnie K. Holcomb. 1986. *Politics and the Ethiopian Famine, 1984–1985.* Cambridge: Cultural Survival.

Cliffe, Lionel. 1989. "The Impact of War and the Response to It in Different Agrarian Systems in Eritrea." *Development and Change* 20: 373–400.

Cline, Ray. 1980. *World Power Trends and U.S. Foreign Policy for the 1980s.* Boulder: Westview Press.

Cobb, Roger, and Charles Elder. 1972. *Participation in American Politics.* Boston: Allyn and Bacon.

Cohen, Youssef, Brian R. Brown, and A.F.K. Organski. 1981. "The Paradoxical Nature of State-Making: The Violent Creation of Order." *American Political Science Review* 75 (4): 901–910.

Collier, David (ed.). 1979. *The New Authoritarians in Latin America.* Princeton: Princeton University Press.

Cook, Chris (ed.). 1992. *The Facts on File Political Almanac.* 2nd ed. New York: Facts on File.

Copson, Raymond. *Ethiopia: War and Famine.* Washington, D.C.: Foreign Affairs and National Defense Division.

Creasey, Pauline, and Simon May (eds.). 1988. *The European Armaments Market and Procurement Cooperation.* New York: St. Martin's Press.

Crone, Donald. 1988. "State, Social Elites, and Government Capacity in Southeast Asia." *World Politics* 40 (2) (January): 252–268.

———. 1991. "Military Regimes and Social Justice in Indonesia and Thailand." *Journal of Asian and African Studies* 26 (1–2): 96–113.

Crouch, Harold. 1978. *The Army and Politics in Indonesia.* Ithaca: Cornell University Press.

———. 1988. "The Military Mind and Economic Development." In J. Soedjati Djiwandono and Mun Cheong Yong (eds.), *Soldiers and Stability in Southeast Asia.* Singapore: Institute of Southeast Asian Studies.

Curtis, Donald, Michael Hubbard, and Andrew Shepherd. 1988. *Preventing Famine: Policies and Prospects for Africa.* New York: Routledge.

Curtis, Gerald L., and Sung-joo Han. 1983. *The U.S.–South Korean Alliance: Evolving Patterns in Security Relations.* Lexington: D. C. Heath.

Cusack, Thomas. 1981. "The Sinews of Power: Labor and Capital in the Production of National Military Force Capability." Discussion Paper. Berlin: International Institute for Comparative Social Research.

———. 1984. "The Evolution of Power, Threat, and Security." Discussion Paper. Berlin: International Institute for Comparative Social Research.

———. 1990. *Exploring Realpolitik: Probing International Relations Theory with Computer Simulation.* Boulder, CO: Lynne Rienner.

Cusack, Thomas, and Michael D. Ward. 1981. "Military Spending in the United States, Soviet Union, and the People's Republic of China." *Journal of Conflict Resolution* 25: 429–469.

Cutler, Peter. 1985. *The Use of Economic and Social Information in Famine Prediction and Response.* London: Overseas Development Administration.

Dawisha, Karen. 1979. *Soviet Foreign Policy Toward Egypt.* London: Macmillan.

Deger, Saadet. 1984. "Optimal Control and Differential Game Models of Military Expenditure in Less Developed Countries." *Journal of Economic Dynamics and Control* 7: 153–169.

———. 1985. "Technology Transfer and Arms Production in Less Developed Countries." *Industry and Development* 15: 1–18.

———. 1986a. *Military Expenditure in Third World Countries: The Economic Effects.* Boston: Routledge and Kegan Paul.

———. 1986b. "Economic Development and Defense Expenditure." *Economic Development and Cultural Change* 35: 179–196.

———. 1986c. "Soviet Arms Sales to the Developing Countries: The Economic Forces." In Robert Cassen (ed.), *Soviet Interests in the Third World.* Beverly Hills: Sage, pp. 159–176.

Deger, Saadet, and Somnath Sen. 1983. "Military Expenditure, Spin-off, and Economic Development." *Journal of Development Economics* 13: 67–83.

Deger, Saadet, and Ron Smith. 1983. "Military Expenditure and Growth in Less Developed Countries." *Journal of Conflict Resolution* 27: 335–353.

Deger, Saadet, and Robert West (eds.). 1987. *Defense, Security and Development.* London: Frances Pinter.

✓DeGrasse, Robert. 1983. *Military Expansion, Economic Decline: The Impact of Military Spending on U.S. Economic Performance*. Armonk, NY: M. E. Sharpe.

de Masi, Paula, and Henri Lorie. 1989. "How Resilient Are Military Expenditures?" IMF Staff Papers: 131–165.

Denny, Lionel, and Tony Addison. 1987. *The Alleviation of Poverty Under Structural Adjustment*. Washington, D.C.: World Bank.

Denoon, David B. 1987. "Defence Spending in ASEAN: An Overview." In Chin Kin Wah (ed.), *Defence Spending in Southeast Asia*. Singapore: Institute of Southeast Asian Studies, pp. 48-71.

Desai, Meghnad, and David Blake. 1981. "Modelling the Ultimate Absurdity: A Comment on a Quantitative Study of the Strategic Arms Race in the Missile Age." *Review of Economics and Statistics* 63: 629–632.

Deudney, Daniel. 1990. "The Case Against Linking Environmental Degradation and National Security." *Millennium* 19 (3): 461–476.

Diamond, Larry. 1987. "Class Formation in the Swollen African State." *Journal of Modern African Studies* 25 (4): 567–596.

Dixon, William, and Bruce Moon. 1986. "Military Burden and Basic Human Needs." *Journal of Conflict Resolution* 30 (4) (December): 660–684.

Djiwandono, J. Soedjati. 1988. "The Military and National Development in Indonesia." In J. Soedjati Djiwandono and Mun Cheong Yong (eds.), *Soldiers and Stability in Southeast Asia*. Singapore: Institute of Southeast Asian Studies.

Domar, E. D. 1957. *Essays in the Theory of Economic Growth*. Oxford: Oxford University Press.

Dommen, Edward, and Alfred Maizels. 1988. "The Military Burden in Developing Countries." *Journal of Modern African Studies* 26: 3.

Dreyer, June Teufel. 1990. "Taiwan in 1989: Democratization and Economic Growth." *Asian Survey* 30 (1): 52–58.

Dunn, Michael Collins. 1986. "Egypt: From Domestic Needs to Export Market." In James Katz (ed.), *The Implications of Third World Military Industrialization*. Lexington: Lexington Books.

Dunnigan, James. 1982. *How to Make War*. New York: William Morrow.

Dunnigan, James, and Austin Bay. 1985. *A Quick and Dirty Guide to War*. New York: William Morrow.

Dupuy, Trevor N. 1979. *Numbers, Predictions, and War*. New York: Bobbs-Merrill.

Dupuy, Trevor N., Grace P. Hayes, and John A. C. Andrews (eds.). 1980. *Almanac of World Military Power*. San Rafael, CA: Presidio Press.

Eckstein, Harry. 1970. "On the Causes of Internal Wars." In Eric A. Nordlinger (ed.), *Politics and Society*. Englewood Cliffs: Prentice-Hall, pp. 287–309.

Economic and Social Council (ECOSOC). 1986. *Report of the Inter-Agency Mission to Sudan*. New York: United Nations.

The Economist. 1990. December 22.

The Economist. 1991. March 9.

The Economist. 1993. January 16.

Edmonds, Martin. 1981. *International Arms Procurement: New Directions*. New York: Pergamon Press.

Eicher, Carl K., and John Staatz. 1984. *Agricultural Development in the Third World*. Baltimore: Johns Hopkins University Press.

Eide, Asbjorn (ed.). 1977. *Bulletin of Peace Proposals* (special issue) 8 (2).

Emmerson, Donald K. 1988. "The Military and Development in Indonesia." In J. Soedjati Djiwandono and Mun Cheong Yong (eds.), *Soldiers and Stability in Southeast Asia*. Singapore: Institute of Southeast Asian Studies.

Evangelista, Matthew. 1988. *Innovation and the Arms Race*. Ithaca: Cornell University Press.

Evans, Carol. 1986. "Reappraising Third-World Arms Production." *Survival* (March/April).

Evans, Peter. 1979. *Dependent Development*. Berkeley: University of California Press.

Faini, Riccardo, Patricia Annez, and Lance Taylor. 1984. "Defense Spending, Economic Structure, and Growth: Evidence Among Countries and Over Time." *Economic Development and Cultural Change* 32: 487–498.

Fairbank, John K. 1983. *The United States and China*. 4th ed. Cambridge, Mass: Harvard University Press.

Fatton, Robert, Jr. 1988. "Bringing the Ruling Class Back In: Class, State and Hegemony in Africa." *Comparative Politics* 20 (3): 252–264.

Federation of Korean Industries. 1987. *Korea's Economic Policies (1945–1985)*. Seoul: Federation of Korean Industries.

Ferrari, Paul L., et al. 1987. *U.S. Arms Exports: Policies and Contractors*. Washington, D.C.: Investor Responsibilities Research Center.

Ferris, Wayne. 1973. *The Power Capabilities of Nation-States*. Lexington: Lexington Books.

Finer, Samuel E. 1975. "State- and Nation-Building in Europe: The Role of the Military." In Charles Tilly (ed.), *The Formation of National States in Western Europe*. Princeton: Princeton University Press, pp. 84–163.

Finnegan, William. 1989. "The Emergency." Parts I and II. *New Yorker Magazine*, May 22 and 29.

Firebrace, James. 1984. *Never Kneel Down: Drought, Development and Liberation in Eritrea*. Nottingham: War on Want.

Firebrace, James, and Gayle Smith. 1982. *The Hidden Revolution: An Analysis of Social Change in Tigray (Northern Ethiopia) Based on Eyewitness Accounts*. London: War on Want.

Food and Agriculture Organization (FAO). 1982. *Estimation of Crop Areas and Yields in Agricultural Statistics*. Rome: FAO

———. Annual. *Production Yearbook*. Rome: FAO.

Forrest, Joshua. 1988. "The Quest for State 'Hardness' in Africa." *Comparative Politics* 20 (4): 423–442.

Foss, Christopher F. 1989. "Brazilian Programmes Being Held up by Fund Shortage." *Jane's Defence Weekly* 11 (21) (May 27): 1009.

Frank, Andre Gunder. 1981. *Crisis in the Third World*. New York: Holmes and Meier.

Franko, Lawrence G., and Sherry Stephenson. 1980. *French Export Behavior in Third-World Markets*. Washington, D.C.: Center for Strategic and International Studies.

Frederiksen, P. C., and Robert E. Looney. 1985. "Another Look at the Defense Spending and Development Hypothesis." *Defense Analysis* 1 (3).

Freeman, John R. 1983. "Granger Causality and the Time Series Analysis of Political Relationships." *American Journal of Political Science* 27: 327–58.

Gaidar, Yegor. 1993. *Report to the Supreme Soviet*. March.

Galli, Rosemary E. 1987. "The Food Crisis and the Socialist State in Lusophone Africa." *African Studies Review* 30 (1): 19–47.

Garnham, David. 1976a. "Power Parity and Lethal International Violence, 1969–1973." *Journal of Conflict Resolution* 20: 379–394.

———. 1976b. "Dyadic International War, 1816–1965." *Western Political Quarterly* 29: 231–242.

George, Susan. 1988. *A Fate Worse Than Debt*. New York: Grove Press.

Gersony, Robert. 1988. *Summary of Mozambican Refugee Accounts of Principally Conflict Related Experience in Mozambique*. Washington, D.C.: Bureau for Refugee Programs, Department of State.

———. 1989. *Why Somalis Flee: Synthesis of Accounts of Conflict Experience in*

Northern Somalia by Somali Refugees, Displaced Persons, and Others. Washington, D.C.: Bureau for Refugee Programs, Department of State.

Ghosh, Pradip K. (ed.). 1984. *Disarmament and Development.* Westport: Greenwood Press.

Gidadhubli, R. G. 1992. "Requiem for Rupee Trade." *Economic and Political Weekly* (May 30).

Gill, Peter. 1986. *A Year in the Death of Africa: Politics, Bureaucracy and the Famine.* London: Paladin.

Gilpin, Robert. 1981. *War and Change in World Politics.* Cambridge: Cambridge University Press.

———. 1987. *The Political Economy of International Relations.* Princeton: Princeton University Press.

Giorgis, Dawit Wolde. 1989. *Red Tears: War, Famine and Revolution in Ethiopia.* Trenton: The Red Sea Press.

Girling, John. 1981. *Thailand: Society and Politics.* Ithaca: Cornell University Press.

Glantz, Michael (ed.). 1987. *Drought and Hunger in Africa: Denying Famine a Future.* Cambridge: Cambridge University Press.

Glebova, Alla, and Natalia Arkhangelskaya. 1993. "MIG Sales to Malaysia: Too Many Cooks in the Kitchen." *Commersant* (March 16): 6–7.

Goodman, Melvin. 1987. "The Soviet Union and the Third World: The Military Dimension." In Andrzej Korbonski and Francis Fukuyama (eds.), *The Soviet Union and the Third World: The Last Three Decades.* Ithaca: Cornell University Press, pp. 46–66.

Graham, Norman A. 1991. "The Role of the Military in the Political and Economic Development of the Republic of Korea." *Journal of Asian and African Studies* 26: 1–2.

Graham, Thomas. 1984. "India." In James Everett Katz (ed.), *Arms Production in the Third World.* Lexington: Lexington Books.

Graves, Ernest, and Steven A. Hildreth (eds.). 1984. *U.S. Security Assistance.* Lexington: Lexington Books.

Gregor, A. James. 1986. "The Republic of China on Taiwan." In James E. Katz (ed.), *The Implications of Third World Military Industrialization.* Lexington, Mass.: Lexington Books.

Gregor, A. James, Robert E. Harkavy, and Stephanie G. Neuman. 1986. "Taiwan: Dependent 'Self-Reliance.'" In Michael Brzoska and Thomas Ohlson (eds.), *Arms Production in the Third World.* Philadelphia: Taylor and Francis.

Greene, William H. 1990. *Econometric Analysis.* New York: Macmillan.

Griffin, Larry J., Michael Wallace, and Joel Devine. 1982a. "The Political Economy of Military Spending: Evidence from the United States." *Cambridge Journal of Economics* 6: 1–14.

———. 1982b. "Monopoly Capital, Organized Labor, and Military Expenditure in the United States, 1949–1976." *American Journal of Sociology* 88: S113–S153.

———. 1985. "One More Time: Militarizing the U.S. Military Budget: Reply to Jencks." *American Journal of Sociology* 91: 384–391.

Grimmett, Richard F. 1992. "Conventional Arms Transfers to the Third World, 1984–1991." *CRS Report for Congress* (July 20).

Grobar, L. M., and R. C. Porter. 1987. "Benoit Revisited: Defense Spending and Economic Growth in LDCs." Discussion Paper No. 119, Center for Research on Economic Development, University of Michigan (June).

Gruber, William H., and Donald G. Marquis (eds.). 1969. *Factors in the Transfer of Technology.* Cambridge: Massachusetts Institute of Technology Press.

Gu Guan-fu. 1983. "Soviet Aid to the Third World, An Analysis of Its Strategy." *Soviet Studies* 35 (1): 71–89.

Gulhati, Ravi. 1989. *The Political Economy of Reform in Sub-Saharan Africa.* Washington, D.C.: World Bank.

Gupta, Amit. 1988. "India's Military Build-Up: Modernization in Search of a Threat?" *Swords and Ploughshares* (December).

———. 1990. "The Indian Arms Industry: A Lumbering Giant?" *Asian Survey* 30 (9) (September): 846–862.

Gurr, Ted Robert. 1970. *Why Men Rebel.* Princeton: Princeton University Press.

———. (ed.). 1980. *The Handbook of Political Conflict: Theory and Research.* New York: Free Press.

Gyimah-Brempong, Kwabena. 1989. "Defense Spending and Economic Growth in Subsaharan Africa: An Econometric Investigation." *Journal of Peace Research* 26 (1) (February): 79–91.

Hagerty, Devin. 1991. "India's Regional Security Doctrine." *Asian Survey* 31 (4) (April): 351–364.

Haggard, Stephan. 1985. "The Politics of Adjustment: Lessons from the IMF's Extended Fund Facility." *International Organization* 38 (3) (Summer): 505–534.

———. 1990. *Pathways from the Periphery.* Ithaca: Cornell University Press.

Hammond, Paul Y., David J. Louscher, Michael D. Salomone, and Norman A. Graham. 1983. *The Reluctant Supplier: U.S. Decision-Making for Arms Sales.* Cambridge: Oelgeschlager, Gunn and Hain.

Han, Sung-joo. 1983. *U.S.-Korea Security Cooperation: Retrospects and Prospects.* Seoul: Asiatic Research Center.

Hansen, Emmanuel (ed.). 1987. *Africa: Perspectives on Peace and Development.* London: Zed Press.

Harkavy, Robert E., and Stephanie G. Neuman (eds.). 1987. *The Lessons of Recent Wars in the Third World.* Lexington, Mass.: Lexington Books.

Harris, Michael. 1991. *Anatomy of Disaster Relief.* London: Frances Pinter.

Hartman, John T. 1989. "Wolpin's Assessment of the Military's Role in Development: An Exercise in Modelling and Measurement Without Theory." *Labor, Capital and Society.*

Hartman, John T., and Wey Hsiao. 1988. "Military Expenditure, Development and Dependency: A Time Series Analysis of Taiwan." Unpublished paper, Indiana University.

———. 1989. "Military Expenditure, Military Assistance and Development: A Time Series Analysis of Taiwan." Unpublished paper, Indiana University.

———. 1992. "Counting Taiwan's Defense Spending." Unpublished paper, State University of New York at Buffalo.

Hartman, John T., Wey Hsiao, and Taufiq Rashid. 1989. "Military Spending and Development: A Causal Analysis of Post-War Taiwan." Unpublished paper, Indiana University.

Hartman, John T., and Pamela Walters. 1985. "Dependency, Military Assistance, and Development: A Cross-National Study." *Politics and Society* 14: 431–458.

Hartung, W. D. 1990. "Breaking the Arms-Sales Addiction: New Directions for U.S. Policy." *World Policy Journal* 8 (Winter): 1–26.

Herz, John. 1976. *The Nation-State and the Crisis of World Politics.* New York: David McKay.

Hewitt, D. 1991. "Military Expenditures in the Developing World." *Finance & Development* 28 (September): 22–25.

Hickey, Dennis Van Vranken. 1986. "U.S. Arms Sales to Taiwan." *Asian Survey* 26 (12): 1324–1336.

Ho, Samuel P. S. 1978. *Economic Development in Taiwan, 1860–1970.* New Haven: Yale University Press.

Holmes, Richard (ed.). 1988. *The World Atlas of Warfare: Military Innovations That Changed the Course of History*. New York: Penguin Viking.

Holsti, K. J. 1972. *International Politics: A Framework for Analysis*. Englewood Cliffs: Prentice-Hall.

Horowitz, Donald L. 1985. *Ethnic Groups in Conflict*. Berkeley: University of California Press.

Howard, Michael. 1984. *The Causes of Wars*. Cambridge: Harvard University Press.

Howarth, Mike. 1986. "Defending the Republic of Korea: Armed Forces and Industry Forge Ahead." *International Defense Review* 2.

Hsiao, Wey. 1990. "The Determinants of Welfare Spending in Postwar Taiwan, 1951–1983." In J. R. Wu and H. N. Yu (eds.), *Proceedings of the 1990 Chinese American Academic and Professional Convention*. New York: Chinese American Academic and Professional Society, pp. 257–260.

Human Rights Watch. Annual. *World Report*. New York.

Hummel, Christopher K. 1992. "Ukrainian Arms Makers Are Left on Their Own." *RFE/RL Reports* (August 14).

Huntington, Samuel P. 1957. *The Soldier and the State: The Theory and Politics of Civil-Military Relations*. Cambridge: Harvard University Press.

———. 1968. *Political Order in Changing Societies*. New Haven: Yale University Press.

Hyden, Goran. 1983. *No Shortcuts to Progress: African Development Management in Perspective*. Berkeley: University of California Press.

International Committee of the Red Cross. Annual. *Annual Report*. Geneva.

———. 1986. *International Committee of the Red Cross Bulletin*. Special Edition—Angola: 85–86.

International Food Policy Research Institute (IFPRI). Annual. *Report*. Washington, D.C.

International Institute for Strategic Studies (IISS). Annual. *The Military Balance*. London: IISS.

International Labor Office (ILO). Annual. *Yearbook of Labour Statistics*. Geneva: ILO.

International Monetary Fund (IMF). Annual. *Government Finance Statistics Yearbook*. Washington, D.C.: IMF.

———. Annual. *International Financial Statistics*. Washington, D.C.: IMF.

Intriligator, Michael D. 1982. "Research on Conflict Theory: Analytical Approaches and Areas of Application." *Journal of Conflict Resolution* 26 (2): 307–327.

Isard, Walter, and Charles H. Anderton. 1985. "Arms Race Models: A Survey and Synthesis." *Conflict Management and Peace Science* 8 (2): 27–98.

Itoh, M. 1990. *The World Economic Crisis and Japanese Capitalism*. New York: St. Martin's Press.

Jackman, Robert. 1976. "Politicians in Uniform: Military Governments and Social Change in the Third World." *American Political Science Review* (70) (December).

———. 1992. *The Political Capacity of Nation States: Institutions and Legitimacy*. Unpublished manuscript.

Jackson, Marvin R. (ed.). 1985. *East-South Trade: Economics and Political Economics*. Special issue of *Soviet and Eastern Foreign Trade*.

Jackson, Robert, and Carl Rosberg. 1982. *Personal Rule in Black Africa*. Berkeley: University of California Press.

Jaeger, William. 1987. "Agricultural Incentives and Policy in Sub-Saharan Africa: Some Recent Trends and Methodological Issues." Unpublished paper.

Janowitz, Morris. 1960. *The Professional Soldier: A Social and Political Portrait*. New York: Free Press.

———. 1964. *The Military in the Political Development of New Nations*. Chicago: University of Chicago Press.

———. 1977. *Military Institutions and Coercion in the Developing Nations: Expanded Edition of the Military in the Political Development of New Nations*. Chicago: University of Chicago Press.

Jansson, Kurt, Michael Harris, and Angela Penrose. 1987. *The Ethiopian Famine*. London: Zed Books.

Jencks, Christopher. 1985. "Methodological Problems in Studying 'Military Keynesianism.'" *American Journal of Sociology* 91 (2) (Sept.): 373–378.

Jervis, Robert. 1976. *Perception and Misperception in International Politics*. Princeton: Princeton University.

Joerding, Wayne. 1986. "Economic Growth and Defense Spending." *Journal of Development Economics* 16 (April): 35–40.

Johnson, H. G. 1971. "A Word to the Third World." *Encounter* 37 (October): 3–10.

Johnson, John J. (ed.). 1962. *The Role of the Military in Underdeveloped Countries*. Princeton, NJ: Princeton University Press.

Johnston, J. 1972. *Econometric Methods*. New York: McGraw-Hill.

Jones, Rodney, and Steven Hildreth. 1984. *Modern Weapons and Third-World Powers*. Boulder: Westview Press.

Jorgensen, L., and R. Landau. 1990. *Technology and Capital Formation*. Cambridge: MIT Press.

Kaldor, Mary. 1982. *The Baroque Arsenal*. London: Andre Deutsch.

Kaminski, Bartlomiej, and Robert Janes. 1988. "Economic Rationale for Eastern Europe's Third World Policy." *Problems of Communism* 37 (2) (March-April): 15–28.

Kaplan, Robert D. 1988. *Surrender or Starve: The Wars Behind the Famine*. Boulder: Westview Press.

Kapstein, Ethan B. 1988. "Economic Development and National Security." In Edward Azar and Chung-in Moon (eds.), *National Security in the Third World*. College Park: Center for International Development and Conflict Management, University of Maryland, pp. 136–151.

Karasapan, Omer. 1987. "Turkey's Armaments Industries." *Middle East Report* (January-February).

Kasfir, Nelson. 1984. *State and Class in Africa*. Totowa: Cass and Company.

Katz, James (ed.). 1984. *Arms Production in Developing Countries*. Lexington: Lexington Books.

———. (ed.) 1986. *The Implications of Third World Military Industrialization*. Lexington, Mass.: Lexington Books.

Kavic, Lorne J. 1967. *India's Quest for Security*. Berkeley: University of California Press.

Keegan, John. 1983. *World Armies*. 2nd ed. Detroit, MI: Gale Research Co.

Keesing's Contemporary Archives. Periodical. London: Keesing's Ltd.

Kennedy, Charles H., and David J. Louscher. 1989. *Military Elites and Politics in Asia and Africa*. London: E. J. Brill.

Kennedy, Paul. 1987. *The Rise and Fall of the Great Powers*. New York: Random House.

Kibreab, Gaim. 1987. *Refugees and Development in Africa: The Case of Eritrea*. Trenton: Red Sea Press.

Kidron, Michael, and Ronald Segal. 1984. *The New State of the World Atlas*. New York: Simon and Schuster.

Kidron, Michael, and Dan Smith. 1983. *The War Atlas*. New York: Simon and Schuster.

Kireyev, Alexei. 1992. "The Former Soviet Union." In *SIPRI Yearbook, 1992*. Oxford: Oxford University Press, pp. 380–390.

Kirk-Greene, Anthony, and Douglas Rimmer. 1981. *Nigeria Since 1970*. London: Hodder and Staughton.

Kirkpatrick, C., and C. J. Green. 1982. "A Cross-Section Analysis of Food Insecurity in Developing Countries: Its Magnitude and Sources." *Journal of Development Studies* 18 (2): 202–228.

Kissinger, Henry. 1977. *American Foreign Policy* (3rd ed.). New York: W. W. Norton.

Klare, Michael. 1984. *American Arms Supermarket*. Austin: University of Texas Press.

———. 1993. "The Next Great Arms Race." *Foreign Affairs* 3: 136–152.

Kolodziej, Edward A. 1987a. *Making and Marketing Arms: The French Experience and*

Its Implications for the International System. Princeton: Princeton University Press.

———. 1987b. "Whither Modernization and Militarisation: Implications for International Peace and Security." In Christian Schmidt (ed.), *Peace Defense and Economic Analysis.* London: Macmillan.

Kolodziej, Edward A. and Robert E. Harkavy (eds.). 1982. *Security Policies of Developing Countries.* Lexington: Lexington Books.

Koo, Anthony Y. C. 1968. *The Role of Land Reform in Economic Development: A Case Study of Taiwan.* New York: Praeger.

Krause, Joachim. 1988. "Soviet Arms Transfer Restraint." In Thomas Ohlson (ed.), *Arms Transfer Limitations and Third World Security.* Oxford: Oxford University Press.

Krause, Keith. 1992. *Arms and the State: Patterns of Military Production and Trade.* Cambridge: Cambridge University Press.

Krauthammer, Charles. 1991. "The Unipolar Moment." *Foreign Affairs* 70 (1): 23–33.

Kuo, Shirley W. Y. 1983. *The Taiwan Economy in Transition.* Boulder: Westview Press.

Lasswell, Harold, and Abraham Kaplan. 1950. *Power and Society.* New Haven: Yale University Press.

Laurance, Edward J. 1992. *The International Arms Trade.* New York: Macmillan.

Lebovic, James H., and Ashfaq Ishaq. 1987. "Military Burden, Security Needs and Economic Growth in the Middle East." *Journal of Conflict Resolution* 31 (March): 106–139.

Lee, Ki-baik. 1984. *A New History of Korea.* Seoul: Ilchokak Publishers.

Lemarchand, René. 1987. "The Dynamics of Factionalism in Contemporary Africa." In Zaki Ergas (ed.), *The African State in Transition.* London: Macmillan, pp. 149–165.

Levy, Jack. 1983. *War in the Modern Great Power System, 1495–1975.* Lexington: University of Kentucky Press.

———. 1986. "Declining Power and the Motivation for Preventive War." Paper presented at the annual meeting of the American Political Science Association. Washington, D.C. August.

Lim, David. 1983. "Another Look at Growth and Defense in Less Developed Countries." *Economic Development and Cultural Change* 31: 2.

Lin, Ching-Yuan. 1973. *Industrialization in Taiwan, 1946–1969: Trade and Import Substitution Policies for Developing Countries.* New York: Praeger.

Lindgren, Goran. 1984. "Review Essay: Armaments and Economic Performance in Industrialized Market Economies." *Journal of Peace Research* 21: 375–387.

Lindgren, Karin, Birger Heldt, Kjell-Ake Nordquist, and Peter Wallensteen. 1991. "Major Armed Conflicts in 1990." In *SIPRI Yearbook 1991: World Armaments and Disarmament.* Oxford: Oxford University Press, pp. 345–380.

Lipietz, Alain. 1987. *Mirages and Miracles: The Crises of Global Fordism.* London: Verso.

Lipton, Michael. 1977. *Why Poor People Stay Poor: Urban Bias in World Development.* Cambridge: Harvard University Press.

Little, I.M.D., and J. A. Mirrlees. 1974. *Project Appraisal and Planning for Developing Countries.* New York: Basic Books.

Liu, Leo Y. 1988. "The Military Capability and Strategic Posture of Taiwan in the 1990s." *Journal of Third World Studies* 5 (1): 19–38.

Lofchie, Michael. 1988. *The Policy Factor: Agricultural Performance in Kenya and Tanzania.* Boulder: Lynne Rienner.

Looney, Robert E. 1986. *The Political Economy of Latin American Defense Expenditures.* Lexington: D. C. Heath/Lexington Books.

———. 1988a. "Financial Constraints on Potential Latin American Arms Producers." *Current Research on Peace and Violence* 10 (4): 159–168.

———. 1988b. "Socio-Economic Environments and the Budgetary Allocation Process in

Developing Countries: The Case of Defense Expenditures." *Socio-Economic Planning Sciences* 22.

———. 1988c. *Third-World Military Expenditure and Arms Production.* New York: St. Martin's Press.

———. 1989a. "The Economic Impact of Rent Seeking and Military Expenditures: A Comparison of Third World Military and Civilian Regimes." *American Journal of Economics and Sociology* 48 (1) (January): 11–31.

———. 1989b. "The Influence of Arms Imports on Third World Debt." *Journal of Developing Areas* 23 (January). 330.5 J8596

———. 1989c. "Internal and External Factors Effecting Third World Military Expenditures." *Journal of Peace Research* 26 (1): 33–46. 341. 105 J86

———. 1990. "Militarization, Military Regimes, and the General Quality of Life in the Third World." *Armed Forces and Society* 17 (1) (Fall): 127–139.

Looney, Robert E., and Peter C. Frederiksen. 1986. "Defense Expenditures, External Public Debt and Growth in Developing Countries." *Journal of Peace Research* 23 (4) (December): 329–338.

Lotz, J. R. 1970. "Patterns of Government Spending in Developing Countries." *Kyklos: The Manchester School* 38 (2).

Louscher, David J. 1987. "Brazil and South Korea: Two Cases of Indigenous Production Development." In David J. Louscher and Michael D. Salomone (eds.), *Marketing Security Assistance: New Perspectives on Arms Sales.* Lexington: D. C. Heath/ Lexington Books.

———. 1990. "International Arms Procurement in the 1990s." Paper presented at the Annual Convention of the International Studies Association, Washington, D.C., April 10–14.

Louscher, David J., and Michael D. Salomone (eds.). 1987. *Marketing Security Assistance: New Perspectives on Arms Sales.* Lexington: D. C. Heath/Lexington Books.

———. 1987a. "The Nature of the Arms Trade in the Late Twentieth Century." In David J. Louscher and Michael D. Salomone (eds.), *Marketing Security Assistance: New Perspectives on Arms Sales.* Lexington: D. C. Heath/Lexington Books, pp. 1– 10.

———. 1987b. *Technology Transfer and U.S. Security Assistance: The Impact of Licensed Production.* Boulder: Westview Press.

Louscher, David J., and Anne Naylor Schwarz. 1989. "Patterns of Third World Military Acquisition." In Kwang-il Baek, Ronald D. McLaurin, and Chung-in Moon (eds.), *The Dilemma of Third World Defense Industries.* Boulder: Westview Press.

Maddison, Angus. 1989. *The World Economy in the 20th Century.* Paris: OECD Development Centre Studies.

Magagna, Victor V. 1991. *Communities of Grain: Rural Rebellion in Contemporary Perspective.* New York: Cornell University Press.

Maizels, Alfred, and Machiko K. Nissanke. 1986. "The Determinants of Military Expenditures in Developing Countries." *World Development* 14 (9): 1125–1140.

Majeski, Stephen J. 1983. "Mathematical Models of the U.S. Defense Expenditure Decision-Making Process." *American Journal of Political Science* 27: 485–514. 330.5 W9276

Majeski, Stephen J., and David L. Jones. 1981. "Arms Race Modeling: Causality Analysis and Model Specification." *Journal of Conflict Resolution* 25: 259–288.

Mandel, Ernst. 1975. *Late Capitalism.* London: Verso Press.

Mann, Michael. 1984. "The Autonomous Power of the State: Its Origins, Mechanisms and Results." *Archives Europeenes de Sociologie* 25 (2).

Mansbach, Richard, and John Vasquez. 1981. *In Search of Theory: A New Paradigm for Global Politics.* New York: Columbia University Press.

Maoz, Zeev. 1982. *Paths to Conflict: International Dispute Initiation, 1816–1976.* Boulder: Westview Press.

Marando, Joseph. 1987. *Life in Liberated Eritrea*. Rome: Research and Information Center on Eritrea.

Marcum, John A. 1988. "Angola." *Survival* 30 (1): 3–13.

Marglin, S. A., and J. B. Schor. 1990. *The Golden Age of Capitalism: Reinterpreting the Postwar Experience*. Oxford: Clarendon Press.

Mason, Edward, et al. 1980. *The Economic and Social Modernization of the Republic of Korea*. Cambridge: Harvard University Press.

Matthews, Ron. 1989. *Defence Production in India*. New Delhi: ABC.

McGinnis, Michael D., and John T. Williams. 1989. "Change and Stability in Superpower Rivalry." *American Political Science Review* 83 (4) (December): 1101–1123.

McGowan, Pat, and Howard Shapiro. 1973. *The Comparative Study of Foreign Policy: A Survey of Scientific Findings*. Beverly Hills: Sage.

McGuire, Martin C. 1977. "A Quantitative Study of the Strategic Arms Race in the Missile Age." *The Review of Economics and Statistics* 59: 328–339.

———. 1981. "A Quantitative Study of the Strategic Arms Race in the Missile Age: A Reply." *The Review of Economics and Statistics* 63: 632–633.

McIntyre, John R., and Daniel S. Papp. 1986. *The Political Economy of International Technology Transfer*. New York: Quorum Books.

McKinlay, Robert. 1989. *Third World Military Expenditure: A Political Economy Approach*. London: Pinter/Columbia University Press.

McLaurin, Ronald D. 1989. "Technology Acquisition: A Case Study of the Supply Side." In Kwang-il Baek, Ronald D. McLaurin, and Chung-in Moon (eds.), *The Dilemma of Third World Defense Industries*. Boulder: Westview Press, pp. 57–100.

McNamara, R. S. 1991. "Reducing Military Expenditures in the Third World." *Finance & Development* 28 (September): 26–28.

McNeil, William. 1982. *The Pursuit of Power: Technology, Armed Force, and Society Since A.D. 1000*. Chicago: University of Chicago Press.

Mead, W. R. 1990. "On the Road to Ruin: Winning the Cold War, Losing the Economic Race." *Harper's* 280 (March): 59–64.

Melman, Seymour. 1978. "Inflation and Unemployment as Products of the War Economy." *Peace Research Reviews* 7: 17–52.

———. 1985. *The Permanent War Economy*. New York: Simon and Schuster.

Menon, Rajan. 1986. *Soviet Power and the Third World*. New Haven: Yale University Press.

Migdal, Joel. 1988. *Strong Societies and Weak States: State-Society Relations and State Capabilities in the Third World*. Princeton: Princeton University Press.

Minear, Larry. 1991. *Humanitarianism Under Seige: A Critical Review of Operation Lifeline*. Trenton: Red Sea Press.

Minority Rights Group. 1983. *Eritrea and Tigray*. London: Minority Rights Group.

Minter, William. 1989. *The Mozambican National Resistance (Renamo) as Described by Ex-Participants*. Submitted to the Ford Foundation and the Swedish International Development Authority.

———. 1990. *The National Union for the Total Independence of Angola as Described by Ex-Participants and Foreign Visitors*. Stockholm: Swedish International Development Authority.

Mintz, Alex, and Alex Hicks. 1984. "Military Keynesianism in the United States, 1949–1976: Disaggregating Military Expenditures and Their Determination." *American Journal of Sociology* 90: 411–417.

Mirskii, Georgi. 1972. *Tretii mir: obshchestvo, vlast', armiia*. Moscow.

Moore, Barrington. 1966. *The Social Origins of Dictatorship and Democracy*. New York: Beacon Press.

Morgenthau, Hans J. 1973. *Politics Among Nations* (5th ed.). New York: Alfred Knopf.

Morrison, Thomas K. 1984. "Cereal Imports by Developing Countries: Trends and Determinants." *Food Policy* 9 (1): 13–26.

Muscat, Robert. 1990. *Thailand and the United States: Development, Security, and Foreign Aid*. New York: Columbia University Press.

Nafziger, Wayne E. 1988. *Inequality in Africa: Political Elites, Proletariat and the Poor*. Cambridge: Cambridge University Press.

Nahm, Andrew C. 1988. *Korea Tradition and Transformation: A History of the Korean People*. Elizabeth: Hollym International.

Nardinelli, Clark, and Gary B. Ackermann. 1976. "Defense Expenditures and the Survival of American Capitalism: A Note." *Armed Forces and Society* 3: 13–16.

National Oceanic and Atmospheric Administration. Periodical. *Monthly Climatic Data for the World*. Asheville, North Carolina.

Nations, Richard. 1984. "Pride and Paranoia." *Far Eastern Economic Review* (August 16).

Naur, Maja. 1980. "Industrialization and Transfer of Civilian and Military Technology to the Arab Countries." *Current Research on Peace and Violence*.

Nelson, D. N. 1991. "Security in a Post-Hegemonic World." *Fletcher Forum of World Affairs* 15 (Summer): 27–37.

Nelson, R. R. 1990. "U.S. Technological Leadership: Where Did It Come from and Where Did It Go?" *Research Policy* 19: 117–132.

———. 1991. "Diffusion of Development: Post–World War II Convergence Among Advanced Industrial Nations." *American Economic Review* 81 (May): 271–275.

Neuman, Stephanie. 1978. "Security, Military Expenditure and Socioeconomic Development: Reflections on Iran." *Orbis* (27) 3.

Neuman, Stephanie G. (ed.). 1984a. *Defense Planning in Less-Industrialized States*. Lexington: D. C. Heath/Lexington Books.

———. 1984b. "International Stratification and Third World Military Industries." *International Organization* 38 (1) (Winter): 167–197.

Neuman, Stephanie G., and Robert E. Harkavy (eds.). 1980. *Arms Transfers in the Modern World*. New York: Praeger.

Newcombe, Alan, and Frank Klaassen. 1977. "A Tensiometer Prediction of Nations Likely to be Involved in International War in the Years 1977–1980." Paper prepared for the Seventh General Conference of the International Peace Research Association, Oaxtepec, Mexico, December 11–16.

Nincic, Miroslav, and Thomas R. Cusack. 1979. "The Political Economy of U.S. Military Spending." *Journal of Peace Research* 16: 101–115.

Nixon, Richard. 1981. *The Real War*. New York: Warner Books.

Nordlinger, Eric. 1970. "Soldiers in Mufti: The Impact of Military Rule upon Economic and Social Change in Non-Western States." *American Political Science Review* 63: 1131–1148.

———. 1977. *Soldiers in Politics: Coups and Governments*. Englewood Cliffs: Prentice-Hall.

Nutter, John J. 1991. "An Inter-Nation Simulation/World Model: A Framework for an All-Computer Simulation of Global Political, Economic, and Strategic Dynamics." Doctoral Diss., Northwestern University.

———. 1992. "Why Nations Arm: A Pooled Time Series Analysis of the Creation of National Military Capability." Paper presented at the Workshop on Third World Security and Development, sponsored by the Midwest Consortium on International Security Studies, East Lansing, Michigan, April.

Nyong'o, Peter Anyang. 1987. *Popular Struggles for Democracy in Africa*. London: Zed Press.

Nzongola-Ntalaja. 1987. "The National Question and the Crisis of Instability in the Horn of Africa." In Emmanuel Hansen (ed.), *Africa: Perspectives on Peace and Development*. London: Zed Press, pp. 55–86.

Odetola, Olatunde. 1982. *Military Regimes and Development: A Comparative Analysis in African Societies.* Boston: George Allen and Unwin.

O'Donnell, Guillermo. 1973. *Modernization and Bureaucratic Authoritarianism.* Berkeley: Institute of International Studies.

Office for Emergency Operations in Africa (OEOA). 1986. *Status Report on the Emergency Situation as of 1 January 1986.* New York: United Nations.

Organski, A.F.K., and Jacek Kugler. 1980. *The War Ledger.* Chicago: University of Chicago Press.

Ostrom, Charles W., Jr. 1978. "A Reactive Linkage Model of the US Defence Expenditure Policy-making Process." *American Political Science Review* 76: 60–74.

———. 1990. *Time Series Analysis* (2nd ed.). Newbury Park: Sage.

Ostrom, Charles W., Jr., and R. F. Marra. 1986. "US Defence Spending and the Soviet Estimate." *American Political Science Review* 80: 819–842.

Paget, Julian. 1967. *Counter-Insurgency Operations: Techniques of Guerrilla Warfare.* New York: Walker and Company.

Paige, Jeffery. 1975. *Agrarian Revolution: Social Movements and Export Agriculture in the Underdeveloped World.* New York: Free Press.

Paszynski, Marian. 1981. "The Economic Interest of the CMEA Countries in Relations with Developing Countries." In Christopher T. Saunders (ed.), *East-West-South: Economic Interactions Between Three Worlds.* London: Macmillan.

Paulino, Leonardo A., and Shen Sheng Tseng. 1980. *A Comparative Study of FAO and USDA Data on Production, Area, and Trade of Major Food Staples.* Research Report 19. Washington, D.C.: International Food Policy Research Institute.

Payne, James. 1981. *The American Threat.* College Station, Tex.: Lytton Publishing.

Perlmutter, Amos. 1969. "The Praetorian State and the Praetorian Army: Toward a Taxonomy of Civil-Military Relations in Developing Polities." *Comparative Politics* 1 (April): 382–404.

Posen, Barry. 1984. *The Sources of Military Doctrine: France, Britain, Germany Between the World Wars.* Ithaca: Cornell University Press.

Prokhorov, G. M. 1972 (quoted in Turpin, *Soviet Foreign Trade*).

Pye, Lucien W. 1962. "Armies in the Process of Political Modernization." In John J. Johnson (ed.), *The Role of the Military in Underdeveloped Countries.* Princeton, NJ: Princeton University Press.

Pye, Lucien W. 1961. "Armies in the Process of Political Modernization." *Archives Europeennes de Sociologie* 2: 82–92.

———. 1966. *Aspects of Political Development.* Boston: Little, Brown.

Pyschas, Paul, and Pentti Malaska. 1989. "An Analysis of the Problematique of African Famine." In Aklilu Lemma and Pentti Malaska (eds.), *Africa Beyond Famine: A Report for the Club of Rome.* New York: Tycooly, pp. 81–131.

Quan, Julia. 1987. *Mozambique: A Cry for Peace.* Oxford: Oxfam.

Rahmato, Desalgen. 1988. "Peasant Survival Strategies in Ethiopia." *Disasters* 12 (4): 326–344.

Ray, George. 1984. *The Diffusion of Mature Technologies.* New York: Cambridge University Press.

Ray, James Lee, and Ayse Vural. 1986. "Power Disparities and Paradoxical Conflict Outcomes." *International Interactions* 12 (4).

Reiser, Stewart. 1989. *The Israeli Arms Industry—Foreign Policy, Arms Transfers and Military Doctrine of a Small State.* London: Holmes and Meier.

Rejai, Mostafa, and Cynthia H. Enloe. 1969. "Nation-States and States-Nations." *International Studies Quarterly* 13 (2): 140–158.

Republic of Korea, Bank of Korea. 1988. *Economic Statistics Yearbook.* Seoul: Bank of Korea.

Republic of Korea, Economic Planning Board. 1983. *Annual Report on the Family Income and Expenditure Survey 1983*. Seoul: Economic Planning Board.

————. 1985. *Annual Report on the Family Income and Expenditure Survey 1985*. Seoul: Economic Planning Board.

————. 1987. *Annual Report on the Family Income and Expenditure Survey 1987*. Seoul: Economic Planning Board.

————. 1988. *Major Statistics of the Korean Economy 1988*. Seoul: Economic Planning Board.

Republic of Korea, Ministry of Health and Social Affairs. 1986. *Yearbook of Health and Social Statistics*. Seoul: Ministry of Health and Social Affairs.

Rice, Edward E. 1988. *Wars of the Third Kind: Conflict in Underdeveloped Countries*. Berkeley: University of California Press.

Richardson, Lewis F. 1960. *Arms and Insecurity: A Mathematical Study of the Causes and Origins of War*. Pittsburgh: Boxwood Press.

Rikhye, Ravi. 1989. "Reorganizing Indian Armor." *Indian Defense Review* (July).

————. 1990. *Militarization of Mother India*. New Delhi: Chanakya.

Rizvi, Hasan-Askari. 1991. "The Military and Politics in Pakistan." *Journal of Asian and African Studies* XXVI (1–2): 27–42.

————. 1993. *Pakistan and the Geostrategic Environment: A Study of Foreign Policy*. New York: St. Martin's Press.

Robison, Richard. 1978. "Toward a Class Analysis of the Indonesian Military Bureaucratic State." *Indonesia* 25 (April): 17–39.

Rogers, Marvin. 1988. "Depoliticization of Indonesia's Political Parties: Attaining Military Stability." *Armed Forces and Society* 14 (2) (Winter): 247–272.

Rokkan, Stein. 1975. "Dimensions of State Formation and Nation-Building: A Possible Paradigm for Research on Variations Within Europe." In Charles Tilly (ed.), *The Formation of National States in Western Europe*. Princeton: Princeton University Press, pp. 562–600.

Rone, Jemera. 1989. *Angola: Violations of the Laws of War by Both Sides*. New York: Human Rights Watch.

Ross, Andrew L. 1981. *Arms Production and Developing Countries: The Continuing Proliferation of Conventional Weapons*. Santa Monica: Rand Corporation.

————. 1989. "Full Circle: Conventional Proliferation, the International Arms Trade, and Third World Arms Exports." In Kwang-il Baek, Ronald D. McLaurin, and Chung-in Moon (eds.), *The Dilemma of Third World Defense Industries*. Boulder: Westview Press, pp. 1–31.

Rothstein, Robert. 1986. "The 'Security Dilemma' and the 'Poverty Trap' in the Third World." *Jerusalem Journal of International Relations* 8 (December).

Rouquie, Alain. 1982. *The Military and the State in Latin America*. Berkeley: University of California Press.

Rudner, Martin. 1976. "The Indonesian Military and Economic Policy." *Modern Asian Studies* 10 (2): 249–284.

Ruiz, C. A., and Jonas Zoninsein. 1979. "The Arms Race, Global Industry and Basic Human Needs Satisfaction: An Application of the Latin American Model to the Issue of Disarmament." Unpublished paper. Rio de Janeiro: Candido Mendes University.

Rummel, R. J. 1979a. *National Attributes and Behavior*. Beverly Hills: Sage.

————. 1979b. *Understanding Conflict and War, Vol. 4: War, Power, Peace*. Beverly Hills: Sage.

Russett, Bruce, and Harvey Starr. 1989. *World Politics: A Menu for Choice*. New York: W. H. Freeman.

Saiyud, Kerdphol. 1986. *The Struggle for Thailand: Counter-Insurgency, 1965–1985*. Bangkok: S Research Center.

Salim, Mohammad El-Sayed. 1987. " Egypt." In James Katz (ed.), *Arms Production in Developing Countries*. Lexington: D. C. Heath/Lexington Books.

Sanger, Clyde. 1982. *Safe and Sound: Disarmament and Development in the Eighties.* London: Zed Press.

Sanjian, Gregory S. 1988. *Arms Transfers to the Third World: Probability Models of Superpower Decisionmaking.* Boulder: Lynne Rienner.

Scheer, Robert. 1982. *With Enough Shovels: Reagan, Bush, and Nuclear War.* New York: Random House.

Schmidt, Christian (ed.). 1987a. *The Economics of Military Expenditures, Economic Growth and Fluctuations.* New York: St. Martin's Press.

———. 1987b. "Semantic Variations on Richardson's Armaments Dynamics." In Christian Schmidt (ed.) *The Economics of Military Expenditures, Economic Growth and Fluctuations.* New York: St. Martin's Press.

Schultheis, Michael. 1989. "Refugees in Africa: The Geopolitics of Forced Displacement." *African Studies Review* 32 (1): 3–30.

Sellers, Robert C. Annual. *Armed Forces of the World.* New York: Praeger.

Sen, Amartya. 1982. *Poverty and Famines: An Essay on Entitlement and Deprivation.* Oxford: Oxford University Press.

Shephard, Jack. 1974. *The Politics of Starvation.* London: Zed Press.

Shindo, Eiichi. 1985. "Hunger and Weapons: The Entropy of Militarisation." *Review of African Political Economy* 33: 6–22.

Shulman, Marshall (ed.). 1986. *East-West Tensions in the Third World.* New York: W. W. Norton.

Simatupang, T. B. 1989. "Indonesia: Leadership and National Security Perceptions." In Mohammed Ayoob and Chai-Anan Samudavanija (eds.), *Leadership Perceptions and National Security: The Southeast Asian Experience.* Singapore: Institute of Southeast Asian Studies.

Singer, J. David. 1958. "Threat Perception and the Armament-Tension Dilemma." *Journal of Conflict Resolution* 2: 90–105.

———. (ed.) 1979. *Explaining War.* Beverly Hills: Sage.

Singer, J. David, Stuart Bremer, and John Stuckey. 1979. "Capability Distribution, Uncertainty, and Major Power War, 1820–1965." In J. David Singer (ed.), *Explaining War.* Beverly Hills: Sage.

Singh, Harjinder. 1977. *Birth of an Air Force.* New Delhi: Palit and Palit.

SIPRI (Stockholm International Peace Research Institute). Annual. *World Armaments and Disarmament* (Yearbook). Stockholm: SIPRI.

Sisson, Richard, and Leo E. Rose. 1990. *War and Secession: Pakistan, India and the Creation of Bangladesh.* Berkeley: University of California Press.

Sivard, Ruth Leger. 1985. *World Military and Social Expenditures: 1985 Edition.* Washington, D.C.: World Priorities.

Siverson, Randolph, and Michael Sullivan. 1983. "The Distribution of Power and the Onset of War." *Journal of Conflict Resolution* 27 (3) (September): 473–494.

Skidmore, Thomas E. 1988. *The Politics of Military Rule in Brazil, 1964–85.* Oxford: Oxford University Press.

Skidmore, Thomas E., and Peter Smith. 1989. *Modern Latin America.* New York: Oxford University Press.

Small, Melvin, and J. David Singer. 1982. *Resort to Arms: International and Civil Wars, 1816–1980.* Beverly Hills: Sage.

Smith, Alan H. 1985. "Soviet Trade Relations with the Third World." In Robert Cassen (ed.), *Soviet Interests in the Third World.* London: Sage.

Smith, Chris, and Bruce George. 1985. "The Defense of India." *Jane's Defence Weekly* (March 2).

Smith, Dan, and Ron Smith. 1979. "Reflections on Neuman." *Orbis* 23: 471–477.

Smith, R. P. 1977. "Military Expenditures and Capitalism." *Cambridge Journal of Economics* 1 (March): 61–76. ℬℴ·ℱℂⅈℱℱ ·

———. 1978. "Military Expenditure and Capitalism: A Reply." *Cambridge Journal of Economics* 2 (June): 299–304.

———. 1980a. "The Demand for Military Expenditure." *Economic Journal* 90 (December): 811–820.

———. 1980b. "Military Expenditures and Investment in OECD Countries, 1954–1973." *Journal of Comparative Economics* 4: 19–32.

———. 1987. "The Demand for Military Expenditure: A Correction." *Economic Journal* 97 (December): 989–990.

———. 1989. "Models of Military Expenditure." *Journal of Applied Econometrics* 4: 345–359.

Smith, Theresa Clair. 1980. "Arms Race Instability and War." *Journal of Conflict Resolution* 24 (2) (June): 253–284.

Snider, Lewis W. 1987. "Identifying the Elements of State Power: Where Do We Begin?" *Comparative Political Studies* 20 (3) (October): 314–356.

———. 1988. "Political Strength, Economic Structure, and the Debt Servicing Potential of Developing Countries." *Comparative Political Studies* 20: 455–488.

———. 1990a. "The Political Dimensions of Military Spending and Debt Service in Southeast Asia." *Contemporary Southeast Asia* 11 (4) (March): 278–305.

———. 1990b. "The Political Performance of Third World Governments and the Debt Crisis." *American Political Science Review* 84: 1263–1280.

———. 1991. "Guns, Debts, and Politics: New Variations on an Old Theme." *Armed Forces and Society* 17 (2) (Winter): 167–190.

Solo, Robert A. 1986. "Review Article: Melman and Reich on Industrial Policy." *Economic Development and Cultural Change* 34: 373–384.

Spanier, John. 1987. *Games Nations Play* (6th ed.). Washington, D.C.: Congressional Quarterly Press.

Spykman, Nicholas. 1942. *America's Strategy in World Politics*. New York: Harcourt Brace.

Staatz, John M. 1989. "Food Supply and Food Demand in Sub-Saharan Africa." Mimeo. Michigan State University.

Steinberg, David I. 1988. *South Korea's Military: Political and Social Roles*. New York: The Asia Society, Background Report.

Stephan, Alfred (ed.). 1973. *Authoritarian Brazil*. New Haven: Yale University Press.

———. 1978. *State and Society: Peru in Comparative Perspective*. Princeton: Princeton University Press.

Stork, Joe. 1987. "Arms Industries of the Middle East." *Middle East Report* (January-February).

Suchit, Bunbongkarn. 1988. "The Military and Development for National Security in Thailand." In J. Soedjati Djiwandono and Mun Cheong Yong (eds.), *Soldiers and Stability in Southeast Asia*. Singapore: Institute of Southeast Asian Studies.

Sweezy, Paul. 1970. *The Theory of Capitalist Development*. New York: Monthly Review Press.

———. 1973. "Comments on Szymanski's Paper 'Military Spending and Economic Stagnation.'" *American Journal of Sociology* 79 (3): 709–710.

Szymanski, Albert. 1973a. "Military Spending and Economic Stagnation." *American Journal of Sociology* 79 (1): 1–14.

———. 1973b. "Reply to Sweezy." *American Journal of Sociology* 79 (3): 710–711.

Taylor, Charles L. 1983. *World Handbook of Political and Social Indicators*. 3rd ed. Vol. I and II. New Haven: Yale University Press.

Taylor, Charles Lewis, and David A. Jodice. 1983. *World Handbook of Political and*

Social Indicators. Ann Arbor: Inter-University Consortium for Political and Social Research.

Tellis, Ashley. 1990. "Securing the Barrack: The Logic, Structure and Objectives of India's Naval Expansion." Part 2. *Naval War College Review* 43 (1) (January).

Terhal, Peter. 1981. "Guns or Grain: Macroeconomic Costs and Indian Defense, 1960–70." *Economic and Political Weekly* (December 5).

———. 1982. "Foreign Exchange Costs of the Indian Military." *Journal of Peace Research* 19.

Teshome, Tadesse. 1990. "Food, Relief Centers and Forced Migration in N.E. Africa: An Analysis of Institutions and Policies." M.A. Thesis, Michigan State University.

Thomas, Raju. 1978. *The Defense of India in a Budgetary Perspective*. New Delhi: Macmillan.

———. 1991. "Security and Democracy in South Asia." Paper presented at the Midwest Consortium for International Security Studies (MCISS) Workshop on South Asian Security, Madison, Wisconsin, October.

Thucydides. 1951. *The Peloponnesian War*. New York: Random House.

Tilly, Charles. 1975. "Reflections on the History of European State-Making." In Charles Tilly (ed.), *The Formation of National States in Western Europe*. Princeton: Princeton University Press, pp. 3–83.

———. 1990. *Coercion, Capital and European States, AD 990–1990*. Cambridge: Basil Blackwell.

Timmer, C. Peter. 1984. "Developing a Food Strategy." In Carl K. Eicher and John M. Staatz (eds.), *Agricultural Development in the Third World*. Baltimore: Johns Hopkins University Press.

Trimberger, Ellen Kay. 1978. *Revolutions from Above*. New Brunswick: Transaction Press.

Tuchman, Barbara. 1980. *The Guns of August*. New York: Bantam Books.

Tullberg, Rita. 1985. "Military-Related Debt in Non-Oil Developing Countries." In *World Armaments and Disarmament: SIPRI Yearbook 1985*. London: Taylor and Francis.

Turpin, William N. 1977. *Soviet Foreign Trade: Purpose and Performance*. Lexington, Mass.: Lexington Books.

United Nations. Annual. *Human Development Report*. New York: United Nations.

———. 1991. *World Economic Survey*. New York: United Nations.

———. Annual. *Yearbook of National Account Statistics*. New York: United Nations.

United Nations Conference on Trade and Development (UNCTAD). Annual. *Handbook of International Trade and Development Statistics*. Geneva: UNCTAD.

United Nations Development Program (UNDP). Emergency Programme—Mozambique. 1988. *Emergency: Mozambique '88*. New York: United Nations.

———. 1989. *African Economic and Financial Data*. New York: United Nations.

United Nations Disaster Relief Organization (UNDRO). 1981. *Displaced and Drought-Affected Persons in Southern and Central Angola*. Geneva: UNDRO.

United States Arms Control and Disarmament Agency (ACDA). Annual. *World Military Expenditures and Arms Transfers*. Washington, D.C.: ACDA.

United States Committee for Refugees (USCR). Annual. *World Refugee Survey*. Washington, D.C.: American Council for Nationalities Service.

———. 1991. *The Long Road Home: Angola's Post-War Inheritance*. Washington, D.C.: American Council for Nationalities Service.

United States Congress, House of Representatives. 1986. Subcommittee on Africa. *Emergency Famine Relief Needs in Ethiopia and Sudan*. Washington, D.C.: U.S. Government Printing Office.

———. 1988. Subcommittee on Rights, Subcommittee on International Organizations, and Subcomittee on Africa. *Update on Recent Developments in Ethiopia: The Famine Crisis.* Washington, D.C.: U.S. Government Printing Office.

———. 1989a. Committee on Foreign Affairs, Select Committee on Hunger, and the Subcommittee on Africa. *Politics of Hunger in the Sudan.* Washington, D.C.: U.S. Government Printing Office.

———. 1989b. Subcommittee on Africa. *New Reports of Human Rights Violations in the Angolan Civil War.* Washington, D.C.: U.S. Government Printing Office.

———. 1989c. Subcommittee on Africa. *Reported Massacres and Indiscriminate Killings in Somalia.* Washington, D.C.: U.S. Government Printing Office.

———. 1989d. Subcommittee on Foreign Operations and the Select Committee on Hunger. *Africa's Uprooted People.* Washington, D.C.: Government Printing Office.

United States Defense Security Assistance Agency (DSAA). 1990 FMS Control and Reports Division, Controller. *Fiscal Year Series.* September.

Valdés, Alberto (ed.). 1981. *Food Security for Developing Countries.* Boulder: Westview Press.

Valkenier, Elizabeth Kridl. 1983. *The USSR and the Third World: An Economic Bind.* New York: Praeger.

———. 1986. "East-West Economic Competition in the Third World." In Marshall Shulman (ed.), *East-West Tensions in the Third World.* New York: W. W. Norton.

Vasquez, John. 1984. "The Role of Capability in the Preservation of Peace and the Onset of War." Paper presented at the Second International Congress of Arts and Sciences, Rotterdam, Netherlands, June 7.

Vneshniaia torgovlia SSSR (Moscow serial publication). Various years.

Vneshnie ekonomicheskie sviazi SSSR (Moscow serial publication). 1989g.

Wallace, Michael. 1979. "Arms Races and Escalation: Some New Evidence." In J. David Singer (ed.), *Explaining War.* Beverly Hills: Sage.

———. 1980. "Accounting for Superpower Arms Spending." In Pat McGowan and Charles Kegley (eds.), *Threats, Weapons, and Foreign Policy.* Beverly Hills: Sage.

———. 1982. "Armaments and Escalation." *International Studies Quarterly* 26 (1) (March): 37–56.

Wallenstein, Peter, et al. 1985. *Global Militarization.* Boulder: Westview Press.

Wassily, Leontief, and Faye Duchin. 1983. *Military Spending Facts and Figures: Worldwide Implications and Future Outlook.* New York: Oxford University Press.

Wayman, Frank William. 1975. *Military Involvement in Politics: A Causal Model.* Beverly Hills: Sage.

Weede, Erich. 1976. "Overwhelming Preponderance as a Pacifying Condition Among Contiguous Asian Dyads, 1950–1969." *Journal of Conflict Resolution* 20 (3) (September): 395–411.

———. 1986. "Rentseeking, Military Participation and Economic Performance in LDCs." *Journal of Conflict Resolution* 30 (2) (June).

Welch, Claude E., Jr., and Arthur K. Smith. 1974. *Military Role and Rule: Perspectives on Civil-Military Relations.* North Scituate: Duxbury Press.

Westlake, M. J. 1987. "The Measurement of Agricultural Price Distortions in Developing Countries." *Journal of Development Studies* 23 (1): 368–381.

Whitaker, Jennifer Seymour. 1988. *How Can Africa Survive?* New York: Harper and Row.

White, Ralph. 1970. *Nobody Wanted War.* Garden City: Doubleday.

Wight, Martin. 1977. *Systems of States.* Leicester: Leicester University Press.

Wilkenfeld, Jonathan, Gerald Hopple, Paul Rossa, and Stephen Andriole. 1980. *Foreign Policy Behavior: The Interstate Behavior Analysis Model.* Beverly Hills: Sage.

Wohlstetter, Albert. 1968. "Illusions of Distance." *Foreign Affairs* 46 (January).

Woldemeskel, Getachew. 1989. "The Consequences of Resettlement in Ethiopia." *African Affairs* 88 (352): 359–375.

Wolpin, Miles. 1986. *Militarization, Internal Repression and Social Welfare in the Third World*. New York: St. Martin's Press.

Woolf, Amy. 1993. *Nuclear Weapons to the Soviet Union: Issues and Prospects*. CRS Issue Brief, updated January 13.

World Bank. 1981. *Accelerated Development in Sub-Saharan Africa*. Washington, D.C.: World Bank.

———. 1984a. *Korea: Development in a Global Context*. Washington, D.C.: World Bank.

———. 1984b. *Toward Sustained Development in Sub-Saharan Africa*. Washington, D.C.: World Bank.

———. 1988. *The Challenge of Hunger in Africa: A Call to Action*. Washington, D.C.: World Bank.

———. 1989. *Africa's Adjustment and Growth in the 1980s*. Washington, D.C.: World Bank.

———. Annual. *World Development Report*. Washington, D.C.: Oxford University Press.

———. Annual. *World Tables*. Washington, D.C.: World Bank.

World Food Program (WFP). Irregular. *Emergency Operation: Report by the Executive Committee*. Rome: WFP.

Woronoff, Jon. 1983. *Korea's Economy: Man-Made Miracle*. Seoul: Si-sa-yong-o-sa Publishers.

Wulf, Herbert. 1983. "Developing Countries." In Nicole Ball and Milton Leitenberg (eds.), *The Structure of the Defense Industry: An International Survey*. London: Croom Helm.

Wulf, Herbert, et al. 1987. *Transitional Arms Production Technology*. Hamburg: University of Hamburg.

Yong, Mun Cheong. 1988. "Perspectives on the Military and Development in Indonesia." In J. Soedjati Djiwandono and Mun Cheong Yong (eds.), *Soldiers and Stability in Southeast Asia*. Singapore: Institute of Southeast Asian Studies.

Yos, Santasombat. 1989. "Leadership and Security in Modern Thai Politics." In Mohammed Ayoob and Chai-Anan Samudavanija (eds.), *Leadership Perceptions and National Security: The Southeast Asian Experience*. Singapore: Institute of Southeast Asian Studies.

Zartman, I. William (ed.). 1984. *The Political Economy of Nigeria*. New York: Praeger.

———. 1989. *Ripe for Resolution: Conflict and Intervention in Africa*. Oxford: Oxford University Press.

Zinnes, Dina. 1980. "Why War? Evidence on the Outbreak of International Conflict." In Ted Robert Gurr (ed.), *The Handbook of Political Conflict*. New York: Free Press.

Zisk, Kimberly Marten. 1993. "Civil Military Relations in the New Russia." Occasional Paper from the Mershon Center Project at Columbus, Ohio, "Assessing Alternative Futures for the United States and Post-Soviet Relations" (March).

Zolberg, Aristide, Astri Suhrke, and Sergio Aguayo. 1989. *Escape from Violence: Conflict and the Refugee Crisis in the Developing World*. Oxford: Oxford University Press.

Zuk, Gary, and W. R. Thompson. 1982. "The Post-Coup Military Spending Question." *American Political Science Review* 76: 60–74.

❖ Index ❖

❖ About the Contributors ❖

Mohammed Ayoob is professor of international relations at James Madison College, Michigan State University. He is also a Ford Foundation Fellow in International Security at the Watson Institute of International Studies, Brown University, for the 1993–1994 academic year.

Marcus Cheatham is director of Survey Research at the Institute for Public Policy and Social Research at Michigan State University.

Donald Crone is professor and chair of politics and international relations at Scripps College, Claremont, California.

Norman A. Graham is associate professor of international relations at James Madison College, Michigan State University, where he is also the director of the Center for European and Russian Studies.

Amit Gupta is a research associate in the Program in South and West Asian Studies at the University of Illinois, Champaign-Urbana.

John Hartman is assistant professor of sociology at the State University of New York, Buffalo.

Wey Hsiao is a research specialist at the Executive Office of Elder Affairs, The Commonwealth of Massachusetts.

Peter M. Lewis is assistant professor of political science at the American University.

David J. Louscher is professor and department head of political science at the University of Akron.

John Jacob Nutter is a visiting assistant professor at James Madison College, Michigan State University.

Warren Phillips is professor of government and politics at the University of Maryland and the Senior Vice Chairman of Maryland Moscow, Inc.

Linda Racioppi is assistant professor of international relations at James Madison College, Michigan State University.

Lewis W. Snider is associate professor of political science in the Center for Politics and Economics at the Claremont Graduate School.

James Sperling is associate professor of political science at the University of Akron.

Jonas Zoninsein is assistant professor at James Madison College, Michigan State University. He specializes in economic development and international economics.

❖ About the Book ❖

Do military expenditures retard economic growth and development, enhance the development process, or neither? How effective are military and military-dominated regimes in promoting economic development? What is the impact of military expenditures and arms acquisitions on conflict patterns?

Exploring the causal links between security concerns, military expenditures and economic development in the Third World, the authors systematically address the concept of security in the Third World context. They trace historical trends in arms transfers and technology diffusion, analyze the relationships between military spending and economic development in several newly industrializing and developing countries, and assess the impact of military regimes in the search for security and development.